PATTERNS
OF
EXPOSITION
4

RANDALL E. DECKER

PATTERNS
OF
EXPOSITION
4

LITTLE, BROWN AND COMPANY
BOSTON

LIBRARY OF CONGRESS CATALOG CARD NUMBER: 73–16696

THIRD PRINTING

Published simultaneously in Canada
by Little, Brown & Company (Canada) Limited

PRINTED IN THE UNITED STATES OF AMERICA

To the Instructor

Patterns of Exposition 4 retains the same principles and format as the three former editions. With the still rapidly expanding usage of the books throughout the country, we continue to question instructors who are using one of the earlier editions about their preferences in essay materials and their needs for any basic changes in the book. They have asked little: this fourth version was frequently requested, but primarily for a continuing change of illustrative selections to keep pace, to some extent, with the changing interests of youth. It is important too, we believe, through fresh materials to maintain the same kind of teaching enthusiasm with which the earlier editions are being used. Many instructors are finding it advantageous to rotate two, sometimes three, editions from year to year.

Nineteen of the most highly regarded selections from the second edition have been retained, and many new selections are here anthologized for the first time. Three essays without questions, each using one or more of the patterns of exposition, are grouped in a separate section at the end.

In this edition, as in the others, we have attempted to bring together the best readings to demonstrate expository techniques. We have also tried to make possible their convenient use in whatever ways instructors think best for their own classes. Versatility was one of the many standards used in choosing materials; therefore only complete essays or free-standing units of larger works have been included. If these, with some inevitable overlap of patterns, are more complicated than excerpts illustrating single principles, they are also more realistic and certainly more useful for other classroom purposes.

Their arrangement here is but one of the many workable orders; the instructor can easily develop another if he so desires. To make such variations convenient, we have nearly always placed interessay questions at the ends of sequences, where they can be quickly detected and, if not suitable, easily eliminated or modified.

We have tried to vary the study questions — and undoubtedly have included far more than any one teacher will want — from the purely objective to those calling for some serious self-examination by the students. (A booklet, *A Manual to Accompany Patterns of Exposition 4*, is available, placing further materials under the instructor's complete control.)

Suggestions for writing assignments to be developed from ideas in the essays are located immediately after each selection. But for classes in which the instructor prefers writing to be done according to the expository pattern under study at the time, regardless of subject matter, topic suggestions are located at the end of each section.

"A Guide to Terms," where matters from *Abstract* to *Unity* are briefly discussed, refers whenever possible to the essays themselves for illustrations. To permit unity and easy access, it is located at the back of the book, but there are continuing cross-references to it in the study questions.

In all respects — in size, content, arrangement, format — we have tried to keep *Patterns of Exposition 4* uncluttered and easy to use.

The editor would like to express appreciation for the helpful criticism and suggestions provided by his friends and colleagues, especially David Skwire, Drury H. Cargill, Carole Clopper, Leo E. Sullivan, David E. Fear, Darlene Strawser, Lucille Johnsen, Terence S. Martin, John Hardaway, John Driscoll, James Antonioli, Joseph S. Marshall, and Helen Everett. He would also like to thank Charles Christensen, Margaret Zusky, and Lynn Settlemyer of the Little, Brown staff.

Table of Contents

Introduction   xiii

1   Illustrating Ideas by Use of *Example*   1

RUSSELL BAKER
Juglipidity 3

JAMES THURBER
Courtship Through the Ages 7

LAURENCE J. PETER and RAYMOND HULL
The Peter Principle 14

DICK GREGORY
The Ghetto Cop 26

2   Analyzing a Subject by *Classification*   39

SAMUEL JOHNSON
Roarers, Whisperers, and Moderators 42

ERIC BERNE
Can People Be Judged by Their Appearance?   46

VANCE PACKARD
New Directions of Marriage   52

JAMES A. MICHENER
The Assumptions of the Middle Class   59

3   Explaining by Means of
    Comparison and *Contrast*   69

ANNE ROIPHE
Confessions of a Female Chauvinist Sow   72

BRUCE CATTON
Grant and Lee: A Study in Contrasts   80

ARTHUR L. CAMPA
Anglo vs. Chicano: Why?   86

TIME
Male and Female: The Differences Between Them   94

4   Using *Analogy* as an Expository Device   105

SYLVIA ASHTON-WARNER
Gate-Crashing a Child's Mind   107

CHARLES OSGOOD
Nations Can Be Schizoid Too   110

ALVIN TOFFLER
Modular Man   114

TOM WOLFE
O Rotten Gotham — Sliding Down into the
Behavioral Sink   119

5   Explaining through *Process Analysis*   **131**

ERNEST HEMINGWAY
The Bull Fight as Symbolism   133

ALEXANDER PETRUNKEVITCH
The Spider and the Wasp   137

RACHEL CARSON
The Other Road   145

JESSICA MITFORD
To Dispel Fears of Live Burial   151

6   Analyzing *Cause* and *Effect* Relationships   **161**

JERZY KOSINSKI
TV as Baby Sitter   164

GAIL SHEEHY
$70,000 a Year, Tax Free   169

LAWRENCE CASLER
This Thing Called Love Is Pathological   174

GLORIA STEINEM
What It Would Be Like if Women Win   182

7   Using *Definition* to Help Explain   191

ALBERT SCHWEITZER
Reverence for Life   194

WOODY ALLEN
A Brief, Yet Helpful, Guide to Civil
Disobedience   199

D. H. LAWRENCE
Pornography   204

CLAUDE BROWN
The Language of Soul   210

8   Reasoning by Use of *Induction* and *Deduction*   221

BENJAMIN FRANKLIN
On the Choice of a Mistress   224

THOMAS JEFFERSON
The Declaration of Independence   228

PETER F. DRUCKER
How Best to Protect the Environment   234

ARTHUR C. CLARKE
The Star of the Magi   242

9   Explaining with the Help of *Description*   253

SHARON CURTIN
Aging in the Land of the Young   256

BARBARA W. TUCHMAN
The Changed and Unchanging   261

MICHAEL J. ARLEN
Griefspeak   266

MARTIN HOFFMAN
The Gay Bar   273

10   Using *Narration* as an Expository Technique   283

MARTIN GANSBERG
38 Who Saw Murder Didn't Call the Police   286

DENNIS SMITH
Malicious False Alarms   292

GEORGE ORWELL
A Hanging   299

JACK KEROUAC
Alone on a Mountaintop   307

Essays for Further Reading and Analysis   319

ALEKSANDER I. SOLZHENITSYN
The Heart of a Nation   320

ALEX HALEY
My Furthest-Back Person — "The African"   325

HENRY DAVID THOREAU
Where I Lived, and What I Lived For   335

A Guide to Terms   343

Introduction

Exposition is one of the four basic forms of communication, more important to most people than any of the others — narration, description, or argumentation (including persuasion). The novelist and to some extent the sports reporter use narration and description; the lawyer, the salesman, the preacher become skilled in logical argument and persuasion. But these persons are in specialized fields, prepared by specialized training. People in such professions, like the rest of us, are also frequent users of exposition in one way or another.

Exposition means explanation, simply an *exposing* of information or ideas. Its primary function is not to tell a story or relate a happening, although exposition often *uses* narration as one of many techniques. Its primary function is not to create vivid pictures for the reader, although description, too, may at times be a valuable technique of exposition. The primary function of exposition is not to convince or persuade, although, conversely, logical argument and persuasion frequently use exposition as one of their techniques. But the primary function of exposition itself is merely *to explain*.

Even beyond our increasing need for informally written and spoken explanations, we use the processes of written exposition throughout college — in reports, term papers, essay examinations. Most of us use exposition throughout our working lives — in letters, in memoranda, in business and professional reports. Hence there are practical reasons why most college composition courses are devoted primarily to study and practice in exposition. And these, of course, are the reasons this book is devoted to the basic patterns of and other techniques commonly used in expository writing.

There is nothing new about these patterns of exposition; we have been using most of them since we first tried to explain why some types of birds fly south in the winter. But mature writing depends partly on the author's being able to use *deliberately* whichever techniques will do the job best, with the least chance of misunderstanding. We study them to get a clearer view of their functions and possibilities, with the aim of being able to use them more effectively in our own writing.

We examine and practice these techniques separately, realizing they are seldom used separately in practical writing. After all, when we observe and practice for hours a skill involved in tennis or golf, we are not assuming that an entire game will be made up of serving or putting. In writing, we know there is no reason why a process analysis should not be used to assist comparison in some explanations, why illustration might not be valuably aided in certain developments by narration. In good writing, if the patterns do not overlap, it is simply because one alone is sufficient for the purpose.

But besides the study of writing techniques in a college anthology, we have a right to expect real benefit from the reading itself. Reading and thinking about new ideas or experiences is an excellent way to widen horizons, to broaden our interests — and that is an important phase of becoming educated. In general, each set of four essays in this book progresses in complexity and depth. Challenges help our understanding to reach an ever higher level.

The manner of approaching each reading, or the study of it, may be suggested by the instructor. If not, a worthwhile system for the student to give at least a fair trial is this:

1. For the first reading relax. Read the selection casually, as you would some magazine article, for whatever enjoyment or new ideas you can get without straining. Do not stop to look up new words unless the sentences in which they are used are meaningless until you do. But have a pencil in hand and mark all words you are doubtful about, then go on.

2. When finished with the first reading, put the book down; for a few minutes think over what you have read.

3. Then use the dictionary to help you understand the words you have marked. Do not make the mistake of finding the first or

the shortest definition and trying to memorize it. Instead, look at the various meanings, and for the word's uses as noun, verb, and modifier. *Think* about them. Pronounce the word. Use it in a few sentences. Identify it with similar words you already know. Then see how the author has used it.

4. After you understand all the words, read and think briefly about the assigned questions and remarks following the selection. (The paragraphs in each selection are numbered for easy reference.)

5. Then reread the essay, pausing sometimes to think and to *question*, underlining important ideas, marking sentences or phrases that seem to you especially interesting, misleading, amusing, or well expressed.

6. Then return to the questions at the end. You will probably find that you have already provided most of the answers. If not, give them further thought, referring again to the essay and to "A Guide to Terms" or earlier explanations wherever necessary for thorough understanding.

7. Next, try to *evaluate* the selection. What was the author trying to explain? Did he succeed in explaining? Was his endeavor worthwhile?

Useful as these selections can be, however, they are not intended as models for imitation by students. Each was written, as all expository projects should be, to give a particular audience a particular explanation. The style of some is much too informal for most college writing. Other styles, perhaps from a slower and more sedate age than ours, would be too stately for today. Pure imitation is not the purpose of our study.

But each of the selections does demonstrate one or more of the *patterns* of exposition, which are as useful now as ever. Each can provide, too, some profitable study of other sound principles of writing — principles of effective sentences and paragraphs, mature diction, forceful introductions and closings. The consideration of all these principles, instead of being handled in separate sections, is a continuing study within the basic framework of the expository patterns. The book is designed so that instructors and students can use it in several ways.

1

Illustrating Ideas by Use of *Example*

The use of examples to illustrate an idea under discussion is the most common, and frequently most efficient, pattern of exposition. It is a method we use almost instinctively; for instance, instead of talking in generalities about the qualities of a good football coach, we cite Coach Smith as an example. We may go further and illustrate Smith's virtues by a specific account of his handling of a crucial situation in the last Homecoming game. In this way we put our abstract ideas into concrete form — a process that is always an aid to clarity. (As a matter of fact, with the "for instance" in this very paragraph, examples are employed to illustrate the *use* of example.)

Lack of clear illustrations may leave the reader with only a hazy conception of the points the writer has tried to make. Even worse, the reader may try to supply examples from his own knowledge or experience, and these might do the job poorly or even lead him to an impression different from that intended by the author. Since the writer is the one trying to communicate, clarity is primarily his responsibility.

Not only do good examples put into clear, concrete form what otherwise might remain vague and abstract, but the writing also becomes more interesting, with a better chance of holding the reader's attention. With something specific to be visualized, a statement also becomes more convincing — but convincing within certain limitations. If we use the Volkswagen as an example of German workmanship, the reader is probably aware that this car may not be entirely typical. Although isolated examples will not hold up well in logical argument, for ordinary purposes of explanation

1

the Volkswagen example could make its point convincingly enough.

As in the selection and use of all materials for composition, of course, the successful writer selects and uses examples cautiously, always keeping in mind the nature of his reader-audience and his own specific purpose for communicating. To be effective, each example must be pertinent, representing the chief qualities of the generality it illustrates. Its function as an example must be either instantly obvious to the reader or fully enough developed so that he learns exactly what it illustrates, and how. Sometimes, however, illustration may be provided best by something other than a real-life example — a fictional anecdote, an analogy, or perhaps a parable that demonstrates the general idea. Here even greater care is needed to be sure these examples are both precise and clear.

Illustration is sometimes used alone as the basic means of development; but it also frequently assists other basic techniques, such as comparison and contrast. In either of its functions, the author may find his purpose best served by one well-developed example, possibly with full background information and descriptive details. But sometimes citing several shorter examples is best, particularly if the author is attempting to show a trend or a prevalence. In more difficult explanations, of course, a careful combination of the two techniques — using both one well-developed example and several shorter examples — may be worth the extra time and effort required.

Whichever method is used, the writer is following at least one sound principle of writing: he is trying to make the general more specific, the abstract more concrete.

RUSSELL BAKER

RUSSELL BAKER, born in Virginia in 1925, is a graduate of Johns Hopkins University and a veteran of World War II. Baker, who lives in Washington, D.C., has spent his career as a newspaperman and columnist on the staffs of the *Baltimore Sun* and *The New York Times*. His wit and subtlety are equally evident in his books: *An American in Washington* (1961), *No Cause for Panic* (1964), *All Things Considered* (1965), and *Poor Russell's Almanac* (1972).

Juglipidity

"Juglipidity" is from *Poor Russell's Almanac*, a collection of Baker's short humorous pieces. This essay provides a convenient beginning illustration of the use of examples as a simple, basic pattern of exposition.

The English language is suffering from a word shortage. This is 1 because the world changes so fast nowadays that word makers cannot produce new words fast enough to keep up with all the new things that are happening.

For example, the Volkswagen has been with us for twenty 2 years, but we still do not have a good word to describe the peculiar state of mind which the Volkswagen induces in its driver. Without such a word, other drivers have no effective way of dealing with the Volkswagen driver as he weaves in and out of heavy traffic, feeling dangerously like a broken-field runner on an asphalt gridiron.

All you can do when you catch one of these people at a red 3 light is lean out the window and say, "You're suffering from lethal delusions of mobility," or something equally cumbersome. The word we need here is, obviously "miniphoria," a descriptive noun

Reprinted by permission of the publisher from *The New York Times* (September 2, 1965). © 1965 by The New York Times Company.

suggesting the odd euphoria that comes over people hunched in miniature machines. When you catch a Volkswagen driver at the light, you simply lean out the window and roar, "You stupid miniphoriac!" and the world becomes a satisfying place again.

Another modern condition for which there is no adequate word is the appearance of women walking along the street in tightly fitting trousers, slacks or jeans. Everyone has seen this modern spectacle, but at present dozens of imprecise words are needed to discuss it. Words like "rippling," "quivering," "bulging," "ballooning," etc.

What we need is a single noun that succinctly sums up the condition. Such a word might be "juglipidity." With "juglipidity," the spectacle will no longer leave us speechless. Seeing one of these poor creatures in public, we will only have to say, "That poor woman's juglipidity is acute," and the situation will be satisfactorily disposed of.

We also need a word for the modern crime of robbery by machine. In the typical mechanized robbery, the victim puts fifteen cents into a soda-pop vending machine. The machine seizes the money, drops it into a metal loot box, and refuses to come across with the soda pop.

The victim is baffled. If he had been robbed by a man with a gun, he would know what to do. He would go to the police, report the commission of a felony and, after the bandit had been caught, testify in court to put the wretch behind bars.

Against a felonious machine, there is no apparent recourse. What is the word for this offense that has been committed? What are the victim's rights once he has futilely punched the coin-return lever a few times? Is it permissible to kick the machine? Should it be turned over to the police?

If there were a familiar word for this all-too-familiar modern crime, the victim could act with reason. The word we need is "slottery," a noun meaning "robbery by a coin-vending machine."

Give crime its proper name and man can deal with it. When the machine grabs his fifteen cents, the victim, no longer faced with an indefinable situation, will cry, "Ah ha! So slottery's your game, eh?" He will then feel perfectly justified in attacking the thief with a jack handle, recovering his money from the loot box and stuffing the machine's slots with chewing gum.

Meanings and Values

1a. What is Baker's central theme? (See Guide to Terms: *Unity*.)
  b. Show how each part of the brief essay does, or does not, act as a tributary flowing into this theme.
  c. Does the writing have unity?
2. What other examples can you suggest which might also have been used as illustrations?
3. Who are the "word makers" (par. 1)?
4. How would you describe the tone of this essay? (Guide: *Style/ Tone.*)
5a. Famous humorist James Thurber once defined humor as "emotional chaos remembered in tranquility." If this is true, can it help explain the funny aspects of even a small piece such as this? Explain your answer.
  b. Is there a deeper significance to this essay than appears on the surface? If so, what is it?

Expository Techniques

1a. What standard method, or methods, does the author employ to introduce the essay? (Guide: *Introductions.*)
  b. How well does it fulfill the basic requirements of a good introduction?
2a. The first sentence is a generalization. (Guide: *Specific/General.*) What purposes are served by the further development of the essay?
  b. Are the examples well chosen? Justify your answer.
3a. What transitional devices are used to introduce each example? (Guide: *Transition; Coherence.*)
  b. How are these transitions also a matter of coherence?
4. Illustrate the meaning of the term *rhetorical question* by use of examples from this essay. (Guide: *Rhetorical Question.*)
5. This author uses no closing other than one of his main points. (Guide: *Closings.*) How successful do you consider the closing for this writing? Why?

Diction and Vocabulary

1a. What specific kind of figure of speech is the last part of paragraph 2? (Guide: *Figures of Speech.*)
  b. What specific kind do you find in paragraph 6?

2. Consider each of the following words, using your dictionary as necessary to be sure of their meanings: lethal, cumbersome, euphoria (par. 3); succinctly (5); felony (7, 8); recourse (8).

Suggestions for Writing and Discussion

1. If you believe there is more than humor to the allegation that we need effective word-labels to deal effectively with frustrating situations, explain this theory more seriously, using whatever means necessary to make your reasoning clear and specific.

2. It is a commonly accepted fact that we *think* only in words (not denying the fact that we can *feel* without them). Either accepting or rejecting this generality, show then the importance of vocabulary, as you see it.

3. One characteristic of this era is the growing feeling by many that we are becoming possessed by machines, perhaps even about to be done in by them. If you sometimes share this apprehension, explain why and what you believe we could, or should, do about the situation.

4. How *do* words get made and adopted into the language?

(NOTE: Suggestions for topics requiring development by use of EXAMPLE are on page 37, at the end of this section.)

JAMES THURBER

JAMES THURBER (1894–1961) was a writer and cartoonist whose essays, short stories, and line drawings have helped enliven and illuminate American life for half a century. After he joined the staff of *The New Yorker* in 1925, most of his writings were first published in that magazine. Some of his collections are in book form: *Is Sex Necessary?* (1929, with E. B. White), *The Owl in the Attic* (1931), *Let Your Mind Alone!* (1937), *The Thurber Carnival* (1945), *The Thurber Album* (1952), and *Thurber Country* (1953). His more recent books are *Alarms and Diversions* (1957), *The Years with Ross* (1959), and *Lanterns and Lances* (1961).

Courtship Through the Ages

"Courtship Through the Ages" was first published in 1939 by *The New Yorker,* and the same year it was included in Thurber's book *My World — and Welcome to It.* Although it would be misleading to call any one selection "typical" of writing as varied as Thurber's, this one is at least representative of the kind of humor that made him famous. It also serves, for us, to illustrate example usage to show a "prevalence."

Surely nothing in the astonishing scheme of life can have nonplussed Nature so much as the fact that none of the females of any of the species she created really cared very much for the male, as such. For the past ten million years Nature has been busily inventing ways to make the male attractive to the female, but the whole business of courtship, from the marine annelids up to man, still lumbers heavily along, like a complicated musical comedy. I have been reading the sad and absorbing story in Volume 6 (Cole to

1

Dama) of the *Encyclopaedia Britannica*. In this volume you can learn all about cricket, cotton, costume designing, crocodiles, crown jewels, and Coleridge, but none of these subjects is so interesting as the Courtship of Animals, which recounts the sorrowful lengths to which all males must go to arouse the interest of a lady.

We all know, I think, that Nature gave man whiskers and a   2 mustache with the quaint idea in mind that these would prove attractive to the female. We all know that, far from attracting her, whiskers and mustaches only made her nervous and gloomy, so that man had to go in for somersaults, tilting with lances, and performing feats of parlor magic to win her attention; he also had to bring her candy, flowers, and the furs of animals. It is common knowledge that in spite of all these "love displays" the male is constantly being turned down, insulted, or thrown out of the house. It is rather comforting, then, to discover that the peacock, for all his gorgeous plumage, does not have a particularly easy time in courtship; none of the males in the world do. The first peahen, it turned out, was only faintly stirred by her suitor's beautiful train. She would often go quietly to sleep while he was whisking it around. The *Britannica* tells us that the peacock actually had to learn a certain little trick to wake her up and revive her interest: he had to learn to vibrate his quills so as to make a rustling sound. In ancient times man himself, observing the ways of the peacock, probably tried vibrating his whiskers to make a rustling sound; if so, it didn't get him anywhere. He had to go in for something else; so, among other things, he went in for gifts. It is not unlikely that he got this idea from certain flies and birds who were making no headway at all with rustling sounds.

One of the flies of the family Empidae, who had tried every-   3 thing, finally hit on something pretty special. He contrived to make a glistening transparent balloon which was even larger than himself. Into this he would put sweetmeats and tidbits and he would carry the whole elaborate envelope through the air to the lady of his choice. This amused her for a time, but she finally got bored with it. She demanded silly little colorful presents, something that you couldn't eat but that would look nice around the house. So the male Empis had to go around gathering flower petals and pieces of bright paper to put into his balloon. On a courtship flight a male Empis cuts quite a figure now, but he can hardly be said to be happy. He never knows how soon the female will demand heavier presents, such as Roman coins and gold collar buttons. It seems probable that one day the courtship of the Empidae will fall down, as man's occasionally does, of its own weight.

The bowerbird is another creature that spends so much time   4 courting the female that he never gets any work done. If all the male bowerbirds became nervous wrecks within the next ten or fifteen years, it would not surprise me. The female bowerbird insists that a playground be built for her with a specially constructed bower at the entrance. This bower is much more elaborate than an ordinary nest and is harder to build; it costs a lot more, too. The female will not come to the playground until the male has filled it up with a great many gifts: silvery leaves, red leaves, rose petals, shells, beads, berries, bones, dice, buttons, cigar bands, Christmas seals, and the Lord knows what else. When the female finally condescends to visit the playground, she is in a coy and silly mood and has to be chased in and out of the bower and up and down the playground before she will quit giggling and stand still long enough even to shake hands. The male bird is, of course, pretty well done in before the chase starts, because he has worn himself out hunting for eyeglass lenses and begonia blossoms. I imagine that many a bowerbird, after chasing a female for two or three hours, says the hell with it and goes home to bed. Next day, of course, he telephones someone else and the same trying ritual is gone through with again. A male bowerbird is as exhausted as a night-club habitué before he is out of his twenties.

The male fiddler crab has a somewhat easier time, but it can   5 hardly be said that he is sitting pretty. He has one enormously large and powerful claw, usually brilliantly colored, and you might suppose that all he had to do was reach out and grab some passing cutie. The very earliest fiddler crabs may have tried this, but, if so, they got slapped for their pains. A female fiddler crab will not tolerate any caveman stuff; she never has and she doesn't intend to start now. To attract a female, a fiddler crab has to stand on tiptoe and brandish his claw in the air. If any female in the neighborhood is interested — and you'd be surprised how many are not — she comes over and engages him in light badinage, for which he is not in the mood. As many as a hundred females may pass the time of day with him and go on about their business. By nightfall of an average courting day, a fiddler crab who has been standing on tiptoe for eight or ten hours waving a heavy claw in the air is in pretty sad shape. As in the case of the males of all species, however, he gets out of bed next morning, dashes some water on his face, and tries again.

The next time you encounter a male web-spinning spider, stop 6 and reflect that he is too busy worrying about his love life to have any desire to bite you. Male web-spinning spiders have a tougher life than any other males in the animal kingdom. This is because the female web-spinning spiders have very poor eyesight. If a male lands on a female's web, she kills him before he has time to lay down his cane and gloves, mistaking him for a fly or a bumblebee who has tumbled into her trap. Before the species figured out what to do about this, millions of males were murdered by ladies they called on. It is the nature of spiders to perform a little dance in front of the female, but before a male spinner could get near enough for the female to see who he was and what he was up to, she would lash out at him with a flat-iron or a pair of garden shears. One night, nobody knows when, a very bright male spinner lay awake worrying about calling on a lady who had been killing suitors right and left. It came to him that this business of dancing as a love display wasn't getting anybody anywhere except the grave. He decided to go in for web-twitching, or strand-vibrating. The next day he tried it on one of the nearsighted girls. Instead of dropping in on her suddenly, he stayed outside the web and began monkeying with one of its strands. He twitched it up and down and in and out with such a lilting rhythm that the female was charmed. The serenade worked beautifully; the female let him live. The *Britannica's* spider-watchers, however, report that this system is not always successful. Once in a while, even now, a female will fire three bullets into a suitor or run him through with a kitchen knife. She keeps threatening him from the moment he strikes the first low notes on the outside strings, but usually by the time he has got up to the high notes played around the center of the web, he is going to town and she spares his life.

Even the butterfly, as handsome a fellow as he is, can't always 7 win a mate merely by fluttering around and showing off. Many butterflies have to have scent scales on their wings. Hepialus carries a powder puff in a perfumed pouch. He throws perfume at the ladies when they pass. The male tree cricket, Oecanthus, goes Hepialus one better by carrying a tiny bottle of wine with him and giving drinks to such doxies as he has designs on. One of the male snails throws darts to entertain the girls. So it goes, through the long list of animals, from the bristle worm and his rudimentary dance steps to man and his gift of diamonds and sapphires. The golden-eye drake raises a jet of water with his feet as he flies over a lake; Hepialus has his powder puff, Oecanthus his wine bottle, man his etchings. It is a bright and melancholy story, the age-old desire of the male for the female, the age-old desire of the female to be amused and entertained. Of all the creatures on earth, the only males who could be figured as putting any irony into their courtship are the grebes and certain other diving birds. Every now and then a courting grebe slips quietly down to the bottom of a lake and then, with a mighty "Whoosh!," pops out suddenly a few feet from his girl friend, splashing water all over her. She seems to be persuaded that this is a purely loving display, but I like to think that the grebe always has a faint hope of drowning her or scaring her to death.

I will close this investigation into the mournful burdens of the male with the *Britannica's* story about a certain Argus pheasant. It appears that the Argus displays himself in front of a female who stands perfectly still without moving a feather. . . . The male Argus the *Britannica* tells about was confined in a cage with a female of another species, a female who kept moving around, emptying ashtrays and fussing with lampshades all the time the male was showing off his talents. Finally, in disgust, he stalked away and began displaying in front of his water trough. He reminds me of a certain male (Homo sapiens) of my acquaintance who one night after dinner asked his wife to put down her detective magazine so that he could read her a poem of which he was very fond. She sat quietly enough until he was well into the middle of the thing, intoning with great ardor and intensity. Then suddenly there came a sharp, disconcerting *slap!* It turned out that all during the male's display, the female had been intent on a circling mosquito and had finally trapped it between the palms of her hands. The male in this case did not stalk away and display in front of a water trough; he went over to Tim's and had a flock of drinks and recited the poem to the fellas. I am sure they all told bitter stories of their own about how their displays had been interrupted by females. I am also sure that they all ended up singing "Honey, Honey, Bless Your Heart."

Meanings and Values

1a. Clarify the meaning of "irony of situation" by using at least one example from this essay. (See Guide to Terms: *Irony*.)
 b. Use at least three examples to illustrate the meaning of "verbal irony."
2. Thurber's writing is sometimes said to have nearly universal appeal — not only because of the humor, but also because of his subjects and his attitude toward them. What appeals would this subject have to various types of people you know?
3a. The author's themes are ordinarily deeper than they may appear to be on the surface, and they are sometimes quite serious. How seriously is he concerned about the mating foolishness of human males? How can you tell?
 b. Explain the relation of this matter of attitude to that of tone in writing. (Guide: *Style/Tone.*)
 c. Describe Thurber's tone in this essay, using no more than two or three descriptive words.
4. How much literal truth, if any, is in the allegation that "none of the females . . . she created really cared very much for the male, as such" (par. 1)?
5. Do you think we are really laughing at the animals themselves when we go to the zoo? If not, what do we laugh at? Explain carefully.

Expository Techniques

1. How does the author remind us with each new example, without making an issue of it, that he is describing people as well as (perhaps even more than) wildlife?
2. List the general ways in which humor is achieved in this selection and illustrate each with a specific example.
3. Briefly explain why some people would classify these examples as personification, whereas others would not. (Guide: *Figures of Speech.*)
4a. Which of the common transitional devices is (or are) used to bridge between paragraphs 2 and 3? (Guide: *Transition.*)
 b. Between 3 and 4?
 c. Between 4 and 5?
 d. How do such matters relate to coherence? (Guide: *Coherence.*)

Diction and Vocabulary

1. Which, if any, of the ways listed in answering question 2 of "Expository Techniques" are matters of diction? Why? (Guide: *Diction.*)

2. If you are not already familiar with the following words as used in this essay, study their meanings as given in the dictionary; nonplussed, lumbers (par. 1); condescends, habitué (4); brandish, badinage (5); doxies (7); intoning, disconcerting (8).

Suggestions for Writing and Discussion

1. Explain fully, using specific examples, the real reasons for amusement at a zoo (or, for some people, a barnyard).

2. How do young men today try to impress the girls they are interested in?

3. Examine the possibility that women are interested in male "displays" because such reactions have been "programmed" into them from their earliest childhood.

4. If you are familiar with the aims and methods of the women's liberation movement, how do you think its more radical members would react to Thurber's impressions of courtship?

(NOTE: Suggestions for topics requiring development by use of EXAMPLE are on page 37, at the end of this section.)

LAURENCE J. PETER and RAYMOND HULL

LAURENCE J. PETER was born in Canada in 1919 and received his Ed.D. from Washington State University. Based on his wide experience as a teacher, counselor, school psychologist, prison instructor, consultant, and university professor, he has written numerous articles for professional journals. His books include *Prescriptive Teaching* (1965), *Teaching System: Vol. 1, Individual Instruction* (1972), and *The Peter Prescription* (1972). Peter is now associate professor of education, director of the Evelyn Frieden Center for Prescriptive Teaching, and coordinator of programs for emotionally disturbed children at the University of Southern California.

RAYMOND HULL, also born in 1919, the son of an English Methodist minister, has lived in British Columbia since 1947. He has been a prolific writer of television and stage plays, several of which have been published. His articles have been featured in such magazines as *Punch, Maclean's,* and *Esquire.*

The Peter Principle

"The Peter Principle," as it follows, combines the first two chapters of the book by that name, which was published in 1969. It is a clear and orderly illustration of the use of developed examples to give concrete form to an abstract central theme.

When I was a boy I was taught that the men upstairs knew what ⓘ they were doing. I was told, "Peter, the more you know, the further you go." So I stayed in school until I graduated from college and then went forth into the world clutching firmly these ideas and my new teaching certificate. During the first year of teaching I was upset to find that a number of teachers, school principals, supervisors and superintendents appeared to be unaware of their professional responsibilities and incompetent in executing their duties. For example my principal's main concerns were that all window shades be at the same level, that classrooms should be quiet and that no one step on or near the rose beds. The superintendent's main concerns were that no minority group, no matter how fanatical, should ever be offended and that all official forms be submitted on time. The children's education appeared farthest from the administrator mind.

At first I thought this was a special weakness of the school ②
system in which I taught so I applied for certification in another province. I filled out the special forms, enclosed the required documents and complied willingly with all the red tape. Several weeks later, back came my application and all the documents!

No, there was nothing wrong with my credentials; the forms ③
were correctly filled out; an official departmental stamp showed that they had been received in good order. But an accompanying letter said, "The new regulations require that such forms cannot be accepted by the Department of Education unless they have been registered at the Post Office to ensure safe delivery. Will you please remail the forms to the Department, making sure to register them this time?"

I began to suspect that the local school system did not have a   4
monopoly on incompetence.

As I looked further afield, I saw that every organization con-   5
tained a number of persons who could not do their jobs.

A UNIVERSAL PHENOMENON

Occupational incompetence is everywhere. Have you noticed it?   6
Probably we all have noticed it.

We see indecisive politicians posing as resolute statesmen and   ⑦
the "authoritative source" who blames his misinformation on "situational imponderables." Limitless are the public servants who are indolent and insolent; military commanders whose behavioral timidity belies their dreadnaught rhetoric, and governors whose innate servility prevents their actually governing. In our sophistication, we virtually shrug aside the immoral cleric, corrupt judge, incoherent attorney, author who cannot write and English teacher who cannot spell. At universities we see proclamations authored by administrators whose own office communications are hopelessly

muddled; and droning lectures from inaudible or incomprehensible instructors.

Seeing incompetence at all levels of every hierarchy—political, 8
legal, educational and industrial — I hypothesized that the cause
was some inherent feature of the rules governing the placement
of employees. Thus began my serious study of the ways in which
employees move upward through a hierarchy, and of what happens
to them after promotion.

For my scientific data hundreds of case histories were collected. 9
Here are three typical examples.

Municipal Government File, Case No. 17. J. S. Minion[1] was a 10
maintenance foreman in the public works department of Excelsior City. He was a favorite of the senior officials at City Hall.
They all praised his unfailing affability.

"I like Minion," said the superintendent of works. "He has 11
good judgment and is always pleasant and agreeable."

This behavior was appropriate for Minion's position: he was 12
not supposed to make policy, so he had no need to disagree with his
superiors.

The superintendent of works retired and Minion succeeded 13
him. Minion continued to agree with everyone. He passed to his
foreman every suggestion that came from above. The resulting conflicts in policy, and the continual changing of plans, soon demoralized the department. Complaints poured in from the Mayor and
other officials, from taxpayers and from the maintenance-workers'
union.

Minion still says "Yes" to everyone, and carries messages 14
briskly back and forth between his superiors and his subordinates.
Nominally a superintendent, he actually does the work of a messenger. The maintenance department regularly exceeds its budget,
yet fails to fulfill its program of work. In short, Minion, a competent foreman, became an incompetent superintendent.

Service Industries File, Case No. 3. E. Tinker was exceptionally 15
zealous and intelligent as an apprentice at G. Reece Auto Repair
Inc., and soon rose to journeyman mechanic. In this job he showed
outstanding ability in diagnosing obscure faults, and endless pa-

---

[1] Some names have been changed, in order to protect the guilty.

tience in correcting them. He was promoted to foreman of the repair shop.

But here his love of things mechanical and his perfectionism became liabilities. He will undertake any job that he thinks looks interesting, no matter how busy the shop may be. "We'll work it in somehow," he says. 16

He will not let a job go until he is fully satisfied with it. 17

He meddles constantly. He is seldom to be found at his desk. He is usually up to his elbows in a dismantled motor and while the man who should be doing the work stands watching, other workmen sit around waiting to be assigned new tasks. As a result the shop is always overcrowded with work, always in a muddle, and delivery times are often missed. 18

Tinker cannot understand that the average customer cares little about perfection — he wants his car back on time! He cannot understand that most of his men are less interested in motors than in their pay checks. So Tinker cannot get on with his customers or with his subordinates. He was a competent mechanic, but is now an incompetent foreman. 19

Military File, Case No. 8. Consider the case of the late renowned General A. Goodwin. His hearty, informal manner, his racy style of speech, his scorn for petty regulations and his undoubted personal bravery made him the idol of his men. He led them to many well-deserved victories. 20

When Goodwin was promoted to field marshall he had to deal, not with ordinary soldiers, but with politicians and allied generalissimos. 21

He would not conform to the necessary protocol. He could not turn his tongue to the conventional courtesies and flatteries. He quarreled with all the dignitaries and took to lying for days at a time, drunk and sulking, in his trailer. The conduct of the war slipped out of his hands into those of his subordinates. He had been promoted to a position that he was incompetent to fill. 22

AN IMPORTANT CLUE!

In time I saw that all such cases had a common feature. The employee had been promoted from a position of competence to a posi- 23 tion of incompetence. I saw that, sooner or later, this could happen to every employee in every hierarchy.

Hypothetical Case File, Case No. 1. Suppose you own a pill-rolling   24
factory, Perfect Pill Incorporated. Your foreman pill roller dies of a perforated ulcer. You need a replacement. You naturally look among your rank-and-file pill rollers.

Miss Oval, Mrs. Cylinder, Mr. Ellipse and Mr. Cube all show   25
various degrees of incompetence. They will naturally be ineligible for promotion. You will choose — other things being equal — your most competent pill roller, Mr. Sphere, and promote him to foreman.

Now suppose Mr. Sphere proves competent as foreman. Later,   26
when your general foreman, Legree, moves up to Works Manager, Sphere will be eligible to take his place.

If, on the other hand, Sphere is an incompetent foreman, he   27
will get no more promotion. He has reached what I call his "level of incompetence." He will stay there till the end of his career.

Some employees, like Ellipse and Cube, reach a level of incom-   28
petence in the lowest grade and are never promoted. Some, like Sphere (assuming he is not a satisfactory foreman), reach it after one promotion.

E. Tinker, the automobile repair-shop foreman, reached his   29
level of incompetence on the third stage of the hierarchy. General Goodwin reached his level of incompetence at the very top of the hierarchy.

So my analysis of hundreds of cases of occupational incom-   30
petence led me on to formulate *The Peter Principle:*

> *In a Hierarchy Every Employee Tends*
> *to Rise to His Level of Incompetence*

A NEW SCIENCE!

Having formulated the Principle, I discovered that I had inad-   31
vertently founded a new science, hierarchiology, the study of hier-archies.

The term "hierarchy" was originally used to describe the sys-   32
tem of church government by priests graded into ranks. The con-temporary meaning includes any organization whose members or employees are arranged in order of rank, grade or class.

Hierarchiology, although a relatively recent discipline, appears   33
to have great applicability to the fields of public and private administration.

THIS MEANS YOU!

My Principle is the key to an understanding of all hierarchal sys-   34
tems, and therefore to an understanding of the whole structure
of civilization. A few eccentrics try to avoid getting involved with
hierarchies, but everyone in business, industry, trade-unionism,
politics, government, the armed forces, religion and education is so
involved. All of them are controlled by the Peter Principle.

Many of them, to be sure, may win a promotion or two, mov-   35
ing from one level of competence to a higher level of competence.
But competence in that new position qualifies them for still another promotion. For each individual, for *you*, for *me*, the final
promotion is from a level of competence to a level of incompetence.[2]

So, given enough time — and assuming the existence of enough   36
ranks in the hierarchy — each employee rises to, and remains at,
his level of incompetence. Peter's Corollary states:

In time, every post tends to be occupied by an employee who   37
is incompetent to carry out its duties.

WHO TURNS THE WHEELS?

You will rarely find, of course, a system in which *every* employee   38
has reached his level of incompetence. In most instances, something
is being done to further the ostensible purposes for which the hierarchy exists.

Work is accomplished by those employees who have not yet   39
reached their level of incompetence.

*   *   *

A study of a typical hierarchy, the Excelsior City school sys-   40
tem, will show how the Peter Principle works within the teaching
profession. Study this example and understand how hierarchiology
operates within every establishment.

[2] The phenomena of "percussive sublimation" (commonly referred to as
"being kicked upstairs") and of "the lateral arabesque" are not, as the casual
observer might think, exceptions to the Principle. They are only pseudo-
promotions. . . .

Let us begin with the rank-and-file classroom teachers. I group   41
them, for this analysis, into three classes: competent, moderately
competent and incompetent.

Distribution theory predicts, and experience confirms, that   42
teachers will be distributed unevenly in these classes: the majority
in the moderately competent class, minorities in the competent and
incompetent classes. This graph illustrates the distribution:

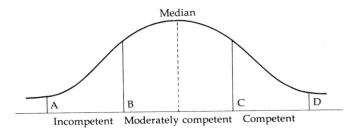

THE CASE OF THE CONFORMIST

An incompetent teacher is ineligible for promotion. Dorothea D.   43
Ditto, for example, had been an extremely conforming student in
college. Her assignments were either plagiarisms from textbooks
and journals, or transcriptions of the professors' lectures. She always did exactly as she was told, no more, no less. *She was considered to be a competent student.* She graduated with honors
from the Excelsior Teachers' College.

When she became a teacher, she taught exactly as she herself   44
had been taught. She followed precisely the textbook, the curriculum guide and the bell schedule.

Her work goes fairly well, except when no rule or precedent is   45
available. For example, when a water pipe burst and flooded the
classroom floor, Miss Ditto kept on teaching until the principal
rushed in and rescued the class.

"Miss Ditto!" he cried. "In the Name of the Superintendent!   46
There are three inches of water on this floor. Why is your class
still here?"

She replied. "I didn't hear the emergency bell signal. I pay   47
attention to those things. You know I do. I'm certain you didn't
sound the bell." Flummoxed before the power of her awesome
non sequitur, the principal invoked a provision of the school code

giving him emergency powers in an extraordinary circumstance and led her sopping class from the building.

So, although she never breaks a rule or disobeys an order, she is often in trouble, and will never gain promotion. Competent as a student, *she has reached her level of incompetence as a classroom teacher, and will therefore remain in that position throughout her teaching career.* 48

THE ELIGIBLE MAJORITY

Most beginning teachers are moderately competent or competent — see the area from B to D on the graph — and *they will all be eligible for promotion.* Here is one such case. 49

A Latent Weakness. Mr. N. Beeker had been a competent student, and became a popular science teacher. His lessons and lab periods were inspiring. His students were co-operative and kept the laboratory in order. Mr. Beeker was not good at paper work, but this weakness was offset, in the judgment of his superiors, by his success as a teacher. 50

Beeker was promoted to head of the science department where he now had to order all science supplies and keep extensive records. *His incompetence is evident!* For three years running he has ordered new Bunsen burners, but no tubing for connecting them. As the old tubing deteriorates, fewer and fewer burners are operable, although new ones accumulate on the shelves. 51

Beeker is not being considered for further promotion. *His ultimate position is one for which he is incompetent.* 52

Higher up the Hierarchy. B. Lunt had been a competent student, teacher and department head, and was promoted to assistant principal. In this post he got on well with teachers, students and parents, and was intellectually competent. He gained a further promotion to the rank of principal. 53

Till now, he had never dealt directly with school-board members, or with the district superintendent of education. It soon appeared that he lacked the required finesse to work with these high officials. *He kept the superintendent waiting* while he settled a dispute between two children. Taking a class for a teacher who 54

was ill, *he missed a curriculum revision committee meeting* called
by the assistant superintendent.

He worked so hard at running his school that *he had no energy*　55
for running community organizations. He declined offers to become
program chairman of the Parent-Teacher Association, president
of the Community Betterment League and consultant to the Committee for Decency in Literature.

His school lost community support and he fell out of favor　56
with the superintendent. Lunt came to be regarded, by the public
and by his superiors, as an incompetent principal. When the assistant superintendent's post became vacant, the school board declined
to give it to Lunt. He remains, and will remain till he retires, unhappy and incompetent as a principal.

The Autocrat. R. Driver, having proved his competence as student,　57
teacher, department head, assistant principal and principal, was
promoted to assistant superintendent. Previously he had only
to interpret the school board's policy and have it efficiently carried
out in his school. Now, as assistant superintendent, he must par-
ticipate in the policy discussions of the board, using democratic
procedures.

But Driver dislikes democratic procedures. He insists on his　58
status as an expert. He lectures the board members much as he
used to lecture his students when he was a classroom teacher. He
tries to dominate the board as he dominated his staff when he was
a principal.

The board now considers Driver an incompetent assistant su-　59
perintendent. He will receive no further promotion.

Soon Parted. G. Spender was a competent student, English teacher,　60
department head, assistant principal and principal. He then worked
competently for six years as an assistant superintendent — patri-
otic, diplomatic, suave and well liked. He was promoted to superintendent. Here he was obliged to enter the field of school finance,
in which he soon found himself at a loss.

From the start of his teaching career, Spender had never both-　61
ered his head about money. His wife handled his pay check, paid
all household accounts and gave him pocket money each week.

Now Spender's incompetence in the area of finance is revealed.　62
He purchased a large number of teaching machines from a fly-by-

night company which went bankrupt without producing any programs to fit the machines. He had every classroom in the city
equipped with television, although the only programs available in
the area were for secondary schools. Spender has found his level
of incompetence.

ANOTHER PROMOTION MECHANISM

The foregoing examples are typical of what are called "line pro-   63
motions." There is another mode of upward movement: the "staff
promotion." The case of Miss T. Totland is typical.

Miss Totland, who had been a competent student and an out-   64
standing primary teacher, was promoted to primary supervisor. She
now has to teach, not children, but teachers. Yet *she still uses the
techniques which worked so well with small children.*

Addressing teachers, singly or in groups, she speaks slowly   65
and distinctly. She uses mostly words of one or two syllables. She
explains each point several times in different ways, to be sure it is
understood. She always wears a bright smile.

Teachers dislike what they call her false cheerfulness and her   66
patronizing attitude. Their resentment is so sharp that, instead of
trying to carry out her suggestions, they spend much time devising
excuses for *not* doing what she recommends.

Miss Totland has proved herself incompetent in communicat-   67
ing with primary teachers. She is therefore ineligible for further
promotion, *and will remain as primary supervisor, at her level of
incompetence.*

YOU BE THE JUDGE

You can find similar examples in any hierarchy. Look around you   68
where you work, and pick out the people who have reached their
level of incompetence. You will see that in every hierarchy *the
cream rises until it sours.* Look in the mirror and ask whether . . .

Meanings and Values

1a. Has it been your experience that incompetence is really widespread
    enough to make this selection worthwhile?

b. Support your answer, either way, by examples from your own or your family's experience. (You will not be *proving* anything — merely supporting an observation.)

2. Does it seem feasible to you that our highly successful, complex industrial and educational systems were devised and are run either by incompetent top executives and engineers or by underlings in the hierarchy? Why, or why not?

3. To what extent are people in elective public office subject to the Peter Principle?

4. Clarify the distinction between "line" and "staff" promotions, as referred to in paragraph 63.

5. Specify at least two ways in which an understanding of the Peter Principle might be of value to an individual.

6. Why do people permit themselves to be promoted to levels of incompetence?

Expository Techniques

1. Show how at least two of the standard methods of introduction are used for this exposition. (See Guide to Terms: *Introductions.*)

2a. Where do the authors first give a simple statement of their central theme? (Guide: *Unity.*)

b. How, if at all, is the statement qualified? (Guide: *Qualification.*)

c. Do all portions of the essay serve as "tributaries" into the central theme, thus giving unity to the writing? If not, what are the exceptions?

3a. Several short, undeveloped examples are used in paragraph 1 to show a "prevalence." What is the generality they support?

b. What generality does the list of short examples in paragraph 7 support?

4a. A brief comparison between the examples of paragraph 1 and those of paragraph 7 can be used to show that examples, like words, can achieve differing degrees of specificity. (Guide: *Specific/General.*) Which of the two sets is more general?

b. Is one set then necessarily more, or less, effective than the other? Explain.

5. Paragraphs 2 and 3 comprise a more fully developed example. Which paragraph contains the generalization it supports?

6. All the author's case file reports, themselves fully developed examples, also *use* example. Analyze any one of these reports for its basic structure, its use of this kind of interior example, and the effectiveness of presentation.

7a. Of the "hundreds of case histories" (par. 9) at the authors' disposal, why do you think cases 17, 3, and 8 were chosen to use as examples?

    b. Were these good choices?

8a. How is the series of developed examples beginning in paragraph 43 organized?

    b. How is this organization superior, or inferior, to a less structured, more casual arrangement?

    c. Can you think of some other order that would have been as effective? Explain.

    d. What advantage is derived from the similar formats and endings of these examples?

Diction and Vocabulary

1. If you are not familiar with the meanings of any of the following words, consult your dictionary: phenomenon (subheading before par. 6); indolent, dreadnaught, innate, servility, incoherent, inaudible (7); hypothesized, inherent (8); succeeded, demoralized (13); protocol (22); inadvertently (31); eccentrics (34); corollary (36); ostensible (38); plagiarisms (43); flummoxed, *non sequitur* (47); latent (50).

Suggestions for Writing and Discussion

1. How is it possible, if at all in this complex society, to avoid getting involved with hierarchies (par. 34), other than in occasional dealings with them in the necessary conduct of family affairs? Consider such pertinent matters as methods, penalties, rewards.

2. If one's work is necessarily involved in a hierarchy, what practical methods would you suggest for reaching and remaining on the highest level of *competence,* thereby defying the Peter Principle?

3. From your own knowledge, select an example of incompetence dis·similar to any of those discussed in this essay. Show as well as you can the way in which this person passed his highest level of competence and, if possible, the results of the mistake for himself and others.

4. If you have reasons to doubt the Peter Principle's rather broad claims, show the nature of and justification for your doubts. You should not try to "prove" the principle wrong unless you have at least as much ammunition as the authors do. Remember that they do qualify most of their major generalizations.

(NOTE: Suggestions for topics requiring development by use of EXAMPLE are on page 37, at the end of this section.)

DICK GREGORY

Dɪᴄᴋ Gʀᴇɢᴏʀʏ, born in St. Louis in 1932, is a popular come-
dian, nightclub entertainer, recording artist, author, and
lecturer. He won the Missouri mile-run championship in 1951
and while attending Southern Illinois University (1951–1953
and 1955–1956) was named the school's outstanding athlete.
He served in the United States Army from 1953 to 1955.
Gregory is one of America's sharpest social satirists. He has
been fasting for several years to protest the war in Southeast
Asia. In 1968 he ran unsuccessfully for President as the U.S.
Peace and Freedom Party candidate. Gregory's books include
the autobiographical *Nigger* (1964), *From the Back of the Bus*
(1964), *What's Happening?* (1965), *No More Lies: The Myths
of American History* (1971), and *Dick Gregory's Political
Primer* (1972). He has also recorded several albums, among
them *Dick Gregory in Living Black and White*. Gregory lives
in Chicago with his wife and ten children.

The Ghetto Cop

"The Ghetto Cop" (editor's title) is an excerpt from Gregory's
book *The Shadow That Scares Me*, published in 1968. Although in this selection Gregory is less dependent on example
as a means of primary development than the previous authors
have been, his liberal and informal use of varied examples is
consistent with his essay's familiar style.

The power structure cannot expect to solve the social problems   1
of the ghetto by the mere physical presence of cops. The violence
and strife in the ghetto cannot be contained or suppressed because
they do not represent a riot. Five disciplined cops can stop a riot,
but the best trained armies in the world cannot contain a legitimate protest.

The attitude of the cop is much more important than his physical presence. If you live in a city whose baseball team has just won the World Series, or which has been chosen by the Shriners as the site for their national convention, you will see people take over the town. They get drunk in the streets, damage property, and bother passersby. The cop will look the other way because a big convention is bringing the city millions of dollars. If a cop can be taught to change his attitude because a convention is bringing a city a lot of money, he had also better be taught not to mistreat people who are demanding human dignity, which is more than all the money in the world can buy.

People insist that it is unfair to generalize about the police. The good cop is held up for public inspection and he is supposed to be the example of law-enforcement officers everywhere. Just as the one rabbi, priest or minister who goes to Alabama to demonstrate is supposed to represent the whole church. The one beautiful cop in a neighborhood *will* stand out. He has pride in his job. He is sensitive to human problems and knows how to talk to the person on the street corner. He has not chosen his job because he couldn't get hired any place else. He is a cop because he wants to be; perhaps his father and grandfather before him had devoted their lives to law enforcement.

The problem cops, and there are many, are those who resented their job when they took it. They are the cops who act like the judge and the jury when they make an arrest. Their resentment shows twenty-four hours a day. This situation will never change until society gives law enforcement a status which is comparable to the job it is expected to do.

Policemen labor under two basic injustices: inadequate salary and lack of proper training. The cop is the most underpaid man in American society today. Cops in the large cities should begin with a minimum salary of ten thousand dollars per year. You must pay a proper dollar for the job required. More and more potential teachers are lost to the vocation of education because industry is able to pay more money. The cop is so important to solving the social problems which beset the ghetto that America should take the chance of overpaying him, not underpaying him.

Being an entertainer, I am constantly reminded of the financial injustice which the cop suffers. I have done benefit performances all over the country for Policemen's Wives, Policemen's

Widows, Policemen's Benevolence Associations, and so on. But I
never did a show for the politician's wife or the nightclub owner's
wife. They are able to provide for their family in case of emergency,
because their earnings are at a higher level than the cop's. If America treated the cop with the respect his job deserves, the family of a
cop killed in the line of duty would automatically become the responsibility of government. Some local governments have accepted
this responsibility, but such legislation should be enacted across the
country in a uniform way.

Imagine yourself a cop in a major urban area. When you put   7
on that uniform in the morning and leave the house, you never
know if you will make it back home in the evening. The policeman
must live daily with a basic human fright which few other professions share. Yet the cop pays the same price for his haircut
that Rockefeller pays. He pays the same amount for the education
of his children that the rich executive pays. If a policeman is killed
in the line of duty, it is an ethical and moral imperative that society
accept the responsibility of scholarships for his children, a home
for his family, and other necessary benefits.

Somehow we seem to be able to give foreign aid to countries   8
all over the world, even those countries who openly tell us to "go
to hell." We should be able to find the money to give some aid to
the cop — proper salary and proper training. Domestic aid to the
cop at home is more important than foreign aid to countries abroad.
We have a crisis in this country which can destroy us from within.
. . . The number one place to begin to solve this problem which calls
attention to itself with the haunting chant, "Burn, baby, burn," is
through enlightened law enforcement.

There is a psychological factor operating in the injustice to the   9
cop. A man knows when he is being mistreated and it is bound to
affect his attitude. This applies to both Negroes and cops. When
we finally create an atmosphere in this country where law-enforcement officers are trained and paid in direct proportion to the importance of their job, a new attitude of vocational pride will be
evident. If society does not have enough pride in its law-enforcement officers to pay them what they are worth, the cop is more
likely to be susceptible to the bribe. If the pay scale is high enough,
the cop does not want to risk getting caught taking a bribe for
fear of losing his job. He knows he cannot get another job at the
same high salary. Honesty and devotion are basic ingredients in
vocational pride.

There is also the consideration of security, which is especially 10 important in a dangerous profession. The soldier has security, although often he is not even aware of it. Count up his benefits and you will find that he has much more security than the cop. And the soldier's job is easier than the cop's, because the soldier knows where his enemy is. The enemy even wears a uniform to identify himself. But the cop doesn't know what his enemy looks like. It might be that nut the Army rejected! The same man who is too crazy to go to Vietnam and kill Vietcong is back home in your neighorhood waiting to assault you. The cop has to deal with him.

Each new technological advance and the prospect of life in a 11 cybernetic society will place more demands upon the cop. We will see unions demanding shorter and shorter work weeks. There will be an increase of leisure time. People will have more time on their hands, perhaps to be out in the streets. When a man works a forty-hour week, the cop can count on the foreman watching him at least eight hours a day!

The prophet Micah insisted that the Lord requires simply that 12 man "do justice." He seems to imply that other problems of human relationship will be solved when a climate of justice is established. Justice in America today requires the investment of funds for the proper training and schooling of law-enforcement officers. The cop's job is too important for him to be allowed to put on the uniform without proper training. When I travel to England, it is frightening to see that the cabdriver in London receives a longer period of training than the average cop in America. Surely we must see our cops as more crucial to the total health of society than England does its cabdrivers. Only through basic research and proper training can just and enlightened law enforcement become a reality. And this enlightment and sensitivity must come *before* the cop gets out into the street. Society simply cannot send the cop out into the street with his nightstick to get on-the-job training on my head or with my problems, which he has not been trained to understand. He must become thoroughly aware of my social problems while he is still in school. All the force in the world will never totally suppress a legitimate problem. Those who would deal with social problems must have a basic human understanding.

The cop must be taught the unique problems of ghetto living 13 *before* he ever goes out on his beat. He must know, for example, why the man in the ghetto rarely shops at the supermarket. The supermarket requires him to pay cash. So the man in the ghetto goes to the white local merchant across the street. The prices in that little store are too high already, and the local merchant will try to cheat even more. The ghetto brother knows he is being cheated and it worries him. So when the white merchant turns his back to get the stale day-old loaf of bread, his customer wipes out the cookie rack. It is the customer's way of making up for the cheat. While the merchant is busy putting his thumb on the scale, his pickles disappear.

The cop must understand this injustice. He will see that there   14
is more to the issue than a customer stealing. But if the customer gets caught stealing, the merchant calls a cop. When the ghetto kid gets caught stealing, the merchant grabs him by the ears and holds him until the cops arrive. But what happens when that same kid gets short-changed by the merchant? The kid can't call a cop and get a fair hearing. Cops must be taught to have a responsive and sympathetic ear and listen when that ghetto mother complains that her kids are being shortchanged. Once a cop becomes aware of such practices from the beginning, he can go immediately to the local merchant and say, "We have tremendously explosive social problems in this neighborhood which you could tip off at any moment. Don't shortchange the kids." And if complaints continue to come in, the cop should investigate the basis of the complaint immediately. Such activity would go a long way toward establishing a new image of respect for the cop in the ghetto. And the resentment and frustration which lead to breaking the local merchant's window and looting his store would begin to be alleviated.

Understanding ghetto kids presents a special problem for the   15
cop. When a riot breaks out in a high school, the damage is already done and there is little the cop can do besides try to contain the violence. But if the cop had been sensitive to the history of the problem, the riot might have been avoided. For example, two kids have a gun duel in the schoolyard. The incident will very probably be hushed up by the school principal to keep his own record clean downtown. He doesn't want the superintendent of schools questioning his ability to control his pupils. But the seed for further trouble has been sown. A full-scale school riot may erupt which is certainly a more destructive mark on the principal's record.

Cops need to learn to work hand in hand with the school.   16
They need to learn to meet ghetto kids on their own level — the " 'cause why" level. It is that basic, raw, instinctive level of life

which seeks honest and open answers to very basic questions. High school kids know that the cops will be on hand when they throw their dance. 'Cause why is that the only time the cops are around? The cop has the image of only coming around to break up a party.

When cops learn to meet kids on their own level, they will learn the answer to many adolescent mysteries. Like why so many kids choose the street corner or the local hangout instead of the brand-new recreational facilities in the neighborhood. It is a simple fact of Nature. Recreational facilities are geared to a program for boys. But the boys are going to choose to be where the girls are. The girls are at the local hangout. There are certain biological factors which take precedence even over basketball! 17

When cops learn the conditions of the home environment in the ghetto, they will find out why kids act as they do. How many cops on the beat have actually seen their mother have an affair with their own daddy, let alone another man? Or how many cops have seen their mother take a needle and stick it in her arm and get high? The ghetto kid has seen this. He has looked at his own mother have an affair with a stranger. Of course, she told him it was one of Daddy's friends who came by to talk to her. So they went into the bedroom to talk, closing the door behind them. But Mother never thought that her little seven-year-old kid would peek through the keyhole. After he peeked through the keyhole and saw what he saw, he came back out into the street. He has just seen his mother have an affair with a stranger and the cop is going to tell him to be good? Naturally he will start swinging on the cop because he has to react against something. He can't swing on Momma. 18

The cop has to go back home with the ghetto kid and find out where he learned that language he uses. Mother and Father would never curse in front of the kid, until they get angry. Then the curse words fly. When you hear these words at age seven, you assume that a dirty word is something to be used as a defensive weapon. So when you walk down the street and a little girl says to you, "You stink," quite naturally you are angry and threatened. It is only natural to turn and say, "Kiss my butt." It is natural because the little seven-year-old has heard Mother and Father use dirty language under the same threatening conditions. The little kid doesn't take a bite out of a good piece of chicken and curse. He smacks his lips and makes funny little grunting noises, just like Momma and Daddy. But when he is threatened, angry, and misused, the little 19 kid curses. His home environment has taught him that response.

Cops must be trained to understand, on the human level, the   20
conditions of life and the home environment. It is amazing to see
the results of juvenile police who have received private grants to
work with kids. They accept the gang leader and work with him.
They do not start out resenting him and trying to force him to behave. A loyalty is established between cop and gang, so that the
cops often know when and where the big rumble is going to be. By
really becoming involved in the life of the gang, and accepting kids
on their own level, juvenile cops have been able to contain potentially troublesome situations.

Just and proper training of cops must take into account the tre-   21
mendous responsibility placed upon law-enforcement officers and
the great pressures under which they live. Can you imagine a cop
running through the streets of New York City, chasing a burglar,
and he shoots, missing the culprit and hitting the Russian diplomat
coming out of the United Nations Building? That is World War
Three! Such is the awesome responsibility placed upon the man
with the gun.

Imagine the mental pressure a cop must live under daily in the   22
ordinary line of duty. He sees daily the horror we only read about
in the newspapers. We read about a three-year-old girl being sexually molested, mutilated, and murdered. The cop sees it for himself. He walks into an apartment minutes after a man has gone
berserk and chopped up his wife and mutilated his kids. Perhaps
the cop has little kids of his own waiting for him to come home.
What does such a gruesome sight do to a man's mind? How does it
affect a man mentally to daily smell and touch dead human beings?
It is the cop's job to live in an atmosphere of death — to see dead
kids, to hear people moaning, groaning, and crying for help. Society
expects the cop to experience such sickening horror and to take it
in his stride. He is expected to forget what he has seen and walk
back out on the street without holding a grudge. Have we done
enough basic research to find out what such an occupational atmosphere does to a cop, as a man? Without such basic research, he
cannot be adequately trained to deal with the conditions which his
job imposes upon him. The cop's daily work is certain to affect him
mentally. One cannot witness daily the horrible reminders of the
worst that man can do without developing a low evaluation of hu-

manity. Just and proper training for the cop must take this inevitable reaction into account.

Respect for law and order can never be expected until a climate 23 of justice is created which encompasses both the cop and the man in the ghetto. The cop has to be an authority before he gets into the neighborhood. He must be trained to be an expert in understanding human behavior. He must be skilled in the art of human relationships. He must be a general practitioner trained to doctor social ills. If the cop is not adequately trained, he may be doing the very best he can given the conditions of his job; but his best is still wrong. A man does not become a brain surgeon by receiving on-the-job training in the emergency room of a hospital. The surgeon receives basic knowledge and training in medical school. Then he is ready to operate on a cracked skull and see the raw horror of an exposed brain. He will become a better surgeon with each new operation. But he is trained for his task before he is allowed to perform his very first operation. Basic knowledge and training precede actual practice. And the same thing must happen with law enforcement.

If the man on the street is to respect law and order, the cop 24 must behave like a trained, enlightened authority. A man does not want his authority getting angry, swinging a nightstick, and cursing. Such behavior is like the brain surgeon panicking at the sight of a skull fracture after an automobile accident. If that happens, you might just as well close down the hospital. The patient will die when he sees the look of horror on the surgeon's face. The surgeon is expected to take the crisis in his stride and do his job.

It is the same with the cop. It is easy for the cop to walk down 25 the street when nothing is going on, beating his stick on the lamppost and waving with a friendly word for everyone sitting on the tenement stoop. But can the cop keep this same air of cool, calm, and authority in the midst of crisis?

Almost every day a cop performs duties as a matter of routine 26 which would scare me to death. A woman giving birth to a baby in the back seat of my car, for example. It doesn't scare the average cop because he has been trained to know what to do when that water bag bursts before the woman gets to the hospital. He recognizes that it is an act of Nature and he knows how to deal with it.

The social revolution in the sore spots of this nation is another 27 act of Nature, a natural response to oppressive conditions. It bears the same marks of pain, violence, and struggle which accompany any birth. From this violent, painful struggle a new America will be born. For the first time, the nation will be christened in the name of freedom, dignity, and justice. During this transitory period of pregnancy, justice demands that the cop be trained to display the same authority and sophistication in the midst of social crisis as he does when a woman gives birth to a baby in the back of his patrol wagon.

It has been said, "Justice belongs to all men, or it belongs to none." Aristotle wrote, "The way to gain good will is to show good will." And the prophet Micah reminds us what the Lord requires for men to live together in peace, love, and harmony, "do justice, love kindness and walk humbly with your God." What better description could there be for a climate in which respect for law and order is guaranteed? To *do* justice means to treat all men with respect and human dignity — Negroes, whites, cops, and all of creation. To love kindness is to consciously seek an atmosphere of human dwelling in which the rights and needs of all men are respected. To walk humbly means to maintain an air of sensitivity which seeks first to understand human expression rather than to thwart or suppress it. Such is the climate of justice. And when that climate is created, respect for law and order—even an increase of genuine love—will follow.

Meanings and Values

1a. What apparently is the author's attitude toward his subject matter? (See Guide to Terms: *Point of View*.)
  b. How did you determine the preceding answer?
  c. How, if at all, is tone involved in the matter? (Guide: *Style/Tone*.)

2a. Is there any evidence of sentimentality in this essay? (Guide: *Sentimentality*.) If so, is it sufficient to damage the writing's effectiveness?
  b. Explain how this is, or would be, a matter of tone.

3a. What criticism, if any, would an ultra-liberal be apt to make of this essay?
  b. An ultra-conservative?
  c. Judging by "The Ghetto Cop," where would you place Gregory on the liberal-conservative spectrum?

4. How valid and appropriate is the comparison with foreign aid in paragraph 8? Explain.

5. If you see any irony in the comparison of cops and cabdrivers in paragraph 12, what kind is it? Why? (Guide: *Irony.*)

6. Give this essay our three-step critical evaluation. (Guide: *Evaluation.*)

7. If you have read "The Peter Principle," do you think the principle applies to police departments as much as to schools and commercial enterprises? Explain.

Expository Techniques

1a. Cite the paragraphs that use example to achieve concreteness.

   b. Which of these examples, if any, would have benefited by further development?

   c. Which examples, if any, seem poorly chosen for their purposes? How could the choice have been improved?

2. By what methods does the author gain emphasis? (Guide: *Emphasis.*) Provide one example of each method.

3. Consider the following sentences in relation to each other and to the essay's general subject matter: the last sentence in paragraph 4, the first in paragraph 5, and the last in paragraph 8.

   a. Which of these three, if any, seems to you a good statement of the overall central theme? (Guide: *Unity.*)

   b. Do *all* parts of the essay pertain to this statement?

   c. If not, does the writing therefore lack unity — or was your answer to 3a incorrect? Explain.

4a. Which of the author's statements, if they are to be taken literally, should have been more carefully qualified? (Guide: *Qualification.*)

   b. Give your reasons for each.

   c. Indicate how qualification for each could have been achieved with least difficulty.

   d. Which of these generalizations, as used in their own context, do you consider permissible as mere obvious exaggerations (a technique sometimes useful for shock value alone)?

   e. Briefly explain how a writer may jeopardize the effectiveness of his writing (even aside from possible damage to other people) by careless generalizing. Illustrate by using quotations from this essay, if any apply.

5a. What standard techniques are used here for closing. (Guide: *Closings.*)

   b. How effectively?

6a. How does its style help qualify this selection as a familiar essay? (Guide: *Essay; Style/Tone.*)

   b. How, if at all, are its organization and development also involved in the matter?

7a. If you have read "The Peter Principle," point out at least three basic ways in which the writing techniques differ decidedly between it and Gregory's essay.

b. Is either more effectively written, considering the subject matter with which the authors were working? Explain.

Diction and Vocabulary

1a. Which of the elements of style discussed in your answer to question 7a in "Expository Techniques" are primarily matters of diction? (Guide: *Diction.*) Cite examples.

b. Which are primarily matters of syntax? (Guide: *Syntax.*) Cite examples.

2a. Gregory consistently uses colloquial and slang terms. (Guide: *Colloquial.*) List or mark these. (Dictionaries will differ as to which are colloquial and which slang, but for our purposes we need not be concerned with the distinction.)

b. Comment briefly on the appropriateness for this essay of such liberal usage.

3a. What do you think is the usual connotation of the word "cop"? (Guide: *Connotation/Denotation.*)

b. Do you think Gregory intends this connotation here? Why, or why not?

c. List the possible alternatives to "cop" and indicate for each whether its choice would have been better or worse.

d. Be prepared to justify your answers.

4. Consult the dictionary as needed for an understanding of the following words: Shriners (par. 2); potential, beset (5); imperative (7); cybernetic (11); alleviated (14); encompasses (23).

Suggestions for Writing and Discussion

1. Consider the statement that "five disciplined cops can stop a riot" (par. 1). If you have had sufficient training or experience to speak with some authority, explain how a relatively small police squad (perhaps five is too small) *can* stop a riot.

2. Compare, with facts if you can, the security of the soldier with that of the policeman (par. 10).

3. What problems other than those of police (par. 11) do you think would multiply or worsen with shorter work weeks? Explain.

4. If you have carefully observed a policeman with special training and the time to work with ghetto children (par. 2), explain how he went about this project and, if possible, how successful and long-lasting were the results.

5. Most British city police (officially designated as *peace* officers) do not carry guns. Weigh objectively and explain the feasibility of such a policy in American cities.

6. Consider the statement that "one cannot witness daily the horrible reminders of the worst that man can do without developing a low evaluation of humanity" (par. 22). If you believe this is even generally true, what kind of advance training could possibly offset that devastating effect? Be objective and as thorough as possible.

Writing Suggestions for Section 1
Illustration by Example

Use one of the following statements or another suggested by them as your central theme. Develop it into a unified composition, using examples from history, current events, or personal experience to illustrate your ideas. Be sure to have your reader-audience clearly in mind, as well as your specific purpose for the communication.

1. Successful businesses keep employees at their highest level of *competence.*

2. Even the "beautiful" cop is still a loser.

3. Laws holding parents responsible for their children's crimes would (or would not) result in serious injustices.

4. You can't always tell a nonconformist just by looking at him.

5. Young people became bored with their "rebellion."

6. Not all women want to be "liberated."

7. One thing is certain about styles: they cannot stay the same.

8. Good sportsmanship is far more than shaking hands with the winner.

9. Religion in the United States is far from dead.

10. Democracy is not always the best form of government.

11. Colonialism was not entirely bad.

12. Nearly anyone can have a creative hobby.

13. The general quality of television commercials may be improving (or deteriorating).

14. Buying a used automobile (or a —————) is a risky endeavor, even at best.

15. "Some books are to be tasted; others swallowed; and some few to be chewed and digested." (*Francis Bacon,* English scientist-author, 1561–1626.)

2

Analyzing a Subject by *Classification*

People naturally like to sort and classify things. The untidiest urchin, moving into a new dresser of his own, will put his handkerchiefs together, socks and underwear in separate stacks, and perhaps his toads and snails (temporarily) into a drawer of their own. He may classify animals as those with legs, those with wings, and those with neither. As he gets older, he finds that schoolteachers have ways of classifying *him*, not only into a reading group but, periodically, into an "A" or "F" category, or somewhere in between. On errands to the grocery store, he discovers the macaroni in the same department as noodles, the pork chops somewhere near the ham. In reading the local newspaper, he observes that its staff has done some classifying for him, putting most of the comics together and seldom mixing sports stories with the news of bridal showers. Eventually he finds courses neatly classified in the college catalogue, and he knows enough not to look for biology courses under "Social Science." (Examples again — used to illustrate a "prevalence.")

However, our main interest in classification here is its use as a structural pattern for explanatory writing. Many subjects about which either student or graduate may need to write will remain a hodgepodge of facts and opinions unless he can find some system of analyzing the material, dividing the subject into categories, and classifying individual elements into those categories. Here we have the distinction usually made between the rhetorical terms *division* and *classification* — for example, dividing "meat" into pork, beef, mutton, and fowl, then classifying ham and pork chops into the category of "pork." But this distinction is one we need scarcely pause for here; once the need for analysis is recognized, the dividing and classifying become inevitable companions and result in the single scheme of "classification" itself, as we have been discussing it. The original division into parts merely sets up the system which, if well chosen, best serves our purpose.

Obviously, no single system of classification is best for all purposes. Our untidy urchin may at some point classify girls according to athletic prowess, then later by size or shape or hair color. Other people may need entirely different systems of classification: the music instructor classifies girls as sopranos, altos, contraltos; the psychologist, according to their behavioral patterns; the sociologist, according to their ethnic origins.

Whatever the purpose, for the more formal uses of classification ("formal," that is, to the extent of most academic and on-the-job writing), we should be careful to use a logical system that is complete and that follows a consistent principle throughout. It would not be logical to divide Protestantism into the categories of Methodist, Baptist, and Lutheran, because the system would be incomplete and misleading. But in classifying Protestants attending some special conference — a different matter entirely — such a limited system might be both complete and logical. In any case, the writer must be careful that classes do not overlap: to classify the persons at the conference as Methodists, Baptists, Lutherans, and clergy would be illogical, because some are undoubtedly both Lutheran, for instance, and "clergy."

In dividing and classifying we are really using the basic process of outlining. Moreover, if we are dealing with classifiable *ideas*, the resulting pattern *is* our outline, which has been our aim all along — a basic organizational plan.

This process of classification frequently does, in fact, organize much less tangible things than the examples mentioned. We might wish to find some orderly basis for discussing the South's post–Civil War problems. Division might give us three primary categories of information: economic, political, and social. But for a full-scale consideration of these, the major divisions themselves may be subdivided for still more orderly explanation: the economic information may be further divided into agriculture and industry. Now it is possible to isolate and clarify such strictly industrial matters as shortage of investment capital, disrupted transportation systems, and lack of power development.

Any plan like this seems almost absurdly obvious, of course — *after* the planning is done. It appears less obvious, however, to the inexperienced writer who is dealing with a jumble of information he must explain to someone else. This is when he should be aware of the patterns at his disposal, and one of the most useful of these, alone or combined with others, is classification.

SAMUEL JOHNSON

SAMUEL JOHNSON (1709–1784) was an English poet, critic, essayist, and lexicographer. After a difficult and often bitter beginning in his field, Johnson gained fame which has lasted for more than two centuries. His writing is perhaps most often remembered for its wit and sharp edge of sarcasm, but much of its effectiveness was due to a characteristic clarity and forthrightness. Among his best-known works are his *Dictionary, The Rambler, The Idler, Rasselas, The Lives of the English Poets,* and several of his many political essays and pamphlets.

Roarers, Whisperers, and Moderators

"Roarers, Whisperers, and Moderators," as it is used here, is taken from Johnson's slightly longer essay by that title. Its classification system, as well as the organization of it, is the simplest possible example of that pattern of exposition.

When any man has endeavoured to deserve distinction, he will be surprised to hear himself censured where he could not expect to have been named; he will find the utmost acrimony of malice among those whom he never could have offended. 1

As there are to be found in the service of envy men of every diversity of temper and degree of understanding, calumny is diffused by all arts and methods of propagation. Nothing is too gross or too refined, too cruel or too trifling to be practised; very little regard is had to the rules of honourable hostility, but every weapon is accounted lawful; and those that cannot make a thrust at life are content to keep themselves in play with petty malevolence, to teaze with feeble blows and impotent disturbance. 2

But as the industry of observation has divided the most miscellaneous and confused assemblages into proper classes, and ranged the insects of the summer, that torment us with their drones or stings, by their several tribes; the persecutors of merit, notwithstanding their numbers, may be likewise commodiously distinguished into Roarers, Whisperers, and Moderators. 3

The Roarer is an enemy rather terrible than dangerous. He has 4
no other qualification for a champion of controversy than a hard-
ened front and strong voice. Having seldom so much desire to confute as to silence, he depends rather upon vociferation than argument, and has very little care to adjust one part of his accusation to
another, to preserve decency in his language, or probability in his
narratives. He has always a store of reproachful epithets and contemptuous appellations, ready to be produced as occasion may require, which by constant use he pours out with resistless volubility.
If the wealth of a trader is mentioned, he without hesitation devotes
him to bankruptcy; if the beauty and elegance of a lady be com-
mended, he wonders how the town can fall in love with rustick
deformity; if a new performance of genius happens to be celebrated, he pronounces the writer a hopeless idiot, without knowledge of books or life, and without the understanding by which it
must be acquired. His exaggerations are generally without effect
upon those whom he compels to hear them; and though it will
sometimes happen that the timorous are awed by his violence, and
the credulous mistake his confidence for knowledge, yet the opinions which he endeavours to suppress soon recover their former
strength, as the trees that bend to the tempest erect themselves
again when its force is past.

The Whisperer is more dangerous. He easily gains attention by 5
a soft address, and excites curiosity by an air of importance. As
secrets are not to be made cheap by promiscuous publication, he
calls a select audience about him, and gratifies their vanity with an
appearance of trust by communicating his intelligence in a low
voice. Of the trader he can tell that though he seems to manage an
extensive commerce, and talks in high terms of the funds, yet his
wealth is not equal to his reputation; he has lately suffered much
by an expensive project, and had a greater share than is acknowl-
edged in the rich ship that perished by the storm. Of the beauty
he has little to say, but that they who see her in a morning do not
discover all these graces which are admired in the park. Of the
writer he affirms with great certainty, that though the excellence
of the work be incontestable, he can claim but a small part of the
reputation; that he owed most of the images and sentiments to a
secret friend; and that the accuracy and equality of the stile was
produced by the successive correction of the chief criticks of the age.

As every one is pleased with imagining that he knows some- 6
thing not commonly divulged, secret history easily gains credit; but

it is for the most part believed only while it circulates in whispers, and when once it is openly told, is openly confuted.

The most pernicious enemy is the man of Moderation. Without [7] interest in the question, or any motive but honest curiosity, this impartial and zealous enquirer after truth, is ready to hear either side, and always disposed to kind interpretations and favourable opinions. He has heard the trader's affairs reported with great variation, and after a diligent comparison of the evidence, concludes it probable that the splendid superstructure of business being originally built upon a narrow basis, has lately been found to totter; but between dilatory payment and bankruptcy there is a great distance; many merchants have supported themselves by expedients for a time, without any final injury to their creditors; and what is lost by one adventure may be recovered by another. He believes that a young lady pleased with admiration, and desirous to make perfect what is already excellent, may heighten her charms by artificial improvements, but surely most of her beauties must be genuine, and who can say that he is wholly what he endeavours to appear? The author he knows to be a man of diligence, who perhaps does not sparkle with the fire of *Homer*, but has the judgment to discover his own deficiencies, and to supply them by the help of others; and in his opinion modesty is a quality so amiable and rare, that it ought to find a patron wherever it appears, and may justly be preferred by the publick suffrage to petulant wit and ostentatious literature.

He who thus discovers failings with unwillingness, and ex- [8] tenuates the faults which cannot be denied, puts an end at once to doubt or vindication; his hearers repose upon his candour and veracity, and admit the charge without allowing the excuse.

Such are the arts by which the envious, the idle, the peevish, [9] and the thoughtless, obstruct that worth which they cannot equal, and by artifices thus easy, sordid, and detestable, is industry defeated, beauty blasted, and genius depressed.

Meanings and Values

1. Clarify the meaning of "cannot make a thrust at life" (par. 2).
2a. Why is the moderate critic more pernicious than the others (par. 7)?
  b. Is this statement a paradox? (See Guide to Terms: *Paradox*.) Why, or why not?

3. Many subjects relevant 200 years ago would be badly out of date today. Explain why this subject is, or is not, one of them.

Expository Techniques

1a. In your estimation, how well does Johnson's classification system meet the requirements of logic as discussed in the introduction to this section?
 b. If it seems inadequate in this respect, how might the fault have been overcome?
2a. What is the basis for arrangement of the three classes?
 b. How, if at all, is this arrangement a matter of emphasis? (Guide: *Emphasis.*)
3. What is gained, or lost, by using the same three examples within each of the categories?

Diction and Vocabulary

1a. It is understandable that styles change in writing as in anything else. What differences in diction, if any, do you find between Johnson's writing and that of modern authors you are familiar with? (Guide: *Diction.*) Be as specific as possible.
 b. What differences are matters of syntax? (Guide: *Syntax.*)
2. Consult the dictionary as needed for the meanings of the following words: censured, acrimony (par. 1); calumny, malevolence (2); commodiously (3); confute, vociferation, epithets, appellations, volubility, timorous, credulous (4); promiscuous (5); pernicious, dilatory, expedients, petulant, ostentatious (7); extenuates, vindication, veracity (8); artifices (9).

Suggestions for Writing and Discussion

1. Provide examples from public figures or your own acquaintances to illustrate each of the three classes — or more, if you think Johnson's classification system was inadequate.
2. What areas of endeavor, if any, seem relatively immune from petty attacks? What could account for any such differences?
3. How can one effectively deal with unjustified calumny, either as the victim or the witness to such attacks?

(NOTE: Suggestions for topics requiring development by CLASSIFICATION are on page 67, at the end of this section.)

ERIC BERNE

Eric Berne (1910–1970) was a graduate of McGill University's School of Medicine. A psychiatrist, he wrote extensively in that field, lectured at various universities, and served on the psychiatric staff of Mount Sinai Hospital in New York City. He later engaged in private practice and research in California. His books include *Games People Play* (1964), *The Happy Valley* (1968), and *Sex in Human Loving* (1970).

Can People Be Judged by Their Appearance?

"Can People Be Judged by Their Appearance?" was originally published in Berne's *The Mind in Action* (1947) and was later included in a revised edition of his book, *A Layman's Guide to Psychiatry and Psychoanalysis*. This explanation of one theory of basic human types is an example of a scientific subject made readable for nonscientists. Using division and classification as his primary pattern of development, Berne also relies to varying extents on most of the other expository patterns: illustration, comparison and contrast, process analysis, cause and effect, definition, and description.

Everyone knows that a human being, like a chicken, comes from an egg. At a very early stage, the human embryo forms a three-layered tube, the inside layer of which grows into the stomach and lungs, the middle layer into bones, muscles, joints, and blood vessels, and the outside layer into the skin and nervous system. 1

Usually these three grow about equally, so that the average human being is a fair mixture of brains, muscles, and inward organs. In some eggs, however, one layer grows more than the others, and when the angels have finished putting the child together, he may have more gut than brain, or more brain than 2

Reprinted by permission of Simon and Schuster, Inc., from *A Layman's Guide to Psychiatry and Psychoanalysis*, by Eric Berne, M.D. Copyright © 1947, 1957, 1967 by Eric Berne, M.D.

muscle. When this happens, the individual's activities will often be mostly with the overgrown layer.

We can thus say that while the average human being is a   3
mixture, some people are mainly "digestion-minded," some "muscle-minded," and some "brain-minded," and correspondingly digestion-bodied, muscle-bodied, or brain-bodied. The digestion-bodied people look thick; the muscle-bodied people look wide; and the brain-bodied people look long. This does not mean the taller a man is the brainier he will be. It means that if a man, even a short man, looks long rather than wide or thick, he will often be more concerned about what goes on in his mind than about what he does or what he eats; but the key factor is slenderness and not height. On the other hand, a man who gives the impression of being thick rather than long or wide will usually be more interested in a good steak than in a good idea or a good long walk.

Medical men use Greek words to describe these types of   4
bodybuild. For the man whose body shape mostly depends on the inside layer of the egg, they use the word *endomorph*. If it depends mostly upon the middle layer, they call him a *mesomorph*. If it depends upon the outside layer, they call him an *ectomorph*. We can see the same roots in our English words "enter," "medium," and "exit," which might just as easily have been spelled "ender," "mesium," and "ectit."

Since the inside skin of the human egg, or endoderm, forms   5
the inner organs of the belly, the viscera, the endomorph is usually belly-minded; since the middle skin forms the body tissues, or soma, the mesomorph is usually muscle-minded; and since the outside skin forms the brain, or cerebrum, the ectomorph is usually brain-minded. Translating this into Greek, we have the viscerotonic endomorph, the somatotonic mesomorph, and the cerebrotonic ectomorph.

Words are beautiful things to a cerebrotonic, but a viscerotonic   6
knows you cannot eat a menu no matter what language it is printed in, and a somatotonic knows you cannot increase your chest expansion by reading a dictionary. So it is advisable to leave these words and see what kinds of people they actually apply to, remembering again that most individuals are fairly equal mixtures and that what we have to say concerns only the extremes. Up to the present, these types have been thoroughly studied only in the male sex.

Viscerotonic Endomorph. If a man is definitely a thick type rather   7
than a broad or long type, he is likely to be round and soft, with
a big chest but a bigger belly. He would rather eat than breathe
comfortably. He is likely to have a wide face, short, thick neck, big
thighs and upper arms, and small hands and feet. He has over-
developed breasts and looks as though he were blown up a little
like a balloon. His skin is soft and smooth, and when he gets bald,
as he does usually quite early, he loses the hair in the middle of his
head first.

The short, jolly, thickset, red-faced politician with a cigar in   8
his mouth, who always looks as though he were about to have a
stroke, is the best example of this type. The reason he often makes
a good politician is that he likes people, banquets, baths, and sleep;
he is easygoing, soothing, and his feelings are easy to understand.

His abdomen is big because he has lots of intestines. He likes
to take in things. He likes to take in food, and affection and ap-   9
proval as well. Going to a banquet with people who like him is his
idea of a fine time. It is important for a psychiatrist to understand
the natures of such men when they come to him for advice.

Somatotonic Mesomorph. If a man is definitely a broad type rather   10
than a thick or long type, he is likely to be rugged and have lots
of muscle. He is apt to have big forearms and legs, and his chest
and belly are well formed and firm, with the chest bigger than the
belly. He would rather breathe than eat. He has a bony head, big
shoulders, and a square jaw. His skin is thick, coarse, and elastic,
and tans easily. If he gets bald, it usually starts on the front of the
head.

Dick Tracy, Li'l Abner, and other men of action belong to this   11
type. Such people make good lifeguards and construction workers.
They like to put out energy. They have lots of muscles and they
like to use them. They go in for adventure, exercise, fighting, and
getting the upper hand. They are bold and unrestrained, and love
to master the people and things around them. If the psychiatrist
knows the things which give such people satisfaction, he is able
to understand why they may be unhappy in certain situations.

Cerebrotonic Ectomorph. The man who is definitely a long type is   12
likely to have thin bones and muscles. His shoulders are apt to sag
and he has a flat belly with a dropped stomach, and long, weak

legs. His neck and fingers are long, and his face is shaped like a long egg. His skin is thin, dry, and pale, and he rarely gets bald. He looks like an absent-minded professor and often is one.

Though such people are jumpy, they like to keep their energy 13 and don't fancy moving around much. They would rather sit quietly by themselves and keep out of difficulties. Trouble upsets them, and they run away from it. Their friends don't understand them very well. They move jerkily and feel jerkily. The psychiatrist who understands how easily they become anxious is often able to help them get along better in the sociable and aggressive world of endomorphs and mesomorphs.

In the special cases where people definitely belong to one type 14 or another, then, one can tell a good deal about their personalities from their appearance. When the human mind is engaged in one of its struggles with itself or with the world outside, the individual's way of handling the struggle will be partly determined by his type. If he is a viscerotonic he will often want to go to a party where he can eat and drink and be in good company at a time when he might be better off attending to business; the somatotonic will want to go out and do something about it, master the situation, even if what he does is foolish and not properly figured out, while the cerebrotonic will go off by himself and think it over, when perhaps he would be better off doing something about it or seeking good company to try to forget it.

Since these personality characteristics depend on the growth of 15 the layers of the little egg from which the person developed, they are very difficult to change. Nevertheless, it is important for the individual to know about these types, so that he can have at least an inkling of what to expect from those around him, and can make allowances for the different kinds of human nature, and so that he can become aware of and learn to control his own natural tendencies, which may sometimes guide him into making the same mistakes over and over again in handling his difficulties.

Meanings and Values

1. Consider men you have known who fit, or nearly fit, into one or another of the three categories of build.
   a. Do they also have the traits described by Berne in paragraphs 8, 9,

11, and 13? Or do you know, perhaps, a "thick" man who hates banquets, a "wide" man who writes poetry, or a "long" man who bullies people?

   b. If so, should we assume that these are learned characteristics? Explain.

2. Illustrate clearly how an understanding of basic types of people can be important to the layman.

3. In view of the fact that so many of a person's characteristics are determined before he is born, what room does the author leave for the possibility of altering or controlling these natural tendencies?

4. If you have read "The Peter Principle" in Section 1, show by use of a clear example how an understanding of Berne's theory might benefit an individual in his personal application of the Peter Principle.

Expository Techniques

1a. Most people, according to the author, are not classifiable in the categories he discusses. Is the classification system then faulty, since it does not include everyone?

   b. Explain the difference, if any, between this system and the faulty classification of Protestants mentioned in the introduction to this section.

2. Study the general organization of this essay.

   a. Which paragraphs give an overall preview of Berne's classification system?

   b. Which paragraphs are devoted to explanations of individual categories?

   c. Where does the author bring the categories together again to show the importance of the whole analysis?

   d. Can you work out another plan that would have presented his material as meaningfully?

3. The author ends each detailed account of type characteristics with a statement of why the psychiatrist needs to know these things (pars. 9, 11, 13). Why is this a valuable technique, even though the essay was not written for psychiatrists?

4. Show the value of the parallel structures in paragraphs 4 and 5. (See Guide to Terms: *Parallel Structure.*)

5. In your opinion, do Berne's occasional attempts at humor — e.g., "the angels" and "cannot eat a menu" — benefit or detract from his explanation? Why?

Diction and Vocabulary

1a. Are the numerous Greek words as bothersome as you expected them to be when you first glanced at the essay? Why, or why not?

b. Do you think the author expects us really to master them? If not, why did he use them?

2. Aside from the Greek words, you probably found no words with which you were not already familiar. Is this a result of the type of subject matter, the author's concern for his audience, or something else? Explain.

Suggestions for Writing and Discussion

1. At the time this essay was written, the types had been "thoroughly studied only in the male sex." Even if the same general traits were characteristic of women, might tradition and social pressures tend to modify the natural tendencies more in women than in men (e.g., women are "not supposed" to go around flexing their muscles or getting into fist fights)? Explain any differences that you would expect.

2. Using examples for illustration, show that basic nature can be changed — or, if you prefer, that such change is very difficult or impossible.

3. Show the practical importance — especially for success in your future career — of understanding people and why they act as they do.

4. Develop the thesis that people of opposite types can sometimes get along more congenially than those of the same type.

(NOTE: Suggestions for topics requiring development by use of CLASSIFI-CATION are on page 67, at the end of this section.)

VANCE PACKARD

Vance Packard, born in Pennsylvania in 1914, spent many years as a newspaper reporter and columnist and as a free-lance contributor to various periodicals. He is a prolific author of books, several of which have been best sellers and are still widely read and quoted. Among them are *The Hidden Persuaders* (1957), *The Status Seekers* (1959), *The Waste Makers* (1960), *The Pyramid Climbers* (1962), *The Naked Society* (1964), and *Nation of Strangers* (1972).

New Directions of Marriage

"New Directions of Marriage" (editor's title) is a section of Packard's *The Sexual Wilderness,* which was published in 1968. Faced with presenting a tangle of predictions and proposals, the author chose to bring order to his subject matter by an informal but workable system of classification. In one form or another, it is probably the only way order could have been achieved.

Most of the rules regulating marriages and their dissolution were 1 made in eras when the bride and groom could look forward to fewer than half the number of years together that the couples marrying in the next few years can anticipate. For that reason alone, entering into wedlock calls for a new high level of prudence. There is now obviously a greater chance the partners will outgrow each other, lose interest, or become restless. In the past quarter-century, instead of greater prudence, however, we have seen a considerable increase in imprudent embarkations upon marriage.

Wives in the future surely will spend an increasing proportion 2 of their married life as equal partners of the husband free of the "motherhood-service role," and so will have more options for the outlet of their surplus energy. They can no longer view marriage as a haven where they will be looked after by a husband in return for traditional services rendered.

Instead, more than ever before, women will have not only the opportunity but the expectation to push out for themselves and function as autonomous individuals who happen to have marriage partners. Marriages will apparently continue to be brittle for some time. Families in the immediate future will be expected to be highly mobile, and ever smaller in size.

While, as noted, the traditional economic functions of marriage have shrunk, there are 2 particularly compelling reasons looming why people will be marrying in the coming decade despite the relatively free availability of unmarried sexual partners:

1. The warm, all-embracing companionship that in marriage can endure through the confusion, mobility, and rapid social change of our times.

2. The opportunity to obtain immortality and personal growth for married individuals who perpetuate themselves through reproduction as they help mold personalities of their children and proudly induct them into the larger community.

This opportunity is so profoundly desired by most adult humans who are capable of reproduction that childlessness by choice would seem to be almost as difficult to popularize on any large scale as singleness by choice. Both would probably require intensive, prolonged social conditioning.

The institution of marriage is obviously in need of modifications to fit the modern needs. Author Jerome Weidman made an important point in his book *Your Daughter Iris* when he wrote of today's marriages: "Human beings do not obtain permanent possession of each other when they marry. All they obtain is the right to work at the job of holding on to each other." In pressing for modification of marriage as an institution we should seek above all to assure that the 2 functions of marriage just stated be fulfilled.

A variety of predictions and proposals are being heard today as to how the male-female liaison will or should evolve in the next few decades to meet the changing conditions of modern life. Here, for example, are 8 possible patterns of marriage or near-marriage that are being discussed:

1. *Serial mating.* Sometimes it is called serial monogamy, sometimes serial polygamy, sometimes consecutive polygamy. But the basic idea is pretty much the same for all. It would assume a turnover of partners over the 50-odd years that a man and a woman can expect to live after they first consider marriage. Swedish sociologist Joachim Israel suggested that 4 or 5 marriages might be about par for a lifetime. The mood behind such proposals was summed up by a New York model when she said, "Why lie to yourself? We know we're not going to love one man all our lives." Among others, a psychologist-social worker in California, Virginia Star, has advocated the adoption of renewable marriage contracts. She suggests the contract lapse unless renewed every 5 years.

2. *Unstructured cohabitation.* These are the prolonged affairs without any assumption of permanence or responsibility. Such so-called unstructured liaisons — long popular in the lower classes — have been springing up in many of the larger universities in the off-campus housing. A psychiatrist at the University of California in Berkeley has suggested these liaisons may be the shape of the future. He said, "Stable, open non-marital relationships are pushing the border of what society is going to face in 10 years." [1]

A man's magazine in the mid-1960s presented some unconventional views of a woman who had been involved in a national controversy. During the presentation, she was asked, "How many lovers have you had, if you don't mind our asking?"

She responded, "You've got a helluva nerve, but I really don't mind. I've had five, if you count my marriage as an affair . . . five affairs, all of them really wing-dings."

3. *Mutual polygamy.* At a conference of marriage specialists in 1966 one expert from a Midwestern university speculated, "If we are moving into a new pattern where we are not claiming that marriage can do all the things that have been assumed, we may be moving into a kind of situation where there will be more than one partner. A compartmentalizing." Each partner in any particular marriage might have several mates, each chosen for a special purpose — for example, economic, recreational, procreational. A more

10

11

12

13

14

[1] "Unstructured Relations," *Newsweek*, July 4, 1966.

informal variant of this would be "flexible monogamy," which in the view of Phyllis and Eberhard Kronhausen would frankly allow "for variety, friendships, and even sexual experiences with other individuals, if these are desired." [2]

4. *Single-parent marriages by intent.* These, on the Swedish model, would be the females — and occasional males — who yearn for parenthood without the burdens of wedlock.

5. *Specialists in parenthood.* Anthropologist Margaret Mead, in looking a few decades ahead, suggests the time may come when pressures to keep the birth rate low will produce a social style "in which parenthood would be limited to a smaller number of families whose principal function would be child-rearing; the rest of the population would be free to function — for the first time in history — as individuals." [3]

6. *Communal living.* In such a situation, several adult females and several adult males might live together in the same large dwelling and consider themselves an enlarged communal family, much as the hippies and other unconventional family groups have already been doing for some time.

7. *Legalized polygamy for senior citizens.* This is a form of polygamy that enables a man to have several wives at the same time. It has been advanced as a way to ease the demographic problem created by the fact that after the age of 60 there are increasingly more females than males in the population. One such proposal was advanced in the magazine *Geriatrics* by Dr. Victor Kassel, of Salt Lake City (the Mormon capital). The idea was taken seriously enough to be debated and unofficially turned down by the National Council of the Aging. A widow in South Carolina gave one feminine viewpoint when she said, "I am lonesome — but not that lonesome!"

8. *A variety of liaison patterns functioning in society simultaneously.* David Mace suggests we are moving toward a 3-layer cake type of society as far as male-female liaisons are concerned. He speculated that there may be a coexistence of several patterns. One pattern, as he sees it, will be that a proportion of the people will settle for sex freedom. They will not marry, but will drift into

15

16

17

18

19

[2] Phyllis and Eberhard Kronhausen, *The Sexually Responsive Woman* (New York: Grove Press, 1964), p. 236.

[3] Margaret Mead, "The Life Cycle and Its Variants: The Division of Roles," *Daedalus*, Summer, 1967.

liaisons of long and short terms. There will be no attempt to punish or suppress such persons. He suggested that the second layer of this cake would involve somewhat more structuring, with a number of people choosing to go in and out of marriage and probably having several marriages in a lifetime, as in the common Hollywood pattern. Probably in this second layer there will be an attitude of freedom regarding extramarital sex while the couples are married. He suggested that in the third layer of the cake will be those who accept the concept of exclusive monogamy, preceded in at least some cases by premarital chastity.

Moral standards aside, one complication of most of the 8 possible patterns cited above is that they do not allow sufficiently for the intense desire that most women have for a secure arrangement — or at least women have had this intense desire until very recent times. They have had greater difficulty accepting fluid arrangements, especially after they pass the age of 30, than males.   20

An even bigger complication is that while most of these arrangements might seem attractive in terms of providing the companionship so important to male-female partnerships today, they do not come to terms with the second crucial ingredient of modern marriages: a partnership where there is a sound environment for reaching for immortality through the rearing of childen. Thus most should be rejected from serious consideration as socially unfeasible — at least for people interested in having children, and we suspect that those who don't will remain a small minority.   21

Meanings and Values

1. If you have also observed that there has been a "considerable increase in imprudent embarkations upon marriage" (par. 1), what probable reasons can you see for this trend?

2. For what other "compelling reasons" (pars. 4–6), if any, do you think people will still be marrying in the coming decade?

3a. Are most of your acquaintances, consciously or not, really after "immortality and personal growth" (par. 6) when they deliberately have children? Explain.

   b. Does either of these really seem to be a valid reason for such an undertaking today? Explain.

4a. Why has it been more difficult for women than for men to accept "fluid arrangements" after the age of 30 (par. 20)?

b. Do you have any reason, or reasons, to think this situation is changing? If so, what are they?

5a. Can you determine, from the writing itself, the author's attitude toward his subject matter — e.g., does he favor an abandoning of the one-love-forever concept, which has been the long-standing ideal in most Western cultures?

b. What effect, if any, does the attitude have on the success of the essay, on its value as a factual report of the way things are now and the way they are likely to be in the future?

Expository Techniques

1a. Which of the customary methods of introducing an exposition does the author employ? (See Guide to Terms: *Introductions*.)

b. How effectively?

2a. Show, by providing fresh examples, that the "8 possible patterns" (par. 9) are actually *divisions*, categories into which can be *classified* numerous, more specific proposals for future marriage. (The author has done this for us in some of the categories.)

b. Is it, then, a completely sound classification system, meeting all the requirements mentioned in the introductory discussion on classification?

c. If so, be prepared to defend your answer. If not, do you think it is sound enough for the author's purpose? Why, or why not?

3a. The author ordinarily avoids overgeneralizations by a cautious use of qualification. (Guide: *Qualification*.) Cite three examples of his use of this precaution.

b. Find statements, if any, that would benefit from greater qualification.

c. If any, why do you think they need it?

Diction and Vocabulary

1a. In this essay Packard often presents his own opinions or impressions — almost inevitable in any summary-analysis, however well rooted in facts — but he never uses the word "I." Cite the ways in which he avoids this usage. (As you know, it is common in student writing — e.g., "I think . . . I am sure . . . I think.")

b. What are the advantages, if any, in eliminating first-person pronouns?

c. Where especially, in college writing, are they generally considered entirely inappropriate?

2a. Cite an example of simile. (Guide: *Figures of Speech*.)
  b. Cite two good examples of metaphor. (*Note:* The author's use of "3-layer cake," par. 19, is analogy, a pattern considered in a later section of this book.)

3a. If you were trying to sell the concept of "serial mating" throughout your county, by which of the four possible labels mentioned in paragraph 10 would you call it, in order to minimize opposition? (Guide: *Connotation/Denotation*.)
  b. Explain your choice.

4. Consult the dictionary as needed for full understanding of the following words: options (par. 2); autonomous (3); perpetuate (6); liaison (9, 11); monogamy (10); cohabitation (11).

Suggestions for Writing and Discussion

1. Considering longer lives and chaotic times (and the opinions of such people as the New York model), is it already too much to expect that a girl really "in love" with a man now will still love the same man fifty years from now? How about his love for her? Explain.

2. What do you consider the chances for survival of the old 'til-death-do-us-part ideal of marriage, even if we go to a "layer cake type of society"? Why?

3. Packard, for the purposes of his essay, puts "moral standards aside." What effects, if any, can moral standards be expected to have on general public acceptance of changed marital structuring? On what grounds have you formed your opinion?

4. Give your own full explanation of the meaning and implications of "reaching for immortality through the rearing of children."

5. We may often read conflicting "preponderant evidence" that broken homes produce, or do not produce, more than their proportion of juvenile crime and/or future psychological and social problems of the children raised in them. What evidence on this question, either way or both, do you find in your own experience or observation?

6. Does it seem to you that many girls and women expect, or want, marriage to be "a haven where they will be looked after by a husband in return for traditional services rendered"? Analyze your observations in terms of overall society.

7. Do many boys or young men of your acquaintance expect or want to provide such a "haven"? Analyze your observations in terms of overall society.

(NOTE: Suggestions for topics requiring development by use of CLASSIFICATION are on page 67, at the end of this section.)

JAMES A. MICHENER

JAMES A. MICHENER, born in 1907 in New York, received numerous degrees from universities in this country and in Europe. He has taught at Colorado State and at Harvard. In 1947 he was awarded the Pulitzer Prize for *Tales of the South Pacific*, published earlier that year. His other well-known books include *Fires of Spring* (1949), *Return to Paradise* (1951), *The Bridges at Tokori* (1953), *Sayonara* (1954), *Hawaii* (1959), *The Drifters* (1971), and *Kent State: What Happened and Why* (1971).

The Assumptions of the Middle Class

"The Assumptions of the Middle Class" was first published in *America Against America: The Revolution in Middle-Class Values* (1969). In this writing, unlike the preceding essays using classification, it is the author's personal remembrances and interpretations that are divided into categories for closer study, but in the belief that they are representative of their era and therefore of special significance today.

THE ASSAULT WIDENS

From all sides the barrage continues. Thoughtful blacks in the cities do not want their children educated along the old middle-class lines which produced obedient stenographers and shipping clerks. 1

Young draftees simply cannot accept the simplistic postulates of World Wars I and II: "Congress has declared war. It's our duty to fight." 2

Young ministers, truly wrestling with the problems their congregations bring to them, cannot advise their younger members "to follow in the old paths and everything will work out all right." 3

Particularly, younger college professors gag at indoctrinating   4
their students with a vision of happiness through working for
I.B.M. or doing research for the Pentagon. Everywhere I look I
find so much rebellion against the values that predominated when
I was growing up that I have been forced to reevaluate them.

It seems to me that the assumptions upon which I operated as   5
a young man can best be understood if they are summarized within
certain categories. What follows is merely one man's recollection of
the forces which formed him. Other men my age will recall other
experiences and will identify other forces, but in general most lists
would include roughly the same components.

THE PURITAN NOOSE

Within the Christian ethic American society has always inclined   6
toward Puritanism. Any local businessman who wanted to get
ahead, any political leader who hoped for long life, has had to pay
public homage to Puritan morality, and even the more liberal
European Catholic Church, when implanted on our shores, found
it expedient to advocate a censorship of, say, films, along ridic-
ulously puritanical lines. I suppose that no single strand of middle-
class values has been rejected more totally in recent years than
this strangling rope of Puritanism which once bound us so strongly,
and against which the young have rebelled with such contempt.

We have lived primarily within a Christian ethic, once largely   7
Protestant, of late increasingly Catholic. Our father figures have
been austere men like John Knox, John Calvin, Martin Luther, and
Thomas Aquinas. To the perceptive young person today these
moral leaders, who used to terrify me with their rectitude, seem
slightly ridiculous. One evening, when I tried to introduce the
matter of religious ethics to a young group, one girl said, "Please!
Today the Pope is just as confused as we are."

THE THREE R'S

A cornerstone of middle-class life has been reliance upon educa-   8
tion. Through it, immigrants were salvaged and the children of the
laboring class set free. A conspicuous feature of American life has
been the fact that the upper classes have done precious little in this
country for the education of anyone but themselves, whereas the
middle and laboring classes have striven consistently for a free,

widely dispersed education. I myself, a product of that middle-class faith in education, believe it has been the principal differentiator between America and the rest of the world.

Some years ago in Hawaii a barefooted Japanese cleaning woman demonstrated the middle-class attitude toward education. She told me one day as she was sweeping my apartment that she was worried about her two sons and asked if she might talk with me. I assumed that her boys had gotten themselves mixed up with girls or had stolen a car, but her problems were rather different. "First son, senior Harvard Law School. Top ten. When he graduate he can go into big law firm New York. Or into government? Which one?" I said that since he was a Japanese boy trying to make his way in a Caucasian society it might be wise to establish himself first with his peers, then move into government. She agreed. "Second son, freshman M.I.T. Next year they starting accelerated course advanced calculus" — those were her exact words. "In regular calculus he get only B-minus. Should he try new course?" With wages earned by sweeping apartments, she had sent her sons to two of the best universities in America, five thousand miles from Hawaii.

MAKING IT

A central belief of the middle class in which I grew up was that the son of a ditchdigger could become a college president, whereas the careless son of the top family in town could easily make mistakes from which he would not recover. These twin beliefs were not legendary; each year they were illustrated by specific lives in our community, and are still being illustrated. I have lived in a good many countries in the world, and in no other is social mobility so easily attainable, or so dominant a factor in national life. I realize that I am begging the core question of "Mobility to what?" Young people ridicule the legendary middle-class struggle to achieve upward mobility because they see that a man is often no better off "ahead" than he was when he started. For the moment I shall avoid that challenge.

COMPETENCE

At home, in school, and in church I was reared on the stern belief that in the long run competence set the limits as to what a man could become, and this was drummed into my generation wherever we turned. If you wanted to play third base in the big leagues you had to learn how to handle ground balls smashed toward the bag. If you shied away from stabbing your hand out at the speeding white bullet, you were not going to be a third baseman. You could be something else, but not that. This was true, we were taught, of all professions. If you wanted to be a lawyer, you went to law school. If you wanted to go into business, you mastered arithmetic and the art of quick decision. The penalty for sliding through life without having mastered any competence was a sentence to mediocrity.

By no means did we equate competence with formal education. 12 Horse traders, garage mechanics, and trainmen stood high in our value judgments; and I can still remember the approval with which one of my teachers read that admirable passage from Emerson in which he described how much he admired the farm girl who knew how to subdue a fractious calf by letting the animal suck on her finger as if it were a teat. "I admire people who know how to do things," said Emerson, the high priest of middle-class values, and we shared his enthusiasm. To this day I retain a sense of awe in the presence of anyone who knows how to do something.

HIERARCHY

I have always felt that in America our middle-class values were 13 strongly rooted in a sense of hierarchy, and the fact that we have eschewed the trappings of royalty has blinded us, I think, to the other fact that we are the most royalist of peoples. I remember when Arnold Bennett unleashed one of his periodic attacks on the British royal family to the great distress of some Englishmen who were at that moment visiting America. They were outraged that Bennett had dared to speak ill of royalty but were consoled by their New Jersey host, who explained, "Never worry about what your English fools like Arnold Bennett say of your royal family. England may go off the gold standard. She may have a Socialist government. But she will never discard or in any way abuse the royal family, because the people of Iowa would not permit it."

I find this principle of hierarchy, or class consciousness if you 14 prefer, strongly ingrained in American life, and much of the protest of the young today has been a legitimate rejection of our country-club pretensions. On the other hand, I do feel that our responsible affection for position and order has been a strong factor in accounting for our stability.

RESPONSIBILITY

At the core of middle-class life has stood the doctrine of responsibility. Not only was a man largely responsible for himself and his family, but groups of families were responsible for their community. If I were asked to specify a major difference between life as it is actually lived in the United States and in Japan or Spain, for example, I would stress the fact that in those other countries there is no public tradition of support for art museums, hospital complexes, universities, and a multitude of other public charities, whereas this sense of responsibility has been strong in America. For tragic and historic reasons, we have not up to now been willing to allow this responsibility to operate in certain areas like race relations or the preservation of our cities, but the tradition for the exercise of such responsibility exists and is available for new creative uses. I would judge this commitment to responsibility to be a major characteristic of American middle-class life.

ACCUMULATION

No one should underestimate the powerful urge felt by the middle class toward accumulation, either of money, or property, or the sillier accouterments of success. I judge this to be one of our strongest motivating factors and one most subject to abuse. The tradition began, I suppose, on the frontier, when it was patently better to have 640 acres of cleared land than a quarter of an acre.

I spoke recently with a man who had just bought a comfortably sized insurance business, and even before he had moved into his new office he was planning for a second, a third, and a fourth office in nearby towns. He explained, "Of course I could make a comfortable living from my new office, but only for a few years. In this business you build volume or the major insurance companies take away your franchise. It's impossible to stay little. You grow big or you perish."

If our middle-class mania for accumulation is subject to abuse, it is also subject to ridicule, and many a father who has spent the years from 22 to 52 in a mad race to accumulate now finds himself powerless to answer his children who ask, "Why did you do it, Pop? What good did you get out of it? What have you to show for the rat race except two cars and three picture windows?" These are terrifying questions to throw at a man in his fifties, for they undermine his hitherto unquestioned faith in accumulating.

OPTIMISM

One of the most appealing of the middle-class virtues has been   19
the tendency toward optimism. There has been reason for this, for in spite of wars, depressions, and other setbacks of considerable dimension, the American middle class has been living in an expanding economy, in which social justice has made conspicuous gains. The middle-class response has been a general euphoria. After all, Kaiser Wilhelm and Adolf Hitler were defeated. Communism was more or less contained, and although a stubborn Democratic party did make frequent incursions to power, the Republican party did return at comforting intervals to run things pretty much as we had grown accustomed to seeing them run. It did not seem preposterous for the middle class to cling to its optimism.

Of course, at its most blatant our optimism took the pathetic   20
form demonstrated by George Babbitt of Zenith City and was properly ridiculed. One of the most disastrous cultural influences ever to hit America was Walt Disney's Mickey Mouse, that idiot optimist who each week marched forth in Technicolor against a battalion of cats, invariably humiliating them with one clever trick after another. I suppose the damage done to the American psyche by this foolish mouse will not be specified for another fifty years, but even now I place much of the blame for Vietnam on the bland attitudes sponsored by our cartoons.

When the original version of this essay was published, I re-   21
ceived much criticism for this passage on Mickey Mouse. Some vilified me for having spoken ill of one of our nation's folk heroes. Others rebuked me for having taken seriously what was intended merely as a fairy tale, and one that they revered. And a great many asked, "You didn't mean what you said seriously, did you? Wasn't it all a put-on?" I supose nothing proves more clearly that I did mean what I said than the seriousness of the criticism that overtook me.

I do indeed believe that the narcotic nonsense of these cartoons 22
— and similar daydreams of American life — dull our sensitiveness
to real problems. . . .

Meanings and Values

1. What *is* the so-called middle class?

2. Today we repeatedly encounter references to "Puritan morality" (par. 6). Just what is it?

3. Examine more fully the author's opinion that "the upper classes" have done precious little for education (par. 8). Do you agree? Why, or why not?

4. Explain more fully how faith in education may be "the principal differentiator between America and the rest of the world" (par. 8).

5a. Do you suppose the people of Iowa really care much about the British royal family (par. 13)? Justify your viewpoint.

  b. If not, what is the value of this example, if any?

6a. What may be one of the "tragic and historic reasons" referred to in paragraph 15?

  b. In what areas other than race relations and city preservation may they apply?

7a. What abuses have resulted from our urge to accumulate (par. 16)?

  b. Among your acquaintances, do you think any sizable proportion of middle-aged men really had an "unquestioned" faith in accumulating until shaken up by the younger generation? Explain.

8. The author implies that the Republican Party has always been the "middle-class" party. Can you recall from your study of history whether this observation is entirely accurate? Explain.

9. Consider carefully the statement (par. 20) that Mickey Mouse was one of the most disastrous cultural influences ever to hit America.

  a. To what extent, if at all, does it function as paradox? Explain. (See Guide to Terms: *Paradox*.)

  b. To what extent does it function as irony of situation? Explain. (Guide: *Irony*.)

10a. Describe what seems to be the author's attitude toward his subject.

  b. How, if at all, does this attitude affect the essay's tone? (Guide: *Style/Tone*.)

  c. His reactions to the deaths of the old assumptions vary considerably. What quality does this variation subtly impart to his tone?

11a. Where would you place this essay on an objective-subjective continuum? (Guide: *Objective/Subjective Writing*.)

  b. If you have read the Gregory and/or Packard essays, how do the three (or two) compare in this respect?

    c. Which degree of objectivity would be preferable for most college term papers?

Expository Techniques

1a. Do the author's "categories" meet all the requirements for a sound system of classification? Explain any exceptions.
  b. Is the system clearly presented, the categories properly differentiated? Explain any exceptions.
2a. Undergraduates are usually discouraged from using subheadings in their college writing, as they may tend to produce choppiness and poor coherence. (Guide: *Coherence.*) Would Michener's essay have been better, or worse, without them?
  b. Explain the reasons for your answer, noting any basic differences between his writing and most college papers.
3a. Are the four examples the author selected for his introduction well chosen for the purpose? Why, or why not?
  b. Is the example of the cleaning woman (par. 9) worth the rather extensive development given it? Justify your answer.
  c. All the categories are illustrated by examples with the exception of "Making It" (par. 10). Would it too have been improved by the use of examples? Why, or why not?
  d. Do you think the rather trivial Emerson example (par. 12) is a good one for its purpose? Why, or why not?
4a. Which, if any, of Michener's statements would have benefited from greater qualification? (Guide: *Qualification.*)
  b. Why?
  c. How might you have done the qualifying?

Diction and Vocabulary

1a. List or mark five figures of speech in this essay. (Guide: *Figures of Speech.*)
  b. Note the specific kind of each, and comment on its effectiveness.
  c. How is the use of such figurative language a matter of style? (Guide: *Style/Tone.*) Use comparison with nonfigurative examples, if necessary, in order to explain how style is affected.
2. Use the dictionary as needed to become familiar with the following words and their meanings: postulates (par. 2); components (5); homage, expedient (6); ethic (6, 7); perceptive, rectitude (7); peers (9); fractious (12); eschewed (13); hierarchy (13, 14); accouterments, patently (16); euphoria, contained, incursions (19); blatant, psyche (20); vilified, revered (21).

Suggestions for Writing and Discussion

Explore the meaning and implications (from your generation's and/or your own standpoint) of any one of the following quotations. Then devise your own statement of central theme, modifying or negating as you prefer, and develop it as a thoughtful oral or written composition, as assigned.

1. "a vision of happiness through working for I.B.M. or doing research for the Pentagon" (par. 4).
2. "the strangling rope of Puritanism . . ." (par. 6).
3. "a sentence to mediocrity" (par. 11).
4. "we are the most royalist of peoples" (par. 13).
5. "legitimate rejection of our country-club pretenses" (par. 14).
6. "responsible affection for position and order . . . a strong factor in accounting for our stability" (par. 14).
7. "commitment to responsibility . . ." (par. 15).
8. "the sillier accouterments of success" (par. 16).

Writing Suggestions for Section 2
Classification

Use division and classification (into at least three categories) as your basic method of analyzing one of the following subjects from one point of view. Narrow the topic as necessary to enable you to do a thorough job.

1. College students.
2. College teachers.
3. Athletes.
4. Coaches.
5. Salespeople.
6. Hunters (or fishermen).
7. Parents.
8. Marijuana users.
9. Policemen.
10. Summer (or part-time) jobs.
11. Motivations for study.
12. Methods for studying for exams.
13. Attitudes toward life.
14. Lies.
15. Selling techniques.
16. Tastes in clothes.
17. Television programs.
18. Sailing vessels.
19. Horses (or other animals).
20. Love.
21. Immorality.
22. Contemporary music.

3

Explaining by Means of
Comparison and *Contrast*

One of the first expository methods we used as children was *comparison*, noticing similarities of objects, qualities, and actions, or *contrast*, noticing their differences. We compared the color of the new puppies with that of their mother, contrasted our father's height with our own. Then the process became more complicated, and we employ it frequently in college essay examinations or term papers when we compare or contrast forms of government, reproductive systems of animals, or ethical philosophies of man. Later, in the business or professional worlds, we may prepare important reports based on comparison and contrast — between kinds of equipment for purchase, the personnel policies of different departments, or precedents in legal matters. Nearly everyone uses the process, though he may not be aware of this, many times a day — in choosing a head of lettuce, in deciding what to wear to school, in selecting a house or a friend or a religion.

In the more formal scholastic and professional uses of comparison and contrast, however, an ordered plan is needed to avoid having a mere list of characteristics or a frustrating jumble of similarities and differences. If the author wants to avoid communication blocks that will prevent his "getting through" to his reader, he will observe a few basic principles of selection and development. These principles apply mostly to comparisons between two subjects only; if three or more are to be considered, the usual method is to compare or contrast them in pairs.

A *logical* comparison or contrast can be made only between

subjects of the same general type. (Analogy, a special form of comparison used for another purpose, is discussed in the next section.) For example, contrasting a pine and a maple could be useful or meaningful, but little would be gained, except exercise in sentence construction, by contrasting the pine and the pansy.

Of course, logical but informal comparisons that are merely incidental to the basic structure, and hence follow no special pattern, may be made in any writing. But once committed to a formal full-scale analysis by comparison or contrast, the careful writer ordinarily gives the subjects similar treatment. Points used for one should also be used for the other, and usually in the same order. All pertinent points should be explored — pertinent, that is, to the purpose of the comparison.

The purpose and the complexity of materials will usually indicate their arrangement and use. Sometimes the purpose is merely to point out *what* the likenesses and differences are, sometimes it is to show the *superiority* of one thing over another — or possibly to convince the reader of the superiority, as this is also a technique of argumentation. The purpose may be to explain the *unfamiliar* (wedding customs in Ethiopia) by comparing to the *familiar* (wedding customs in Kansas). Or it may be to explain or emphasize some other type of *central idea,* as in most of the essays in this section.

One of the two basic methods of comparison is to present all the information on the two subjects, one at a time, and to summarize by combining their most important similarities and differences. This method may be desirable if there are few points to compare, or if the individual points are less important than the overall picture they present. Therefore, this procedure might be a satisfactory means of showing the relative difficulty of two college courses, or comparing two viewpoints concerning an automobile accident. (Of course, as in all other matters of expository arrangement, the last subject discussed is in the most emphatic position.)

However, if there are several points of comparison to be considered, or if the points are of individual importance, alternation of the material would be a better arrangement. Hence, in a detailed comparison of Oak Valley and Elm Hill hospitals, we might compare their sizes, locations, surgical facilities, staffs, and so on, always in the same order. To tell all about Oak Valley and then all about Elm Hill would create a serious communication block, requiring the reader constantly to call on his memory of what was cited earlier, or to turn back to the first group of facts again and again in order to make the meaningful comparisons that the author should have made for him.

Often the subject matter or the purpose itself will suggest a more casual treatment, or some combination or variation of the two basic methods. We might present the complete information on the first subject, then summarize it point by point within the complete information on the second. In other circumstances (as in "The Spider and the Wasp" in Section 5), it may be desirable simply to set up the thesis of likeness or difference, and then to explain a *process* that demonstrates this thesis. And, although expository comparisons and contrasts are frequently handled together, it is sometimes best to present all similarities first, then all differences — or vice versa, depending on the emphasis desired.

In any basic use of "comparison" (conveniently, the term is most often used in a general sense to cover both comparison and contrast), the important thing is to have a plan that is selected to suit the purpose and materials and thoughtfully worked out in advance.

ANNE ROIPHE

ANNE RICHARDSON ROIPHE (born 1935) is a native New Yorker. After graduating from Sarah Lawrence she pursued further studies in Munich, Germany. Upon her return to the United States Ms. Roiphe worked for a public relations firm and did research for Forbes. Her first novel, *Digging Out*, published in 1968, was met with great enthusiasm. She has since published *Up The Sandbox* (1971) which was made into a major motion picture. Her latest book, *Long Division*, was published in 1973. Ms. Roiphe and her husband, a psychoanalyst, live in New York City with their five daughters who range in age from 1 to 17 years.

Confessions of a Female Chauvinist Sow

"Confessions of a Female Chauvinist Sow" first appeared in the magazine *New York*. This is an informal essay (which some would classify as "familiar"), and the author uses personal examples liberally to illustrate her central theme. It is a theme, however, that depends directly on comparison and contrast for its primary development.

1 I once married a man I thought was totally unlike my father and I imagined a whole new world of freedom emerging. Five years later it was clear even to me — floating face down in a wash of despair — that I had simply chosen a replica of my handsome daddy-true. The updated version spoke English like an angel but — good God! — underneath he was my father exactly: wonderful, but not the right man for me.

2 Most people I know have at one time or another been fouled up by their childhood experiences. Patterns tend to sink into the unconscious only to reappear, disguised, unseen, like marionette

Reprinted by permission of the author from *New York* Magazine (October 30, 1972).

strings, pulling us this way or that. Whatever ails people — keeps them up at night, tossing and turning — also ails movements no matter how historically huge or politically important. The women's movement cannot remake consciousness, or reshape the future, without acknowledging and shedding all the unnecessary and ugly baggage of the past. It's easy enough now to see where men have kept us out of clubs, baseball games, graduate schools; its easy enough to recognize the hidden directions that limit Sis to cake-baking and Junior to bridge-building; it's now possible for even Miss America herself to identify what *they* have done to us, and, of course, *they* have and *they* did and *they* are. . . . But along the way we also developed our own hidden prejudices, class assumptions and an anti-male humor and collection of expectations that gave us, like all oppressed groups, a secret sense of superiority (co-existing with a poor self-image — it's not news that people can believe two contradictory things at once).

Listen to any group that suffers materially and socially. They have a lexicon with which they tease the enemy: ofay, goy, honky gringo. "Poor pale devils," said Malcolm X loud enough for us to hear, although blacks had joked about that to each other for years. Behind some of the women's liberation thinking lurk the rumors, the prejudices, the defense systems of generations of oppressed women whispering in the kitchen together, presenting one face to their menfolk and another to their card clubs, their mothers and sisters. All this is natural enough but potentially dangerous in a revolutionary situation in which you hope to create a future that does not mirror the past. The hidden anti-male feelings, a result of the old system, will foul us up if they are allowed to persist. 3

During my teen years I never left the house on my Saturday night dates without my mother slipping me a few extra dollars — mad money, it was called. I'll explain what it was for the benefit of the new generation in which people just sleep with each other: the fellow was supposed to bring me home, lead me safely through the asphalt jungle, protect me from slithering snakes, rapists and the like. But my mother and I knew young men were apt to drink too much, to slosh down so many rye-and-gingers that some hero might well lead me in front of an oncoming bus, smash his daddy's car into Tiffany's window or, less gallantly, throw up on my new dress. Mad money was for getting home on your own, no matter what form of insanity your date happened to evidence. Mad money 4

was also a wallflower's rope ladder; if the guy you came with
suddenly fancied someone else, well, you didn't have to stay there
and suffer, you could go home. Boys were fickle and likely to be
unkind; my mother and I knew that, as surely as we knew they
tried to make you do things in the dark they wouldn't respect you
for afterwards, and in fact would spread the word and spoil your
rep. Boys liked to be flattered; if you made them feel important
they would eat out of your hand. So talk to them about their interests, don't alarm them with displays of intelligence — we all
knew that, we groups of girls talking into the wee hours of the
night in a kind of easy companionship we thought impossible with
boys. Boys were prone to have a good time, get you pregnant, and
then pretend they didn't know your name when you came knock-
ing on their door for finances or comfort. In short, we believed
boys were less moral than we were. They appeared to be hypocrit-
ical, self-seeking, exploitative, untrustworthy and very likely to be
showing off their precious masculinity. I never had a girl friend
I thought would be unkind or embarrass me in public. I never
expected a girl to lie to me about her marks or sports skill or
how good she was in bed. Altogether — without anyone's directly
coming out and saying so — I gathered that men were sexy, powerful, very interesting, but not very nice, not very moral, humane and
tender, like us. Girls played fairly while men, unfortunately, re-
served their honor for the battlefield.

Why are there laws insisting on alimony and child support?   5
Well, everyone knows that men don't have an instinct to protect
their young and, given half a chance, with the moon in the right
phase, they will run off and disappear. Everyone assumes a mother
will not let her child starve, yet it is necessary to legislate that a
father must not do so. We are taught to accept the idea that men
are less than decent; their charms may be manifold but their characters are riddled with faults. To this day I never blink if I hear
that a man has gone to find his fortune in South America, having
left his pregnant wife, his blind mother and taken the family car.
I still gasp in horror when I hear of a woman leaving her asthmatic
infant for a rock group in Taos because I can't seem to avoid the
assumption that men are naturally heels and women the ordained
carriers of what little is moral in our dubious civilization.

My mother never gave me mad money thinking I would ditch   6
a fellow for some other guy or that I would pass out drunk on the

floor. She knew I would be considerate of my companion because, after all, I was more mature than the boys that gathered about. Why was I more mature? Women just are people-oriented; they learn to be empathetic at an early age. Most English students (students interested in humanity, not artifacts) are women. Men and boys — so the myth goes — conceal their feelings and lose interest in anybody else's. Everyone knows that even little boys can tell the difference between one kind of a car and another — proof that their souls are mechanical, their attention directed to the non-human.

I remember shivering in the cold vestibule of a famous men's 7 athletic club. Women and girls are not permitted inside the club's door. What are they doing in there, I asked? They're naked, said my mother, they're sweating, jumping up and down a lot, telling each other dirty jokes and bragging about their stock market exploits. Why can't we go in? I asked. Well, my mother told me, they're afraid we'd laugh at them.

The prejudices of childhood are hard to outgrow. I confess 8 that every time my business takes me past that club, I shudder. Images of large bellies resting on massage tables and flaccid penises rising and falling with the Dow Jones average flash through my head. There it is, chauvinism waving its cancerous tentacles from the depths of my psyche.

Minorities automatically feel superior to the oppressor be- 9 cause, after all, they are not hurting anybody. In fact, they feel morally better. The old canard that women need love, men need sex — believed for too long by both sexes — attributes moral and spiritual superiority to women and makes of men beasts whose urges send them prowling into the night. This false division of good and bad, placing deforming pressures on everyone, doesn't have to contaminate the future. We know that the assumptions we make about each other become a part of the cultural air we breathe and, in fact, become social truths. Women who want equality must be prepared to give it and to believe in it, and in order to do that it is not enough to state that you are as good as any man, but also it must be stated that he is as good as you and both will be humans together. If we want men to share in the care of the family in a new way, we must assume them as capable of consistent loving tenderness as we.

I rummage about and find in my thinking all kinds of anti- 10 male prejudices. Some are just jokes and others I will have a hard time abandoning. First, I share an emotional conviction with many sisters that women given power would not create wars. Intellectually I know that's ridiculous; great queens have waged war before; the likes of Lurleen Wallace, Pat Nixon and Mrs. General Lavelle can be depended upon in the future to guiltlessly condemn to death other people's children in the name of some ideal of their own. Little girls, of course, don't take toy guns out of their hip pockets and say "Pow, pow" to all their neighbors and friends like the average well-adjusted little boy. However, if we gave little girls the six-shooters, we would soon have double the pretend body count.

Aggression is not, as I secretly think, a male-sex-linked characteristic: brutality is masculine only by virtue of opportunity. True, there are 1,000 Jack the Rippers for every Lizzie Borden, but that surely is the result of social forms. Women as a group are indeed more masochistic than men. The practical result of this division is that women seem nicer and kinder, but when the world changes, women will have a fuller opportunity to be just as rotten as men and there will be fewer claims of female moral superiority. 11

Now that I am entering early middle age, I hear many women complaining of husbands and ex-husbands who are attracted to younger females. This strikes the older woman as unfair, of course. But I remember a time when I thought all boys around my age and grade were creeps and bores. I wanted to go out with an older man: a senior or, miraculously, a college man. I had a certain contempt for my coevals, not realizing that the freshman in college I thought so desirable, was some older girl's creep. Some women never lose that contempt for men of their own age. That isn't fair either and may be one reason why some sensible men of middle years find solace in young women. 12

I remember coming home from school one day to find my mother's card game dissolved in hysterical laughter. The cards were floating in black rivers of running mascara. What was so funny? A woman named Helen was lying on a couch pretending to be her husband with a cold. She was issuing demands for orange juice, aspirin, suggesting a call to a specialist, complaining of neglect, of fate's cruel finger, of heat, of cold, of sharp pains on the bridge of the nose that might indicate brain involvement. What was so funny? The ladies explained to me that all men behave just like that with colds, they are reduced to temper tantrums by simple 13 nasal congestion, men cannot stand any little physical discomfort — on and on the laughter went.

The point of this vignette is the nature of the laughter — us laughing at them, us feeling superior to them, us ridiculing them behind their backs. If they were doing it to us we'd call it male chauvinist pigness; if we do it to them, it is inescapably female chauvinist sowness and, whatever its roots, it leads to the same isolation. Boys are messy, boys are mean, boys are rough, boys are stupid and have sloppy handwriting. A cacophony of childhood memories rushes through my head, balanced, of course, by all the well-documented feelings of inferiority and envy. But the important thing. the hard thing, is to wipe the slate clean, to start again without the meanness of the past. That's why it's so important that the women's movement not become anti-male and allow its most prejudiced spokesmen total leadership. The much-chewed-over abortion issue illustrates this. The women's-liberation position, insisting on a woman's right to determine her own body's destiny, leads in fanatical extreme to a kind of emotional immaculate conception in which the father is not judged even half-responsible — he has no rights, and no consideration is to be given to his concern for either the woman or the fetus. 14

Woman, who once was abandoned and disgraced by an unwanted pregnancy, has recently arrived at a new pride of ownership or disposal. She has traveled in a straight line that still excludes her sexual partner from an equal share in the wanted or unwanted pregnancy. A better style of life may develop from an assumption that men are as human as we. Why not ask the child's father if he would like to bring up the child? Why not share decisions, when possible, with the male? If we cut them out, assuming an old-style indifference on their part, we perpetuate the ugly divisiveness that has characterized relations between the sexes so far. 15

Hard as it is for many of us to believe, women are not really superior to men in intelligence or humanity — they are only equal. 16

Meanings and Values

1a. How would you describe the author's point of view in this selection? (See Guide to Terms: *Point of View*.)
   b. How did the tone help determine your answer? (Guide: *Style/Tone*.)

2. In the last sentence of paragraph 2 is an example of irony. (Guide: *Irony.*)
   a. What kind is it?
   b. Could it also be used to illustrate the meaning of "paradox"? (Guide: *Paradox.*) Why, or why not?

3a. Exactly what is the "myth" with which Roiphe is primarily concerned?
   b. Is it explained more by comparison or by contrast?
   c. Which aspects of it, if any, do young women of your acquaintance still seem to believe? Explain.

4. Show the special significance, in relation to the theme, of the author's mother's last answer in paragraph 7.

5. How is it possible, if at all, to "guiltlessly" condemn to death other people's children (par. 10)?

6. If you have read Michener's "The Assumptions of the Middle Class" in Section 2, what relationship, if any, do you see between it and Roiphe's ideas?

Expository Techniques

1. The central theme of this essay becomes clear more slowly than in most expository writings. (Guide: *Unity.*)
   a. At what point did you first become aware of it?
   b. Where is it first clearly stated?
   c. Is this a specific or a general statement? (Guide: *Specific/General.*)
   d. What then is the primary function of the rest of the essay?

2a. Is the further development accomplished more by comparison or contrast? Explain.
   b. Cite paragraphs by which your answer to 2a can best be illustrated.
   c. Which pattern of exposition previously studied does the author use more freely in her comparison/contrast? How effectively?

3. Which of the standard means of introducing an exposition are used in this essay? (Guide: *Introductions.*)

4a. In paragraphs 6 and 7 can be found examples of both rhetorical and non-rhetorical questions. (Guide: *Rhetorical Question.*) Identify one of each and show the difference.
   b. Cite one further question used as a rhetorical device.

5a. Cite two examples of parallel structure in paragraph 14. (Guide: *Parallel Structure.*)
   b. What advantage, if any, is gained by use of this technique.

6. How effective is the brief closing paragraph? (Guide: *Closings.*) Why?

Diction and Vocabulary

1a. What is the significance of the word "sow," as used in the title?
 b. How, if at all, is this significance a matter of connotation? (Guide: *Connotation/Denotation.*)

2a. Cite five figures of speech that you consider particularly effective. (Guide: *Figures of Speech.*)
 b. Indicate the kind of each.

3a. Which, if any, of the author's figures of speech could also be classed as a cliché. (Guide: *Clichés.*)
 b. If any, is its use justified here? Why, or why not?

4. Would you consider any of the author's expressions colloquial? (Guide: *Colloquial.*) If so, which?

5. Explain briefly how your answers to questions 2–4 are related to matters of style. (Guide: *Style/Tone.*)

6. Use the dictionary as necessary to understand the meanings of the following words: lexicon (par. 3); empathetic, artifacts (6); flaccid (8); chauvinism (8, 14); canard (9); masochistic (11); coevals, solace (12); vignette, cacophony (14).

Suggestions for Writing and Discussion

1. Show by use of examples that it is also possible in other matters to "believe two contradictory things at once" (par. 2).

2. Has it been your observation that girls are less likely than boys to embarrass one in public or to lie about such things as grades or sexual prowess (par. 4)? Explain the difference, if any.

3. What justification is there for laws forcing men to pay alimony and/or child support (par. 5)?

4. Is there any *natural* reason that mothers are less apt to desert their children than fathers? In your estimation, is one desertion more reprehensible than the other? Explain.

5. Explore the author's assertion (par. 11) that women are more masochistic than men.

6. If applicable, select any one aspect of Roiphe's "myth" about men-women differences and show why you still consider the difference more fact than myth.

(NOTE: Suggestions for topics requiring development by use of COMPARISON and CONTRAST are on page 104, at the end of this section.)

BRUCE CATTON

BRUCE CATTON, born in Michigan in 1899, is a Civil War specialist whose early career included reporting for various newspapers. He was the recipient of both the Pulitzer Prize for historical work and the National Book Award in 1954. He has served as director of information for the United States Department of Commerce and has written many books, including *Mr. Lincoln's Army* (1951), *Glory Road* (1952), *A Stillness at Appomattox* (1953), *The Hallowed Ground* (1956), *America Goes to War* (1958), *The Coming Fury* (1961), *Terrible Swift Sword* (1963), *Never Call Retreat* (1966), and *Waiting for the Morning Train: An American Boyhood* 1972). Since 1954 Catton has been editor of *American Heritage*.

Grant and Lee: A Study in Contrasts

"Grant and Lee: A Study in Contrasts" was written as a chapter of *The American Story*, a collection of essays by noted historians. In this study, as in most of his other writing, Catton does more than recount the facts of history: he shows the significance within them. It is a carefully constructed essay, using contrast and comparison as the entire framework for his explanation.

When Ulysses S. Grant and Robert E. Lee met in the parlor of a 1
modest house at Appomattox Court House, Virginia, on April 9, 1865, to work out the terms for the surrender of Lee's Army of Northern Virginia, a great chapter in American life came to a close, and a great new chapter began.

These men were bringing the Civil War to its virtual finish. To 2
be sure, other armies had yet to surrender, and for a few days the fugitive Confederate government would struggle desperately and vainly, trying to find some way to go on living now that its chief

support was gone. But in effect it was all over when Grant and Lee signed the papers. And the little room where they wrote out the terms was the scene of one of the poignant, dramatic contrasts in American history.

They were two strong men, these oddly different generals, and they represented the strengths of two conflicting currents that, through them, had come into final collision. 3

Back of Robert E. Lee was the notion that the old aristocratic concept might somehow survive and be dominant in American life. 4

Lee was tidewater Virginia, and in his background were family, culture, and tradition . . . the age of chivalry transplanted to a New World which was making its own legends and its own myths. He embodied a way of life that had come down through the age of knighthood and the English country squire. America was a land that was beginning all over again, dedicated to nothing much more complicated than the rather hazy belief that all men had equal rights and should have an equal chance in the world. In such a land Lee stood for the feeling that it was somehow of advantage to human society to have a pronounced inequality in the social structure. There should be a leisure class, backed by ownership of land; in turn, society itself should be keyed to the land as the chief source of wealth and influence. It would bring forth (according to this ideal) a class of men with a strong sense of obligation to the community; men who lived not to gain advantage for themselves, but to meet the solemn obligations which had been laid on them by the very fact that they were privileged. From them the country would get its leadership; to them it could look for the higher values — of thought, of conduct, of personal deportment — to give it strength and virtue. 5

Lee embodied the noblest elements of this aristocratic ideal. Through him, the landed nobility justified itself. For four years, the Southern states had fought a desperate war to uphold the ideals for which Lee stood. In the end, it almost seemed as if the Confederacy fought for Lee; as if he himself was the Confederacy . . . the best thing that the way of life for which the Confederacy stood could ever have to offer. He had passed into legend before Appomattox. Thousands of tired, underfed, poorly clothed Confederate soldiers, long since past the simple enthusiasm of the early days of the struggle, somehow considered Lee the symbol of everything for which they had been willing to die. But they could not 6 quite put this feeling into words. If the Lost Cause, sanctified by so much heroism and so many deaths, had a living justification, its justification was General Lee.

Grant, the son of a tanner on the Western frontier, was everything Lee was not. He had come up the hard way and embodied nothing in particular except the eternal toughness and sinewy fiber of the men who grew up beyond the mountains. He was one of a body of men who owed reverence and obeisance to no one, who were self-reliant to a fault, who cared hardly anything for the past but who had a sharp eye for the future. [7]

These frontier men were the precise opposites of the tidewater aristocrats. Back of them, in the great surge that had taken people over the Alleghenies and into the opening Western country, there was a deep, implicit dissatisfaction with a past that had settled into grooves. They stood for democracy, not from any reasoned conclusion about the proper ordering of human society, but simply because they had grown up in the middle of democracy and knew how it worked. Their society might have privileges, but they would be privileges each man had won for himself. Forms and patterns meant nothing. No man was born to anything, except perhaps to a chance to show how far he could rise. Life was competition. [8]

Yet along with this feeling had come a deep sense of belonging to a national community. The Westerner who developed a farm, opened a shop, or set up in business as a trader, could hope to prosper only as his own community prospered — and his community ran from the Atlantic to the Pacific and from Canada down to Mexico. If the land was settled, with towns and highways and accessible markets, he could better himself. He saw his fate in terms of the nation's own destiny. As its horizons expanded, so did his. He had, in other words, an acute dollars-and-cents stake in the continued growth and development of his country. [9]

And that, perhaps, is where the contrast between Grant and Lee becomes most striking. The Virginia aristocrat, inevitably, saw himself in relation to his own region. He lived in a static society which could endure almost anything except change. Instinctively, his first loyalty would go to the locality in which that society existed. He would fight to the limit of endurance to defend it, because in defending it he was defending everything that gave his own life its deepest meaning. [10]

The Westerner, on the other hand, would fight with an equal [11] tenacity for the broader concept of society. He fought so because everything he lived by was tied to growth, expansion, and a constantly widening horizon. What he lived by would survive or fall with the nation itself. He could not possibly stand by unmoved in the face of an attempt to destroy the Union. He would combat it with everything he had, because he could only see it as an effort to cut the ground out from under his feet.

So Grant and Lee were in complete contrast, representing two diametrically opposed elements in American life. Grant was the modern man emerging; beyond him, ready to come on the stage, was the great age of steel and machinery, of crowded cities and a restless, burgeoning vitality. Lee might have ridden down from the old age of chivalry, lance in hand, silken banner fluttering over his head. Each man was the perfect champion of his cause, drawing both his strengths and his weaknesses from the people he led. 12

Yet it was not all contrast, after all. Different as they were — in background, in personality, in underlying aspiration — these two great soldiers had much in common. Under everything else, they were marvelous fighters. Furthermore, their fighting qualities were really very much alike. 13

Each man had, to begin with, the great virtue of utter tenacity and fidelity. Grant fought his way down the Mississippi Valley in spite of acute personal discouragement and profound military handicaps. Lee hung on in the trenches at Petersburg after hope itself had died. In each man there was an indomitable quality . . . the born fighter's refusal to give up as long as he can still remain on his feet and lift his two fists. 14

Daring and resourcefulness they had, too; the ability to think faster and move faster than the enemy. These were the qualities which gave Lee the dazzling campaigns of Second Manassas and Chancellorsville and won Vicksburg for Grant. 15

Lastly, and perhaps greatest of all, there was the ability, at the end, to turn quickly from war to peace once the fighting was over. Out of the way these two men behaved at Appomattox came the possibility of a peace of reconciliation. It was a possibility not wholly realized, in the years to come, but which did, in the end, help the two sections to become one nation again . . . after a war whose bitterness might have seemed to make such a reunion wholly impossible. No part of either man's life became him more than the part he played in their brief meeting in the McLean house at 16

Appomattox. Their behavior there put all succeeding generations of Americans in their debt. Two great Americans, Grant and Lee — very different, yet under everything very much alike. Their encounter at Appomattox was one of the great moments of American history.

Meanings and Values

1a. Clarify the assertions that through Lee "the landed nobility justified itself" and that "if the Lost Cause . . . had a living justification," it was General Lee (par. 6).
 b. Why are these assertions pertinent to the central theme?

2a. Does it seem reasonable that "thousands of tired, underfed, poorly clothed Confederate soldiers" had been willing to fight for the aristocratic system in which they would never have had even a chance to be aristocrats? Why, or why not?
 b. Can you think of more likely reasons why they were willing to fight?

3. Under any circumstances today might such a social structure as the South's be best for a country? Explain.

4a. What countries of the world have recently been so torn by internal war and bitterness that reunion has seemed, or still seems, impossible?
 b. Do you see any basic differences between the trouble in those countries and that in America at the time of the Civil War?

5a. The author calls Lee a symbol (par. 6). Was Grant also a symbol? If so, of what?
 b. How would you classify this kind of symbolism? (See Guide to Terms: *Symbol*.)

Expository Techniques

1. Make an informal list of paragraph numbers from 3 to 16, and note by each whether the paragraph is devoted primarily to Lee, to Grant, or to direct comparison or contrast of the two. This chart will show you Catton's basic pattern of development. (Notice, for instance, how the broad information of paragraphs 4–6 and 7–9 seems almost to "funnel" down through the narrower summaries in 10 and 11 and into paragraph 12, where the converging elements meet and the contrast is made specific.)

2. What new technique of development is started in paragraph 13?

3a. What is gained, or lost, by the use of a single sentence for paragraph 3?
 b. For paragraph 4?

4a. How many paragraphs does the introduction comprise?

b. How successfully does it fulfill the three basic requirements of a good introduction? (Guide: *Introductions*.)

5. Show how Catton has constructed the beginning of each paragraph so that there is a smooth transition from the one preceding it. (Guide: *Transition*.)

6. The author's conclusion is really only the explanation of one of his integral points — and this method, if not carefully planned, runs the risk of ending too abruptly and leaving the reader unsatisfied. How has Catton avoided this hazard? (Guide: *Closings*.)

7a. What seems to be the author's attitude toward Grant and Lee?

b. Show how his tone reflects this attitude. (Guide: *Study/Tone*.)

Diction and Vocabulary

1. Why would a use of colloquialisms have been inconsistent with the tone of this writing?

2a. List or mark all metaphors in paragraphs 1, 3, 5, 7–11, 16. (Guide: *Figures of Speech*.)

b. Comment on their general effectiveness.

3. If you are not already familiar with the following words, study their meanings as given in the dictionary and as used in this essay: virtual, poignant (par. 2); concept (4); sinewy, obeisance (7); implicit (8); tenacity (11); diametrically, burgeoning (12); aspiration (13); fidelity, profound, indomitable (14); succeeding (16).

4. Explain how the word "poignant" aptly describes this contrast of two men (par. 2).

Suggestions for Writing and Discussion

1. Find, by minor research, an account of some incident in the life of Grant or Lee which can be used, in suitable essay form, to illustrate one of Catton's points.

2. Select some other dramatic moment in history and show its long-range significance.

3. Select some important moment in your life and show its long-range significance.

4. Explain how someone you know symbolizes a philosophy or way of life.

(Note: Suggestions for topics requiring development by use of COMPARISON and CONTRAST are on page 104, at the end of this section.)

ARTHUR L. CAMPA

ARTHUR L. CAMPA, born in 1905 of missionary parents in Guaymas, Mexico, received degrees at the University of New Mexico and Columbia University. Before becoming chairman of the Department of Modern Languages at the University of Denver in 1946, Campa served in the U.S. Air Force, had moved from instructor to professor at the University of New Mexico, and had already become a versatile and prolific writer. Campa has served the Department of State as cultural affairs officer in foreign embassies and as director of training projects for the Peace Corps. Since 1946 Campa has been director of the Center of Latin American Studies in Denver. His books include *Spanish Folk Poetry in New Mexico* (1946) and *Treasure of the Sangres des Christos* (1963).

Anglo vs. Chicano: Why?

"Anglo vs. Chicano: Why?" was written for *Western Review* and condensed somewhat for *Intellectual Digest*; we use the briefer version here. Campa goes further than most writers on this subject to develop a careful, point-by-point analysis of not only differences, but their origins and implications as well.

The cultural differences between Hispanic and Anglo-American 1 people have been dwelt upon by so many writers that we should all be well informed about the values of both. But audiences are usually of the same persuasion as the speakers, and those who consult published works are for the most part specialists looking for affirmation of what they believe. So, let us consider the same subject, exploring briefly some of the basic cultural differences that cause conflict in the Southwest, where Hispanic and Anglo-American cultures meet.

Cultural differences are implicit in the conceptual content of 2

Reprinted by permission of the author and publishers from *Intellectual Digest* (January 1973). First published in *Western Review*, vol. IX (Spring 1972).

the languages of these two civilizations, and their value systems stem from a long series of historical circumstances. Therefore, it may be well to consider some of the English and Spanish cultural configurations before these Europeans set foot on American soil. English culture was basically insular, geographically and ideologically; was more integrated on the whole, except for some strong theological differences; and was particularly zealous of its racial purity. Spanish culture was peninsular, a geographical circumstance that made it a catchall of Mediterranean, central European and north African peoples. The composite nature of the population produced a market regionalism that prevented close integration, except for religion, and led to a strong sense of individualism. These differences were reflected in the colonizing enterprise of the two cultures. The English isolated themselves from the Indians physically and culturally; the Spanish, who had strong notions about *pureza de sangre* [purity of blood] among the nobility, were not collectively averse to adding one more strain to their racial cocktail. Cortés led the way by siring the first *mestizo* in North America, and the rest of the conquistadores followed suit. The ultimate products of these two orientations meet today in the Southwest.

    Anglo-American culture was absolutist at the onset; that is, all the dominant values were considered identical for all, regardless of time and place. Such values as justice, charity, honesty were considered the superior social order for all men and were later embodied in the American Constitution. The Spaniard brought with him a relativistic viewpoint and saw fewer moral implications in man's actions. Values were looked upon as the result of social and economic conditions. 3

    The motives that brought Spaniards and Englishmen to America also differed. The former came on an enterprise of discovery, searching for a new route to India initially, and later for new lands to conquer, the fountain of youth, minerals, the Seven Cities of Cíbola and, in the case of the missionaries, new souls to win for the Kingdom of Heaven. The English came to escape religious persecution, and once having found a haven, they settled down to cultivate the soil and establish their homes. Since the Spaniards were not seeking a refuge or running away from anything, they continued their explorations and circled the globe 25 years after the discovery of the New World. 4

    This peripatetic tendency of the Spaniard may be accounted 5 for in part by the fact that he was the product of an equestrian culture. Men on foot do not venture far into the unknown. It was almost a century after the landing on Plymouth Rock that Governor Alexander Spotswood of Virginia crossed the Blue Ridge Mountains, and it was not until the nineteenth century that the Anglo-Americans began to move west of the Mississippi.

The Spaniard's equestrian role meant that he was not close to the soil, as was the Anglo-American pioneer, who tilled the land and built the greatest agricultural industry in history. The Spaniard cultivated the land only when he had Indians available to do it for him. The uses to which the horse was put also varied. The Spanish horse was essentially a mount, while the more robust English horse was used in cultivating the soil. It is therefore not surprising that the viewpoints of these two cultures should differ when we consider that the pioneer is looking at the world at the level of his eyes while the *caballero* [horseman] is looking beyond and down at the rest of the world.   6

One of the most commonly quoted, and often misinterpreted, characteristics of Hispanic peoples is the deeply ingrained individualism in all walks of life. Hispanic individualism is a revolt against the incursion of collectivity, strongly asserted when it is felt that the ego is being fenced in. This attitude leads to a deficiency in those social qualities based on collective standards, an attitude that Hispanos do not consider negative because it manifests a measure of resistance to standardization in order to achieve a measure of individual freedom. Naturally, such an attitude has no *reglas fijas* [fixed rules].   7

Anglo-Americans who achieve a measure of success and security through institutional guidance not only do not mind a few fixed rules but demand them. The lack of a concerted plan of action, whether in business or in politics, appears unreasonable to Anglo-Americans. They have a sense of individualism, but they achieve it through action and self-determination. Spanish individualism is based on feeling, on something that is the result not of rules and collective standards but of a person's momentary, emotional reaction. And it is subject to change when the mood changes. In contrast to Spanish emotional individualism, the Anglo-American strives for objectivity when choosing a course of action or making a decision.   8

The Southwestern Hispanos voiced strong objections to the   9 lack of courtesy of the Anglo-Americans when they first met them in the early days of the Santa Fe trade. The same accusation is leveled at the *Americanos* today in many quarters of the Hispanic world. Some of this results from their different conceptions of polite behavior. Here too one can say that the Spanish have no *reglas fijas* because for them courtesy is simply an expression of the way one person feels toward another. To some they extend the hand, to some they bow and for the more *íntimos* there is the well-known *abrazo*. The concepts of "good or bad" or "right and wrong" in polite behavior are moral considerations of an absolutist culture.

Another cultural contrast appears in the way both cultures share part of their material substance with others. The pragmatic Anglo-American contributes regularly to such institutions as the Red Cross, the United Fund and a myriad of associations. He also establishes foundations and quite often leaves millions to such institutions. The Hispano prefers to give his contribution directly to the recipient so he can see the person he is helping. 10

A century of association has inevitably acculturated both Hispanos and Anglo-Americans to some extent, but there still persist a number of culture traits that neither group has relinquished altogether. Nothing is more disquieting to an Anglo-American who believes that time is money than the time perspective of Hispanos. They usually refer to this attitude as the "*mañana* psychology." Actually, it is more of a "today psychology," because Hispanos cultivate the present to the exclusion of the future; because the latter has not arrived yet, it is not a reality. They are reluctant to relinquish the present, so they hold on to it until it becomes the past. To an Hispano, nine is nine until it is ten, so when he arrives at nine-thirty, he jubilantly exclaims: "¡Justo!" [right on time]. This may be why the clock is slowed down to a walk in Spanish while in English it runs. In the United States, our future-oriented civilization plans our lives so far in advance that the present loses its meaning. January magazine issues [including ID's] are out in December; 1973 cars have been out since October; cemetery plots and even funeral arrangements are bought on the installment plan. To a person engrossed in living today the very idea of planning his funeral sounds like the tolling of the bells. 11

It is a natural corollary that a person who is present oriented should be compensated by being good at improvising. An Anglo- 12

American is told in advance to prepare for an "impromptu speech," but an Hispano usually can improvise a speech because "*Nosotros lo improvisamos todo*" [we improvise everything].

Another source of cultural conflict arises from the difference 13 between *being* and *doing*. Even when trying to be individualistic, the Anglo-American achieves it by what he does. Today's young generation decided to be themselves, to get away from standardization, so they let their hair grow, wore ragged clothes and even went barefoot in order to be different from the Establishment. As a result they all ended up doing the same things and created another stereotype. The freedom enjoyed by the individuality of *being* makes it unnecessary for Hispanos to strive to be different.

In 1963 a team of psychologists from the University of 14 Guadalajara in Mexico and the University of Michigan compared 74 upper-middle-class students from each university. Individualism and personalism were found to be central values for the Mexican students. This was explained by saying that a Mexican's value as a person lies in his *being* rather than, as is the case of the Anglo-Americans, in concrete accomplishments. Efficiency and accomplishments are derived characteristics that do not affect worthiness in the Mexican, whereas in the American it is equated with success, a value of highest priority in the American culture. Hispanic people disassociate themselves from material things or from actions that may impugn a person's sense of being, but the Anglo-American shows great concern for material things and assumes responsibility for his actions. This is expressed in the language of each culture. In Spanish one says, "*Se me cayó la taza*" [the cup fell away from me] instead of "I dropped the cup."

In English, one speaks of money, cash and all related trans- 15 actions with frankness because material things of this high order do not trouble Anglo-Americans. In Spanish such materialistic concepts are circumvented by referring to cash as *efectivo* [effective] and when buying or selling as something *al contado* [counted out], and when without it by saying *No tengo fondos* [I have no funds]. This disassociation from material things is what produces *sobriedad* [sobriety] in the Spaniard according to Miguel de Unamuno, but in the Southwest the disassociation from materialism leads to *dejadez* [lassitude] and *desprendimiento* [disinterestedness]. A man may lose his life defending his honor but is unconcerned about the lack of material things. *Desprendimiento* causes a man to spend his last cent on a friend, which when added to lack of concern for the future may mean that tomorrow he will eat beans as a result of today's binge.

The implicit differences in words that appear to be identical 16 in meaning are astonishing. *Versatile* is a compliment in English and an insult in Spanish. An Hispano student who is told to apologize cannot do it, because the word doesn't exist in Spanish. *Apologia* means words in praise of a person. The Anglo-American either apologizes, which is a form of retraction abhorrent in Spanish, or compromises, another concept foreign to Hispanic culture. *Compromiso* means a date, not a compromise. In colonial Mexico City, two hidalgos once entered a narrow street from opposite sides, and when they could not go around, they sat in their coaches for three days until the viceroy ordered them to back out. All this because they could not work out a compromise.

It was that way then and to some extent now. Many of today's 17 conflicts in the Southwest have their roots in polarized cultural differences, which need not be irreconcilable when approached with mutual respect and understanding.

Meanings and Values

1a. What is this author's point of view? (See Guide to Terms: *Point of View*.)
 b. Does he maintain this viewpoint consistently? If not where does he lose it?
2. Where, if at all, does he engage in sentimentality? (Guide: *Sentimentality*.)
3. Differentiate the meanings of "objective" and/or "subjective" by citing portions of this essay. (Guide: *Objective/Subjective*.)
4. Why do you suppose the author ignored Indian influence in explaining present-day Chicano culture?
5. What type of essay is "Anglo vs. Chicano: Why?" (Guide: *Essay*.)
6. Give this selection our three-step critical evaluation. (Guide: *Evaluation*.)

Expository Techniques

1a. Is Campa's development primarily by comparison or by contrast?
 b. Are there any exceptions? If so, where?

   c. Given his particular subject, does this seem to indicate a one-sided analysis? Explain.

2a. Which of the basic means of organizing comparison/contrast does the author use?

   b. Would the other method have been better? Why, or why not?

3a. How many individual items of comparison/contrast has he developed?

   b. Cite the paragraphs devoted to each.

4. Would the essay have benefited by greater use of qualification? (Guide: *Qualification.*) If so, how?

5. Demonstrate by specific passages how generalizations can be made more specific through the use of examples. (Guide: *Specific/General.*)

6. Does the last sentence seem fully justified, prepared for by the preceding analysis? Why, or why not?

Diction and Vocabulary

1a. For the average American reader, does this author overuse foreign words and expressions? Explain the reasons for your answer.

   b. Most of these words are defined, but not all of them — e.g., *mestizo* (par. 2) and *abrazo* (9). Why do you think he made exceptions of these?

   c. The Spanish word "conquistadores" is not printed in italics (par. 2). Why?

2. Familiarize yourself with the following words and their meanings, consulting a dictionary as necessary: implicit, conceptual, configurations, insular, ideological, peninsular (par. 2); relativistic (3); peripatetic (5); equestrian (5, 6); incursion (7); recipient (10); acculturated (11); corollary (12); impugn (14); retraction (16).

3. Can the relatively large number of "dictionary-type" words be explained in terms of Campa's expected reader-audience? If so, how?

Suggestions for Writing and Discussion

1. Use one of Campa's major points for still further development or for analytic refutation.

2. If you can do so with any reliable knowledge of the subject, show what effects Indian culture had on that of today's Chicano.

3. In areas where Anglo and Chicano cultures have long been in contact, what effects have they already had on each other?

4. Select some other American ethnic group and show how cultural background differences have also caused conflict when confronted

with Anglo culture. If possible, show how this conflict was, or is being, resolved.

5. Agree or disagree with Campa's assertion that the young generation of Anglo-Americans merely created another stereotype (par. 13). Support your stand.

6. If you have read Michener's "The Assumptions of the Middle Class" in Section Two, what points of similarity do you find between his views and Campa's?

(NOTE: Suggestions for topics requiring development by use of COMPARISON and CONTRAST are on page 104, at the end of this section.)

TIME magazine essays are sometimes the result of group effort by members of the staff and are therefore printed without a by-line. The following selection is one of these.

Male and Female:
The Differences Between Them

"Male and Female: The Differences Between Them" was a *Time* essay in March 1972. It delves into a subject of widespread current interest and dispute; in so doing, it also provides us with another example of point-by-point comparative analysis.

"The Book of Genesis had it wrong. In the beginning God created Eve," says Johns Hopkins Medical Psychologist John Money. What he means is that the basic tendency of the human fetus is to develop as a female. If the genes order the gonads to become testicles and put out the male hormone androgen, the embryo will turn into a boy; otherwise it becomes a girl: "You have to add something to get a male," Money notes. "Nature's first intention is to create a female."   1

Nature may prefer women, but virtually every culture has been partial to men. That contradiction raises an increasingly pertinent question (as well as the hackles of militant feminists): Are women immutably different from men? Women's Liberationists believe that any differences — other than anatomical — are a result of conditioning by society. The opposing view is that all of the differences are fixed in the genes. To scientists, however, the nature-nurture controversy is oversimplified. To them, what human beings are results from a complex interaction between both forces.   2

94

Says Oxford Biologist Christopher Ounsted: "It is a false dichotomy to say that this difference is acquired and that one genetic. To try and differentiate is like asking a penny whether it is really a heads penny or a tails penny." As Berkeley Psychologist Frank Beach suggests, "Predispositions may be genetic; complex behavior patterns are probably not."

The idea that genetic predispositions exist is based on three kinds of evidence. First, there are the "cultural universals" cited by Margaret Mead. Almost everywhere, the mother is the principal caretaker of the child, and male dominance and aggression are the rule. Some anthropologists believe there has been an occasional female-dominated society; others insist that none have existed.

SEX TYPING

Then there is the fact that among most ground-dwelling primates, males are dominant and have as a major function the protection of females and offspring. Some research suggests that this is true even when the young are raised apart from adults, which seems to mean that they do not learn their roles from their society.

Finally, behavioral sex differences show up long before any baby could possibly perceive subtle differences between his parents or know which parent he is expected to imitate. "A useful strategy," says Harvard Psychologist Jerome Kagan, "is to assume that the earlier a particular difference appears, the more likely it is to be influenced by biological factors."

Physical differences appear even before birth. The heart of the female fetus often beats faster, and girls develop more rapidly. "Physiologically," says Sociologist Barbette Blackington, "women are better-made animals." Males do have more strength and endurance — though that hardly matters in a technological society.

Recent research hints that there may even be sex differences in the brain. According to some experimenters, the presence of the male hormone testosterone in the fetus may "masculinize" the brain, organizing the fetal nerve centers in characteristic ways. This possible "sex typing" of the central nervous system before birth may make men and women respond differently to incoming stimuli, Sociologist John Gagnon believes.

In fact, newborn girls do show different responses in some situations. They react more strongly to the removal of a blanket and more quickly to touch and pain. Moreover, experiments demonstrate that twelve-week-old girls gaze longer at photographs of faces than at geometric figures. Boys show no preference then, though eventually they pay more attention to figures. Kagan acknowledges the effect of environment, but he has found that it exerts a greater influence on girls than on boys. The female infants who experienced the most "face-to-face interaction" with their mothers were more attentive to faces than girls whose mothers did not exchange looks with them so much. Among boys, there was no consistent relationship.

INTERNAL ORGANS

As some psychologists see it, this very early female attention to the human face suggests that women may have a greater and even partly innate sensitivity to other human beings. Perhaps this explains why girls seem to get more satisfaction from relationships with people.

Even after infancy, the sexes show differential interests that do not seem to grow solely out of experience. Psychoanalyst Erik Erikson has found that boys and girls aged ten to twelve use space differently when asked to construct a scene with toys. Girls often build a low wall, sometimes with an elaborate doorway, surrounding a quiet interior scene. Boys are likely to construct towers, façades with cannons, and lively exterior scenes. Erikson acknowledges that cultural influences are at work, but he is convinced that they do not fully explain the nature of children's play. The differences, he says, "seem to parallel the morphology [shape and form] of genital differentiation itself: in the male, an external organ, erectible and intrusive; internal organs in the female, with vestibular access, leading to statically expectant ova."

In aptitude as well as in interest, sex differences become apparent early in life. Though girls are generally less adept than boys at mathematical and spatial reasoning, they learn to count sooner and to talk earlier and better. Some scientists think this female verbal superiority may be caused by sex-linked differences in the brain. Others believe it may exist because, as observation proves, mothers talk to infant girls more than to baby boys. But does the mother's talking cause the child to do likewise, or could it be the other way round? Psychologist Michael Lewis suggests the possibility that girls are talked to more because, for biological reasons, they respond more than boys to words and thus stimulate their mothers to keep talking.

Evidence that parental behavior does affect speech comes from tests made by Kagan among poor Guatemalan children. There, boys are more highly valued than girls, are talked to more and become more verbal. In the U.S., Psychiatrist David Levy has found that boys who are atypically good with words and inept with figures have been overprotected by their mothers. Psychologist Elizabeth Bing has observed that girls who excel at math and spatial problems have often been left to work alone by their mothers, while highly verbal girls have mothers who offer frequent suggestions, praise and criticism.   12

While girls outdo boys verbally, they often lag behind in solving analytical problems, those that require attention to detail. Girls seem to think "globally," responding to situations as a whole instead of abstracting single elements. In the "rod and frame test," for instance, a subject sits in a dark room before a luminous rod inside a slightly tilted frame, and is asked to move the rod to an upright position. Boys can separate the rod visually from the frame and make it stand straight; girls, misled by the tipped frame, usually adjust the rod not to the true vertical but to a position parallel with the sides of the frame.   13

In another experiment, children are asked to group related pictures. Boys again pay attention to details, perhaps putting together pictures that show people with an arm raised; girls make functional groups of, for example, a doctor, a nurse and a wheelchair.   14

In all such differences, environmental influence is suggested by the fact that children who think analytically most often prove to have mothers who have encouraged initiative and exploration, while youngsters who think globally have generally been tied to their mother's apron strings. In Western society, of course, it is usually boys who are urged toward adventure. Herein, perhaps — there is no proof — lies an explanation for the apparent male capacity to think analytically.   15

In IQ tests, males and females score pretty much alike. Since this is true, why do women seem less creative? Many social scientists are convinced that the reasons are cultural. Women, they say, learn early in life that female accomplishment brings few   16 rewards. In some cases, women cannot be creative because they are discriminated against. In other instances, a woman's creativity may well be blunted by fear of nonconformity, failure or even success itself. Unlike men, Kagan says, women are trained to have strong anxiety about being wrong.

To many psychoanalysts, however, the explanation lies in the   17
fact that women possess the greatest creative power of all: bringing new life into being; thus they need not compensate by producing works of art. Men, it is theorized, are driven to make up for what seem to them a deficiency. That they feel keenly, though unconsciously, their inability to bear children is shown in dreams reported on the analyst's couch, in the behavior of small boys who play with dolls and walk around with their stomachs thrust forward in imitation of their pregnant mothers and in primitive rites and ancient myths. According to these myths, presumably conceived by males, Adam delivered Eve from his rib cage, Zeus gave birth to Athena out of his head, and when Semele was burned to death, Zeus seized Dionysus from her womb and sewed him up in his thigh until the infant had developed.

There are personality differences between the sexes too. Al-   18
though no trait is confined to one sex — there are women who exceed the male average even in supposedly masculine characteristics — some distinctions turn up remarkably early. At New York University, for example, researchers have found that a female infant stops sucking a bottle and looks up when someone comes into the room; a male pays no attention to the visitor.

Another Kagan experiment shows that girls of twelve months   19
who become frightened in a strange room drift toward their mothers, while boys look for something interesting to do. At four months, twice as many girls as boys cry when frightened in a strange laboratory. What is more, Kagan says, similar differences can be seen in monkeys and baboons, which "forces us to consider the possibility that some of the psychological differences between men and women may not be the product of experience alone but of subtle biological differences."

FEMALE PASSIVITY

Many researchers have found greater dependence and docility in   20
very young girls, greater autonomy and activity in boys. When a

barrier is set up to separate youngsters from their mothers, boys try to knock it down; girls cry helplessly. There is little doubt that maternal encouragement — or discouragement — of such behavior plays a major role in determining adult personality. For example, a mother often stimulates male autonomy by throwing a toy far away from her young son, thus tacitly suggesting to him that he leave her to get it.

Animal studies suggest that there may be a biological factor in   21 maternal behavior; mothers of rhesus monkeys punish their male babies earlier and more often than their female offspring; they also touch their female babies more often and act more protective toward them.

As for the controversial question of female "passivity," Psy-   22 choanalyst Helene Deutsch believes that the concept has been misunderstood. "There is no contradiction between being feminine and working. The ego can be active in both men and women," she says. It is only in love and in sex that passivity is particularly appropriate for women. As she sees it, passivity is no more than a kind of openness and warmth; it does not mean "inactivity, emptiness or immobility."

Another controversy rages over the effect of hormones. Mil-   23 itant women, who discount hormonal influence, disagree violently with scientific researchers, who almost unanimously agree that hormones help determine how people feel and act. So far, there have been few studies of male hormones, but scientists think they may eventually discover hormonal cycles in men that produce cyclic changes in mood and behavior. As for females, studies have indicated that 49% of female medical and surgical hospital admissions, most psychiatric hospital admissions and 62% of violent crimes among women prisoners occur on premenstrual and menstrual days. At Worcester State Hospital in Massachusetts, Psychologists Donald and Inge Broverman have found that estrogen sharpens sensory perception. They believe that this heightened sensitivity may lead more women than men to shy away from situations of stress.

FIERCE BULLS

One trait thought to be affected by hormones is agressiveness. In   24 all cultures, investigators report, male infants tend to play more aggressively than females. While scientists think a genetic factor may be involved, they also observe that society fosters the difference by permitting male aggression and encouraging female adaptability. Some suggest that females may be as aggressive as men — but with words instead of deeds.

The definitive research on hormones and aggression is still to   25
be done. However, it has been established that the female hormone estrogen inhibits aggression in both animal and human males. It has also been proved that the male hormone androgen influences aggression in animals. For example, castration produces tractable steers rather than fierce bulls.

The influence of androgen begins even before birth. Admin-   26
istered to pregnant primates, the hormone makes newborn females play more aggressively than ordinary females. Moreover, such masculinized animals are usually aggressive as long as they live, even if they are never again exposed to androgen.

According to some experts, this long-lasting effect of hor-   27
mones administered or secreted before birth may help explain why boys are more aggressive than girls even during their early years when both sexes appear to produce equal amounts of male and female hormones. Other observers have suggested that the spurt in male-hormone production at puberty could be one of the causes of delinquency in adolescent boys, but there is no proof that this is so.

Will there some day be a "unisex" society with no differences   28
between men and women, except anatomical ones? It seems unlikely. Anatomy, parturition and gender, observes Psychologist Joseph Adelson, cannot be wished away "in a spasm of the distended will, as though the will, in pursuit of total human possibility, can amplify itself to overcome the given." Or, as Psychoanalyst Therese Benedek sees it, "biology precedes personality."

"Nature has been the oppressor," observes Michael Lewis.   29
Women's role as caretaker "was the evolutionary result of their biological role in birth and feeding." The baby bottle has freed women from some of the tasks of that role, but, says University of Michigan Psychologist Judith Bardwick, "the major responsibility for child rearing is the woman's, even in the Soviet Union, the Israeli kibbutz, Scandinavia and mainland China." Furthermore, though mothering skills are mostly learned, it is a fact that if animals are raised in isolation and then put in a room with the young of the species, it is the females who go to the infants and take care of them.

"Perhaps the known biological differences can be totally over-   30
come, and society can approach a state in which a person's sex is of
no consequence for any significant activity except childbearing,"
admits Jerome Kagan. "But we must ask if such a society will be
satisfying to its members." As he see it, "complementarity" is what
makes relationships stable and pleasurable.

Psychoanalyst Martin Symonds agrees. "The basic reason why   31
unisex must fail is that in the sexual act itself, the man has to be
assertive, if tenderly, and the woman has to be receptive. What
gives trouble is when men see assertiveness as aggression and
women see receptiveness as submission." Unisex, he sums up,
would be "a disaster," because children need roles to identify with
and rebel against. "You can't identify with a blur. A unisex world
would be a frictionless environment in which nobody would be
able to grow up."

The crucial point is that a difference is not a deficiency. As   32
Biologist Ounsted puts it, "We are all human beings and in this
sense equal. We are not, however, the same." In the opinion of
John Money, "You can play fair only if you recognize and respect
authentic differences."

Though scientists disagree about the precise nature and   33
causes of these differences, there is no argument about two points:
society plays a tremendous part in shaping the differences, and
most women are capable of doing whatever they want. Only in the
top ranges of ability, says Kagan, are innate differences significant;
for typical men and women, "the biological differences are totally
irrelevant." Psychiatrist Donald Lunde agrees. "There is no evidence," he asserts, "that men are any more or less qualified by
biological sex differences alone to perform the tasks generally re-
served for them in today's societies."

Meanings and Values

1a. Undoubtedly the intent of this essay was to offer an unbiased, completely objective analysis. Does it succeed in this respect?
 b. Provide specific support for your answer.
2a. If "militant women" (par. 23) deny the findings of scientific researchers, on whose authority do you think they base their dis-
   counting of hormonal influences?
 b. Does it seem to be a sound basis for dispute?

3. Do you think the closing paragraph is sufficiently prepared for in the text itself? Why, or why not?

Expository Techniques

1. Does the fact that this essay uses contrast almost exclusively, showing only differences, indicate bias on the part of the authors? Why, or why not?

2. Would some plan of organization other than point-by-point contrast have been as effective? Why, or why not?

3a. At least three standard techniques for introducing exposition are combined in paragraph 1. (See Guide to Terms: *Introductions*.) What are they?
   b. How effectively are they used?
   c. What other methods might have been used?

4a. Paragraphs 3–5 employ another "pattern of exposition" already studied, to assist in the primary comparative analysis. What pattern is it?
   b. Paragraph 5 also serves a subtle but important purpose in the further development of the essay. What is this function?

5a. Most paragraphs of this essay are linked to preceding paragraphs by transitional devices. (Guide: *Transition*.) Cite five such transitions.
   b. Explain how this is also a matter of coherence. (Guide: *Coherence*.)

6a. Is more confusion than benefit derived from the extensive use of quotations and references to scientists whose names mean nothing to average readers?
   b. What useful purpose, if any, does this practice serve?

7a. Cite examples of five differing types of qualification. (Guide: *Qualification*.)
   b. Is this practice overused — e.g., does it promote, or hinder, good credibility?

Diction and Vocabulary

1. Do you think that for *Time* readers the essay should have avoided such physiological terms as "testosterone," "estrogen," and "androgen"? Why, or why not?

2. Explain why references to mythological characters in paragraph 17 should, or should not, be considered rhetorical allusions. (Guide: *Allusions*.)

3. Use the dictionary as needed to understand the meanings of the following words: hackles, immutably, dichotomy, predispositions

(par. 2); innate (9); façades, vestibular (10); atypically (12); autonomy, tacitly (20); definitive (25); parturition (28).

Suggestions for Writing and Discussion

1. What trends do you see which may indicate that we are moving toward a "unisex" society (par. 28). Or, if you prefer, show why you consider reports of such trends and their probable outcomes to be greatly exaggerated.

2. Frequently people object to having human personality traits compared to and explained by those of animals (pars. 4, 19, 21, 25–26, 29). Does this seem to you a valid objection?

3. Select one or more of the following quotations as a basis for further discussion.

   a. "Males do have more strength and endurance — though that hardly matters in a technological society" (par. 6).

   b. "[G]irls seem to get more satisfaction from relationships with people" (par. 9).

   c. "[B]oys who are atypically good with words and inept with figures have been overprotected by their mothers" (par. 12).

   d. "Men, it is theorized, are driven to make up for what seems to them a deficiency" (par. 17).

   e. " '[C]omplementarity' is what makes relationships stable and pleasurable" (par. 30).

Writing Suggestions for Section 3
Comparison and Contrast

Base your central theme on one of the following, and develop your composition primarily by use of comparison and/or contrast. Use examples liberally for clarity and concreteness, chosen always with your purpose and reader-audience in mind.

1. The working conditions of two jobs.
2. Two kinds of home life.
3. The sea at two different times.
4. Two ways to quit smoking.
5. Two modes of travel.
6. The innate qualifications needed for success in two careers.
7. The natural temperaments of two acquaintances.
8. Two types of protesters.
9. Two styles in protest demonstrations.
10. Two restaurants.
11. Two poets.
12. Two policemen.
13. The teaching techniques of two instructors or former teachers.
14. Two methods of parental handling of teenage problems.
15. Two family attitudes toward the practice of religion.
16. Two "moods" of the same town at different times.
17. The personalities (or atmospheres) of two cities or towns of similar size.
18. Two acquaintances who exemplify different ways of serving humanity.
19. Two acquaintances who seem to symbolize different philosophies of life.
20. Two different attitudes toward the same thing or activity: one "practical," the other romantic or aesthetic.
21. The beliefs and practices of two religions or denominations concerning *one* aspect of religion.
22. Two courses on the same subject: one in high school and one in college.
23. The differing styles of two players of some sport or game.
24. *One* aspect of city life and of life on a farm, in a small town, or in a suburb.
25. *One* aspect of military life and of civilian life.
26. The hazards of frontier life and those of today.

4

Using *Analogy* as an Expository Device

Analogy is a special form of comparison that is used for a specific purpose: to explain something abstract or difficult to understand by showing its similarity to something concrete or easy to understand. A much less commonly used technique than logical comparison (and contrast), analogy is, nonetheless, a highly efficient means of explaining some difficult concepts or of giving added force to the explanations.

Logical comparison is made between two members of the same general class, usually assuming the same kind of interest in the subject matter of both. But in analogy we are really concerned only with the subject matter of one, using a second just to help explain the first. The two subjects, quite incomparable in most respects, are never of the same general class; if they are, we then have logical comparison, not analogy.

If the analogy is to be effective, the writer should be able to assume that his reader is familiar enough with the easier subject, or can quickly be made so, that it really helps explain the more difficult one. A common example is the explanation of the human circulatory system, which we may have trouble comprehending, by comparing the heart and arteries with a pump forcing water through the pipes of a plumbing system. This analogy has been carried further to liken the effect of cholesterol deposits on the inner walls of the arteries to mineral deposits that accumulate inside water pipes and eventually close them entirely. Although there is little logical similarity between a steel pipe and a human artery, the *analogical* similarity would be apparent to most readers — but the analogy might cause even greater confusion for any who did not know about pumps.

Distinguishing between analogy and metaphor is sometimes difficult. The difference is basically in their purpose: the function of a metaphor is merely *to describe,* to create a brief, vivid image for the reader; the function of analogy is primarily one of exposition, *to explain,* rather than to describe. In this sense, however, the function of a metaphor is actually *to suggest* an analogy: instead of showing the similarities of the heart and the pump, a metaphor might simply refer to "that faithful pump inside my chest," implying enough of a comparison to serve its purpose as description. (We can see here why some people refer to analogy as "extended" metaphor.) The analogist, when trying to explain the wide selection of college subjects and the need for balance in a course of study, could use the easily understood principle of a cafeteria, which serves Jell-O and lemon meringue pie, as well as meat and potatoes. If his purpose had been only to create an image, to describe, he might have referred simply to the bewildering variety in "the cafeteria of college courses" — and that would have been a metaphor. (For another example of analogy, see the explanation of *Unity,* in Guide to Terms.)

As useful as analogy can be in exposition, however, it is a risky technique to use in logical argument. It should never be offered anywhere as *proof.* The two subjects of any analogy, although similar in one or more useful ways, are basically too unlike to form any kind of dependable evidence.

SYLVIA ASHTON-WARNER

SYLVIA ASHTON-WARNER lived her early life in New Zealand. From her experiences there teaching the native Maoris she developed the educational theories expounded in her books and lectures. Ms. Ashton-Warner's best-known books are *Teacher* and *Spearpoint: "Teacher" in America* (1972). She has also written five novels, among them *Spinster* (1958) and *Three* (1970). Now living in Vancouver, Canada, Ms. Ashton-Warner has spent the past few years teaching and lecturing extensively in India, England, Israel, the United States, and Canada.

Gate-Crashing a Child's Mind

"Gate-Crashing a Child's Mind" (editor's title) is an excerpt from the book *Spearpoint*. It offers a brief but clear example of analogy at work, while also serving to illustrate this author's imaginative and sensitive style of writing which, among other qualities, has earned wide admiration by readers across several continents.

I like the picture of the mind of our child as a house owned by his   1
soul, inhabited by his instincts; his wants, fears, desires and loves, his hates and happinesses. A merry, motley, moving company, some potential homicides, others pure saints, rubbing shoulders and elbows with one another, all together going for it, like a carnival of celebrants dancing madly. At times, from the pressures within, they venture outside into the street for a breath of fresh air, exercise themselves and encounter others, bring back food and something new to talk about, returning somewhat civilised.

But now you see the unskilled teacher outside in the street   2
come to the door, not knock and wait, but gate-crash with his own

company of imagery, join battle with the defendants, rout them and take over occupancy, so that the native images flee and hide under beds, behind doors, beneath the staircase or in the toolshed at the back, where they die of wounds and deprivation. The house is now full of alien imagery belonging to the teacher. What's wrong with it . . . it's imagery, isn't it? But the thing is that the replacing imagery is not alive as the native inhabitants were. It is static. It can't dance. It can only do what it's told to do and what it sees to copy. It doesn't go out and see the world and make a contribution. It can't make you think and do things . . . and the ravished soul vacates. Absentee landlord.

Simultaneously the teacher takes over occupancy of the other   3
houses in the street, the minds of the other children in his class, so that now we have the same kind of imagery in every one of the houses, all copies of the teacher, in a street named Conformity. As for all the former native occupants of the houses, now deceased, it's what I call murder of the imagery. Spiritually speaking, millions of children are murdered annually. Trained and paid to do it.

On the other hand, here is the enlightened skillful teacher   4
strolling in the street, agog with interest in whom he meets, engaging in conversation. An interesting person at the least, so that people from the houses, the native inhabitants, are disposed to come out and meet him, exchange greetings and ideas with him. Sometimes with him and often without him, they feel free to think and do things . . . outside in the world. A street named Variation.

Meanings and Values

1a. What actually are the "exercise" and the "food" in the street outside the mind (par. 1)?
 b. Provide examples of both.
2. What is the irony, if any, in the latter part of paragraph 3? (See Guide to Terms: *Irony*.)
3. In what respects other than artistic could the murder of a child's native imagery be a serious loss?
4. Use this selection to illustrate the meaning of the term "subjective writing." (Guide: *Objective/Subjective*.)
5. Compare and/or contrast the style and tone of this writing with those of any other selection already studied. (Guide: *Style/Tone*.)

Expository Techniques

1. Does this selection fulfill all the requirements for analogy? Explain.
2. Does "Gate-Crashing a Child's Mind" exemplify good coherence? (Guide: *Coherence.*) Support your answer, being as specific as possible.
3a. Can Ashton-Warner's frequent use of unconventional sentence structures be justified in this particular writing? Explain why, or why not.
   b. Why would they be less suitable in ordinary college writing, such as research papers?

Diction and Vocabulary

1a. Within this analogy (primary function of which is always to *explain*) the author also uses figurative language liberally. Cite five examples of metaphors or similes and indicate which each is. (Guide: *Figures of Speech.*)
   b. Why is the use of figurative language especially appropriate to this writing?
2. How important is diction to Ashton-Warner's style? (Guide: *Style/Tone.*) Cite examples.

Suggestions for Writing and Discussion

1. What far-reaching effects could a preponderance of "gate-crashing" teachers have on culture itself, perhaps on the kind of civilization future generations will inherit?
2. Choose two teachers of your experience or acquaintance who seem to exemplify the extremes described by Ashton-Warner. Contrast their methods and results, using concrete examples wherever possible.
3. If you see her first type of teacher as less devastating than she does, provide a thoughtful defense. Or you may wish to consider, practically our very real problems of mass education on a scale that few generations have ever before attempted.

(NOTE: Suggestions for topics requiring development by use of ANALOGY are on page 128, at the end of this section.)

CHARLES OSGOOD

CHARLES OSGOOD, born in 1933, is a native New Yorker who is known for his work as a news correspondent and feature reporter on radio and television. In 1954 he graduated from Fordham University with a degree in economics. Osgood was program director, general manager, and general assignment reporter for various networks; in 1967 he joined CBS where he is known as "poet in residence" for his reporting in lyric verse. He can be seen regularly on the CBS Morning News.

Nations Can Be Schizoid Too

"Nations Can Be Schizoid Too" (editor's title) was written as a CBS broadcast commentary. An experienced commentator such as Osgood, however, devotes as much attention to sound principles of composition as would any other careful writer. Such essays as this, in fact, are usually prepared with both oral and (later) written communication in mind.

One mark of schizophrenia or a schizoid personality according to R.D. Laing, one of the world's experts on the subject, is that a person gets to feeling that at least part of his life and experience is somehow unreal. There's a real self and an unreal self. The real self, his actual core personality, is what he calls me. But it's the me nobody knows. The other part, the unreal, accidental, or artificial self, is the one he projects to the world. The sicker he gets the more he thinks it is the unreal self and not the real self that is acting when he acts. The him that is driving a car, listening to the radio, fighting with his wife, or robbing a bank is not the real him. However, if you have to deal with this individual the real him is the one that's doing these things. What he thinks of as the real him is what is unreal to everybody else. The individual they see walking, talking, acting one way or another, is what that individual

Charles Osgood's *Profile* (CBS News, November 10, 1971) reprinted by permission of CBS News.

really is as far as they are concerned. That inner him that nobody knows, nobody knows — so it is unreal to them.

Now all of us are a little bit schizoid. We all do this thing of distinguishing between ourselves as we conceive of ourselves and the superficial, at least from our point of view superficial, us that faces the rest of the world. Of course to the rest of the world that superficial face is us.

Nations can be schizoid, too. We can, for example, get to feeling that the real America is something quite distinct from the day-to-day way that America is and acts. We can say yes there are awful problems in the cities but the cities are not the real America. We can say yes there are economic and social problems but that unemployed people, black people, or poor people are not the real Americans. We can say yes there is injustice but the real America is just. We can acknowledge the American military is the biggest, strongest, and most expensive in the world . . . yet know on another level that the real America is not militaristic, is peaceloving and would never act the bully. We can say the polluted lakes and streams and rivers are just an accident of progress — they are not the real American waters — any more than the air over New York or LA is the real American air.

To the outside world the real America is what they see and hear — what we say and how we act. To them the real America is homes and radio and newspapers, highways, our television, our politicians and policemen, our criminals and prisons — it is our businesses, science, schools, hospitals, cities, suburbs, farms — everything visible, audible, and tangible about us. The point is that we are all these things and that to the extent we disassociate from them and feel that they have nothing to do with us to that extent we are schizoid. Finally if we get to the point where we think that there is a real America only we can see, if our inner vision does not correspond to what other people think about us, we shouldn't be too surprised if they think we are crazy.

Meanings and Values

1. Most rhetoricians maintain that an individual cannot properly be used to analogize a group of individuals of the same class, however *representative* he may be of the group.

a. Does it seem to you that a nation is merely a collection of individuals — or is it more? If the latter, what else is it?
b. Do you consider this selection a proper example of analogy?

2a. Does the author seem to be implying a moralistic judgment on the United States? Cite specific references that support your answer.
b. Is this a better example of objective or subjective writing — or would you place it somewhere in between? Why?

3a. What other countries, if any, seem to be afflicted with schizophrenia?
b. In what ways?

4. Use the three-point system of evaluation to judge the success of this selection. (See Guide to Terms: *Evaluation.*)

Expository Techniques

1a. How successful is the author's gradual revealing of his central theme? (Guide: *Unity.*)
b. Has he sacrificed unity because of not divulging his basic premise earlier? Explain why, or why not.

2. What, if anything, is gained by quoting an expert, even indirectly, in the introduction?

3a. Which of the first two sentences of paragraph 3 is more specific? (Guide: *Specific/General.*) Why?
b. How does the second sentence compare in this respect with the remaining sentences of the paragraph?
c. Construct a sentence of your own by which to demonstrate a still greater degree of specificity than the third sentence.

4. What advantages, if any, are gained by the extensive use of parallel construction in paragraph 3? (Guide: *Parallel Structure.*)

Diction and Vocabulary

1a. Considering the original purpose of this composition, why is it not surprising that we find few, if any, "difficult" words?
b. Is the term "schizoid" defined sufficiently to accomplish its function here?

2a. The author's concluding word was undoubtedly a deliberate choice, selected for its effect. (These things seldom "just happen," even for a professional writer or speaker.) How effective is it? Analyze the reasons for your answer.
b. How, if at all, is this a matter of connotation? (Guide: *Connotation/Denotation.*)

Suggestions for Writing and Discussion

1. Select one of the apparent contradictions mentioned in paragraph 3, or provide one of your own, and show how it is, or is not, a valid indication of national schizophrenia. (Some of the subjects, such as America's militarism, have become so riddled with clichés that a real effort will be needed to achieve any degree of originality.)

2. Develop further your answer to question 1a of "Meanings and Values" to show what a nation really is, if not merely a collection of people.

3. Refer, if you like, to question 3 of "Meanings and Values" and select another country which seems, from what you have read or observed, to show definite signs of schizoid personality. Show the contrast between its two "faces."

(NOTE: Suggestions for topics requiring development by use of ANALOGY are on page 128, at the end of this section.)

ALVIN TOFFLER

ALVIN TOFFLER, a native of New York City and graduate of New York University, has been a Washington correspondent for various newspapers and magazines and has contributed to numerous other magazines and professional journals. At one time he was an associate editor of *Fortune*. He has served on the faculty of New School for Social Research and has lectured at Cornell and other universities. Toffler wrote *The Culture Consumers* (1964), and edited *Schoolhouse in the City* (1968).

Modular Man

"Modular Man" (editor's title) is from the chapter "The Cost of Involvement" in Toffler's record-breaking best seller *Future Shock*, published in 1970. Here he has used simple analogy to help explain his concept of one personal problem imposed on city dwellers by increasing "urbanism."

Urbanism — the city dweller's way of life — has preoccupied sociology since the turn of the century. Max Weber pointed out the obvious fact that people in cities cannot know all their neighbors as intimately as it was possible for them to do in small communities. Georg Simmel carried this idea one step further when he declared, rather quaintly, that if the urban individual reacted emotionally to each and every person with whom he came into contact, or cluttered his mind with information about them, he would be "completely atomized internally and would fall into an unthinkable mental condition." 1

Louis Wirth, in turn, noted the fragmented nature of urban relationships. "Characteristically, urbanites meet one another in highly segmental roles ..." he wrote, "Their dependence upon 2 others is confined to a highly fractionalized aspect of the other's round of activity." Rather than becoming deeply involved with the total personality of every individual we meet, he explained, we necessarily maintain superficial and partial contact with some. We are interested only in the efficiency of the shoe salesman in meeting our needs; we couldn't care less that his wife is an alcoholic.

What this means is that we form limited involvement relationships with most of the people around us. Consciously or not we define our relationships with most people in functional terms. So long as we do not become involved with the shoe salesman's problems at home, or his more general hopes, dreams and frustrations, he is, for us, fully interchangeable with any other salesman of equal competence. In effect, we have applied the modular principle to human relationships. We have created the disposable person: Modular Man.

Rather than entangling ourselves with the whole man, we plug into a module of his personality. Each personality can be imagined as a unique configuration of thousands of such modules. Thus no whole person is interchangeable with any other. But certain modules are. Since we are seeking only to buy a pair of shoes, and not the friendship, love or hate of the salesman, it is not necessary for us to tap into or engage with all the other modules that form his personality. Our relationship is safely limited. There is limited liability on both sides. The relationship entails certain accepted forms of behavior and communication. Both sides understand, consciously or otherwise, the limitations and laws. Difficulties arise only when one or another party oversteps the tacitly understood limits, when he attempts to connect up with some module not relevant to the function at hand.

Today a vast sociological and psychological literature is devoted to the alienation presumed to flow from this fragmentation of relationships. Much of the rhetoric of existentialism and the student revolt decries this fragmentation. It is said that we are not sufficiently "involved" with our fellow man. Millions of young people go about seeking "total involvement."

Before leaping to the popular conclusion that modularization is all bad, however, it might be well to look more closely at the matter. Theologian Harvey Cox, echoing Simmel, has pointed out that in an urban environment the attempt to "involve" oneself fully with everyone can lead only to self-destruction and emotional emptiness.

Urban man, he writes, "must have more or less impersonal relationships with most of the people with whom he comes in contact precisely in order to choose certain friendships to nourish and cultivate ... His life represents a point touched by dozens of systems and hundreds of people. His capacity to know some of them better necessitates his minimizing the depth of his relationship to many others. Listening to the postman gossip becomes for the urban man an act of sheer graciousness, since he probably has no interest in the people the postman wants to talk about."

Moreover, before lamenting modularization, it is necessary to   7
ask ourselves whether we really would prefer to return to the traditional condition of man in which each individual presumably related to the whole personality of a few people rather than to the personality modules of many. Traditional man has been so sentimentalized, so cloyingly romanticized, that we frequently overlook the consequences of such a return. The very same writers who lament fragmentation also demand freedom — yet overlook the un-freedom of people bound together in totalistic relationships. For any relationship implies mutual demands and expectations. The more intimately involved a relationship, the greater the pressure the parties exert on one another to fulfill these expectations. The tighter and more totalistic the relationship, the more modules, so to speak, are brought into play, and the more numerous are the demands we make.

In a modular relationship, the demands are strictly bounded.   8
So long as the shoe salesman performs his rather limited service for us, thereby fulfilling our rather limited expectations, we do not insist that he believe in our God, or that he be tidy at home, or share our political values, or enjoy the same kind of food or music that we do. We leave him free in all other matters — as he leaves us free to be atheist or Jew, heterosexual or homosexual, John Bircher or Communist. This is not true of the total relationship and cannot be. To a certain point, fragmentation and freedom go together.

All of us seem to need some totalistic relationships in our   9
lives. But to decry the fact that we cannot have *only* such relationships is nonsense. And to prefer a society in which the individual has holistic relationships with a few, *rather than* modular relationships with many, is to wish for a return to the imprisonment of the past — a past when individuals may have been more tightly bound to one another, but when they were also more tightly regimented

by social conventions, sexual mores, political and religious restrictions.

This is not to say that modular relationships entail no risks or   10
that this is the best of all possible worlds. There are, in fact, profound risks in the situation. . . . Until now, however, the entire public and professional discussion of these issues has been badly out of
focus.

Meanings and Values

1a. Explain further, using examples, the "limitations and laws" which
    "both sides" understand in typical urban contact with other people
    (par. 4).
  b. Just what is it that happens when one of the parties oversteps the
     limits?
2. Why is it necessary to limit relationships with most people to know
    a few others well (par. 6) — e.g., is this merely a matter of the
    limitation of time?
3a. How is it that "traditional man" has become romanticized (par. 7)?
  b. Is there anything ironical in thus overlooking the "unfreedom" of
     people totally involved with each other? (See Guide to Terms:
     Irony.) Explain.
4. Use the three-point system of evaluation to measure the success of
    this selection. (Guide: *Evaluation.*)

Expository Techniques

1a. Where does Toffler's analogy begin?
  b. Why can it not qualify as logical comparison?
  c. Why not as metaphor?
  d. How successfully does it fulfill the basic purpose of analogy?
2a. Cite two examples each of loose and periodic sentences. (Guide:
    Emphasis.)
  b. In what way is the use of these a matter of emphasis?
  c. How, if at all, is such usage related to syntax? (Guide: *Syntax.*)
3a. Illustrate the meaning of "parallel structure" by examples from
    paragraph 8. (Guide: *Parallel Structure.*)
  b. If the use of such structures is also a matter of syntax, explain how.
4a. How does Toffler make the highly generalized statement of Louis
    Wirth more specific (par. 2)? (Guide: *Specific/General.*)
  b. In which paragraphs is this specific put to still further uses?

Diction and Vocabulary

1a. The word "modular" has in very recent years taken on new meaning in everyday parlance. Supply as many examples as possible of this newer usage. (The word itself could be used, of course, to illustrate the fact that our language is in a constant state of change.)

 b. How appropriate is the word to the purposes of this analogy?

2. If not already familiar with the following words as they are used in this selection, consult your dictionary for their meanings: configuration, entails, tacitly (4); existentialism (5); cloyingly (7).

Suggestions for Writing and Discussion

1. Explain fully, using examples as necessary, what may happen to the urban dweller who gets too involved with too many "total personalities."

2. Trace the process by which an increasing intimacy of relationship between two people (preferably *not* romantic) increases the pressures on each other (par. 7).

3. Do you agree that all of us need some totalistic relationships in our lives (par. 9)? How can this be, with the inevitable result of restriction on our own freedom?

4. Where may we still find situations in which individuals are "tightly bound to one another" within a group (par. 9), with modular relationships severely limited? If you have had experience in such a situation, explain its effect on freedom.

5. Discuss some of the most apparent "profound risks" entailed in modular relationships (par. 10).

(NOTE: Suggestions for topics requiring development by use of ANALOGY are on page 128, at the end of this section.)

TOM WOLFE

Tom Wolfe grew up in Richmond, Virginia, was graduated from Washington and Lee University, and took his doctorate at Yale. After working for several years as a reporter for the Washington *Post*, he joined the staff of the New York *Herald Tribune* in 1962. He has won two Washington Newspaper Guild Awards, one for humor and the other for foreign news. Wolfe has been a regular contributor to *New York, Esquire*, and other magazines. His books include *The Kandy-Kolored Tangerine-Flake Streamline Baby* (1965), *The Electric Kool-Aid Acid Test* (1968), and *Radical Chic and Mau-mauing the Flak Catchers* (1970).

O Rotten Gotham—
Sliding Down into the Behavioral Sink

"O Rotten Gotham — Sliding Down into the Behavioral Sink," as used here, is excerpted from a longer selection by that title in Wolfe's book *The Pump House Gang* (1968). Here, as he frequently does, this author investigates an important aspect of modern life — seriously, but in his characteristic and seemingly freewheeling style. It is a style that is sometimes ridiculed by scholars but is far more often admired. (Wolfe, as the serious student can discover for himself, is always in complete control of his materials and methods, using them to create certain effects, to reinforce his ideas.) In this piece his analogy is particularly noteworthy for the extensive usage he is able to get from it.

I just spent two days with Edward T. Hall, an anthropologist, watching thousands of my fellow New Yorkers short-circuiting themselves into hot little twitching death balls with jolts of their

Reprinted by permission of Farrar, Straus & Giroux, Inc., from *The Pump House Gang*, by Tom Wolfe. Copyright © 1968 by Tom Wolfe. Copyright © 1966 by the World Journal Tribune Corporation. Copyright © 1964, 1965, 1966 by the New York Herald Tribune, Inc.

own adrenalin. Dr. Hall says it is overcrowding that does it. Overcrowding gets the adrenalin going, and the adrenalin gets them
queer, autistic, sadistic, barren, batty, sloppy, hot-in-the-pants,
chancred-on-the-flankers, leering, puling, numb — the usual in
New York, in other words, and God knows what else. Dr. Hall has
the theory that overcrowding has already thrown New York into a
state of behavioral sink. Behavorial sink is a term from ethology,
which is the study of how animals relate to their environment.
Among animals, the sink winds up with a "population collapse" or
"massive die-off." O rotten Gotham.

It got to be easy to look at New Yorkers as animals, especially   2
looking down from some place like a balcony at Grand Central at
the rush hour Friday afternoon. The floor was filled with the poor
white humans, running around, dodging, blinking their eyes, making a sound like a pen full of starlings or rats or something.

"Listen to them skid," says Dr. Hall.   3

He was right. The poor old etiolate animals were out there   4
skidding on their rubber soles. You could hear it once he pointed it
out. They stop short to keep from hitting somebody or because they
are disoriented and they suddenly stop and look around, and they
skid on their rubber-soled shoes, and a screech goes up. They pour
out onto the floor down the escalators from the Pan-Am Building,
from 42nd Street, from Lexington Avenue, up out of subways,
down into subways, railroad trains, up into helicopters —

"You can also hear the helicopters all the way down here," says   5
Dr. Hall. The sound of the helicopters using the roof of the Pan-
Am Building nearly fifty stories up beats right through. "If it
weren't for this ceiling" — he is referring to the very high ceiling
in Grand Central — "this place would be unbearable with this kind
of crowding. And yet they'll probably never 'waste' space like this
again."

They screech! And the adrenal glands in all those poor white   6
animals enlarge, micrometer by micrometer, to the size of canta-
loupes. Dr. Hall pulls a Minox camera out of a holster he has on his
belt and starts shooting away at the human scurry. The Sink!

Dr. Hall has the Minox up to his eye — he is a slender man,   7
calm, 52 years old, young-looking, an anthropologist who has
worked with Navajos, Hopis, Spanish-Americans, Negroes, Trukese.
He was the most important anthropologist in the government during the crucial years of the foreign aid program, the 1950's. He di-

rected both the Point Four training program and the Human Relations Area Files. He wrote *The Silent Language* and *The Hidden Dimension*, two books that are picking up the kind of "underground" following his friend Marshall McLuhan started picking up about five years ago. He teaches at the Illinois Institute of Technology, lives with his wife, Mildred, in a high-ceilinged town house on one of the last great residential streets in downtown Chicago, Astor Street; has a grown son and daughter, loves good food, good wine, the relaxed, civilized life — but comes to New York with a Minox at his eye to record! — perfect — The Sink.

We really got down in there by walking down into the Lexing-   8
ton Avenue line subway stop under Grand Central. We inhaled those nice big fluffy fumes of human sweat, urine, effluvia, and sebaceous secretions. One old female human was already stroked out on the upper level, on a stretcher, with two policemen standing by. The other humans barely looked at her. They rushed into line. They bellied each other, haunch to paunch, down the stairs. Human heads shone through the gratings. The species North European tried to create bubbles of space around themselves, about a foot and a half in diameter —

"See, he's reacting against the line," says Dr. Hall.   9

— but the species Mediterranean presses on in. The hell with   10
bubbles of space. The species North European resents that, this male human behind him presses forward toward the booth ... *breathing* on him, he's disgusted, he pulls out of the line entirely, the species Mediterranean resents him for resenting it, and neither of them realizes what the hell they are getting irritable about exactly. And in all of them the old adrenals grow another micrometer.

Dr. Hall whips out the Minox. Too perfect! The bottom of The   11
Sink.

It is the sheer overcrowding, such as occurs in the business   12
sections of Manhattan five days a week and in Harlem, Bedford-Stuyvesant, southeast Bronx every day — sheer overcrowding is converting New Yorkers into animals in a sink pen. Dr. Hall's argument runs as follows: all animals, including birds, seem to have a built-in, inherited requirement to have a certain amount of territory, space, to lead their lives in. Even if they have all the food they need, and there are no predatory animals threatening them, they cannot tolerate crowding beyond a certain point. No more

than two hundred wild Norway rats can survive on a quarter acre
of ground, for example, even when they are given all the food they
can eat. They just die off.

But why? To find out, ethologists have run experiments on all   13
sorts of animals, from stickleback crabs to Sika deer. In one major
experiment, an ethologist named John Calhoun put some domes-
ticated white Norway rats in a pen with four sections to it, connected by ramps. Calhoun knew from previous experiments that
the rats tend to split up into groups of ten to twelve and that the
pen, therefore, would hold forty to forty-eight rats comfortably,
assuming they formed four equal groups. He allowed them to reproduce until there were eighty rats, balanced between male and
female, but did not let it get any more crowded. He kept them supplied with plenty of food, water, and nesting materials. In other
words, all their more obvious needs were taken care of. A less
obvious need — space — was not. To the human eye, the pen did
not even look especially crowded. But to the rats, it was crowded
beyond endurance.

The entire colony was soon plunged into a profound be-   14
havioral sink. "The sink," said Calhoun, "is the outcome of any
behavioral process that collects animals together in unusually great
numbers. The unhealthy connotations of the term are not accidental: a behavioral sink does act to aggravate all forms of pathology that can be found within a group."

For a start, long before the rat population reached eighty, a   15
status hierarchy had developed in the pen. Two dominant male rats
took over the two end sections, acquired harems of eight to ten
females each, and forced the rest of the rats into the two middle
pens. All the overcrowding took place in the middle pens. That was
where the "sink" hit. The aristocrat rats at the end grew bigger,
sleeker, healthier, and more secure the whole time.

In The Sink, meanwhile, nest building, courting, sex behavior,   16
reproduction, social organization, health — all of it went to pieces.
Normally, Norway rats have a mating ritual in which the male
chases the female, the female ducks down into a burrow and sticks
her head up to watch the male. He performs a little dance outside
the burrow, then she comes out, and he mounts her, usually for a
few seconds. When The Sink set in, however, no more than three
males — the dominant males in the middle sections — kept up the
old customs. The rest tried everything from satyrism to homo-

sexuality or else gave up on sex altogether. Some of the subordinate males spent all their time chasing females. Three or four might chase one female at the same time, and instead of stopping at the burrow entrance for the ritual, they would charge right in. Once mounted, they would hold on for minutes instead of the usual seconds.

Homosexuality rose sharply. So did bisexuality. Some males would mount anything — males, females, babies, senescent rats anything. Still other males dropped sexual activity altogether, wouldn't fight and, in fact, would hardly move except when the other rats slept. Occasionally a female from the aristocrat rats' harems would come over the ramps and into the middle sections to sample life in The Sink. When she had had enough, she would run back up the ramp. Sink males would give chase up to the top of the ramp, which is to say, to the very edge of the aristocratic preserve. But one glance from one of the king rats would stop them cold and they would return to The Sink. 17

The slumming females from the harems had their adventures and then returned to a placid, healthy life. Females in The Sink, however, were ravaged, physically and psychologically. Pregnant rats had trouble continuing pregnancy. The rate of miscarriages increased significantly, and females started dying from tumors and other disorders of the mammary glands, sex organs, uterus, ovaries, and Fallopian tubes. Typically, their kidneys, livers, and adrenals were also enlarged or diseased or showed other signs associated with stress. 18

Child-rearing became totally disorganized. The females lost the interest or the stamina to build nests and did not keep them up if they did build them. In the general filth and confusion, they would not put themselves out to save offspring they were momentarily separated from. Frantic, even sadistic competition among the males were going on all around them and rendering their lives chaotic. The males began unprovoked and senseless assaults upon one another, often in the form of tail-biting. Ordinarily, rats will suppress this kind of behavior when it crops up. In The Sink, male rats gave up all policing and just looked out for themselves. The "pecking order" among males in The Sink was never stable. Normally, male rats set up a three-class structure. Under the pressure of overcrowding, however, they broke up into all sorts of unstable subclasses, cliques, packs — and constantly pushed, probed, ex- 19

plored, tested one another's power. Anyone was fair game, except
for the aristocrats in the end pens.

Calhoun kept the population down to eighty, so that the next   20
stage, "population collapse" or "massive die-off," did not occur.
But the autopsies showed that the pattern — as in the diseases
among the female rats — was already there.

The classic study of die-off was John J. Christian's study of   21
Sika deer on James Island in the Chesapeake Bay, west of Cam-
bridge, Maryland. Four or five of the deer had been released on the
island, which was 280 acres and uninhabited, in 1916. By 1955 they
had bred freely into a herd of 280 to 300. The population density
was only about one deer per acre at this point, but Christian knew
that this was already too high for the Sikas' inborn space requirements, and something would give before long. For two years the
number of deer remained 280 to 300. But suddenly, in 1958,
over half the deer died; 161 carcasses were recovered. In 1959
more deer died and the population steadied at about 80.

In two years, two-thirds of the herd had died. Why? It was not   22
starvation. In fact, all the deer collected were in excellent condition,
with well-developed muscles, shining coats, and fat deposits between the muscles. In practically all the deer, however, the adrenal
glands had enlarged by 50 percent. Christian concluded that the
die-off was due to "shock following severe metabolic disturbance,
probably as a result of prolonged adrenocortical hyperactivity. . . .
There was no evidence of infection, starvation, or other obvious
cause to explain the mass mortality." In other words, the constant
stress of overpopulation, plus the normal stress of the cold of the
winter, had kept the adrenalin flowing so constantly in the deer
that their systems were depleted of blood sugar and they died of
shock.

Well, the white humans are still skidding and darting across   23
the floor of Grand Central. Dr. Hall listens a moment longer to the
skidding and the darting noises, and then says, "You know, I've
been on commuter trains here after everyone has been through one
of these rushes, and I'll tell you, there is enough acid flowing in the
stomachs in every car to dissolve the rails underneath."

Just a little invisible acid bath for the linings to round off the   24
day. The ulcers the acids cause, of course, are the one disease people have already been taught to associate with the stress of city life.
But overcrowding, as Dr. Hall sees it, raises a lot more hell with
the body than just ulcers. In everyday life in New York — just the

usual, getting to work, working in massively congested areas like 42nd Street between Fifth Avenue and Lexington, especially now that the Pan-Am Building is set in there, working in cubicles such as those in the editorial offices at Time-Life, Inc., which Dr. Hall cites as typical of New York's poor handling of space, working in cubicles with low ceilings and, often, no access to a window, while construction crews all over Manhattan drive everybody up the Masonite wall with air-pressure generators with noises up to the boil-a-brain decibel levels, then rushing to get home, piling into subways and trains, fighting for time and for space, the usual day in New York — the whole now-normal thing keeps shooting jolts of adrenalin into the body, breaking down the body's defenses and winding up with the work-a-daddy human animal stroked out at the breakfast table with his head apoplexed like a cauliflower out of his $6.95 semi-spread Pima-cotton shirt, and nosed over into a plate of No-Kloresto egg substitute, signing off with the black thrombosis, cancer, kidney, liver, or stomach failure, and the adrenals ooze to a halt, the size of eggplants in July.

One of the people whose work Dr. Hall is interested in on this score is Rene Dubos at the Rockefeller Institute. Dubos's work indicates that specific organisms, such as the tuberculosis bacillus or a pneumonia virus, can seldom be considered "the cause" of a disease. The germ or virus, apparently, has to work in combination with other things that have already broken the body down in some way — such as the old adrenal hyperactivity. Dr. Hall would like to see some autopsy studies made to record the size of adrenal glands in New York, especially of people crowded into slums and people who go through the full rush-hour-work-rush-hour cycle every day. He is afraid that until there is some clinical, statistical data on how overcrowding actually ravages the human body, no one will be willing to do anything about it. Even in so obvious a thing as air pollution, the pattern is familiar. Until people can actually see the smoke or smell the sulphur or feel the sting in their eyes, politicians will not get excited about it, even though it is well known that many of the lethal substances polluting the air are invisible and odorless. For one thing, most politicians are like the aristocrat rats. They are insulated from The Sink by practically sultanic buffers — limousines, chauffeurs, secretaries, aides-de-camp, doormen, shuttered houses, high-floor apartments. They almost never ride subways, fight rush hours, much less live in the slums or work in the Pan-Am Building.

Meanings and Values

1a. Who are members of the "species Mediterranean"?
 b. Who belong to the "species North European"?
 c. What could account for their difference in space requirements (pars. 8–10)?

2. Is this writing primarily objective or subjective? (See Guide to Terms: *Objective/Subjective*.) Why?

3a. Do you get the impression that the author is being unkind, "making fun" of the harried New Yorkers?
 b. What positive step does he take early in the essay which should help to prevent such an impression?

4a. How would you describe the author's rather unique point of view? (Guide: *Point of View*.)
 b. What, if anything, does it have to do with the writing's tone? (Guide: *Style/Tone*.)

5. Compare the tone of this selection with that of any of the preceding essays you have read.

Expository Techniques

1a. Using whatever criteria we have available for judging the success of analogy, appraise the effectiveness of this one.
 b. Does the author work it *too* hard? Be prepared to defend your answer.

2. What are the benefits of the frequent return to what Dr. Hall is doing or saying (e.g., in pars. 3, 5, 7, 9, 11, 23)?

3. Paragraph 12 has a useful function beyond the simple information it imparts — a sort of organic relation to the coming development. Explain how this is accomplished.

4. How is the switch to Sika deer (par. 21) prepared for, avoiding bumpy transition?

5. The preceding three questions have been related in some manner to the problems of transition. How, if at all, are such problems also matters of coherence? (Guide: *Coherence*.)

6. Wolfe is adept at creating just the effect he wants, and the careful student of writing can detect a subtle change of style and pace with each change of subpurpose. (Guide: *Style/Tone*.)
 a. Analyze stylistic differences, with resulting effects, between the description of chaos at Grand Central and the information about Dr. Hall in paragraph 7.
 b. Between the Grand Central scene and the account of the laboratory experiment with rats.
 c. Between the Grand Central scene and the last paragraph.

7. Explain how the style of the more descriptive portions is also a matter of emphasis. (Guide: *Emphasis*.)

8a. Illustrate as many as possible of the elements of effective syntax (itself a matter of style) by examples from this selection. (Guide: *Syntax*.)

 b. What is gained or lost by the unusual length and design of the last sentence of paragraph 24? (We can be sure that it did not "just happen" to Wolfe — and equally sure that one of such length would be disastrous in most writing.)

Diction and Vocabulary

1. What is the significance of the word "Gotham"?

2a. Why do you think the author referred (deliberately, no doubt) to "my fellow New Yorkers" in the first sentence?

 b. What soon could have been the effect if he had not taken such a step?

3. Why does he consistently, after paragraph 2, refer to the people as "poor white humans," "poor human animals," etc?

4. In paragraph 14 he refers to the connotations of the word "sink." What are its possible connotations? (Guide: *Connotation/Denotation*.)

5. Cite examples of verbal irony to be found in paragraphs 5, 8, 24. (Guide: *Irony*.)

6. Which of the elements of style mentioned in your answer to question 6 of "Meanings and Values" are also matters of diction?

7a. Compare Wolfe's diction with that of Catton, Campa (Section 3), Osgood, or Toffler (Sec. 4).

 b. Could their respective uses of diction have been interchanged without detriment to one or both writings? Explain.

8. Consult your dictionary as needed for full understanding of the following words: nephritic, autistic, puling (par. 1); etiolate (4); effluvia, sebaceous (8); pathology (14); satyrism (16); senescent (17); decibel, thrombosis (24); lethal (25).

Suggestions for Writing and Discussion

1. Carrying Wolfe's analogy still further, trace the steps by which a rise in serious crime must result from the overcrowding of "poor human animals."

2. If you are familiar with another city, particularly during rush hours, which appears to you much like New York in this respect, explain what it is like.

3. If you are familiar with some area of high density population that has solved this problem of overcrowding, explain how it was achieved.

4. What practical steps can the *individual* take, if forced to live and/or work in overcrowded conditions, to prevent becoming the victim of his own adrenals?

Writing Suggestions for Section 4
Analogy

(In any normal situation, of course, the analogy is chosen to help explain a theme-idea that already exists — such as those in the first group below. But for classroom training, which even at best is bound to be somewhat artificial, it is sometimes permissible to work from the other direction, to develop a theme that fits some preselected analogy-symbol. Your instructor will indicate which of the groups he prefers you to use.)

1. State a central theme about one of the following general topics or a suitable one of your own, and develop it into a composition by use of an analogy of your own choosing.

   a. A well-organized school system or business establishment.
   b. Starting a new kind of business or other enterprise.
   c. The long-range value of programs for underprivileged children.
   d. The complexity of narcotics control.
   e. The need for cooperation between management and labor.
   f. Today's intense competition for success.
   g. Women's liberation in a "man's world."
   h. The results of ignorance.
   i. The dangers of propaganda.

2. Select an analogy-symbol from the following list and fashion a worthwhile theme that it can illustrate. Develop your composition as instructed.

   a. A freeway at commuting time.
   b. Building a road through a wilderness.
   c. Building a bridge across a river.
   d. A merry-go-round.
   e. A wedding.
   f. A car-wash.
   g. Flood-destruction of a levee.
   h. The tending of a young orchard.
   i. An animal predator stalking prey.
   j. A medical clinic.
   k. A juggling act.

l. An oasis.
m. The game of baseball.
n. A spider's web.
o. A kaleidoscope.
p. A fine clock.

3. Use one of the following suggestions on which to build a complete statement of the central theme for your writing. Develop your composition as instructed.

a. A college education as a savings account.
b. A good book as a long hike.
c. A freshman at registration (or orientation) as a mouse in a maze.
d. The church as a giant oak standing alone.
e. "Playing the field" as a smorgasbord.
f. The college curriculum as a smorgasbord.
g. Racial projudice as a malignant growth.
h. A selling technique as that of catching a fish.
i. A military unit as a machine.
j. College as a mountain to be climbed.
k. Success as a magnet.

Explaining through *Process Analysis*

Process analysis explains how the steps of an operation lead to its completion. Although in one narrow sense it may be considered a kind of narration, process analysis has an important difference in purpose, and hence in approach. Other narration is mostly concerned with the story itself, or with a general concept illustrated by it, but process tells of methods that end in specified results. We might narrate a story about a rifle — its purchase, its role in colorful episodes, perhaps its eventual retirement from active service. (We could, for other purposes, *define* "rifle," or *classify* the types of rifles, no doubt *compare* and *contrast* these types and *illustrate* by examples.) But to show how a rifle works, or how it is manufactured, or how it should be cared for — this is process, and it sometimes becomes the basic pattern of an exposition.

Most writers are especially concerned with two kinds of process, both of them apparent in the preceding example of rifles: the directional, which explains how to *do* something (how to shoot a gun or how to clean it); and the informational, which explains how something is or was *done* (how guns are manufactured). The directional process can vary from the instructions on a shampoo bottle to a detailed plan showing how to make the United Nations more effective. The informational process, on the other hand, might explain the steps of a wide variety of operations or actions or mental processes, with no how-to-do-it purpose at all — how someone went about choosing a college or how the planet Earth was formed. Informational process analysis has been seen in earlier selections: Peter and Hull explained how the Peter Principle works, Wolfe how the experiment with Norway rats was conducted.

Most process analyses are explained in simple, chronological steps. Indeed, the exact order is sometimes of greatest importance, as in a recipe. But occasionally there are problems in organization. The step-by-step format may need to be interrupted for descriptions, definitions, or other explanatory asides. And, still more of a problem, some processes defy a strict chronological treatment, because several things occur simultaneously. To explain the operating process of a gasoline engine, for example, the writer would be unable to convey at once everything that happens at the same time. Some way must be found to present the material in *general* stages, organized as subdivisions, so that the reader can see the step-by-step process through the confusion of interacting relationships.

Another difficulty in explaining by process analysis is estimating what knowledge the reader may already have. Presuming too little background may quickly result in his boredom or even irritability, with a resulting communication block; presuming too much will almost certainly lose him through bewilderment. Like a chain dependent on its weakest line for its strength, the entire process analysis can fail because of just one unclear point that makes the rest unintelligible.

ERNEST HEMINGWAY

ERNEST HEMINGWAY (1899–1961), an American best known as a novelist and short-story writer, began his writing career as a cub reporter on the *Kansas City Star*. During World War I he was wounded while serving with the Italian infantry as an ambulance driver. After the war he did some writing in the United States and for several years in Europe, supporting himself as a foreign correspondent for the *Toronto Star*. Among Hemingway's many famous novels are *The Sun Also Rises* (1926), *A Farewell to Arms* (1929), *For Whom the Bell Tolls* (1940), *Across the River and Into the Trees* (1950), and *The Old Man and the Sea* (1952). The latter won the 1953 Pulitzer Prize in fiction and was instrumental in winning Hemingway the Nobel Prize for Literature in 1954. The Nobel Prize committee praised his "forceful and style-making mastery of the art of modern narration."

The Bull Fight as Symbolism

"The Bull Fight as Symbolism" (editor's title) is from Hemingway's book *By-Line* (1967), a collection of his articles and dispatches of four decades. This piece was written early in Hemingway's career as a writer, and his later famous prose style was only beginning to develop. But the selection gives us an example of simple, step-by-step analysis of uncomplicated process.

Bull fighting is not a sport. It is a tragedy, and it symbolizes the struggle between man and the beasts. There are usually six bulls to a fight. A fight is called a cordia de toros. Fighting bulls are bred like race horses, some of the oldest breeding establishments being several hundred years old. A good bull is worth about $2,000. They are bred for speed, strength and viciousness. In other words a good fighting bull is an absolutely incorrigible bad bull.   1

Bull fighting is an exceedingly dangerous occupation. In six- 2
teen fights I saw there were only two in which there was no one
badly hurt. On the other hand it is very remunerative. A popular
espada gets $5,000 for his afternoon's work. An unpopular espada
though may not get $500. Both run the same risks. It is a good deal
like Grand Opera for the really great matadors except they run the
chance of being killed every time they cannot hit high C.

No one at any time in the fight can approach the bull at any 3
time except directly from the front. That is where the danger
comes. There are also all sorts of complicated passes that must be
done with the cape, each requiring as much technique as a champion billiard player. And underneath it all is the necessity for playing the old tragedy in the absolutely custom bound, law-laid-down
way. It must all be done gracefully, seemingly effortlessly and always with dignity. The worst criticism the Spaniards ever make of
a bull fighter is that his work is "vulgar."

The three absolute acts of the tragedy are first the entry of the 4
bull when the picadors receive the shock of his attacks and attempt to protect their horses with their lances. Then the horses
go out and the second act is the planting of the banderillos. This
is one of the most interesting and difficult parts but among the
easiest for a new bull fight fan to appreciate in technique. The
banderillos are three-foot, gaily colored darts with a small fish
hook prong in the end. The man who is going to plant them walks
out into the arena alone with the bull. He lifts the banderillos at
arm's length and points them toward the bull. Then he calls "Toro!
Toro!" The bull charges and the banderillero rises to his toes,
bends in a curve forward and just as the bull is about to hit him
drops the darts into the bull's hump just back of his horns.

They must go in evenly, one on each side. They must not be 5
shoved, or thrown or stuck in from the side. This is the first time
the bull has been completely baffled, there is the prick of the darts
that he cannot escape and there are no horses for him to charge
into. But he charges the man again and again and each time he
gets a pair of the long banderillos that hang from his hump by their
tiny barbs and flop like porcupine quills.

Last is the death of the bull, which is in the hands of the 6
matador who has had charge of the bull since his first attack. Each
matador has two bulls in the afternoon. The death of the bull is
most formal and can only be brought about in one way, directly

from the front by the matador who must receive the bull in full charge and kill him with a sword thrust between the shoulders just back of the neck and between the horns. Before killing the bull he must first do a series of passes with the muleta, a piece of red cloth he carries about the size of a large napkin. With the muleta the torero must show his complete mastery of the bull, must make the bull miss him again and again by inches, before he is allowed to kill him. It is in this phase that most of the fatal accidents occur.

The word "toreador" is obsolete Spanish and is never used. The torero is usually called an espada or swordsman. He must be proficient in all three acts of the fight. In the first he uses the cape and does veronicas and protects the picadors by taking the bull out and away from them when they are spilled to the ground. In the second act he plants the banderillos. In the third act he masters the bull with the muleta and kills him.   7

Few toreros excel in all three departments. Some, like young Chicuelo, are unapproachable in their cape work. Others like the late Joselito are wonderful banderilleros. Only a few are great killers. Most of the greatest killers are gypsies.   8

Meanings and Values

1. Show precisely how Hemingway's use of "symbolizes" (par. 1) fits our own meaning of the term, or that it does not. (See Guide to Terms: *Symbolism*.)

2a. How would you describe the tone of this writing? (Guide: *Style/Tone*.)

  b. How, if at all, is such tone presumably related to the author's personal attitude toward his subject?

3. Evaluate this selection by use of the three-point system. (Guide: *Evaluation*.)

Expository Techniques

1. In what important respect is a process of this sort more readily analyzed and clearly explained than are many others?

2. Should the author's beginning reference to symbolism have been picked up later, perhaps woven through the process explanation itself? Why, or why not?

3. This essay shows the beginning of Hemingway's later characteristic syntax style. (Guide: *Syntax*.) What distinctiveness of syntax do you find, especially in sentence structures? Use examples to illustrate.

Diction and Vocabulary

1. Is the author's use of Spanish terms excessive? Why, or why not?
2. Does he clarify the meanings of Spanish words sufficiently for a reader who understands neither Spanish nor bull fighting? Support your answer with examples.

Suggestions for Writing and Discussion

1. Why do you think the conduct of such an event as a bull fight is so closely prescribed by rules? What counterparts, in this respect, do you see in our own sports?
2. Is bull fighting more brutal and barbaric (a common accusation in the United States) than any of our own sports? Be specific, and use developed examples to support your theme.
3. Select one sport popular in the United States, and show the symbolism inherent in it. If possible, also show the effect of this symbolism on the sport's popularity.
4. Why do you think people *really* go to such events as a bull fight?
5. Is bull fighting likely to be legalized in the United States? Do you think it should be?

(NOTE: Suggestions for topics requiring development by PROCESS ANALYSIS are on page 159, at the end of this section.)

ALEXANDER PETRUNKEVITCH

ALEXANDER PETRUNKEVITCH (1875–1964) was a Russian-born zoologist who taught at several leading American universities and received honors from others. He was one of the world's foremost authorities on spiders, and his first important book, published in 1911, was *Index Catalogue of Spiders of North, Central, and South America.* He later achieved distinction for his writings on zoological subjects as well as for his translations of English poetry into Russian and Russian poetry into English. Two of his other books are *Choice and Responsibility* (1947) and *Principles of Classification* (1952).

The Spider and the Wasp

"The Spider and the Wasp" was first published in the August 1952 issue of *Scientific American.* This essay should be particularly interesting to students of composition because it demonstrates not only exposition of natural process but also semiscientific writing that has been made understandable, perhaps even fascinating, for completely nonscientific readers. It is also a good illustration of the successful interweaving of several expository techniques.

In the feeding and safeguarding of their progeny insects·and spiders exhibit some interesting analogies to reasoning and some crass examples of blind instinct. The case I propose to describe here is that of the tarantula spiders and their archenemy, the digger wasps of the genus Pepsis. It is a classic example of what looks like intelligence pitted against instinct — a strange situation in which the victim, though fully able to defend itself, submits unwittingly to its destruction. 1

Most tarantulas live in the tropics, but several species occur in the temperate zone and a few are common in the southern U.S. 2

Some varieties are large and have powerful fangs with which they can inflict a deep wound. These formidable looking spiders do not, however, attack man; you can hold one in your hand, if you are gentle, without being bitten. Their bite is dangerous only to insects and small mammals such as mice; for man it is no worse than a hornet's sting.

Tarantulas customarily live in deep cylindrical burrows, from   3
which they emerge at dusk and into which they retire at dawn. Mature males wander about after dark in search of females and occasionally stray into houses. After mating, the male dies in a few weeks, but a female lives much longer and can mate several years in succession. In a Paris museum is a tropical specimen which is said to have been living in captivity for 25 years.

A fertilized female tarantula lays from 200 to 400 eggs at a   4
time; thus it is possible for a single tarantula to produce several thousand young. She takes no care of them beyond weaving a cocoon of silk to enclose the eggs. After they hatch, the young walk away, find convenient places in which to dig their burrows and spend the rest of their lives in solitude. The eyesight of tarantulas is poor, being limited to a sensing of change in the intensity of light and to the perception of moving objects. They apparently have little or no sense of hearing, for a hungry tarantula will pay no attention to a loudly chirping cricket placed in its cage unless the insect happens to touch one of its legs.

But all spiders, and especially hairy ones, have an extremely   5
delicate sense of touch. Laboratory experiments prove that tarantulas can distinguish three types of touch: pressure against the body wall, stroking of the body hair, and riffling of certain very fine hairs on the legs called trichobothria. Pressure against the body, by the finger or the end of a pencil, causes the tarantula to move off slowly for a short distance. The touch excites no defensive response unless the approach is from above where the spider can see the motion, in which case it rises on its hind legs, lifts its front legs, opens its fangs and holds this threatening posture as long as the object continues to move.

The entire body of a tarantula, especially its legs, is thickly   6
clothed with hair. Some of it is short and wooly, some long and stiff. Touching this body hair produces one of two distinct reactions. When the spider is hungry, it responds with an immediate and swift attack. At the touch of a cricket's antennae the tarantula

seizes the insect so swiftly that a motion picture taken at the rate of 64 frames per second shows only the result and not the process of capture. But when the spider is not hungry, the stimulation of its hairs merely causes it to shake the touched limb. An insect can walk under its hairy belly unharmed.

The trichobothria, very fine hairs growing from dislike mem- 7
branes on the legs, are sensitive only to air movement. A light breeze makes them vibrate slowly, without disturbing the common hair. When one blows gently on the trichobothria, the tarantula reacts with a quick jerk of its four front legs. If the front and hind legs are stimulated at the same time, the spider makes a sudden jump. This reaction is quite independent of the state of its appetite

These three tactile responses — to pressure on the body wall, 8
to moving of the common hair, and to flexing of the trichobothria — are so different from one another that there is no possibility of confusing them. They serve the tarantula adequately for most of its needs and enable it to avoid most annoyances and dangers. But they fail the spider completely when it meets its deadly enemy, the digger wasp Pepsis.

These solitary wasps are beautiful and formidable creatures. 9
Most species are either a deep shiny blue all over, or deep blue with rusty wings. The largest have a wing span of about four inches. They live on nectar. When excited, they give off a pungent odor — a warning that they are ready to attack. The sting is much worse than that of a bee or common wasp, and the pain and swelling last longer. In the adult stage the wasp lives only a few months. The female produces but a few eggs, one at a time at intervals of two or three days. For each egg the mother must provide one adult tarantula, alive but paralyzed. The mother wasp attaches the egg to the paralyzed spider's abdomen. Upon hatching from the egg, the larva is many hundreds of times smaller than its living but helpless victim. It eats no other food and drinks no water. By the time it has finished its single Gargantuan meal and become ready for wasphood, nothing remains of the tarantula but its indigestible chitinous skeleton.

The mother wasp goes tarantula-hunting when the egg in her 10
ovary is almost ready to be laid. Flying low over the ground late on a sunny afternoon, the wasp looks for its victim or for the mouth of a tarantula burrow, a round hole edged by a bit of silk.

The sex of the spider makes no difference, but the mother is highly discriminating as to species. Each species of Pepsis requires a certain species of tarantula, and the wasp will not attack the wrong species. In a cage with a tarantula which is not its normal prey, the wasp avoids the spider and is usually killed by it in the night.

Yet when a wasp finds the correct species, it is the other way   11
about. To identify the species the wasp apparently must explore the spider with her antennae. The tarantula shows an amazing tolerance to this exploration. The wasp crawls under it and walks over it without evoking any hostile response. The molestation is so great and so persistent that the tarantula often rises on all eight legs, as if it were on stilts. It may stand this way for several minutes. Meanwhile the wasp, having satisfied itself that the victim is of the right species, moves off a few inches to dig the spider's grave. Working vigorously with legs and jaws, it excavates a hole 8 to 10 inches deep with a diameter slightly larger than the spider's girth. Now and again the wasp pops out of the hole to make sure that the spider is still there.

When the grave is finished, the wasp returns to the tarantula   12
to complete her ghastly enterprise. First she feels it all over once more with her antennae. Then her behavior becomes more aggressive. She bends her abdomen, protruding her sting, and searches for the soft membrane at the point where the spider's legs join its body — the only spot where she can penetrate the horny skeleton. From time to time, as the exasperated spider slowly shifts ground, the wasp turns on her back and slides along with the aid of her wings, trying to get under the tarantula for a shot at the vital spot. During all this maneuvering, which can last for several minutes, the tarantula makes no move to save itself. Finally the wasp corners it against some obstruction and grasps one of its legs in her powerful jaws. Now at last the harassed spider tries a desperate but vain defense. The two contestants roll over and over on the ground. It is a terrifying sight and the outcome is always the same. The wasp finally manages to thrust her sting into the soft spot and holds it there for a few seconds while she pumps in the poison. Almost immediately the tarantula falls paralyzed on its back. Its legs stop twitching; its heart stops beating. Yet it is not dead, as is shown by the fact that if taken from the wasp it can be restored to some sensitivity by being kept in a moist chamber for several months.

After paralyzing the tarantula, the wasp cleans herself by 13
dragging her body along the ground and rubbing her feet, sucks
the drop of blood oozing from the wound in the spider's abdomen,
then grabs a leg of the flabby, helpless animal in her jaws and drags
it down to the bottom of the grave. She stays there for many minutes, sometimes for several hours, and what she does all that time
in the dark we do not know. Eventually she lays her egg and attaches it to the side of the spider's abdomen with a sticky secretion.
Then she emerges, fills the grave with soil carried bit by bit in her
jaws, and finally tramples the ground all around to hide any trace
of the grave from prowlers. Then she flies away, leaving her de-
scendant safely started in life.

In all this the behavior of the wasp evidently is qualitatively 14
different from that of the spider. The wasp acts like an intelligent
animal. This is not to say that instinct plays no part or that she
reasons as man does. But her actions are to the point; they are not
automatic and can be modified to fit the situation. We do not
know for certain how she identifies the tarantula — probably it is
by some olfactory or chemo-tactile sense — but she does it pur-
posefully and does not blindly tackle a wrong species.

On the other hand, the tarantula's behavior shows only con- 15
fusion. Evidently the wasp's pawing gives it no pleasure, for it
tries to move away. That the wasp is not simulating sexual stimulation is certain because male and female tarantulas react in the
same way to its advances. That the spider is not anesthetized by
some odorless secretion is easily shown by blowing lightly at the
tarantula and making it jump suddenly. What, then, makes the
tarantula behave as stupidly as it does?

No clear, simple answer is available. Possibly the stimulation 16
by the wasp's antennae is masked by a heavier pressure on the
spider's body, so that it reacts as when prodded by a pencil. But
the explanation may be much more complex. Initiative in attack
is not in the nature of tarantulas; most species fight only when
cornered so that escape is impossible. Their inherited patterns of
behavior apparently prompt them to avoid problems rather than
attack them. For example, spiders always weave their webs in
three dimensions, and when a spider finds that there is insufficient
space to attach certain threads in the third dimension, it leaves the
place and seeks another, instead of finishing the web in a single
plane. This urge to escape seems to arise under all circumstances,

in all phases of life, and to take the place of reasoning. For a spider to change the pattern of its web is as impossible as for an inexperienced man to build a bridge across a chasm obstructing his way.

In a way the instinctive urge to escape is not only easier but   17
often more efficient than reasoning. The tarantula does exactly what is most efficient in all cases except in an encounter with a ruthless and determined attacker dependent for the existence of her own species on killing as many tarantulas as she can lay eggs. Perhaps in this case the spider follows its usual pattern of trying to escape, instead of seizing and killing the wasp, because it is not aware of its danger. In any case, the survival of the tarantula species as a whole is protected by the fact that the spider is much more fertile than the wasp.

Meanings and Values

1. Briefly summarize the "qualitative" differences between the behavior of the tarantula and that of the wasp.
2. What is the likelihood that some humans also have inherited patterns of behavior that "prompt them to avoid problems rather than attack them" (par. 16)? Use concrete examples, if possible, to support your view.
3. What parallels to the tarantula-wasp relationship can you find in the history of nations? Be explicit and explain.
4a. Describe the type, or types, of readers for whom you think *Scientific American* is meant to appeal. (Do not jump to conclusions: if not familiar with the magazine, you may have to browse through a few issues.)
  b. If you had been the editor, why would you have selected (or not selected) this piece to publish?

Expository Techniques

1a. Where does the author state his central theme?
  b. Is this a desirable location? Why, or why not?
2a. What is the primary function of the process analysis in relation to the central theme?
  b. How successfully does it accomplish its purpose?
3. In paragraph 9 the author goes from pure description of the wasp

into the narrative account that involves both wasp and spider. How does he arrange the content itself to provide smooth and natural transition, hence ensuring coherence? (See Guide to Terms: *Transition* and *Coherence*.)

4. The author also usually arranges his subject materials to help achieve effective *inter*paragraph transitions so that one gets an echo of the last part of one paragraph when reading the topic sentence of the next. List or mark the uses of this transitional device.

5. Effective coherence also depends to a great extent on smooth sentence-to-sentence transitions. The time sequence is often the most difficult of these to write so that "then . . . then . . . then" is avoided. List or mark the eight introductory devices showing time relationship in paragraph 12, and notice their variety.

6a. How many paragraphs constitute the closing?
 b. What function do they serve in addition to concluding the selection?

7. This essay utilizes, to varying extents, the expository patterns of cause and effect, definition, induction, and description. It can also be used to illustrate three patterns we have already studied.
 a. What are the patterns?
 b. Explain their use in this essay.

Diction and Vocabulary

1. Do such informal expressions as "pops out of the hole" (par. 11), "for a shot at the vital spot," and "pumps in the poison" (12) help or hinder the essay's success? Why?

2. Consider such expressions as "beautiful and formidable creatures" (par. 9), "terrifying sight" (12), and "ghastly enterprise" (13).
 a. Are these expressions objective or subjective? (Guide: *Objective/ Subjective*.) Explain why.
 b. Why would they be, or not be, suitable in a scientific report?
 c. What useful purpose, if any, do they serve here?

3a. What do your answers to questions 1 and 2 indicate about the author's tone? (Guide: *Style/Tone*.)
 b. How would you describe his tone?
 c. Explain why it is, or is not, suitable to his subject matter and to his audience.

4. Any specialist writing on a technical subject for a lay audience (as much of *Scientific American's* audience is) has a problem with professional terminology. Consider this author's use of "trichobothria" (par. 5), "chitinous" (9), "olfactory," and "chemo-tactile" (14).
 a. Does there seem to be an excessive use of technical language?
 b. Do you think these words could have been avoided without weakening scientific exactness? If so, how?

   c. Does their use create a communication block for the lay reader, or does the author succeed in avoiding this fault?

   d. Why has be bothered to define "trichobothria" — even repeating his definition — but not the others?

5. The use of "Gargantuan" (par. 9) is an allusion. (Guide: *Figures of Speech*.) Explain the source to which the author alludes and the word's meaning in this essay.

6. Consult the dictionary as needed for a full understanding of the following words, especially as used in this essay: progeny, archenemy, classic (par. 1); formidable (2); perception (4); riffling (5); dislike (7); tactile (8); pungent, chitinous (9); discriminating (10); evoking, molestation (11); harassed (12); secretion (13); qualitatively, olfactory, chemo-tactile (14); ruthless (17).

Suggestions for Writing and Discussion

1. Use the tarantula-wasp relationship as the basis of an analogy to explain the relationship between two persons that you know.

2. Use analogy as suggested above to explain the historical relationship between two specific countries.

3. Using patterns of illustration and comparison, distinguish between intellectual and instinctive human behavior.

4. Compare or contrast man's motives for killing with those of animals. Some use of classification might also be helpful in this assignment.

(NOTE: Suggestions for topics requiring development by PROCESS ANALYSIS are on page 159, at the end of this section.)

RACHEL CARSON

RACHEL CARSON (1907–1964), a native Pennsylvanian and respected marine biologist, was a member of the U.S. Fish and Wildlife Service for several years before her death. She received numerous scientific awards and became famous for a highly developed ability which most scientists lack: the ability to create literature out of scientific information, in language the average layman can understand and appreciate. Some of her many successful books are *Under the Sea Wind* (1952), *The Sea Around Us* (1954), *The Edge of the Sea* (1955), and *A Sense of Wonder* (1965).

The Other Road

"The Other Road" (editor's title) is from Carson's *Silent Spring*. Although it was her most controversial book for several years after its publication in 1962 — at that time she was commonly considered an alarmist, a real menace to progress — she has since been vindicated as more and more people came to understand the tremendous scope of the problem of insecticides. "The Other Road" employs a simple form of process analysis to demonstrate one alternative to poisons.

We stand now where two roads diverge. But unlike the roads in 1
Robert Frost's familiar poem, they are not equally fair. The road we have long been traveling is deceptively easy, a smooth super-highway on which we progress with great speed, but at its end lies disaster. The other fork of the road — the one "less traveled by" — offers our last, our only chance to reach a destination that assures the preservation of our earth.

The choice, after all, is ours to make. If, having endured much, 2
we have at last asserted our "right to know," and if, knowing, we have concluded that we are being asked to take senseless and

145

frightening risks, then we should no longer accept the counsel of those who tell us we must fill our world with poisonous chemicals; we should look about and see what other course is open to us.

A truly extraordinary variety of alternatives to the chemical control of insects is available. Some are already in use and have achieved brilliant success. Others are in the stage of laboratory testing. Still others are little more than ideas in the minds of imaginative scientists, waiting for the opportunity to put them to the test. All have this in common: they are *biological* solutions, based on understanding of the living organisms they seek to control, and of the whole fabric of life to which these organisms belong. Specialists representing various areas of the vast field of biology are contributing — entomologists, pathologists, geneticists, physiologists, biochemists, ecologists — all pouring their knowledge and their creative inspirations into the formation of a new science of biotic controls.

"Any science may be likened to a river," says a Johns Hopkins biologist, Professor Carl P. Swanson. "It has its obscure and unpretentious beginning; its quiet stretches as well as its rapids; its periods of drought as well as of fullness. It gathers momentum with the work of many investigators and as it is fed by other streams of thought; it is deepened and broadened by the concepts and generalizations that are gradually evolved."

So it is with the science of biological control in its modern sense. In America it had its obscure beginnings a century ago with the first attempts to introduce natural enemies of insects that were proving troublesome to farmers, an effort that sometimes moved slowly or not at all, but now and again gathered speed and momentum under the impetus of an outstanding success. It had its period of drought when workers in applied entomology, dazzled by the spectacular new insecticides of the 1940's, turned their backs on all biological methods and set foot on "the treadmill of chemical control." But the goal of an insect-free world continued to recede. Now at last, as it has become apparent that the heedless and unrestrained use of chemicals is a greater menace to ourselves than to the targets, the river which is the science of biotic control flows again, fed by new streams of thought.

Some of the most fascinating of the new methods are those that seek to turn the strength of a species against itself — to use the drive of an insect's life forces to destroy it. The most spectacular of these approaches is the "male sterilization" technique developed by the chief of the United States Department of Agriculture's Entomology Research Branch, Dr. Edward Knipling, and his associates.

About a quarter of a century ago Dr. Knipling startled his [7] colleagues by proposing a unique method of insect control. If it were possible to sterilize and release large numbers of insects, he theorized, the sterilized males would, under certain conditions, compete with the normal wild males so successfully that, after repeated releases, only infertile eggs would be produced and the population would die out.

The proposal was met with bureaucratic inertia and with [8] skepticism from scientists, but the idea persisted in Dr. Knipling's mind. One major problem remained to be solved before it could be put to the test — a practical method of insect sterilization had to be found. Academically, the fact that insects could be sterilized by exposure to X-ray had been known since 1916, when an entomologist by the name of G. A. Runner reported such sterilization of cigarette beetles. Hermann Muller's pioneering work on the production of mutations by X-ray opened up vast new areas of thought in the late 1920's, and by the middle of the century various workers had reported the sterilization by X-rays or gamma rays of at least a dozen species of insects.

But these were laboratory experiments, still a long way from [9] practical application. About 1950, Dr. Knipling launched a serious effort to turn insect sterilization into a weapon that would wipe out a major insect enemy of livestock in the South, the screw-worm fly. The females of this species lay their eggs in any open wound of a warm-blooded animal. The hatching larvae are parasitic, feeding on the flesh of the host. A full-grown steer may succumb to a heavy infestation in 10 days, and livestock losses in the United States have been estimated at $40,000,000 a year. The toll of wildlife is harder to measure, but it must be great. Scarcity of deer in some areas of Texas is attributed to the screw-worm. This is a tropical or subtropical insect, inhabiting South and Central America and Mexico, and in the United States normally restricted to the Southwest. About 1933, however, it was accidentally introduced into Florida, where the climate allowed it to survive over winter and to establish populations. It even pushed into southern Alabama and Georgia, and soon the livestock industry of the southeastern states was faced with annual losses running to $20,000,000.

A vast amount of information on the biology of the screw- [10]

worm had been accumulated over the years by Agriculture Department scientists in Texas. By 1954, after some preliminary field trials on Florida islands, Dr. Knipling was ready for a full-scale test of his theory. For this, by arrangement with the Dutch Government, he went to the island of Curaçao in the Caribbean, cut off from the mainland by at least 50 miles of sea.

Beginning in August 1954, screw-worms reared and sterilized [11] in an Agriculture Department laboratory in Florida were flown to Curaçao and released from airplanes at the rate of about 400 per square mile per week. Almost at once the number of egg masses deposited on experimental goats began to decrease, as did their fertility. Only seven weeks after the releases were started, all eggs were infertile. Soon it was impossible to find a single egg mass, sterile or otherwise. The screw-worm had indeed been eradicated on Curaçao.

The resounding success of the Curaçao experiment whetted [12] the appetites of Florida livestock raisers for a similar feat that would relieve them of the scourge of screw-worms. Although the difficulties here were relatively enormous — an area 300 times as large as the small Caribbean island — in 1957 the United States Department of Agriculture and the State of Florida joined in providing funds for an eradication effort. The project involved the weekly production of about 50 million screw-worms at a specially constructed "fly factory," the use of 20 light airplanes to fly prearranged flight patterns, five to six hours daily, each plane carrying a thousand paper cartons, each carton containing 200 to 400 irradiated flies.

The cold winter of 1957–58, when freezing temperatures [13] gripped northern Florida, gave an unexpected opportunity to start the program while the screw-worm populations were reduced and confined to a small area. By the time the program was considered complete at the end of 17 months, 3½ billion artificially reared, sterilized flies had been released over Florida and sections of Georgia and Alabama. The last-known animal wound infestation that could be attributed to screw-worms occurred in February 1959. In the next few weeks several adults were taken in traps. Thereafter no trace of the screw-worm could be discovered. Its extinction in the Southeast had been accomplished — a triumphant demonstration of the worth of scientific creativity, aided by thorough basic research, persistence, and determination.

Meanings and Values

1. How suitable would this selection have been for use in Section 1 of this book? Why?

2a. What is the author's point of view? (See Guide to Terms: *Point of View.*)

b. What effect, if any, does this have on the tone of the writing. (Guide: *Style/Tone.*)

c. From what other points of view might other writers have discussed the same basic material? Be specific.

3. In view of the fact that the author felt strongly about her subject, one might expect to find at least traces of sentimentality. (Guide: *Sentimentality.*) Do you find any? If so, where?

4a. In paragraph 5 there is an example of irony. (Guide: *Irony.*) What is it?

b. What kind of irony?

5. Illustrate the meaning of "paradox" by use of some portion of paragraph 6. (Guide: *Paradox.*)

Expository Techniques

1a. Which of the two basic kinds of process analysis is this one?

b. What would you assume to be its extreme importance in a book attacking poisonous insecticides?

2. Can the brief comparison in paragraph 1 be correctly called an analogy? Why, or why not?

3a. In which other paragraphs do you find analogy?

b. How effective is it, as used?

4. Several of the standard techniques for opening an expository writing are combined in this two-paragraph introduction. (Guide: *Introductions.*) What are they?

5. The introduction, with the first sentence of paragraph 3, can also provide a clear example of the general becoming more specific. (Guide: *Specific/General.*) Demonstrate how this is accomplished.

Diction and Vocabulary

1a. Do you find an excess of heavy or scientific words as might be expected in a scientist's writing? If so, cite them and show how they could have been avoided.

b. Why is the list of scientific specialties in paragraph 3 not apt to give the average reader any trouble?

2. If you are not familiar with the meanings of the following words, consult your dictionary: entomologists, pathologists, geneticists, physiologists, biochemists, ecologists, biotic (par. 3); impetus (5); inertia (8); succumb (9); eradication (12).

Suggestions for Writing and Discussion

1. Present-day environmentalists are often accused of wanting prematurely to ban all poisonous insecticides. Explain objectively what could be the far-reaching *ill* effects of such premature actions.

2. In view of the relatively small number of citizens raising cattle, how could the governments justify the apparently huge expense of eradicating the screw-worm fly?

3. If you know of more recent successes in biotic control of insects or diseases, explain how they were accomplished.

(NOTE: Suggestions for topics requiring development by PROCESS ANALYSIS are on page 159, at the end of this section.)

JESSICA MITFORD

JESSICA MITFORD was born in England in 1917, a sister of the late novelist and biographer, Nancy Mitford. She is married to an American lawyer and lives in California. Her books are her autobiography, *Daughters and Rebels* (1960); the famous best seller, *The American Way of Death* (1963); *The Trial of Dr. Spock* (1969); and *Kind and Unusual Punishment* (1973), a devastating study of the American penal system.

To Dispel Fears of Live Burial

"To Dispel Fears of Live Burial" (editor's title) is a portion of *The American Way of Death,* a book described in the *New York Times* as a "savagely witty and well-documented exposé." The "savagely witty" style, evident in this selection, does not obscure the fact of its being a tightly organized, step-by-step process analysis.

Embalming is indeed a most extraordinary procedure, and one 1 must wonder at the docility of Americans who each year pay hundreds of millions of dollars for its perpetuation, blissfully ignorant of what it is all about, what is done, how it is done. Not one in ten thousand has any idea of what actually takes place. Books on the subject are extremly hard to come by. They are not to be found in most libraries or bookshops.

In an era when huge television audiences watch surgical opera- 2 tions in the comfort of their living rooms, when, thanks to the animated cartoon, the geography of the digestive system has become familiar territory even to the nursery school set, in a land where the satisfaction of curiosity about almost all matters is a national pastime, the secrecy surrounding embalming can, surely, hardly be attributed to the inherent gruesomeness of the subject.

Custom in this regard has within this century suffered a complete reversal. In the early days of American embalming, when it was performed in the home of the deceased, it was almost mandatory for some relative to stay by the embalmer's side and witness the procedure. Today, family members who might wish to be in attendance would certainly be dissuaded by the funeral director. All others, except apprentices, are excluded by law from the preparation room.

A close look at what does actually take place may explain in large measure the undertaker's intractable reticence concerning a procedure that has become his major *raison d'être*. Is it possible he fears that public information about embalming might lead patrons to wonder if they really want this service? If the funeral men are loath to discuss the subject outside the trade, the reader may, understandably, be equally loath to go on reading at this point. For those who have the stomach for it, let us part the formaldehyde curtain. . . .   3

The body is first laid out in the undertaker's morgue — or rather, Mr. Jones is reposing in the preparation room — to be readied to bid the world farewell.   4

The preparation room in any of the better funeral establishments has the tiled and sterile look of a surgery, and indeed the embalmer–restorative artist who does his chores there is beginning to adopt the term "dermasurgeon" (appropriately corrupted by some mortician-writers as "demisurgeon") to describe his calling. His equipment, consisting of scalpels, scissors, augers, forceps, clamps, needles, pumps, tubes, bowls and basins, is crudely imitative of the surgeon's as is his technique, acquired in a nine- or twelve-month post-high-school course in an embalming school. He is supplied by an advanced chemical industry with a bewildering array of fluids, sprays, pastes, oils, powders, creams, to fix or soften tissue, shrink or distend it as needed, dry it here, restore the moisture there. There are cosmetics, waxes and paints to fill and cover features, even plaster of Paris to replace entire limbs. There are ingenious aids to prop and stabilize the cadaver: a Vari-Pose Head Rest, the Edwards Arm and Hand Positioner, the Repose Block (to support the shoulders during the embalming), and the Throop Foot Positioner, which resembles an old-fashioned stocks.   5

Mr. John H. Eckels, president of the Eckels College of Mortuary Science, thus describes the first part of the embalming pro-   6 cedure: "In the hands of a skilled practitioner, this work may be done in a comparatively short time and without multilating the body other than by slight incision — so slight that it scarcely would cause serious inconvenience if made upon a living person. It is necessary to remove the blood, and doing this not only helps in the disinfecting, but removes the principal cause of disfigurements due to discoloration."

Another textbook discusses the all-important time element: "The earlier this is done, the better, for every hour that elapses between death and embalming will add to the problems and complications encountered. . . ." Just how soon should one get going on the embalming? The author tells us, "On the basis of such scanty information made available to this profession through its rudimentary and haphazard system of technical research, we must conclude that the best results are to be obtained if the subject is embalmed before life is completely extinct — that is, before cellular death has occurred. In the average case, this would mean within an hour after somatic death." For those who feel that there is something a little rudimentary, not to say haphazard, about this advice, a comforting thought is offered by another writer. Speaking of fears entertained in early days of premature burial, he points out, "One of the effects of embalming by chemical injection, however, has been to dispel fears of live burial." How true; once the blood is removed, chances of live burial are indeed remote.

To return to Mr. Jones, the blood is drained out though the veins and replaced by embalming fluid pumped in through the arteries. As noted in *The Principles and Practices of Embalming,* "every operator has a favorite injection and drainage point — a fact which becomes a handicap only if he fails or refuses to forsake his favorites when conditions demand it." Typical favorites are the carotid artery, femoral artery, jugular vein, subclavian vein. There are various choices of embalming fluid. If Flextone is used, it will produce a "mild, flexible rigidity. The skin retains a velvety softness, the tissues are rubbery and pliable. Ideal for women and children." It may be blended with B. and G. Products Company's Lyf-Lyk tint, which is guaranteed to reproduce "nature's own skin texture . . . the velvety appearance of living tissue." Suntone comes in three separate tints: Suntan; Special Cosmetic Tint, a pink shade "especially indicated for young female subjects"; and Regular Cosmetic Tint, moderately pink.

About three to six gallons of a dyed and perfumed solution of   9
formaldehyde, glycerin, borax, phenol, alcohol and water is soon
circulating through Mr. Jones, whose mouth has been sewn together with a "needle directed upward between the upper lip and
gum and brought out through the left nostril," with the corners
raised slightly "for a more pleasant expression." If he should be
bucktoothed, his teeth are cleaned with Bon Ami and coated with
colorless nail polish. His eyes, meanwhile, are closed with flesh-
tinted eye caps and eye cement.

The next step is to have at Mr. Jones with a thing called a tro-   10
car. This is a long, hollow needle attached to a tube. It is jabbed into
the abdomen, poked around the entrails and chest cavity, the con-
tents of which are pumped out and replaced with "cavity fluid."
This done, and the hole in the abdomen sewn up, Mr. Jones's face is
heavily creamed (to protect the skin from burns which may be
caused by leakage of the chemicals), and he is covered with a sheet
and left unmolested for a while. But not for long — there is more,
much more, in store for him. He has been embalmed, but not yet
restored, and the best time to start the restorative work is eight to
ten hours after embalming, when the tissues have become firm and
dry.

The object of all this attention to the corpse, it must be remem-   11
bered, is to make it presentable for viewing in an attitude of healthy
repose. "Our customs require the presentation of our dead in the
semblance of normality . . . unmarred by the ravages of illness,
disease or mutilation," says Mr. J. Sheridan Mayer in his *Restorative Art*. This is rather a large order since few people die in the full
bloom of health, unravaged by illness and unmarked by some dis-
figurement. The funeral industry is equal to the challenge: "In
some cases the gruesome appearance of a mutilated or disease-
ridden subject may be quite discouraging. The task of restoration
may seem impossible and shake the confidence of the embalmer.
This is the time for intestinal fortitude and determination. Once the
formative work is begun and affected tissues are cleaned or removed, all doubts of success vanish. It is surprising and gratifying
to discover the results which may be obtained."

The embalmer, having allowed an appropriate interval to   12
elapse, returns to the attack, but now he brings into play the skill
and equipment of sculptor and cosmetician. Is a hand missing?
Casting one in plaster of Paris is a simple matter. "For replacement
purposes, only a cast of the back of the hand is necessary; this is

within the ability of the average operator and is quite adequate." If a lip or two, a nose or an ear should be missing, the embalmer has at hand a variety of restorative waxes with which to model replacements. Pores and skin texture are simulated by stippling with a little brush, and over this cosmetics are laid on. Head off? Decapitation cases are rather routinely handled. Ragged edges are trimmed, and head joined to torso with a series of splints, wires and sutures. It is a good idea to have a little something at the neck — a scarf or high collar — when time for viewing comes. Swollen mouth? Cut out tissue as needed from inside the lips. If too much is removed, the surface contour can easily be restored by padding with cotton. Swollen necks and cheeks are reduced by removing tissue through vertical incisions made down each side of the neck. "When the deceased is casketed, the pillow will hide the suture incisions . . . as an extra precaution against leakage, the suture may be painted with liquid sealer."

The opposite condition is more likely to present itself — that of emaciation. His hypodermic syringe now loaded with massage cream, the embalmer seeks out and fills the hollowed and sunken areas by injection. In this procedure the backs of the hands and fingers and the under-chin area should not be neglected.

Positioning the lips is a problem that recurrently challenges the ingenuity of the embalmer. Closed too tightly, they tend to give a stern, even disapproving expression. Ideally, embalmers feel, the lips should give the impression of being ever so slightly parted, the upper lip protruding slightly for a more youthful appearance. This takes some engineering, however, as the lips tend to drift apart. Lip drift can sometimes be remedied by pushing one or two straight pins through the inner margin of the lower lip and then inserting them between the two front upper teeth. If Mr. Jones happens to have no teeth, the pins can just as easily be anchored in his Armstrong Face Former and Denture Replacer. Another method to maintain lip closure is to dislocate the lower jaw, which is then held in its new position by a wire run through holes which have been drilled through the upper and lower jaws at the midline. As the French are fond of saying, *il faut souffrir pour être belle.*[1]

If Mr. Jones has died of jaundice, the embalming fluid will very likely turn him green. Does this deter the embalmer? Not if he has intestinal fortitude. Masking pastes and cosmetics are heavily laid

---

[1] You have to suffer if you want to be beautiful.

on, burial garments and casket interiors are color-correlated with particular care, and Jones is displayed beneath rose-colored lights. Friends will say, "How *well* he looks." Death by carbon monoxide, on the other hand, can be rather a good thing from the embalmer's viewpoint: "One advantage is the fact that this type of discoloration is an exaggerated form of a natural pink coloration." This is nice because the healthy glow is already present and needs but little attention.

The patching and filling completed, Mr. Jones is now shaved,   16
washed and dressed. Cream-based cosmetic, available in pink, flesh, suntan, brunette and blond, is applied to his hands and face, his hair is shampooed and combed (and, in the case of Mrs. Jones, set), his hands manicured. For the horny-handed son of toil special care must be taken; cream should be applied to remove ingrained grime, and the nails cleaned. "If he were not in the habit of having them manicured in life, trimming and shaping is advised for better appearance — never questioned by kin."

Jones is now ready for casketing (this is the present participle   17
of the verb "to casket"). In this operation, his right shoulder should be depressed slightly "to turn the body a bit to the right and soften the appearance of lying flat on the back." Positioning the hands is a matter of importance, and special rubber positioning blocks may be used. The hands should be cupped slightly for a more lifelike, relaxed appearance. Proper placement of the body requires a delicate sense of balance. It should lie as high as possible in the casket, yet not so high that the lid, when lowered, will hit the nose. On the other hand, we are cautioned, placing the body too low "creates the impression that the body is in a box."

Jones is next wheeled into the appointed slumber room where   18
a few last touches may be added — his favorite pipe placed in his hand or, if he was a great reader, a book propped into position. (In the case of little Master Jones a Teddy bear may be clutched.) Here he will hold open house for a few days, visiting hours 10 A.M to 9 P.M.

Meanings and Values

  1a. What is the author's tone? (See Guide to Terms: *Style/Tone.*)
    b. Try to analyze the effect this tone had, at first reading, on your impressions of the subject matter itself.

c. Form a specific comparison between this effect of tone and the effect of "tone of voice" in spoken language.

2. Why was it formerly "almost mandatory" for some relative to witness the embalming procedure (par. 2)?

3a. Do you believe that public information about this procedure would cost mortuaries much embalming business (par. 3)? Why, or why not?

b. Why *do* people subject their dead to such a process?

4. Use the three-part system of evaluation to judge the success of this process analysis. (Guide: *Evaluation.*)

Expository Techniques

1a. What is the central theme? (Guide: *Unity.*)

b. Which parts of the writing, if any, do not contribute to the theme, thus damaging unity?

c. What other elements of the writing contribute to, or damage, good unity?

2a. Beginning with paragraph 4, list or mark the transitional devices that help to bridge between paragraphs. (Guide: *Transition.*)

b. Briefly explain how coherence is aided by such interparagraph transitions.

3. In this selection, far more than in most, emphasis can best be studied in connection with style. In fact, the two are almost indistinguishable here, and few, if any, of the other methods of achieving emphasis are used at all. (Guide: *Emphasis; Style/Tone.*) Consider each of the following stylistic qualities (some may overlap; others are included in diction) and illustrate, by examples, how each does create emphasis.

a. Number and selection of details — e.g., the equipment and "aids" of paragraph 5.

b. Understatement — e.g., the "chances of live burial," paragraph 7.

c. Special use of quotations — e.g., "that the body is in a box," paragraph 17.

d. Sarcasm and/or other forms of irony (Guide: *Irony*) — e.g., "How *well* he looks," paragraph 15.

Diction and Vocabulary

1. Much of the essay's unique style (with resulting emphasis) is also classifiable as qualities of diction. Use examples to illustrate the following. (Some may be identical to those of the preceding answer, but they need not be.)

a. Choice of common, low-key words to achieve sarcasm through understatement — e.g., "This is nice . . . ," paragraph 15.

b. Terms of violence — e.g., "returns to the attack," paragraph 12.

c. Terms of the living — e.g., "will hold open house," paragraph 18.

d. The continuing use of "Mr. Jones."

2a. Illustrate the meaning of "connotation" with examples of quotations from morticians. (Guide: *Connotation/Denotation.*)

b. Are these also examples of "euphemism"?

c. Show how the author uses these facts to her own advantage — i.e., again, to achieve emphasis.

3a. Comment briefly on the quality and appropriateness of the metaphor that ends the introduction. (Guide: *Figures of Speech.*)

b. Is this, in any sense, also an allusion? Why, or why not?

4. Use the dictionary as needed to understand the meanings of the following words: docility, perpetuation (par. 1); inherent, mandatory (2); intractable, reticence, *raison d'être* (3); ingenious (5); rudimentary, cellular, somatic (7); carotid artery, femoral artery, subclavian vein (8); semblance (11); simulated, stippling, sutures (12); emaciation (13); dispel (7, title).

Suggestions for Writing and Discussion

1. What evidence can you find that "the satisfaction of curiosity about almost all matters is a national pastime" (par. 2)? Is this a good thing or not? Why?

2. Burial customs differ widely from country to country, sometimes from area to area in this country. If you can, describe one of the more distinctive customs and, if possible, show its sources — e.g., nature of the climate, "old country" tradition.

3. What do you foresee as near- and far-future trends or radical changes in American burial practices? Why?

4. You may wish to develop further your answers to question 3 of "Meanings and Values"; the rationale of a large majority of people who do use this mortuary "service" for their departed relatives.

5. If you like, explain your personal preferences and the reasons for them.

Writing Suggestions for Section 5
Process Analysis

1. From one of the following topics develop a central theme into an *informational* process analysis showing:

    a. How you selected a college.
    b. How you selected your future career or major field of study.
    c. How your family selected a home.
    d. How a potential riot was stopped.
    e. How religious faith is achieved.
    f. How gasoline is made.
    g. How the air in _____ becomes polluted.
    h. How lightning kills.
    i. How foreign policy is made.
    j. How political campaigns are financed.
    k. How _____ Church was rebuilt.
    l. How fruit blossoms are pollinated.

2. Select a specific reader-audience and write a *directional* process analysis on one of the following topics. (Although none of the four illustrative essays is of this type, it is widely used in certain kinds of textbooks and for various utilitarian, how-to-do-it purposes. Few of these, however, achieve any noteworthy literary value.) Show:

    a. How to *do* any of the processes suggested by topics 1a–e. (This treatment will require a different viewpoint, completely objective, and may require a different organization.)
    b. How to overcome shyness.
    c. How to overcome stage fright.
    d. How to make the best use of study time.
    e. How to write a college composition.
    f. How to sell an ugly house.
    g. How to prepare a livestock or any other entry for a fair.
    h. How to start a club (or some other kind of recurring activity).
    i. How to reduce the number of highway accidents in an area.
    j. How to survive a tornado (or other natural disaster).
    k. How to select a car.
    l. How to develop moral (or physical) courage.

6

Analyzing *Cause* and *Effect* Relationships

Unlike process analysis, which merely tells *how*, causal analysis seeks to explain *why*. The two may be combined, but they need not be — many people have driven a car successfully after being told how to do it, never knowing or caring why the thing moved when the key was turned and a pedal or two manipulated.

Some causes and effects are not very complicated; at least the need for their explanation requires only a simple statement. A car may sit in the garage for a while because its owner has no money for a license tag, and sometimes this is explanation enough. But frequently a much more thorough analysis is required, and this may even become the basic pattern of an exposition.

To explain fully the causes of a war or depression or election results the writer must seek not only *immediate* causes (the ones he encounters first) but also *ultimate* causes (the basic, underlying factors that help to explain the more apparent ones). The business or professional man, as well as the student, often has pressing need for this type of analysis. How else could he fully understand or report on a failing sales campaign, diminishing church membership, a local increase of traffic accidents, or teenage use of hard drugs? The immediate cause of a disastrous warehouse fire could be faulty electrical wiring, but this might be attributed in turn to the company's unwise economy measures, which might be traced even further to undue pressures on the management to show large profits. The written analysis might logically stop at any point, of course, depending entirely on its purpose and the reader-audience for which it is intended.

Similarly, both the immediate and ultimate *effects* of an action or situation may, or may not, need to be fully explored. If a 5 per cent pay raise is granted, what will be the immediate effect on the cost of production, leading to what ultimate effects on prices and, in some cases, on the whole economy of a business, a town, or perhaps the entire nation?

In earlier selections of this book we have seen several examples of causal analysis. In Section 1, for instance, Peter and Hull are concerned with the ultimate causes of incompetence in public life, and Gregory is to some extent concerned with both immediate and ultimate causes of police-ghetto strife.

Causal analysis is one of the chief techniques of reasoning; and if the method is used at all, the reader must always have confidence in its thoroughness and logic. Some faults in causal reasoning are these:

1. Never mistake the fact that something happens with or after another occurrence as evidence of a causal relationship — for example, that a black cat crossing the road caused the flat tire a few minutes later, or that a course in English composition caused a student's nervous breakdown that same semester.

2. Consider all possibly relevant factors before attributing causes. Perhaps studying English did result in a nervous breakdown, but the cause may also have been ill health, trouble at home, or the anguish of a love affair. (The composition course, by providing an "emotional" outlet, may even have helped *postpone* the breakdown!)

3. Support the analysis by more than mere assertions: offer evidence. It would not often be enough to *tell* why Shakespeare's wise Othello believed the villainous Iago — the dramatist's lines should be used as evidence, possibly supported by the opinions of at least one literary scholar. If explaining that capital punishment deters crime, do not expect the reader to take your word for it — give before-and-after statistics or the testimony of reliable authorities.

4. Be careful not to omit any links in the chain of causes or effects unless you are certain that the readers for whom the writing is intended will automatically make the right connections themselves — and this is frequently a dangerous assumption. To unwisely omit one or more of the links might leave the reader with

only a vague, or even erroneous, impression of the causal connection, possibly invalidating all that follows and thus making the entire writing ineffective.

5. Be honest and objective. The writer (or thinker) who brings his old prejudices to the task of causal analysis, or who fails to see the probability of *multiple* causes or effects, is almost certain to distort his analysis or to make it so superficial, so thin, as to be almost worthless.

Ordinarily the method of causal analysis is either to work logically from the immediate cause (or effect) down toward the most basic, or to start with the basic and work up toward the immediate. But after he has at least analyzed the subject in his mind and decided what his purpose requires in the paragraph or entire composition, the writer will usually find that a satisfactory pattern suggests itself.

JERZY KOSINSKI

JERZY KOSINSKI, born in Poland in 1933, attended college there. He came to the United States in 1957 and for the next several years did graduate study at Columbia University. In 1965 he became an American citizen. A teacher of English prose, he has served on the faculties of Wesleyan, Princeton, and Yale Universities. Kosinski's first novel, *The Painted Bird*, was translated into 36 languages and brought him France's highest award for a foreign novel; his second, *Steps*, won the 1969 National Book Award. His more recent books are *Being There* (1971) and *The Devil Tree* (1973).

TV as Baby Sitter

"TV as Baby Sitter" is not the usual attack on the quality of TV programs or the effects of their portrayals of violence. First used as a TV commentary itself, the selection is nonetheless an "essay" and no doubt was prepared with at least as much attention to sound principles of composition as if its first use had been for publication. The structure is almost entirely a tightly woven cause/effect analysis.

With the advent of television, for the first time in history, all 1 aspects of animal and human life and death, of societal and individual behavior have been condensed on the average to a 19 inch diagonal screen and a 30 minute time slot. Television, a unique medium, claiming to be neither a reality nor art, has become reality for many of us, particularly for our children who are growing up in front of it.

Imagine a child watching this little world within which Pres- 2 idents and commoners walk; mice and lions, kissing lovers and dy-

Reprinted by permission of the author and the National Broadcasting Company, Inc., from *Comment* program (September 3, 1972). © 1972 by Jerzy Kosinski.

ing soldiers, skyscrapers and dog houses, flowers and detergents, all are reduced to the same size, mixed together, given the same rank, and set in the same screen to be looked at. The child watches this crowded world as he or she pleases, while eating, yawning, playing. What is the outlook of such a child? What does it expect of the world? What can it expect?

It expects all things to be as equal as on television: neither bad nor good, neither pleasant nor painful, neither real nor unreal, merely more or less interesting, merely in better or worse color. It is a world without rank. To such a child, the world is to be looked upon; it is there to entertain its viewer. If it doesn't, one alters it by switching the channel.   3

In the little world of television, all is solved within its magic 30 minutes. In spite of the commercials, the wounded hero either rises or quickly dies, lovers marry or divorce, villains kill or are killed, addicts are cured, justice usually wins, and war ends. All problems are solved again this week, as they were last, and will be next week. Life on TV must be visual. This means single-faceted, revealed in a simple speech and through the obvious gesture. No matter how deep the mystery, the TV camera penetrates it.   4

Parents leave their children in front of the TV as baby sitter, because many feel it is infinitely safer to watch the Sesame world of television than to walk in the world outside of their home. But is it?   5

Unlike television, the child grows older. One day it walks out of the TV room. Against his expectations, he's finally put in a classroom full of other children. A child who has been trained to control the little world, by changing the channels when he didn't like it, and was accustomed to maintaining the same distance between himself and the world televised for his amusement, is naturally threatened by the presence of people he cannot control. Others push him around, make faces at him, encroach. There is nothing he can do to stop them. He begins to feel that this real world unjustly limits him; it offers no channels to turn to.   6

In this unpredictable world of real life, there are no neatly ordered thirty-minute private slots. Here, in life, the child brought up only as a viewer must feel persecuted. Ironically, our industrial state offers few things that can be resolved in thirty minutes. But the teenager keeps expecting it; when it is not, he grows impatient,   7 then adamant, disillusioned, oscillating between the revolutionary scream, "Now," and a political cool "So what?" He is easily depressed and beaten down. In this world of hierarchy and brutish competition, he is challenged and outranked by others. Soon he believes he is defective; instead of coming of age, he's coming apart. This breeding of weak and vulnerable beings knows few exceptions. The kids of the upper classes counteract TV by being involved with real events — real horses, real forests, real mountains — all things they have seen, touched, experienced. They have been given an opportunity to exist outside the television room. However, many middle class children, and almost all from poor families are at the mercy of five or six hours of television a day.

My own attitude toward television is neutral. The medium is here to stay. The danger is in the use we make of it. I'm involved with TV the way I am with the motor car. The motor car has been with us for over 50 years, but it is only recently that we learned its exhaust pollutes our very environment. 8

In today's atomized, disjointed technological society, with so little attention paid to the individual, men need more than ever the inner strength to carry him through the daily pressures. This strength should come from early exposure to life at its most real — its sudden pleasures, joys and abandonment; but also its violence, its lack of justice, its pain, illness, and death. There is subtlety to man's fate which lies beyond the thirteen channels. 9

Meanings and Values

1. Clarify the meaning of "the obvious gesture" referred to in paragraph 4.

2a. Why is it ironical that our industrial state offers few things that can be resolved in thirty minutes. (See Guide to Terms: *Irony*.)

  b. What kind of irony is it?

3a. Do you agree that "almost all" children from poor families — e.g., ghetto children — are insulated by TV from "exposure to life at its most real" (pars. 7, 9)? (You may refer, if you like, to the Gregory selection in Section 1.)

  b. Would better use of qualification make the statement more credible — or would you perhaps eliminate it completely? (Guide: *Qualification*.) Why?

4. If you have read the Ashton-Warner selection in Section 4, what effects do you think TV could have on the "native occupants" of a child's mind?

Expository Techniques

1. Through the first half of this exposition the author subtly alternates effects and causes, paragraph by paragraph, achieving a kind of woven effect.
   a. Indicate which is the primary function of each of the first six paragraphs.
   b. To what specific type of effects is paragraph 7 mostly devoted?
   c. Overall is it an effective pattern for this particular cause/effect analysis? Why, or why not?
2. Which of the standard techniques of closing is used in the last paragraph? (Guide: *Closings.*)
3a. Cite two paragraphs containing rhetorical questions. (Guide: *Rhetorical Question.*)
   b. Why are they classifiable as such?
4. In an exposition this short, it is not surprising that ideas would be expressed in somewhat general, even abstract, terms. (Guide: *Specific/General, Concrete/Abstract.*) Explain how this writing could have been made more specific, if length were no factor, using brief examples to illustrate your point.
5a. Two noticeable features of Kosinski's style may be examined in each of paragraphs 2–4, where they are used together: an interesting selection of details, presented in parallel structure. (Guide: *Parallel Structure, Style.*) Cite one example in each of these paragraphs.
   b. Briefly analyze the value of this combination.

Diction and Vocabulary

1. Some women's liberationists resent use of the pronouns "he" and "him" to designate both male and female. This author has frequent need to use this practice or to provide some alternative.
   a. What method, or methods, do you find used?
   b. What seems to be the best policy for your own writing? Why?
2a. In paragraph 5 do you think Kosinski intends to single out one TV program?
   b. What is the broader meaning of "Sesame"?
   c. How appropriate is its use here?

3. Use your dictionary as necessary to be sure of the meanings of the following words: advent (par. 1); faceted (4); adamant, oscillating, hierarchy, vulnerable (7); subtlety (9).

Suggestions for Writing and Discussion

1. Weigh the relative "safety" of watching TV and walking in the real streets outside (par. 5). Why is this problem likely to be seen differently by a concerned parent than by an objective observer?

2. Reexamine your answers to question 3 of "Meanings and Values." If you like (and if you can with some actual knowledge or experience), build on those answers to present a refutation of Kosinski's assertation about TV and children of poor families.

3. Explain how "inner strength" can come from early exposure to real violence and pain. What, if anything, may be sacrificed in the process?

4. What alternatives to either excessive use of TV or exposure to street violence outside might be worth trying by ordinary parents genuinely concerned about the welfare of their children?

(NOTE: Suggestions for topics requiring development by analysis of CAUSE and EFFECT are on page 190, at the end of this section.)

GAIL SHEEHY

GAIL SHEEHY (born 1937) is a native New Yorker. After graduating from the University of Vermont she was a department
store consumer representative and fashion coordinator. Ms.
Sheehy broke into journalism as a fashion editor for a Roch-
ester, New York newspaper and then became a women's
feature writer for the New York Herald Tribune. Since 1968
Ms. Sheehy has been a contributing editor for *New York*
magazine. She has gathered her material on the sexual subculture by studying New York's prostitutes. Her articles have
appeared in *McCall's, Cosmopolitan, Holiday, Family Circle,*
and *Glamour*. Her books include *Lovesounds* (1970), *Speed Is
of the Essence* (1971), and *Panthermania* (1971). Ms. Sheehy's
most recent book, *Hustling* (1973), is a collection of her articles on the sex scene.

$70,000 a Year, Tax Free

"$70,000 a Year, Tax Free" (editor's title) was written for
NBC's "Comment" series and for later publication. Its brevity,
due to time limitations on the original presentation, obviously
precluded a really thorough analysis of the topic. Observing
how the author did use the time at her disposal provides some
of the value of studying the essay here.

How many women do you know who can take home seventy   1
thousand dollars a year? A psychiatrist? She might take home half
that. A congresswoman? Shirley Chisholm's salary is forty-two-
five.

No, the quickest way for a woman to get ahead in this country   2
is to take up the oldest profession: prostitution.

As one veteran streetwalker explained to a runaway she was   3
breaking in: "You have no status, no power, and no way to get it

except by using your body. Why give it away? You're sitting on a gold mine!"

And so, every summer, in New York City, the hue and cry   4
goes up: Crack down on prostitution! Close the massage parlors! But why has New York become a boomtown for hustlers? Not because of the increased use of drugs, as most people assume. It began with a change in New York's penal code four years ago. Loitering for the purpose of prostitution was reduced by former Police Commissioner Leary from a misdemeanor to a violation. Even girls found guilty on the more serious "pross collar" rarely go to jail. Most judges let them go for a twenty-five to fifty dollar fine — and a week to pay. It amounts to a license.

Word of this change spread with interest through the pimp   5
grapevine around the country: New York was wide open. Today, you'd hardly guess which four states have the largest pipeline shipping prostitutes to New York: in order, they are Minnesota, Massachusetts, Michigan, and Ohio. There are lots of fair haired girls from Minnesota with street names like Little Tiffany, and Marion the Librarian. But why do they come? It couldn't be a more American phenomenon: The prostitute's dream is the most upward mobile, middle class, American pie dream of all.

Number one: she wants money — high-style clothes, a model   6
apartment, candy color wigs and her teeth capped.

Number two: she's looking for a "family." Most of the girls   7
have one or two children — illegitimate. On top of that, the girl is often white and her illegitimate child is black. Back home in Minneapolis, she was already a social pariah, and she couldn't make a go of living and working while dragging a baby from room to rented room. So she comes to New York, looking for a new kind of family — exactly what the pimp provides.

He puts up his stable of three or four girls in a high-rise apart-   8
ment, pays their rent, buys their clothes, foots their doctor bills. Top woman in this "family" — the pimp's favorite, who brings in the most money — is called his "wife." The rest are known as "wife-in-laws." Remarkably enough, they all get along quite well. The tie that really binds is the baby sitter — the girls share one for seventy-five dollars a week and this is what frees them to work.

As a midtown hooker from Virginia put it to me: "Most of the   9
girls are here doing it for their kids. I don't want my daughter to have the kind of childhood I had. She's going to have the best!"

So now the prostitute has money, a family, a baby sitter. The other thing she craves is "glamour and excitement," things she probably dreamed of finding in a career as a model or actress. But those fields are fiercely competitive. Besides, as a prostitute sees it, models and actresses are treated like dress hangers or pieces of meat: they give their bodies away to advance their careers, while so-called straight women exchange sex for the financial security of marriage. A "working girl," as the prostitute refers to herself, is the only honest one: She sets the price, delivers the goods, and concludes her business within the hour — no romantic nonsense about it.

And finally, after she is on the street for a few months, the pace of peeping and hiding, the game of stinging johns and ducking police vans becomes a way of life. It gets into the blood like gambler's fever.

The hooker with the heart of gold? That's a male myth. Many of our street girls can be as vicious and money mad as any corporation president. Moreover, they can be less emotional than men in conducting acts of personal violence. The bulk of their business is not the dispensation of pleasure: it is to mug, rob, swindle, knife, and possibly, even murder their patrons. Police drags against them are about as effective as pacification programs in Vietnam. Apply police pressure to streetwalkers and robberies generally go up. If a girl doesn't bring in that fixed amount, two hundred and fifty a night, she'll go home to a beating from her pimp.

People are puzzled: why this boom in prostitution when young America is bursting with sexual freedom? They forget about men over forty, men who learned their sexual fantasies from nudie calendars in the gas station. To be fun, the bedmate must be a no-no. "You can't fantasize about your wife or girlfriend," one man explained. "The woman has to be an unknown." And where is this illicit thrill of forbidden flesh still to be found? On the black market of course. Furthermore, the prostitute makes no emotional demands. She would never call his office the next day. It is her stock in trade to encourage men's sexual fantasies and exploit them. How else can a girl make seventy thousand dollars a year, tax free!

Meanings and Values

1a. Briefly summarize the author's reasons for a girl's becoming a prostitute.

  b. Do you consider these ultimate or immediate causes — or would you classify them somewhere in between? Why?

2a. Why does the author consider these motivations as an "American pie dream" (par. 5)?

  b. To which of the causes, if any, does the description seem to you not to apply? Why?

3. Why does she assume that we'd "hardly guess" which four states have the largest pipelines into New York prostitution (par. 5)?

4. Do you see anything ironical in the prostitute's comments in paragraph 9? (See Guide to Terms: *Irony*.) If so, explain.

5a. How can perpetuation of the "male myth" (par. 12) be explained?

  b. Why would it be more difficult to "fantasize" about one's wife or girlfriend (par. 13)?

6a. Where would you locate this selection on an objective-to-subjective continuum? (Guide: *Objective/Subjective*.)

  b. Is the author guilty of any sentimentality? (Guide: *Sentimentality*.) If so, where?

Expository Techniques

1a. In which paragraphs does the author explain why prostitution has increased greatly in New York City?

  b. Does this seem to be a thorough cause-and-effect analysis?

  c. Is it sufficient for the purpose? Why, or why not?

2a. In paragraphs 6–11 she outlines a different set of causes. Would they have been more effective for her purpose if she had gone deeper into the more ultimate causes?

  b. Why do you think she did not?

  c. What function is served by the first sentence of paragraph 10? Why would the author have considered it a useful device in this particular exposition?

3a. What is Sheehy's central theme? (Guide: *Unity*.)

  b. Do all portions of the essay serve as "tributaries" into this theme, thus giving unity to the writing? If not, what are the exceptions?

4a. Which of the standard techniques of introduction does this author use? (Guide: *Introductions*.)

  b. Why do they seem particularly well chosen, considering the basic purpose of this exposition?

5a. The last sentence is a good example of at least one standard technique of closing. (Guide: *Closings*.) What is it?

b. Suggest a different kind of closing and compare the potential effectiveness of the two.

6. Which of the patterns of exposition already studied does Sheehy employ in paragraph 10?

7. In your opinion, would any of her statements have benefited by further qualification? (Guide: *Qualification*.) If so, explain why.

Diction and Vocabulary

1. Illustrate the meaning of the following terms by use of one or more examples from this selection.
   a. Colloquialism. (Guide: *Colloquial*.)
   b. Simile. (Guide: *Figures of Speech*.)
   c. Cliché. (Guide: *Clichés*.)

2. What is a "social pariah" (par. 7)?

3. Considering this exposition's original purpose, why do you think the author used few, if any, "dictionary-type" words?

Suggestions for Writing and Discussion

1. The author says most people assume that the increase of prostitution is related to an increased use of drugs. How logical does this assumption appear to you? Explain.

2. Explore parallels in other, more legitimate fields in which motivation may be provided by the "upward mobile, middle class, American pie dream" (par. 5).

3. In view of the five reasons for a girl's becoming a prostitute — all seeming to be fairly common desires — why it is that even more girls do not engage in prostitution?

4. Which of her five reasons do you think would also apply to the thriving business (in some cities especially) of male prostitution? Are there other reasons that apply here?

5. How logical and/or just do you consider the move in many areas toward "equal guilt" laws, whereby the male is considered as guilty as the prostitute he employs?

6. Should there even *be* laws prohibiting prostitution?

7. The word "prostitution" is often used with broader meaning than in Sheehy's analysis — e.g., prostitution of talent or prostitution of science. Select one such usage and examine motivations in terms of this author's "upward mobility" theories.

(NOTE: Suggestions for topics requiring development by analysis of CAUSE and EFFECT are on page 190, at the end of this section.)

LAWRENCE CASLER

LAWRENCE CASLER, born in 1932, is professor of psychology at
the State University of Genesco, New York. He received his
Ph.D. in social psychology from Columbia University in 1962.
Casler has published articles on the development psychology
of infants, the social psychology of marriage, nudism, hypnosis, and ESP.

This Thing Called Love Is Pathological

"This Thing Called Love Is Pathological," of which the following selection is a greater part, was first published in the December 1969 issue of *Psychology Today*. In his search for
ultimate causes and effects of romantic love Casler is far
from romantic and may even draw sparks from some of his
readers. (But personal agreement has never been requisite for
objective analysis of another's views and methods.)

> *Men have died from time to time and worms*
> *have eaten them, but not for love.*
> — Act IV, Scene 1, *As You Like It*

Magazines, movies and television teach us the joys of love. Adver-   1
tisers insist that we must look good and smell good in order to
escape loveless solitude. Artists, philosophers and hippies wage
their varying versions of Love; and most psychotherapists hold
that the ability to love is a sign — sometimes *the* sign — of mental
health.

To suggest that this emphasis on lovingness is misplaced is to   2
risk being accused of arrested development, coldness, low self-
image, or some unmentionable deficiency. Still, the expanding
frontiers of psychology require a reconsideration of love at this
time.

We shall be concerned, chiefly, with what is generally called 3 "romantic" love. But many of these observations may be applicable to other varieties as well.

Love, like other emotions, has causes ... and consequences. 4 Temporarily setting aside an inquiry into why, or whether love makes the world go 'round, makes life worth living, and conquers all, let us consider the somewhat more manageable question of causality. Love between man and woman has many determinants, but instinct is not one of them. Anthropologists have described entire societies in which love is absent, and there are many individuals in our society who have never loved. To argue that such societies and individuals are "sick" or "the exception that proves the rule" (whatever *that* means) is sheer arrogance. Love, when it exists, is a learned emotion. Explanations for its current prevalence must be sought elsewhere than in the genes.

Most individuals in our society, beset by parent-bred, competi- 5 tion-bred insecurity, need acceptance, confirmation, justification. Part of this need is inescapable. Life requires continual decision-making: white vs. red wine, honesty vs. dishonesty, etc. In the presence of uncertainty, most of us need to know that we are making the right decisions, so we seek external validation. We are, therefore, absurdly pleased when we meet someone who shares our penchant for Palestrina or peanut butter. Should we find one person whose choices in many different matters coincide with our own, we will value this buttress of our self-esteem. This attachment to a source of self-validation constitutes one important basis for love.

While the relationship between loving and being loved is an 6 intimate one, this is not to say that love is automatically reciprocated. Indeed, it may lead to feelings of revulsion if the individual's self-image is already irretrievably low: "Anyone who says he loves *me* must be either a fool or a fraud." Still a person is relatively likely to love someone who loves him. Indirect support for this generalization comes from a number of experiments in which persons are falsely informed that they are liked (or disliked) by other members of their group. This misinformation is enough to elicit congruent feelings in most of the deceived subjects. A similar kind of feedback often operates in the elaborate American game of dating. The young woman, for any of several reasons, may pretend to like her escort more than is actually the case. The man, hungry for precisely this kind of response, responds favorably and in kind.

And the woman, gratified by this expression of affection, now feels the fondness she had formerly feigned. Falling in love may be regarded, in cases such as these, as a snowball with a hollow core.

Nevertheless, we do not fall in love with everyone who shows   7
acceptance of us. Other needs clamor for satisfaction. And the more needs that one person satisfies, the more likely are we to love that person. One of the foremost needs is called, very loosely, sex. Our love is elicited not simply by the ego-booster, but by the ego-booster with sex appeal.

The mores of our society discourage us from seeking sexual   8
gratification from anyone with whom we do not have a preexisting relationship. As a result, the more ego-boosting a relationship is, the greater the tendency will be for the booster to serve — actually or potentially — as a sex-satisfier. But it is also true that a person who gives one sexual pleasure tends to boost one's ego. Once again, the snowball effect is obvious.

Society emphasizes, furthermore, the necessity for love to pre-   9
cede sex. Although many disregard this restriction, others remain frightened or disturbed by the idea of a purely sexual relationship. The only way for many sexually aroused individuals to avoid frustration or anxiety is to fall in love — as quickly as possible. More declarations of love have probably been uttered in parked cars than in any other location. Some of these surely are nothing more than seduction ploys, but it is likely that self-seduction is involved in many cases.

For most of us, the internal and external pressures are so great   10
that we can no longer "choose" to love or not love. Loving becomes inevitable, like dying or getting married. We are so thoroughly brainwashed that we come to pity or scorn the person who is not in love. (Of course, the pity or scorn may be self-directed, but not for long: anyone who does not have the inner resources to stand alone can usually impose himself upon somebody else who is equally incapacitated.)

Our society, besides being love-oriented, is marriage-oriented.   11
From early childhood on, we hear countless statements beginning, "When (not *if*) you get married. . . ." And, just as love is regarded as a prerequisite for sex, it is regarded as a prerequisite for marriage. Consequently, the insecurity and the fear of social punishment that force most of us into marriage provide additional powerful motives for falling in love. (The current value of marriage as a

social institution, while open to question, is beyond the scope of this essay.)

To summarize, the *causes* of love are the needs for security,   12
sexual satisfaction, and social conformity. Thus viewed, love loses its uniqueness. Hatred, too, in societies that are as aggression-oriented as ours is love-oriented, may reflect these same needs. To state that love is a superior emotion is to express a current cultural bias. Nothing is good or bad but culture makes it so. . . .

Let us turn now to a consideration of the *consequences* of love.   13
First, being in love makes it easier to have guilt-free sex, to marry, and to view oneself as a normal, healthy citizen of the Western world. Love also tends to alter certain psychological processes. According to a charming quotation that I've been able to trace back no further than its utterance in an old movie called *Mr. Skeffington*, "A woman is beautiful only when she is loved." The statement, however, is not quite accurate. A woman (likewise a man, a worm, a grain of sand) may become beautiful when the perceiver has been primed with LSD, hypnosis, or anything else that can induce hallucinations. In short, love may create the error of over-evaluation. The doting lover is doomed either to painful disillusion or to the permanent delusion that so closely resembles psychosis.

Some may argue that I am speaking of immature infatuation,   14
rather than real love. Mature love, they may insist, is a broadening, deepening experience. This postulation of the salutary effects of love is so pervasive that we must examine its validity. First, there is the matter of evidence. Subjective reports are notoriously unreliable, and experimental studies are nonexistent. The claim that love promotes maturity is unpersuasive without some indication that the individual would not have matured just as readily in the absence of love. Indeed, to the extent that love fosters dependency, it may be viewed as a deterrent to maturity.

I am not asserting that the effects of love always border on the   15
pathological. I *am* saying that the person who seeks love in order to obtain security will become, like the alcoholic, increasingly dependent on this source of illusory well-being. The secure person who seeks love would probably not trap himself in this way. But would the secure person seek love at all?

One inference to be drawn from the material here is that the   16
nonloving person in our society is likely to be in a state of either very good or very poor mental health. The latter possibility re-

quires no extended explanation. One of the standard stigmata of emotional disturbance is the inability to love. Most schools of psychotherapy aim specifically at the development of this ability. Some therapies go so far as to designate the therapist himself as a proper recipient of the patient's newly released love impulses (perhaps on the assumption that if the patient can love his therapist, he can love anybody).

The other part of the statement — that a love-free person can   17
be in excellent mental health — may seem less acceptable. But if the need for a love relationship is based largely on insecurity, conformity to social pressures, and sexual frustration, then the person who is secure, independent, and has a satisfying sex life will not need to love. He will, rather, be a person who does not find his own company boring — a person whose inner resources are such that other persons, although they provide pleasure and stimulation, are not absolutely necessary. We have long been enjoined to love others as we love ourselves. But perhaps we seek love relationships with others only because we do not love ourselves sufficiently.

What would a healthy love-free person be like? One might as-   18
sume that coldness would be among his most salient characteristics. But a cold person is simply one who does not give us the warmth we want or need. The attribution of coldness says more about the person doing the attributing than it does about the person being characterized. Absence of warmth is responded to negatively only by those insecure persons who interpret it as rejection. (Similarly, a nymphomaniac has been defined as a woman whose sex drive is stronger than that of the person who is calling her a nymphomaniac.)

Would the love-free person be egotistical? Perhaps, but only   19
if that term is relieved of its ugly connotations. To be self-centered does not mean to disregard the worth of other people. It does imply that other people are reacted to within a frame of reference that is centered on the self. There is nothing reprehensible about this. In fact, most psychologists would probably accept the position that we are *all* self-centered. No matter how other-directed our actions may appear, they are functions of *our* perception of the world, based, in turn, on *our* previous experiences. Since every act is a "self-ish" one, evaluative criteria should be applied only to the effects of selfishness, rather than to selfishness, *per se*.

This essay has not been anti-love, but pro-people. I view so-   20 ciety's emphasis on love as both an effect and a cause of the insecurity, dependency, and frightened conformity that may be the death of us all. To love a person means, all too often, to use that person. And exploitation, even if mutual, is incompatible with human growth. Finally, like a crutch, love may impede the exercise of our own potential for growth, and thus tend to perpetuate itself.

Perhaps the goal of social reformers should be not love, but respect — for others and, most of all, for self.   21

Meanings and Values

1. If the author's ideas of romantic love and its causes are even partially correct, to what other "varieties" of love might they also apply (par. 3)?

2a. The author states that most individuals are beset by insecurity (par. 5). How is this insecurity "parent-bred"?
 b. How is it "competition-bred"?

3. Is anyone you know so "secure" that he has no need for love at all (par. 15)? Briefly provide some support for your answer.

4. Clarify the author's concept of "self-seduction" (par. 9).

5. In paragraph 18, is the author saying that there is no such being as a "cold" person, except in the view of the person wanting to relate to him? Clarify.

6. How convincingly does the author demonstrate that "love as it exists, is a learned emotion" (par. 4)? Justify your answer objectively.

7a. The author states that his essay has not been "anti-love" (par. 20). Do you agree? Why, or why not?
 b. Has reading it in any way affected your own attitude toward love? Explain.

8. If you have read Packard's "New Directions of Marriage," show whatever significant relationship you find between his ideas and Casler's statement (par. 11) that "insecurity and the fear of social punishment . . . force most of us into marriage."

Expository Techniques

1a. Which, if any, of the author's causes do you consider immediate and which ultimate? Why?
 b. Which of the consequences would you so classify in each category? Why?

2a. Cite the specific devices by which this author keeps us oriented to his step-by-step development — no doubt to prevent any sense of disorder, with resulting frustration and loss of attention.

b. Explain how unity is served by this attention to orderliness. (See Guide to Terms: *Unity.*)

c. How is coherence served. (Guide: *Coherence.*)

3. Which of the common introductory techniques does the author employ? (Guide: *Introduction.*)

4a. Which of the methods for closing are used? (Guide: *Closings.*)

b. Suggest one other way this writing might have been concluded.

5. Would greater use of qualification have improved the effectiveness of this writing? (Guide: *Qualification.*) If so, cite instances and show how the qualifying could be achieved.

Diction and Vocabulary

1a. Cite three clichés in paragraph 4. (Guide: *Clichés.*)

b. Is their use careless or intentional? Why?

2. Is the "snowball" (pars. 6, 8) used as a figure of speech, as analogy, or as a sort of hybrid? Why? (Guide: *Figures of Speech.*)

3a. What is your dictionary's denotative meaning of "egotistical" (par. 19)?

b. Does this differ appreciably from the usual connotation of the word? If so, why?

c. Is it apt to be "relieved of its ugly connotations"?

4. Use the dictionary as necessary in order to understand the meanings of the following words, especially as Casler uses them: pathological (title and par. 15); psychotherapists (1); causality, determinants, anthropologists (4); validation, penchant, Palestrina (5); reciprocated, irretrievably, elicit, congruent, feigned (6); mores (8); ploys (9); prerequisite (11); psychosis (13); postulation, salutary (14); stigmata (16); enjoined (17); salient, attribution, nymphomaniac (18); reprehensible, *per se* (19); impede, perpetuate (20).

Suggestions for Writing and Discussion

1. In raising our own children, how can we be certain to prevent "parent-bred" insecurity (par. 5)?

2. Are our society's old mores against "having sex" without a pre-existing relationship (par. 8) among those mores the younger generation is rebelling against? Are they included, perhaps, in the "Puritan noose" to which Michener refers in his essay in Section 2?

3. If you agree that pressures on most people are so great that loving becomes inevitable (par. 10), provide specific, concrete examples (for the author's pure abstractions) of how this pressure system works.

4. Compose an answer, as you see it, to the author's question (par. 15), "would the secure person seek love at all?"

5. Carefully consider the definition composed by an American psychiatrist, Harry Stack Sullivan: "When the satisfaction or security of another person becomes as significant to one as is one's own, then a state of love exists. So far as I know, under no other circumstances is a state of love present, regardless of popular usage." Show the relation, contradictory or otherwise, between this view of love and that of Casler.

6. Either further develop the idea that "nothing is good or bad but culture makes it so" (par. 12) or shows its weaknesses. Use clear examples liberally to illustrate your views.

(NOTE: Suggestions for topics requiring development by analysis of CAUSE and EFFECT are on page 190, at the end of this section.)

GLORIA STEINEM

GLORIA STEINEM, born in Ohio in 1936, was graduated from Smith College and did graduate work on fellowships at the universities of Calcutta and Delphi. She has been director of educational foundations and research services and has worked as a script writer for television (including "That Was the Week That Was," 1964–1965). Ms. Steinem is a versatile and prolific writer who has contributed to *Esquire, Life, Harper's, Vogue, Glamour, New York Times Magazine, McCall's, Ladies Home Journal, New York, Look,* and others. As a result of her involvement with the women's liberation movement, Ms. Steinem founded and is editor of the unconventional women's magazine, *Ms.* which first appeared in 1972. Her books are *The Thousand Indias* (1957) and *The Beach Book* (1963).

What It Would Be Like if Women Win

"What It Would Be Like . . ." was a *Time* essay in 1970. Generally regarded as being among the more moderate and "reasonable" of the active Women's Liberationists, Ms. Steinem is able nonetheless to draw sparks when she approaches this still-controversial subject. Our selection is no exception, but you will note differences between it and the broadsides of the more militant feminists.

Any change is fearful, especially one affecting both politics and sex 1
roles, so let me begin these utopian speculations with a fact. To break the ice.

Women don't want to exchange places with men. Male chau- 2
vinists, science-fiction writers and comedians may favor that idea for its shock value, but psychologists say it is a fantasy based on ruling-class ego and guilt. Men assume that women want to imitate them, which is just what white people assumed about blacks.

An assumption so strong that it may convince the second-class group of the need to imitate, but for both women and blacks that stage has passed. Guilt produces the question: What if they could treat us as we have treated them?

That is not our goal. But we do want to change the economic system to one more based on merit. In Women's Lib Utopia, there will be free access to good jobs — and decent pay for the bad ones women have been performing all along, including housework. Increased skilled labor might lead to a four-hour workday, and higher wages would encourage further mechanization of repetitive jobs now kept alive by cheap labor. 3

With women as half the country's elected representatives, and a woman President once in a while, the country's *machismo* problems would be greatly reduced. The old-fashioned idea that manhood depends on violence and victory is, after all, an important part of our troubles in the streets ... I'm not saying that women leaders would eliminate violence. We are not more moral than men; we are only uncorrupted by power so far. When we do acquire power, we might turn out to have an equal impulse toward aggression. Even now, Margaret Mead believes that women fight less often but more fiercely than men, because women are not taught the rules of the war game and fight only when cornered. But for the next 50 years or so, women in politics will be very valuable by tempering the idea of manhood into something less aggressive and better suited to this crowded, post-atomic planet. Consumer protection and children's rights, for instance, might get more legislative attention. 4

Men will have to give up ruling-class privileges, but in return they will no longer be the only ones to support the family, get drafted, bear the strain of power and responsibility. Freud to the contrary, anatomy is not destiny, at least not for more than nine months at a time. In Israel, women are drafted, and some have gone to war. In England, more men type and run switchboards. In India and Israel, a woman rules. In Sweden, both parents take care of the children. In this country, come Utopia, men and women won't reverse roles; they will be free to choose according to individual talents and preference. 5

If role reform sounds sexually unsettling, think how it will change the sexual hypocrisy we have now. No more sex arranged 6 on the barter system, with women pretending interest, and men never sure whether they are loved for themselves or for the security few women can get any other way. (Married or not, for sexual reasons or social ones, most women still find it second nature to Uncle-Tom.) No more men who are encouraged to spend a lifetime living with inferiors; with housekeepers, or dependent creatures who are still children. No more domineering wives, emasculating women, and "Jewish mothers," all of whom are simply human beings with all their normal ambition and drive confined to the home. No more unequal partnerships that eventually doom love and sex.

In order to produce that kind of confidence and individuality, child rearing will train according to talent. Little girls will no longer be surrounded by air-tight, self-fulfilling prophecies of natural passivity, lack of ambition and objectivity, inability to exercise power, and dexterity (so long as special aptitude for jobs requiring patience and dexterity is confined to poorly paid jobs; brain surgery is for males).

Schools and universities will help to break down traditional sex roles, even when parents will not. Half the teachers will be men, a rarity now at preschool and elementary levels; girls will not necessarily serve cookies or boys hoist up the flag. Athletic teams will be picked only by strength and skill. Sexually segregated courses like auto mechanics and home economics will be taken by boys and girls together. New courses in sexual politics will explore female subjugation as the model for political oppression, and women's history will be an academic staple, along with black history, at least until the white-male-oriented textbooks are integrated and rewritten.

As for the American child's classic problem — too much mother, too little father — that would be cured by an equalization of parental responsibility. Free nurseries, school lunches, family cafeterias built into every housing complex, service companies that will do household cleaning chores in a regular, businesslike way, and more responsibility by the entire community for the children: all these will make it possible for both mother and father to work, and to have equal leisure time with the children at home. For parents of very young children, however, a special job category, created by Government and unions, would allow such parents a shorter work day.

The revolution would not take away the option of being a   10
housewife. A woman who prefers to be her husband's housekeeper
and/or hostess would receive a percentage of his pay determined
by the domestic relations courts. If divorced, she might be eligible
for a pension fund, and for a job-training allowance. Or a divorce
could be treated the same way that the dissolution of a business
partnership is now.

If these proposals seem farfetched, consider Sweden, where   11
most of them are already in effect. Sweden is not yet a working
Women's Lib model; most of the role-reform programs began less
than a decade ago, and are just beginning to take hold. But that
country is so far ahead of us in recognizing the problem that
Swedish statements on sex and equality sound like bulletins from
the moon.

Our marriage laws, for instance, are so reactionary that   12
Women's Lib groups want couples to take a compulsory written
exam on the law, as for a driver's license, before going through
with the wedding. A man has alimony and wifely debts to worry
about, but a woman may lose so many of her civil rights that in the
U.S. now, in important legal ways, she becomes a child again. In
some states, she cannot sign credit agreements, use her maiden
name, incorporate a business, or establish a legal residence of her
own. Being a wife, according to most social and legal definitions,
is still a 19th century thing.

Assuming, however, that these blatantly sexist laws are abol-   13
ished or reformed, that job discrimination is forbidden, that parents
share financial responsibility for each other and the children, and
that sexual relationships become partnerships of equal adults (some
pretty big assumptions), then marriage will probably go right on.
Men and women are, after all, physically complementary. When
society stops encouraging men to be exploiters and women to be
parasites, they may turn out to be more complementary in emotion
as well. Women's Lib is not trying to destroy the American family.
A look at the statistics on divorce — plus the way in which old
people are farmed out with strangers and young people flee the
home — shows the destruction that has already been done. Liberated women are just trying to point out the disaster, and build
compassionate and practical alternatives from the ruins.

What will exist is a variety of alternative life-styles. Since the   14
population explosion dictates that childbearing be kept to a min-

imum, parents-and-children will be only one of many "families":
couples, age groups, working groups, mixed communes, blood-
related clans, class groups, creative groups. Single women will have
the right to stay single without ridicule, without the attitudes now
betrayed by "spinster" and "bachelor." Lesbians or homosexuals
will no longer be denied legally binding marriages, complete with
mutual-support agreements and inheritance rights. Paradoxically,
the number of homosexuals may get smaller. With fewer over-
possessive mothers and fewer fathers who hold up an impossibly
cruel or perfectionist idea of manhood, boys will be less likely to be
denied or reject their identity as males.

Changes that now seem smaller may get bigger: 15

Men's Lib. Men now suffer from more diseases due to stress, heart   16
attacks, ulcers, a higher suicide rate, greater difficulty living alone,
less adaptability to change and, in general, a shorter life span than
women. There is some scientific evidence that what produces
physical problems is not work itself, but the inability to choose
which work, and how much. With women bearing half the financial
responsibility, and with the idea of "masculine" jobs gone, men
might well feel freer and live longer.

Religion. Protestant women are already becoming ordained min-   17
isters; radical nuns are carrying out liturgical functions that were
once the exclusive property of priests; Jewish women are rewriting
prayers — particularly those that Orthodox Jews recite every morning thanking God they are not female. In the future, the church will
become an area of equal participation by women. This means, of
course, that organized religion will have to give up one of its great
historical weapons: sexual repression. In most structured faiths,
from Hinduism through Roman Catholicism, the status of women
went down as the position of priests ascended. Male clergy implied,
if they did not teach, that women were unclean, unworthy and
sources of ungodly temptation, in order to remove them as rivals
for the emotional for es of men. Full participation of women in
ecclesiastical life might involve certain changes in theology, such
as, for instance, a radical redefinition of sin.

Literary Problems. Revised sex roles will outdate more children's   18
books than civil rights ever did. Only a few children had the prob-

lem of a *Little Black Sambo*, but most have the male-female stereotypes of "Dick and Jane." A boomlet of children's books about
mothers who work has already begun, and liberated parents and
editors are beginning to pressure for change in the textbook industry. Fiction writing will change more gradually, but romantic
novels with wilting heroines and swashbuckling heroes will be
reduced to historical value. Or perhaps to the sado-masochist trade.
(*Marjorie Morningstar*, a romantic novel that took the '50's by
storm, has already begun to seem as unreal as its '20's predecessor,
The Sheik.) As for the literary plots that turn on forced marriages
or horrific abortions, they will seem as dated as Prohibition stories.
Free legal abortions and free birth control will force writers to give
up pregnancy as the *deus ex machina*.

Manners and Fashion. Dress will be more androgynous, with class   19
symbols becoming more important than sexual ones. Pro- or anti-
Establishment styles may already be more vital than who is wearing them. Hardhats are just as likely to rough up antiwar girls as
antiwar men in the street, and police understand that women are
just as likely to be pushers or bombers. Dances haven't required
that one partner lead the other for years, anyway. Chivalry will
transfer itself to those who need it, or deserve respect: old people,
admired people, anyone with an armload of packages. Women with
normal work identities will be less likely to attach their whole sense
of self to youth and appearance; thus there will be fewer nervous
breakdowns when the first wrinkles appear. Lighting cigarettes and
other treasured niceties will become gestures of mutual affection.
"I like to be helped on with my coat," says one Women's Lib
worker, "but not if it costs me $2,000 a year in salary."

For those with nostalgia for a simpler past, here is a word of   20
comfort. Anthropologist Geoffrey Gorer studied the few peaceful
human tribes and discovered one common characteristic: sex roles
were not polarized. Differences of dress and occupation were at a
minimum. Society, in other words, was not using sexual blackmail
as a way of getting women to do cheap labor, or men to be aggressive.

Thus Women's Lib may achieve a more peaceful society on   21
the way toward its other goals. That is why the Swedish government considers reform to bring about greater equality in the sex

roles one of its most important concerns. As Prime Minister Olof Palme explained in a widely ignored speech delivered in Washington this spring: "It is *human beings* we shall emancipate. In Sweden today, if a politician should declare that the woman ought to have a different role from man's, he would be regarded as something from the Stone Age." In other words, the most radical goal of the movement is egalitarianism.

If Women's Lib wins, perhaps we all do.   22

Meanings and Values

1a. In general what seems to be the author's attitude toward her subject matter? (See Guide to Terms: *Style/Tone.*)
  b. To what extent is this attitude reflected by her tone?

2a. If you have read articles on Women's Lib by any of the more radical feminists, what seems to be the most noteworthy differences between their approach and that of Steinem, at least in this essay?
  b. Which is better? Or, if this question depends on purpose and/or reader-audience, explain specifically how.

3. Comment on the following remarks in respect to their effect on the tone:
  a. "decent pay for the bad ones . . . including housework . . ." (par. 3).
  b. "to spend a lifetime living with inferiors; with housekeepers, or dependent creatures . . ." (6).
  c. "A woman who prefers to be her husband's housekeeper . . . would receive a percentage of his pay determined by the domestic relations courts" (10).
  d. "If divorced, she might be eligible for a pension fund . . ." (10).

4a. Why would it be paradoxical if making legal marriages possible between homosexuals resulted in less homosexuality (par. 14)? (Guide: *Paradox.*)
  b. Explain why you do, or do not, assume this might be true?

5a. Explain the significance of the references to *Little Black Sambo* and "Dick and Jane" (par. 18).
  b. How is it, if at all, that either or both of these may now have become symbols? (Guide: *Symbol.*)

6a. If you have read "Male and Female: The Differences Between Them" in Section 3, cite any significant differences in minor or major conclusions of the two essays.
  b. If any, which essay seems based on sounder reasoning?

Expository Techniques

1a. Is Steinem, in this essay, primarily concerned with immediate or ultimate effects?
 b. Is the nearly total exclusion of the other fully justified? Why, or why not?

2a. Few of the paragraphs in this selection have any apparent transitional connections with each other. (Guide: *Transition.*) How, if at all, can this lack be justified by the nature of the writing?
 b. What is the effect, if any, on coherence? (Guide: *Coherence.*)

3. Many of the paragraphs are ideal for demonstrating the technique and value of making the general more specific in order to clarify. (Guide: *Specific/General.*) Select two such paragraphs and use them to illustrate this principle.

4. How successful is the one-sentence closing? Why?

Diction and Vocabulary

1. If you know the meaning of the word *machismo* (par. 4), why might it be regarded as a key word in the whole matter of Women's Liberation? (If you are not familiar with the term, perhaps you know a Spanish speaker who will explain it to you.)

2a. What is the meaning of *deus ex machina* (18)?
 b. Why is it italicized?

3a. In paragraph 6 you may find two colloquialisms. (Guide: *Colloquial.*) What are they?
 b. One of these is also an allusion. (Guide: *Figures of Speech.*) Identify which and explain why it is an allusion.
 c. Cite another example of colloquialism in paragraph 19.

4. Use the dictionary as necessary to understand the following words and their meanings: utopian (par. 1); chauvinists (2); emasculating (6); blatantly (13); swashbuckling (18); androgynous (19); egalitarianism (21).

Suggestions for Writing and Discussion

1. Considering the last sentence of paragraph 3, does it seem to you that Steinem has an overoptimistic view of the labor market? Why, or why not?

2. Is there any inconsistency between the assumption that for the "next 50 years or so" women in politics would be less warlike than men (par. 4) and the somewhat prideful pointing to Indira Gandhi

and Golda Meir as women who already rule (par. 5)? (Has either of these rulers, for example, shown remarkable gentleness when their own country's interests were at stake?)

3. Select one or more of the following statements and explain why it may be controversial. If you like, you may emphasize the view you favor.
   a. "Half the teachers will be men . . ." (par. 8).
   b. "Athletic teams will be picked only by strength and skill" (8).
   c. "with the idea of 'masculine' jobs gone, men might well feel freer and live longer" (16).
   d. "there will be fewer nervous breakdowns when the first wrinkles occur" (19).

Writing Suggestions for Section 6
Analysis of Cause and Effect

Analyze the immediate and ultimate causes and/or effects of one of the following subjects, or another suggested by them. (Be careful that your analysis does not develop into a mere listing of superficial "reasons.")

1. The shortage of summer jobs for students.
2. The ethnic makeup of a neighborhood.
3. Some *minor* discovery or invention.
4. The popularity of some modern singer or other celebrity admired especially by young people.
5. The popularity of some fad of clothing or hair style.
6. The widespread fascination for antique cars (or guns, furniture, dishes, etc.).
7. The widespread enjoyment of fishing or hunting.
8. Student cheating.
9. Failure of the "perfect" vacation.
10. One person's decision to join a "hippie" commune.
11. Too much pressure (on you or an acquaintance) for good school grades.
12. Your being a member of some minority ethnic or religious group.
13. Your association, as an outsider, with members of such a group.
14. The decision of some close acquaintance to enter the religious life.
15. Some unreasonable fear or anxiety that afflicts you or someone you know well.
16. Your need to conform.
17. Your tendency toward individualism.

7

Using *Definition* to Help Explain

Few writing faults can cause a more serious communication block between writer and reader than using key terms that can have various meanings or shades of meaning. Such terms, to be useful rather than detrimental, must be adequately defined.

Of the two basic types of definition, only one is our special concern as a pattern of exposition. But the other, the simpler form, is often useful to clarify meanings of concrete or noncontroversial terms. This simple process is similar to that used most in dictionaries: either providing a synonym (for example, cinema: a motion picture), or placing the word in a class and then showing how it differs from others of the same class (for example, metheglin: an alcoholic liquor made of fermented honey — here the general class is "liquor," and the differences between metheglin and other liquors are that it is "alcoholic" and "made of fermented honey").

More pertinent to our study of structural patterns, however, is *extended* definition, a technique that may be vitally important when using an abstract term. Packard and Michener (Section 2) carefully define most of their terms as they develop classification systems, and Osgood (Section 4) must define "schizoid" in order to gain full benefit from his analogy.

Even with abstract terms that are less scientific, such as "liberal" or "conservative," "loyalty" or "freedom," most readers are too limited by their own experiences and opinions (and no two sets are identical) for the writer to expect understanding of the exact sense in which he uses the terms. He has a right, of course, to use such abstract words any way he chooses — as long as his readers know what that way is. The importance of making this meaning clear becomes crucial when the term is used as a key element of the overall explanation. And sometimes the term being defined is even more than a key element: it may be the subject itself. For instance, to define "The Peter Principle" (Section 1) was really the primary purpose of the writing, even though the authors use examples almost exclusively as a *means* of defining.

Extended definition, unlike the simple, dictionary type, follows no set and formal pattern. Often the reader is not even aware of the process. Because it is an integral part of the overall subject, extended definition is written in the same tone as the rest of the exposition, usually with an attempt to interest the reader, as well as to inform him.

There are some expository techniques peculiar to definition alone. The purpose may be served by giving the background of the term. Or the definition may be clarified by negation, sometimes called "exclusion" or "differentiation," by showing what is *not* meant by the term. Still another way is to enumerate the characteristics of what is defined, sometimes isolating an essential one for special treatment.

To demonstrate the possibilities in these patterns, we can use the term "juvenile delinquency," which might need defining in some contexts since it certainly means different things to different people. (Where do we draw the line, for instance, between "boyish pranks" and delinquency, or between delinquent and nondelinquent experimentation with sex or marijuana?) We might show how attitudes toward juvenile crime have changed: "youthful high spirits" was the label for some of our grandfathers' activities that would be called "delinquency" today. Or we could use negation, eliminating any classes of juvenile wrongdoing not considered delinquency in the current discussion. Or we could simply list characteristics of the juvenile delinquent or isolate one of these — disrespect for authority or lack of consideration for other people — as a universal.

But perhaps the most dependable techniques for defining are the basic expository patterns already studied. The writer could illustrate his meaning of "juvenile delinquency" by giving *examples* from his own experience, from newspaper accounts, or from other sources. (Every one of the introductions to the ten sections of this book, each a definition, relies greatly on illustration by example, as does the Peter/Hull selection.) He could analyze the subject by *classification* of types or degrees of delinquency. He could use the process of *comparison* and *contrast*, perhaps between delinquent and nondelinquent youth. Showing the *causes* and *effects* of juvenile crime could help explain his attitude toward it, and hence its meaning for him. He might choose to use *analogy*, perhaps comparing the child to a young tree growing grotesque because of poor care and attention. Or a step-by-step analysis of the *process* by which a child becomes delinquent might, in some cases, help explain the intended meaning.

Few extended definitions would use all these methods, but the extent of their use must always depend on three factors: (1) the term itself, since some are more elusive and subject to misunderstanding than others; (2) the function the term is to serve in the writing, since it would be foolish to devote several pages to defining a term that serves only a casual or unimportant purpose; and (3) the prospective reader-audience, since the writer wants to avoid insulting the intelligence or background of his readers, yet wants to go far enough to be sure of their understanding.

But this, of course, is a basic challenge in any good writing — analyzing the prospective reader and writing for the best effect on *him.*

ALBERT SCHWEITZER

ALBERT SCHWEITZER (1875–1965), a few months before his death, celebrated his ninetieth birthday near Lambarene, Gabon (in Equatorial Africa), at the sprawling hospital complex he had founded and where he had spent most of his last fifty-three years. Dr. Schweitzer, an Alsatian, became eminent early in his life as a teacher and scholar (with doctoral degrees in both philosophy and theology), noted musician, and expert in organ construction. At the age of thirty, having decided to devote the rest of his life to service in Africa, he began his medical education. Dr. Schweitzer received many international awards, including the Nobel Peace Prize for 1952.

Reverence for Life

"Reverence for Life" is excerpted from Schweitzer's book by that title, which was published in Germany in 1966 and, translated by Reginald H. Fuller, in the United States in 1969. In this selection the author defines his key term — a matter of vital importance since the term might otherwise be open to diverse connotations and interpretations.

Explore everything around you, penetrate to the furthest limits of 1
human knowledge, and always you will come up against something inexplicable in the end. It is called life. It is a mystery so inexplicable that the knowledge of the educated and the ignorant is purely relative when contemplating it.

But what is the difference between the scientist who observes 2
in his microscope the most minute and unexpected signs of life; and the old farmer who by contrast can barely read or write, who stands in springtime in his garden and contemplates the buds opening on

the branches of his trees? Both are confronted with the riddle of life. One may be able to describe life in greater detail, but for both it remains equally inscrutable. All knowledge is, in the final analysis, the knowledge of life. All realization is amazement at this riddle of life — a reverence for life in its infinite and yet ever-fresh manifestations. How amazing this coming into being, living, and dying! How fantastic that in other existences something comes into being, passes away again, comes into being once more, and so forth from eternity to eternity! How can it be? We can do all things, and we can do nothing. For in all our wisdom we cannot create life. What we create is dead.

Life means strength, will, arising from the abyss, dissolving into the abyss again. Life is feeling, experience, suffering. If you study life deeply, looking with perceptive eyes into the vast animated chaos of this creation, its profundity will seize you suddenly with dizziness. In everything you recognize yourself. The tiny beetle that lies dead in your path — it was a living creature, struggling for existence like yourself, rejoicing in the sun like you, knowing fear and pain like you. And now it is no more than decaying matter — which is what you will be sooner or later, too. . . .   3

What is this recognition, this knowledge within the reach of the most scientific and the most childlike? It is reverence for life, reverence for the unfathomable mystery we confront in our universe, an existence different in its outward appearance and yet inwardly of the same character as our own, terribly similar, awesomely related. The strangeness between us and other creatures is here removed.   4

Reverence for the infinity of life means removal of the alienation, restoration of empathy, compassion, sympathy. And so the final result of knowledge is the same as that required of us by the commandment of love. Heart and reason agree together when we desire and dare to be men who seek to fathom the depths of the universe.   5

Reason discovers the bridge between love for God and love for men — love for all creatures, reverence for all being, compassion with all life, however dissimilar to our own.   6

I cannot but have reverence for all that is called life. I cannot avoid compassion for everything that is called life. That is the beginning and foundation of morality. Once a man has experienced it and continues to do so — and he who has once experienced it will   7 continue to do so — he is ethical. He carries his morality within him and can never lose it, for it continues to develop within him. He who has never experienced this has only a set of superficial principles. These theories have no root in him, they do not belong to him, and they fall off him. The worst is that the whole of our generation had only such a set of superficial principles. Then the time came to put the ethical code to the test, and it evaporated. For centuries the human race had been educated with only a set of superficial principles. We were brutal, ignorant, and heartless without being aware of it. We had no scale of values, for we had no reverence for life.

It is our duty to share and maintain life. Reverence concerning all life is the greatest commandment in its most elementary form. Or expressed in negative terms: "Thou shalt not kill." We take this prohibition so lightly, thoughtlessly plucking a flower, thoughtlessly stepping on a poor insect, thoughtlessly, in terrible blindness because everything takes its revenge, disregarding the suffering and lives of our fellow men, sacrificing them to trivial earthly goals. 8

Much talk is heard in our times about building a new human race. How are we to build a new humanity? Only by leading men toward a true, inalienable ethic of our own, which is capable of further development. But this goal cannot be reached unless countless individuals will transform themselves from blind men into seeing ones and begin to spell out the great commandment which is: Reverence for Life. Existence depends more on reverence for life than the law and the prophets. Reverence for life comprises the whole ethic of love in its deepest and highest sense. It is the source of constant renewal for the individual and for mankind. 9

Meanings and Values

1. Demonstrate, by using two seemingly unlikely examples, that "all knowledge is [or is not], in the final analysis, the knowledge of life" (par. 2).

2. What is meant by the reference to "other existences" in paragraph 2? (Can the author, a Christian, be referring to reincarnations?)

3a. Consider the statement that "we can do all things, and we can do nothing" (par. 2). Can this qualify as paradox? As irony? (See Guide to Terms: *Paradox; Irony.*)
   b. If the latter, what kind? Justify your answers.

4. Explain more fully the meaning of the last sentence of paragraph 5.

5. The author says, "Then the time came to put the ethical code to the test, and it evaporated" (par. 7). To what "test" do you think he was referring? Why?

6. Clarify how, in Schweitzer's view, "thoughtlessly stepping on a poor insect . . . takes its revenge" (par. 8).

7. Do you think that the author is trying to make a case against killing at all? Why, or why not?

8. What other possible meanings, or shades of meaning, might the key phrase "reverence for life" seem to have, without a thorough defining?

Expository Techniques

1a. Do you consider this essay primarily abstract or concrete? Why? (Guide: *Abstract/Concrete.*)

b. Would the definition have been much improved by more of either the concrete or the abstract? Why, or why not?

c. Why do you suppose the author selected the beetle (par. 3), a flower, and an insect (par. 8) to serve his purposes? (Remember that a good writer always *selects*: details seldom "just happen" to best advantage.)

2a. Cite two examples of parallel structure in this essay. (Guide: *Parallel Structure.*)

b. What advantage, if any, is gained by their use?

3a. How does the author achieve emphasis on the points he wants stressed? (Guide: *Emphasis.*)

b. Cite at least one example of each method used.

4a. The author obviously feels strongly about this subject, which makes it difficult, no doubt, to avoid sentimentality or melodrama. Do you think that he did avoid it?

b. If not, precisely where not?

c. To what extent, if at all, does or would sentimentality damage the credibility of his message?

Diction and Vocabulary

1a. Why would it be difficult to determine much, from your reading of this selection, about the quality of Schweitzer's diction and syntax? (Guide: *Diction; Syntax.*)

b. Use examples to illustrate the elements of these that we *can* appraise with some certainty.

2. Consult the dictionary as necessary for the meanings of the following words: inexplicable (par. 1); inscrutable, manifestations (2); abyss, perceptive, profundity (3); unfathomable (4); alienation, empathy, (5); superficial (7); comprises (9).

Suggestions for Writing and Discussion

1. The author says that "in all our wisdom we cannot create life" (par. 2). Do you believe this? Why, or why not?

2. If you fully understand and agree with the following statement, use it as your central theme on which to develop your oral or written composition: "All realization is amazement at this riddle of life . . ." (par. 2).

3. If you have ever studied life deeply and been seized by "its profundity" (par. 3), relate this experience and analyze its significance in your life.

4. If you agree that reverence for life is "the beginning and foundation of morality" (par. 7), explain this relation more concretely than did Schweitzer.

5. If you understand Schweitzer's meaning, concretely explain the "set of superficial principles" with which the human race had been educated for centuries (par. 7).

6. Show clearly the practical connection, if you see one, between reverence for insect life and respect for human life. If you do not, show how Schweitzer's idea (par. 8) is more a romantic notion than a practical fact.

(NOTE: Suggestions for topics requiring development by use of DEFINITION are on page 219, at the end of this section.)

WOODY ALLEN

WOODY ALLEN, born Allen Stewart Konigsberg in 1935, is a well-known movie, Broadway, and TV satirist. While still in his teens, Allen wrote TV comedy for Gary Moore, Art Carney, and Sid Caesar. Not until 1961 did Allen himself become a performer. He has contributed pieces to magazines including *Playboy* and the *New Yorker;* these have been collected in his book *Getting Even* (1971). His latest achievements are the movies *Play It Again, Sam* (a take-off on *Casablanca*) and *Everything You Always Wanted To Know About Sex (But Were Afraid to Ask),* a spoof on Dr. Reuben's book of the same name.

A Brief, Yet Helpful, Guide to Civil Disobedience

"A Brief, Yet Helpful, Guide to Civil Disobedience" first appeared in *The New York Times* in October 1972. As is true in most of Allen's writing, it is a humorous "put-on" — selected for inclusion here partially to lighten our way through "Definition," but also because the author uses that particular pattern of exposition in unexpected ways that merit our attention.

In perpetrating a revolution, there are two requirements; someone 1 or something to revolt against and someone to actually show up and do the revolting. Dress is usually casual and both parties may be flexible about time and place but if either faction fails to attend, the whole enterprise is likely to come off badly. In the Chinese Revolution of 1650 neither party showed up and the deposit on the hall was forfeited.

The people or parties revolted against are called the "oppres- 2 sors" and are easily recognized as they seem to be the ones having

Reprinted by permission of the publisher from *The New York Times* (October 15, 1972). © 1972 by The New York Times Company.

all the fun. The "oppressors" generally get to wear suits, own land, and play their radios late at night without being yelled at. Their job is to maintain the "status quo," a condition where everything remains the same although they may be willing to paint every two years.

When the "oppressors" become too strict, we have what is known as a police state wherein all dissent is forbidden as is chuckling, showing up in a bow tie, or referring to the mayor as "Fats." Civil liberties are greatly curtailed in a police state and freedom of speech is unheard of although one is allowed to mime to a record. Opinions critical of the government are not tolerated, particularly about their dancing. Freedom of the press is also curtailed and the ruling party "manages" the news, permitting the citizens to hear only acceptable political ideas and ball scores that will not cause unrest.   3

The groups who revolt are called the "oppressed" and can generally be seen milling about and grumbling or claiming to have headaches. (It should be noted that the oppressors never revolt and attempt to become the oppressed as that would entail a change of underwear.)   4

Some famous examples of revolutions are: 5

The French Revolution, in which the peasants seized power by force and quickly changed all locks on the palace doors so the nobles could not get back in. Then they had a large party and gorged themselves. When the nobles finally recaptured the palace they were forced to clean up and found many stains and cigarette burns.   6

The Russian Revolution, which simmered for years and suddenly erupted when the serfs finally realized that the Czar and the Tsar were the same person.   7

It should be noted that after a revolution is over, the "oppressed" frequently take over and begin acting like the "oppressors." Of course by then it is very hard to get them on the phone and money lent for cigarettes and gum during the fighting may as well be forgotten about.   8

Methods of Civil disobedience: 9

Hunger strike. Here the oppressed goes without food until his demands are met. Insidious politicians will often leave biscuits   10 within easy reach or perhaps some cheddar cheese but they must be resisted. If the party in power can get the striker to eat, they usually have little trouble putting down the insurrection. If they can get him to eat and also lift the check, they have won for sure. In Pakistan, a hunger strike was broken when the Government produced an exceptionally fine veal cordon bleu which the masses found was too appealing to turn down but such gourmet dishes are rare.

The problem with the hunger strike is that after several days one can get quite hungry, particularly since sound-trucks are paid to go through the street saying, "Um . . . what nice chicken — umm . . . some peas . . . umm. . . ."   11

A modified form of the Hunger Strike for those whose political convictions are not quite so radical is giving up chives. This small gesture, when used properly, can greatly influence a government and it is well known that Mahatma Gandhi's insistence on eating his salads untossed shamed the British Government into many concessions. Other things besides food one can give up are: whist, smiling, and standing on one foot and imitating a crane.   12

Sit-down Strike. Proceed to a designated spot and then sit down, but sit all the way down. Otherwise you are squatting, a position that makes no political point unless the government is also squatting. (This is rare, although a government will occasionally crouch in cold weather.) The trick is to remain seated until concessions are made but as in the Hunger Strike, the government will try subtle means of making the striker rise. They may say, "Okay, everybody up, we're closing." Or, "Can you get up for a minute, we'd just like to see how tall you are?"   13

Demonstration and Marches. The key point about a demonstration is that it must be seen. Hence the term, "demonstration." If a person demonstrates privately in his own home, this is not technically a demonstration but merely "acting silly," or "behaving like an ass."   14

A fine example of a demonstration was The Boston Tea Party where outraged Americans disguised as Indians dumped British tea into the harbor. Later, Indians disguised as outraged Americans dumped actual British into the harbor. Following that, the British disguised as tea, dumped each other into the harbor. Finally, German mercenaries clad only in costumes from "The Trojan Women" leapt into the harbor for no apparent reason.   15

When demonstrating, it is good to carry a placard stating one's   16 position. Some suggested positions are: (1) lower taxes, (2) raise taxes, and (3) stop grinning at Persians.

Miscellaneous methods of Civil Disobedience: 17

Standing in front of City Hall and chanting the word "pud- 18
ding" until one's demands are met.

Tying up traffic by leading a flock of sheep into the shopping 19
area.

Phoning members of "the establishment" and singing "Bess, 20
You Is My Woman, Now" into the phone.

Dressing as a policeman and then skipping. 21

Pretending to be an artichoke but punching people as they 22
pass.

Meanings and Values

1. If you find this essay amusing, what do you think is its basic *source* of humor? If not, analyze briefly why (for you, at least) it misses its mark.

2. Writers often use humor, in widely varying degrees, as a vehicle to convey some more serious theme, to share some observation of the human condition. (Humor merely for humor's sake, of course, with no function at all except to make people laugh, is a perfectly legitimate art form in its own right!)

   a. What, if any, more serious purpose does this author apparently have, either in overall theme or in individual parts? Cite examples as needed to support your answer.

   b. What do you consider his *primary* purpose? His secondary purpose, if any?

   c. How successful was he in achieving these aims?

3a. What is Allen's point of view in this essay? (See Guide to Terms: *Point of View*.)

   b. How, if at all, is this related to the tone of the writing? (Guide: *Style/Tone*.)

Expository Techniques

1. Despite the loose organization and humorous tone, the "definitions" in this essay still use some of the standard techniques of more serious definition. Isolate as many of these as possible and cite examples for support.

2. In what respects is Allen's humorous style a matter of syntax? (Guide: *Syntax*.) Be specific, citing examples.

3. One important element of Allen's style of humor is his selection of details, the constant use of surprise. (Only the greenest beginner would assume that even apparently minor details in successful writing are apt to "just happen" — even to an old pro like Woody Allen. They are carefully selected, weighed, and *placed*.)
   a. Cite five good examples of this use of surprise details.
   b. Briefly analyze why this is, or is not, a successful technique.

Diction and Vocabulary

1. How, if at all, is Allen's humorous style a matter of diction? (Guide: *Diction*.) Provide examples to help clarify your ideas.

2. Use the dictionary as necessary to understand the meanings of the following words: perpetrating (par. 1); mime (3); entail (4); insidious, gourmet (10); mercenaries (15).

Suggestions for Writing and Discussion

1. Explore the possibility that humor in itself may have real and very practical value.

2. Use current or historical examples to demonstrate that civil disobedience, while seldom totally successful, is sometimes an effective instrument of change.

(NOTE: Suggestions for topics requiring development by use of DEFINITION are on page 219, at the end of this section.)

D. H. LAWRENCE

Davɪᴅ Hᴇʀʙᴇʀᴛ Lᴀᴡʀᴇɴᴄᴇ (1885–1930), British novelist, poet, essayist, and playwright, was for many years a controversial literary figure because of his frank and, for his time, obsessive treatment of sex in some of his novels. The son of a coal miner, Lawrence began his career as a schoolmaster and with the success of his first novel, *The White Peacock* (1911), he decided to live by writing. A few of his books are *Sons and Lovers* (1913), *The Rainbow* (1915), *Women in Love* (1921), and *Lady Chatterly's Lover* (1928). Lawrence has been admired by many for his insightful and artistic power in prose. E. M. Forster referred to him as "the greatest imaginative novelist of our generation."

Pornography

"Pornography" is excerpted from "Pornography and Obscenity," first published in 1930. Providing us with one man's definition of a still highly controversial term, this selection also illustrates the naturalness and vivid spontaneity of style, which is characteristic of Lawrence's writing.

What is pornography to one man is the laughter of genius to another.   1

The word itself, we are told, means "pertaining to harlots" —   2
the graph of the harlot. But nowadays, what is a harlot? If she was a woman who took money from a man in return for going to bed with him — really, most wives sold themselves, in the past, and plenty of harlots gave themselves, when they felt like it, for nothing. If a woman hasn't got a tiny streak of harlot in her, she's a dry stick as a rule. And probably most harlots had somewhere a streak of womanly generosity. Why be so cut and dried? The law

is a dreary thing, and its judgments have nothing to do with life. . . .

One essay on pornography, I remember, comes to the conclusion that pornography in art is that which is calculated to arouse sexual desire, or sexual excitement. And stress is laid on the fact, whether the author or artist *intended* to arouse sexual feelings. It is the old vexed question of intention, becomes so dull today, when we know how strong and influential our unconscious intentions are. And why a man should be held guilty of his conscious intentions, and innocent of his unconscious intentions, I don't know, since every man is more made up of unconscious intentions than of conscious ones. I am what I am, not merely what I think I am.

However! We take it, I assume, that *pornography* is something base, something unpleasant. In short, we don't like it. And why don't we like it? Because it arouses sexual feelings?

I think not. No matter how hard we may pretend otherwise, most of us rather like a moderate rousing of our sex. It warms us, stimulates us like sunshine on a grey day. After a century or two of Puritanism, this is still true of most people. Only the mob-habit of condemning any form of sex is too strong to let us admit it naturally. And there are, of course, many people who are genuinely repelled by the simplest and most natural stirrings of sexual feeling. But these people are perverts who have fallen into hatred of their fellow-men: thwarted, disappointed, unfulfilled people, of whom, alas, our civilisation contains so many. And they nearly always enjoy some unsimple and unnatural form of sex excitement, secretly.

Even quite advanced art critics would try to make us believe that any picture or book which had "sex appeal" was *ipso facto* a bad book or picture. This is just canting hypocrisy. Half the great poems, pictures, music, stories of the whole world are great by virtue of the beauty of their sex appeal. Titian or Renoir, the Song of Solomon or *Jane Eyre*, Mozart or "Annie Laurie," the loveliness is all interwoven with sex appeal, sex stimulus, call it what you will. Even Michelangelo, who rather hated sex, can't help filling the Cornucopia with phallic acorns. Sex is a very powerful, beneficial and necessary stimulus in human life, and we are all grateful when we feel its warm, natural flow through us, like a form of sunshine. . . .

Then what is pornography, after all this? It isn't sex appeal or   7
sex stimulus in art. It isn't even a deliberate intention on the part
of the artist to arouse or excite sexual feelings. There's nothing
wrong with sexual feelings in themselves, so long as they are
straightforward and not sneaking or sly. The right sort of sex
stimulus is invaluable to human daily life. Without it the world
grows grey. I would give everybody the gay Renaissance stories to
read, they would help to shake off a lot of grey self-importance,
which is our modern civilised disease.

But even I would censor genuine pornography, rigorously. It   8
would not be very difficult. In the first place, genuine pornography
is almost always underworld, it doesn't come into the open. In the
second, you can recognise it by the insult it offers, invariably, to
sex, and to the human spirit.

Pornography is the attempt to insult sex, to do dirt on it. This   9
is unpardonable. Take the very lowest instance, the picture post-
card sold underhand, by the underworld, in most cities. What I
have seen of them have been of an ugliness to make you cry. The
insult to the human body, the insult to a vital human relationship!
Ugly and cheap they make the human nudity, ugly and degraded
they make the sexual act, trivial and cheap and nasty.

It is the same with the books they sell in the underworld. They   10
are either so ugly they make you ill, or so fatuous you can't
imagine anybody but a cretin or a moron reading them, or writing
them.

It is the same with the dirty limericks that people tell after   11
dinner, or the dirty stories one hears commercial travellers telling
each other in a smoke-room. Occasionally there is a really funny
one, that redeems a great deal. But usually they are just ugly and
repellent, and the so-called "humour" is just a trick of doing dirt
on sex.

Now the human nudity of a great many modern people is just   12
ugly and degraded, and the sexual act between modern people is
just the same, merely ugly and degrading. But this is nothing to be
proud of. It is the catastrophe of our civilisation. I am sure no other
civilisation, not even the Roman, has showed such a vast proportion of ignominious and degraded nudity, and ugly, squalid dirty
sex. Because no other civilisation has driven sex into the underworld, and nudity to the w.c.

The intelligent young, thank heaven, seem determined to   13 alter in these two respects. They are rescuing their young nudity from the stuffy, pornographical hole-and-corner underworld of their elders, and they refuse to sneak about the sexual relation. This is a change the elderly grey ones of course deplore, but it is in fact a very great change for the better, and a real revolution.

But it is amazing how strong is the will in ordinary, vulgar 14
people, to do dirt on sex. It was one of my fond illusions, when I was young, that the ordinary healthy-seeming sort of men in railway carriages, or the smoke-room of an hotel or a pullman, were healthy in their feelings and had a wholesome rough devil-may-care attitude towards sex. All wrong! All wrong! Experience teaches that common individuals of this sort have a disgusting attitude towards sex, a disgusting contempt of it, a disgusting desire to insult it. If such fellows have intercourse with a woman, they triumphantly feel that they have done her dirt, and now she is lower, cheaper, more contemptible than she was before.

It is individuals of this sort that tell dirty stories, carry in- 15
decent picture postcards, and know the indecent books. This is the great pornographical class — the really common men-in-the-street and women-in-the-street. They have as great a hate and contempt of sex as the greyest Puritan, and when an appeal is made to them, they are always on the side of the angels. They insist that a film-heroine shall be a neuter, a sexless thing of washed-out purity. They insist that real sex-feeling shall only be shown by the villain or villainess, low lust. They find a Titian or a Renoir really indecent, and they don't want their wives and daughters to see it.

Why? Because they have the grey disease of sex-hatred, 16
coupled with the yellow disease of dirt-lust. The sex functions and the excrementory functions in the human body work so close together, yet they are, so to speak, utterly different in direction. Sex is a creative flow, the excrementory flow is towards dissolution, de-creation, if we may use such a word. In the really healthy human being the distinction between the two is instant, our profoundest instincts are perhaps our instincts of opposition between the two flows.

But in the degraded human being the deep instincts have gone 17
dead, and then the two flows become identical. *This* is the secret of really vulgar and of pornographical people: the sex flow and the excrement flow is the same to them. It happens when the psyche deteriorates, and the profound controlling instincts collapse. Then

sex is dirt and dirt is sex, and sexual excitement becomes a playing with dirt, and any sign of sex in a woman becomes a show
of her dirt. This is the condition of the common, vulgar human
being whose name is legion, and who lifts his voice and it is the
Vox populi, vox Dei. And this is the source of all pornography.

Meanings and Values

1. Could this selection best serve to illustrate subjective or objective
    writing? (See Guide to Terms: *Objective/Subjective.*) Justify your
    answer, citing specific examples.
2. Would you classify it as formal or informal writing? (Guide: *Essay.*)
    Why?
3a. Do you think that a person should, in general, be held responsible
    for his "unconscious intentions" (par. 3)?
 b. Does the law do so?
4a. Does it seem to you that the author may be overgeneralizing in the
    last sentence of paragraph 5?
 b. If such forms of sex excitement are enjoyed "secretly," how could
    he know enough about the matter to make such a broad assertion?
5. What, if anything, is paradoxical in the fact that the type of men
    described early in paragraph 14 have the "grey disease" (par. 16)?
    (Guide: *Paradox.*)

Expository Techniques

1a. In developing his definition of pornography, Lawrence uses nega-
    tion, or exclusion. What is negated?
 b. Which paragraphs are devoted to negation?
 c. Why do you suppose he considers them important enough for so
    much attention? Do you agree?
2a. Which of the other methods of extended definition does he use?
 b. In which paragraphs may they be found?
3. In your estimation, are rhetorical questions overused in this selec-
    tion? (Guide: *Rhetorical Question.*) Be prepared to justify your
    answer.
4a. Cite examples of as many as possible of the standard methods of
    achieving emphasis. (Guide: *Emphasis.*)
 b. What, to you, is the overall effect?
5. Several of the most noticeable features of Lawrence's style are also
    matters of syntax. (Guide: *Style/Tone; Syntax.*) Illustrate as many
    of these as possible by examples from the writing.

Diction and Vocabulary

1a. In the second paragraph is a metaphor that is also a cliché. (Guide: *Clichés.*) What is it?

 b. How, if at all, can we justify its use?

2. Cite at least two other examples of metaphor and one of simile. (Guide: *Figures of Speech.*)

3. What is the meaning of "w.c." (par. 12)?

4a. What is the meaning of *ipso facto* (par. 6)?

 b. Why is it italicized?

5. What is the meaning of *Vox populi, vox Dei* (par. 17)?

6a. In at least five paragraphs Lawrence uses a euphemism. (Guide: *Connotation/Denotation.*) What is it?

 b. In which paragraphs do you find it used?

 c. If sex-hatred is the "grey disease," why do you suppose he chose "yellow" to describe the disease of "dirt-lust"?

7. Consult your dictionary as necessary to be sure of the following words: canting, phallic (par. 6); fatuous, cretin (10); ignominious (12).

Suggestions for Writing and Discussion

1. Select one or more of the artists or works of art listed in paragraph 6, analyze, and explain fully why you agree or disagree that "the loveliness is all interwoven with sex appeal [or] sex stimulus."

2. The "intelligent young" of 1930 (par. 13) are now the grey "establishment" of parents and grandparents against whom the intelligent young of the '60's and '70's have been staging a so-called sexual revolution. Trace the process by which such irony came about. Do you believe this is an inevitable result of generation-aging — e.g., will *your* children and grandchildren also be engaging in sexual revolution?

3. Both of the author's "negated" definitions have been used repeatedly in the attempt to get a fair and workable *legal* distinction between pornography and nonpornography. Usually these attempts failed, and no one felt that the problem had been really solved. How well would Lawrence's definition work as a legal definition — perhaps with some modification you can suggest?

4. What, if anything, do you think should be done about "hard-core" pornography?

(NOTE: Suggestions for topics requiring development by use of DEFINITION are on page 219, at the end of this section.)

CLAUDE BROWN

CLAUDE BROWN, a playwright and versatile author, was born in New York in 1937 and attended Howard University from 1961 to 1965. Some of his plays were performed by the American Afro-Negro Theater Guild in New York. Brown's autobiographical book, *Manchild in the Promised Land* (1965), was well received by readers and critics alike; his articles and essays have been published in numerous periodicals.

The Language of Soul

"The Language of Soul" was originally published in *Esquire* in April 1968. "Soul," Brown's key term, is extremely fluid and elusive, and he has extensively illustrated and explained in order to make its definition fully understood and appreciated.

Perhaps the most soulful word in the world is "nigger." Despite its very definite fundamental meaning (the Negro man), and disregarding the deprecatory connotation of the term, "nigger" has a multiplicity of nuances when used by soul people. Dictionaries define the term as being synonymous with Negro, and they generally point out that it is regarded as a vulgar expression. Nevertheless, to those of chitlins-and-neck-bones background the word nigger is neither a synonym for Negro nor an obscene expression.

"Nigger" has virtually as many shades of meaning in Colored English as the demonstrative pronoun "that", prior to application to a noun. To some Americans of African ancestry (I avoid using the term Negro whenever feasible, for fear of offending the Brothers X, a pressure group to be reckoned with), nigger seems preferable to Negro and has a unique kind of sentiment attached to it. This is exemplified in the frequent — and perhaps even excessive — usage of the term to denote either fondness or hostility.

It is probable that numerous transitional niggers and even es-   3
tablished exsoul brothers can — with pangs of nostalgia — reflect
upon a day in the lollipop epoch of lives when an adorable lady
named Mama bemoaned her spouse's fastidiousness with the
strictly secular utterance: "Lord, how can one nigger be so hard
to please?" Others are likely to recall a time when that drastically
lovable colored woman, who was forever wiping our noses and
darning our clothing, bellowed in a moment of exasperation: "Nigger, you gonna be the death o' me." And some of the brethren who
have had the precarious fortune to be raised up, wised up, thrown
up or simply left alone to get up as best they could, on one of the
nation's South Streets or Lenox Avenues, might remember having
affectionately referred to a best friend as "My nigger."

The vast majority of "back-door Americans" are apt to agree   4
with Webster — a nigger is simply a Negro or black man. But the
really profound contemporary thinkers of this distinguished ethnic
group — Dick Gregory, Redd Foxx, Moms Mabley, Slappy White,
etc. — are likely to differ with Mr. Webster and define nigger as
"something else" — a soulful "something else." The major difference between the nigger and the Negro, who have many traits
in common, is that the nigger is the more soulful.

Certain foods, customs and artistic expressions are associated   5
almost solely with nigger: collard greens, neck bones, hog maws,
black-eyed peas, pigs' feet, etc. A nigger has no desire to conceal
or disavow any of these favorite dishes or restrain other behavioral
practices such as bobbing his head, patting his feet to funky jazz,
and shouting and jumping in church. This is not to be construed
that all niggers eat chitlins and shout in church, nor that only niggers eat the aforementioned dishes and exhibit this type of behavior. It is to say, however, that the soulful usage of the term
nigger implies all of the foregoing and considerably more.

The Language of Soul — or, as it might also be called, Spoken   6
Soul or Colored English — is simply an honest vocal portrayal of
black America. The roots of it are more than three hundred years
old.

Before the Civil War there were numerous restrictions placed   7
on the speech of slaves. The newly arrived Africans had the problem of learning to speak a new language, but also there were in-
hibitions placed on the topics of the slaves' conversation by slave
masters and overseers. The slaves made up songs to inform one

another of, say, the underground railroads' activity. When they sang *Steal Away* they were planning to steal away to the North, not to heaven. Slaves who dared to speak of rebellion or even freedom usually were severely punished. Consequently, Negro slaves were compelled to create a semi-clandestine vernacular in the way that the criminal underworld has historically created words to confound law-enforcement agents. It is said that numerous Negro spirituals were inspired by the hardships of slavery, and that what later became songs were initially moanings and coded cotton-field lyrics. To hear these songs sung today by a talented soul brother or sister or by a group is to be reminded of an historical spiritual bond that cannot be satisfactorily described by the mere spoken word.

The American Negro, for virtually all of his history, has con- 8 stituted a vastly disproportionate number of the country's illiterates. Illiteracy has a way of showing itself in all attempts at vocal expression by the uneducated. With the aid of colloquialisms, malapropisms, battered and fractured grammar, and a considerable amount of creativity, Colored English, the sound of soul, evolved.

The progress has been cyclical. Often terms that have been 9 discarded from the soul people's vocabulary for one reason or another are reaccepted years later, but usually with completely different meaning. In the Thirties and Forties "stuff" was used to mean vagina. In the middle Fifties it was revived and used to refer to heroin. Why certain expressions are thus reactivated is practically an indeterminable question. But it is not difficult to see why certain terms are dropped from the soul language. Whenever a soul term becomes popular with whites it is common practice for the soul folks to relinquish it. The reasoning is that "if white people can use it, it isn't hip enough for me." To many soul brothers there is just no such creature as a genuinely hip white person. And there is nothing more detrimental to anything hip than to have it fall into the square hands of the hopelessly unhip.

White Americans wrecked the expression "something else." It 10 was bad enough that they couldn't say "sump'n else," but they weren't even able to get out "somethin' else." They had to go around saying *something else* with perfect or nearly perfect enunciation. The white folks invariably fail to perceive the soul sound in soulful terms. They get hung up in diction and grammar, and when they vocalize the expression it's no longer a soulful thing. In fact, it can be asserted that spoken soul is more of a sound than a language. It generally possesses a pronounced lyrical quality which is frequently incompatible to any music other than that ceaseless and relentlessly driving rhythm that flows from poignantly spent lives. Spoken soul has a way of coming out metered without the intention of the speaker to invoke it. There are specific phonetic traits. To the soulless ear the vast majority of these sounds are dismissed as incorrect usage of the English language and, not infrequently, as speech impediments. To those so blessed as to have had bestowed upon them at birth the lifetime gift of soul, these are the most communicative and meaningful sounds ever to fall upon human ears: the familiar "mah" instead of "my," "gonna" for "going to," "yo" for "your." "Ain't" is pronounced "ain' "; "bread" and "bed," "brayud" and "bay-ud"; "baby" is never "bay-bee" but "bay-buh"; Sammy Davis Jr. is not "Sammee" but a kind of "Sam-eh"; the same goes for "Eddeh" Jefferson. No matter how many "man's" you put into your talk, it isn't soulful unless the word has the proper plaintive, nasal "maee-yun."

Spoken soul is distinguished from slang primarily by the fact   11 that the former lends itself easily to conventional English, and the latter is diametrically opposed to adaptations within the realm of conventional English. Police (pronounced pō'lice) is a soul term, whereas "The Man" is merely slang for the same thing. Negroes seldom adopt slang terms from the white world and when they do the terms are usually given a different meaning. Such was the case with the term "bag." White racketeers used it in the Thirties to refer to the graft that was paid to the police. For the past five years soul people have used it when referring to a person's vocation, hobby, fancy, etc. And once the appropriate term is given the treatment (soul vocalization) it becomes soulful.

However, borrowings from spoken soul by white men's slang   12 — particularly teen-age slang — are plentiful. Perhaps because soul is probably the most graphic language of modern times, everybody who is excluded from Soulville wants to usurp it, ignoring the formidable fettering to the soul folks that has brought the language about. Consider "uptight," "strung-out," "cop," "boss," "kill 'em," all now widely used outside Soulville. Soul people never question the origin of a slang term; they either dig it and make it a part of their vocabulary or don't and forget it. The expression "uptight," which meant being in financial straits, appeared on the soul scene in the general vicinity of 1953. Junkies were very fond of the word and used it literally to describe what was a perpetual condition with them. The word was pictorial and pointed; therefore it caught on quickly in Soulville across the country. In the early Sixties when "uptight" was on the move, a younger generation of soul people in the black urban communities along the Eastern Seaboard regenerated it with a new meaning: "everything is cool, under control, going my way." At present the term has the former meaning for the older generation and the latter construction for those under thirty years of age.

It is difficult to ascertain if the term "strung-out" was coined   13
by junkies or just applied to them and accepted without protest. Like the term "uptight" in its initial interpretation, "strung-out" aptly described the constant plight of the junkie. "Strung-out" had a connotation of hopeless finality about it. "Uptight" implied a temporary situation and lacked the overwhelming despair of "strung-out."

The term "cop," (meaning "to get"), is an abbreviation of the   14
word "copulation." "Cop," as originally used by soulful teen-agers in the early Fifties, was deciphered to mean sexual coition, nothing more. By 1955 "cop" was being uttered throughout national Soulville as a synonym for the verb "to get," especially in reference to illegal purchases, drugs, pot, hot goods, pistols, etc. ("Man, where can I cop now?") But by 1955 the meaning was all-encompassing. Anything that could be obtained could be "copped."

The word "boss," denoting something extraordinarily good or   15
great, was a redefined term that had been popular in Soulville during the Forties and Fifties as a complimentary remark from one soul brother to another. Later it was replaced by several terms such as "groovy," "tough," "beautiful" and, most recently, "out of sight." This last expression is an outgrowth of the former term "way out," the meaning of which was equivocal. "Way out" had an ad hoc hickish ring to it which made it intolerably unsoulful and consequently it was soon replaced by "out of sight," which is also likely to experience a relatively brief period of popular usage. "Out of sight" is better than "way out," but it has some of the same negative, childish taint of its predecessor.

The expression, "kill 'em," has neither a violent nor a malicious   16
interpretation. It means "good luck," "give 'em hell," or "I'm pulling for you," and originated in Harlem from six to nine years ago.

There are certain classic soul terms which, no matter how often   17
borrowed, remain in the canon and are reactivated every so often,
just as standard jazz tunes are continuously experiencing renaissances. Among the classical expressions are: "solid," "cool," "jive"
(generally as a noun), "stuff," "thing," "swing" (or "swinging"),
"pimp," "dirt," "freak," "heat," "larceny," "busted," "okee doke,"
"piece," "sheet" (a jail record), "squat," "square," "stash," "lay,"
"sting," "mire," "gone," "smooth," "joint," "blow," "play,"
"shot," and there are many more.

Soul language can be heard in practically all communities   18
throughout the country, but for pure, undiluted spoken soul one
must go to Soul Street. There are several. Soul is located at Seventh
and "T" in Washington, D.C., on One Two Five Street in New
York City; on Springfield Avenue in Newark; on South Street in
Philadelphia; on Tremont Street in Boston; on Forty-seventh Street
in Chicago, on Fillmore in San Francisco, and dozens of similar
locations in dozens of other cities.

As increasingly more Negroes desert Soulville for honorary   19
membership in the Establishment clique, they experience a metamorphosis, the repercussions of which have a marked influence on
the young and impressionable citizens of Soulville. The expatriates
of Soulville are often greatly admired by the youth of Soulville, who
emulate the behavior of such expatriates as Nancy Wilson, Ella
Fitzgerald, Eartha Kitt, Lena Horne, Diahann Carroll, Billy Daniels,
or Leslie Uggams. The result — more often than not — is a trend
away from spoken soul among the young soul folks. This abandonment of the soul language is facilitated by the fact that more Negro
youngsters than ever are acquiring college educations (which, incidentally, is not the best treatment for the continued good health
and growth of soul); integration and television, too, are contributing significantly to the gradual demise of spoken soul.

Perhaps colleges in America should commence to teach a   20
course in spoken soul. It could be entitled the Vocal History of
Black America, or simply Spoken Soul. Undoubtedly there would be
no difficulty finding teachers. There are literally thousands of these
experts throughout the country whose talents lie idle while they
await the call to duty.

Meanwhile the picture looks dark for soul. The two extremities   21
in the Negro spectrum — the conservative and the militant — are
both trying diligently to relinquish and repudiate whatever vestige

they may still possess of soul. The semi-Negro — the soul brother intent on gaining admission to the Establishment even on an honorary basis — is anxiously embracing and assuming conventional English. The other extremity, the Ultra-Blacks, are frantically adopting everything from a Western version of Islam that would shock the Caliph right out of his snugly fitting shintiyan to anything that vaguely hints of that big, beautiful, bountiful black bitch lying in the arms of the Indian and Atlantic Oceans and crowned by the majestic Mediterranean Sea. Whatever the Ultra-Black is after, it's anything but soulful.

Meanings and Values

1a. Describe what seems to be the author's attitude toward his subject in general.
  b. What is his attitude toward the "Ultra-Black"? How can you tell?
  c. What is it toward the "semi-Negro"? How can you tell?
  d. Where do you suppose he would class himself from one soul "extremity" to the other? Why?

2a. Show the relation between Brown's attitude toward his subject in general and the general tone of the writing. (See Guide to Terms: *Style/Tone*.)
  b. Describe his tone when he refers to the "Ultra-Black."
  c. Does tone help or hinder the effectiveness of the writing? If either, explain the reason for your answer and cite any important exceptions.

3. How do you account for the fact that soul expressions spread so easily through the much larger white youth subculture?

4. What value do you see, if any, in reading about a highly colloquial "language" used by only a portion of a minority people — a language, at that, which even the author regards as dying?

Expository Techniques

1a. What are the hazards of using, without preliminaries or explanation, a developed example as an introduction? (Guide: *Introductions*.)
  b. How well, if at all, has Brown avoided these hazards?
  c. Show where, and how, the author achieves smooth transition into the basic definition, in this case also the central theme.

2. The introductory example itself is, of course, an extended definition. What methods are used in its development?

3a. Where else, if at all, are extended definitions used to develop the larger one?

b. Cite two examples of the simpler, nonextended type of definition.

4a. Does the author handle the extensive use of examples well, or does he allow them to move in and take over the essay (perhaps really using a framework of definition merely for the purpose of the examples, rather than vice versa)? Be specific in justifying your answer.

b. How is this a matter of unity? (Guide: *Unity.*)

c. Does this essay have desirable unity?

5. Several other techniques are used in the major definition. Cite any uses you can find of the following methods:

a. Giving historical background.

b. Showing by negation.

c. Enumerating characteristics.

d. Comparing and/or contrasting.

e. Analyzing causes and/or effects.

6. Demonstrate, by use of at least two well-chosen paragraphs, how the author makes his abstract statements concrete. (Guide: *Concrete/ Abstract.*)

Diction and Vocabulary

1. Demonstrate, by using examples (other than "nigger") from this essay, the importance of connotation in differentiating soul language from standard English. (Guide: *Connotation/Denotation.*)

2. Undoubtedly, spoken soul includes more earthy expressions than any examples used. Is the author justified in ignoring these? Why, or why not?

3a. Select two sentences from this essay in which you think the syntax is notably either good or bad, and analyze them to determine why. (Guide: *Syntax.*)

b. Comment briefly on the quality of syntax in general.

4a. You may notice an unusually large proportion of difficult, or at least multisyllable, words in this selection. How, if at all, does this fact hurt, or help, the overall effectiveness?

b. If you find any words whose same precise function could have been served by simpler words, list or mark them and supply the substitutions.

c. Would such changes improve the style? (Guide: *Style/Tone.*) The readability for an average educated reader? Explain.

5. Use the dictionary as necessary to become familiar with the following words and their meanings: deprecatory, nuances (par. 1); feasible (2); nostalgia, fastidiousness, secular, precarious (3); profound

(4); maws, funky, construed (5); clandestine, vernacular (7); malapropisms (8); cyclical (9); poignantly, phonetic, impediments, plaintive (10); diametrically (11); graphic, formidable, fettering, regenerated (12); ascertain (13); coition (14); equivocal, ad hoc (15); canon, renaissances (17); clique, metamorphosis, repercussions, expatriates, facilitated, demise (19); repudiate, vestige, caliph, shintiyan (21).

Suggestions for Writing and Discussion

1. Show why many soul brothers are correct, or incorrect, in their belief that there is "no such creature as a genuinely hip white person" (par. 9).

2. Objectively present the reasons for *and* against the offering of college courses in "Spoken Soul" (par. 20).

3. If you can do so with some degree of authority, explain what the "Ultra-Black" *is* after (par. 21).

4. You may wish to expand your answer to question 3 of "Meanings and Values." For example, explain the irony that at the very time when large numbers of young Negroes are deserting soul, the usage of soul-derived expressions has become widespread among white youths.

5. Explain how one can tell genuine soul music from the imitation and from other similar types of music.

6. Describe some other "spiritual bond" or bonds (par. 7), not necessarily pertaining to race, that are sometimes formed by hardship or tragedy.

Writing Suggestions for Section 7
Definition

Develop a composition for a specified purpose and audience, using whatever expository patterns will hep convey a clear understanding of your
meaning of one of the following terms:

1. Soul music.
2. "Establishment."
3. Conscience.
4. Religion.
5. Bigotry.
6. War "atrocity."
7. Evolution.
8. Rationalization.
9. Empathy.
10. Altruism.
11. Hypocrisy.
12. Humor.

13. Sophistication.
14. Naiveté
15. Cowardice.
16. Wisdom.
17. Integrity.
18. Morality.
19. Sin.
20. Social poise.
21. Intellectual (the person).
22. Conservationist.
23. Pornography (if your opinions
    differ appreciably from
    Lawrence's).

Reasoning by Use of *Induction* and *Deduction*

Induction and deduction, important as they are in argumentation, may also be useful methods of exposition. They are often used simply to explain a stand or conclusion, without any effort or need to win converts.

Induction is the process by which we accumulate evidence until, at some point, we can make the "inductive leap" and thus reach a useful *generalization*. The science laboratory employs this technique; hundreds of tests and experiments and analyses may be required before the scientist will generalize, for instance, that polio is caused by a certain virus. It is also the primary technique of the prosecuting attorney who presents pieces of inductive evidence, asking the jury to make the inductive leap and conclude that the accused did indeed kill the victim. On a more personal level, of course, we all learned to use induction at a very early age. We may have disliked the taste of orange juice, winter squash, and carrots, and we were not too young to make a generalization: orange-colored food tastes bad.

Whereas induction is the method of reaching a potentially useful generalization (for example, Professor Kalowski always gives an "F" to students who cut his class three times), *deduction* is the method of *using* such a generality, now accepted as a fact (for example, if we cut this class again today, we will get an "F"). Working from a generalization already formulated — by ourselves, by someone else, or by tradition — we may deduce that a specific thing or circumstance that fits into that generality will act the same. Hence, if convinced that orange-colored food tastes bad, we will be reluctant to try pumpkin pie.

A personnel manager may have discovered over the years that electronics majors from Central College are invariably well trained in their field. His induction may have been based on the evidence of observations, records, and the opinions of fellow Rotary members; and, perhaps without realizing it, he has made the usable generalization about the training of Central College electronics majors. Later, when he has an application from Tom Ortega, a graduate of Central College, his *deductive* process will probably work as follows: Central College turns out well-trained electronics majors; Ortega was trained at Central; therefore, Ortega must be well trained. Here he has used a generalization to apply to a specific case.

Put in this simplified form (which, in writing, it seldom is),* the deductive process is also called a "syllogism" — with the beginning generality known as the "major premise" and the specific that fits into the generality known as the "minor premise." For example:

Major premise — Orange-colored food is not fit to eat.
Minor premise — Pumpkin pie is orange-colored.
Conclusion — Pumpkin pie is not fit to eat.

Frequently, however, the validity of one or both of the premises may be questionable, and here is one of the functions of *induction*: to give needed support — with evidence such as opinions of experts, statistics, and results of experiments or surveys — to the *deductive* syllogism, whether stated or implied. Deductive reasoning, in whatever form presented, is only as sound as both its premises. The child's conviction that orange-colored food is not fit to eat was not necessarily true; therefore his conclusion about pumpkin pie is not very trustworthy. The other conclusions, that we will automatically get an "F" by cutting Kalowski's class and that Ortega is well trained in electronics, can be only as reliable as

---

* Neither induction nor deduction is confined even to a particular order of presentation. If we use specific evidence to *reach* a generalization, it is induction regardless of which part is stated first in a written or spoken account. (Very likely, both the prosecutor's opening remarks and Dr. Salk's written reports first presented their generalizations and then the inductive evidence by which they had been reached.) But if we use a generality in which to *place* a specific, it is still deduction, however stated. (Hence, the reasoning of the personnel manager might be: "Ortega must be well trained because he was educated at C.C., and there's where they really know how to do it.")

the original generalizations that were used as deductive premises. If the generalizations themselves were based on flimsy or insufficient evidence, any future deduction using them is likely to be erroneous.

These two faults are common in induction: (1) the use of *flimsy* evidence — mere opinion, hearsay, or analogy, none of which can support a valid generalization — instead of verified facts or opinions of reliable authorities; and (2) the use of *too little* evidence, leading to a premature inductive leap.

The amount of evidence needed in any situation depends, of course, on purpose and audience. The success of two Central College graduates might be enough to convince some careless personnel director that all Central electronics graduates would be good employees, but two laboratory tests would not have convinced Dr. Salk, or any of his colleagues, that he had learned anything worthwhile about the polio virus. The authors of the Declaration of Independence, in explaining to a wide variety of readers and listeners why they considered the king tyrannical, listed twenty-eight despotic acts of his government, each of which was a verifiable fact, a matter of public record.

Induction and deduction are highly logical processes, and any trace of weakness can seriously undermine an exposition that depends on their reasonableness. (Such weakness can, of course, be even more disastrous in argument.) Although no induction or deduction ever reaches absolute, 100 per cent certainty, we should try to get from these methods as high a degree of *probability* as possible. (We can never positively prove for instance, that the sun will rise in the east tomorrow, but thousands of years of inductive observation and theorizing make the fact extremely probable — and certainly sound enough for any working generalization.)

The student using induction and deduction in compositions, essay examinations, or term papers — showing that Stephen Crane was a naturalistic writer, or that our national policies are unfair to revolutionary movements — should always assume that he will have a skeptical audience that wants to know the logical basis for *all* generalizations and conclusions.

BENJAMIN FRANKLIN

BENJAMIN FRANKLIN (1706–1790) was born in Boston, but lived most of his life in Philadelphia. His versatility as statesman and diplomat, author, scientist, and inventor is well known, both in this country and abroad, and his biography is a rags-to-riches classic. Many people of his time agreed with the noted French economist, Robert Jacques Turgot, who stated, "He snatched the lightning from the skies and the sceptre from tyrants." Franklin's interest in an astonishing variety of fields remained acute until his death at eighty-four. To quote from the *Encyclopaedia Britannica*: "Of all the founding fathers of the United States, Franklin, were there such a thing as reincarnation, would adapt himself most readily to the complexities of the latter half of the 20th century."

On the Choice of a Mistress

"On the Choice of a Mistress" (editor's title) has had a unique history under many titles, but its existence was not even known to the public until many years after Franklin's death. Three versions of it were found in 1850 among the papers of his then deceased grandson, William Temple Franklin. Thereafter it passed through a variety of ownerships and was occasionally printed, but furtively and in limited supply — once under the title "A Philosopher in Undress." Although the piece had enjoyed a sort of locker-room fame for some time, not until 1926 was it published in a widely read biography, written by Phillips Russell, who called Benjamin Franklin "the first civilized American."

June 25, 1745

My dear Friend,[1]

I know of no Medicine fit to diminish the violent natural Inclinations you mention; and if I did, I think I should not com-   1

Reprinted by permission of Yale University Press from *The Papers of Benjamin Franklin*, Volume 3, edited by Leonard W. Labaree (1961).

[1] The addressee is unknown; the letter may in fact be an essay in the form of a letter.

municate it to you. Marriage is the proper Remedy. It is the most natural State of Man, and therefore the State in which you are most likely to find solid Happiness. Your Reasons against entring into it at present, appear to me not well-founded. The circumstantial Advantages you have in View by postponing it, are not only uncertain, but they are small in comparison with that of the Thing itself, the being *married and settled*. It is the Man and Woman united that make the compleat human Being. Separate, she wants his Force of Body and Strength of Reason; he, her Softness, Sensibility and acute Discernment. Together they are more likely to succeed in the World. A single Man has not nearly the Value he would have in that State of Union. He is an incomplete Animal. He resembles the odd Half of a Pair of Scissars. If you get a prudent healthy Wife, your industry in your Profession, with her good Economy, will be a Fortune sufficient.

But if you will not take this Counsel, and persist in thinking 　　2 a Commerce with the Sex inevitable, then I repeat my former Advice, that in all your Amours you should *prefer old Women* to *young ones.* You call this a Paradox, and demand my Reasons. They are these:

1. Because as they have more Knowledge of the World and 　　3 their Minds are better stor'd with Observations, their Conversation is more improving and more lastingly agreable.

2. Because when Women cease to be handsome, they study to 　　4 be good. To maintain their Influence over Men, they supply the Diminution of Beauty by an Augmentation of Utility. They learn to do a 1000 Services small and great, and are the most tender and useful of all Friends when you are sick. Thus they continue amiable. And hence there is hardly such a thing to be found as an old Woman who is not a good Woman.

3. Because there is no hazard of Children, which irregularly 　　5 produc'd may be attended with much Inconvenience.

4. Because thro' more Experience, they are more prudent and 　　6 discrete in conducting an Intrigue to prevent Suspicion. The Commerce with them is therefore safer with regard to your Reputation. And with regard to theirs, if the Affair should happen to be known, considerate People might be rather inclin'd to excuse an old Woman who would kindly take care of a young Man, form his Manners

by her good Counsels, and prevent his ruining his Health and
Fortune among mercenary Prostitutes.

5. Because in every Animal that walks upright, the Deficiency   7
of the Fluids that fill the Muscles appears first in the highest Part:
The Face first grows lank and wrinkled; then the Neck; then the
Breast and Arms; the lower Parts continuing to the last as plump
as ever: So that covering all above with a Basket, and regarding
only what is below the Girdle, it is impossible of two Women to
know an old from a young one. And as in the dark all Cats are
grey, the Pleasure of corporal Enjoyment with an old Woman is
at least equal, and frequently superior, every Knack being by
Practice capable of Improvement.

6. Because the Sin is less. The debauching a Virgin may be   8
her Ruin, and make her for Life unhappy.

7. Because the Compunction is less. The having made a young   9
Girl *miserable* may give you frequent bitter Reflections; none of
which can attend the making an old Woman *happy.*

8[thly and Lastly] They are *so grateful!!*   10

Thus much for my Paradox. But still I advise you to marry directly;   11
being sincerely Your affectionate Friend.

Meanings and Values

1. The author refers to his thesis as a paradox. Explain how it does, or
   does not, fit our own definition of paradox. (See Guide to Terms:
   Paradox.)

2. What is to be gained and/or lost by learning that great men, past
   or present, are not always perfect models of propriety (contrary, of
   course, to what we are sometimes led to believe as small children)?

3. How seriously do you think Franklin meant this to be taken? Why?

4a. Why do you suppose Franklin's grandson, having changed his mind
    at least once about publication, kept the letter's existence a secret
    from the public until his death?

  b. Would you do the same today, in similar circumstances? Why, or
     why not? (Refer, if you like, to Michener's "Assumptions of the
     Middle Class," Section 2.)

Expository Techniques

1. Is the reasoning of this piece inductive or deductive? Explain your reasons carefully, as though to a person who was not aware of any difference between the two.

2. Is the numbering of parts in exposition such as this a good technique, or not? Why?

3. If this, as many believe, was really not a letter at all, but an essay intended for public readership, what is gained by framing it in the form of a letter?

Diction and Vocabulary

1. Writing styles change with the years and centuries. Identify the elements of diction and syntax in this writing which you think distinguish it from the style of modern authors. Use examples from the essay to clarify. (Guide: *Diction; Syntax.*)

2. What kind of figure of speech, if any, is the reference to "Scissars" in paragraph 1? (Guide: *Figures of Speech.*)

3. The words "commerce" (pars. 2, 6) and "want" (par. 1) are used here with somewhat different meanings than are common today. What do they mean in this writing?

4. Use your dictionary as necessary to be sure of the meanings of the following words: discernment (par. 1); amours (2); diminution, augmentation, amiable (4); corporal (7); debauching (8); compunction (9).

Suggestions for Writing and Discussion

1. Develop your answer to question 2 of "Meanings and Values" into a full-scale composition or discussion, using examples for illustration. State your purpose clearly, show effects, and avoid a mere cataloging of sins and foibles.

2. If you have experienced or seriously observed the women's liberation movement, use its viewpoint to comment on one or more of Franklin's "Reasons" or on his argument for marrying. (You might assume this essay to have been published in a modern advice column, perhaps in *Playboy* or *Esquire.*)

3. If you have read Michener's essay in Section 2, what effect do you think the "Puritan Noose" had on middle-class Franklin, who was much closer to it in time than we are (and by geography than many of us)? Or, if it seems more feasible, what does this reading suggest about the "Noose" in colonial America itself?

(Note: Suggestions for topics requiring development by INDUCTION and DEDUCTION are on page 252, at the end of this section.)

THOMAS JEFFERSON

THOMAS JEFFERSON (1743–1826) was born in Virginia, where he lived during his childhood and later attended William and Mary College. He became a lawyer, a member of the Virginia House of Burgesses and of the Continental Congress in 1775. His influence as a liberal democrat was always aided by his prolific and forceful writing. During the Revolutionary War he became Governor of Virginia. After the war he served the new government in various capacities, including those of special minister to France, Secretary of State under Washington, Vice-President, and, for two terms, the country's third President. He died on July 4, the fiftieth anniversary of the signing of the Declaration of Independence.

The Declaration of Independence

The Declaration of Independence, written and revised by Jefferson, was later further revised by the Continental Congress, meeting then in Philadelphia. In this way, as Jefferson later remarked, it drew its authority from "the harmonizing sentiments of the day"; it was, when signed on July 4, 1776, "an expression of the American mind." However, the document still retained much of the form and style of Jefferson's writing, and as literature it has long been admired for its lean and forthright prose. We can find no clearer example of the practical combination of deductive and inductive writing.

When in the course of human events, it becomes necessary for one 1 people to dissolve the political bands which have connected them with another, and to assume among the Powers of the earth, the separate and equal station to which the Laws of Nature and of Nature's God entitle them, a decent respect to the opinions of mankind requires that they should declare the causes which impel them to the separation.

We hold these truths to be self-evident, that all men are 2 created equal, that they are endowed by their Creator with certain unalienable Rights, that among these are Life, Liberty and the pursuit of Happiness. That to secure these rights, Governments are instituted among Men, deriving their just powers from the consent of the governed. That whenever any Form of Government becomes destructive of these ends, it is the Right of the People to alter or to abolish it, and to institute new Government, laying its foundation on such principles and organizing its powers in such form, as to them shall seem most likely to effect their Safety and Happiness. Prudence, indeed, will dictate that Governments long established should not be changed for light and transient causes; and accordingly all experience hath shown, that mankind are more disposed to suffer, while evils are sufferable, than to right themselves by abolishing the forms to which they are accustomed. But when a long train of abuses and usurpations pursuing invariably the same Object evinces a design to reduce them under absolute Despotism, it is their right, it is their duty, to throw off such government, and to provide new Guards for their future security. Such has been the patient sufferance of these Colonies; and such is now the necessity which constrains them to alter their former Systems of Government. The history of the present King of Great Britain is a history of repeated injuries and usurpations, all having in direct object the establishment of an absolute Tyranny over these States. To prove this, let Facts be submitted to a candid world.

He has refused his Assent to Laws, the most wholesome and 3
necessary for the public good.

He has forbidden his Governors to pass Laws of immediate and 4
pressing importance, unless suspended in their operation till his Assent should be obtained; and when so suspended, he has utterly neglected to attend to them.

He has refused to pass other Laws for the accommodation of 5
large districts of people, unless those people would relinquish the right of Representation in the Legislature, a right inestimable to them and formidable to tyrants only.

He has called together legislative bodies at places unusual, un· 6
comfortable, and distant from the depository of their Public Records, for the sole purpose of fatiguing them into compliance with his measures.

He has dissolved Representative Houses repeatedly, for op- 7
posing with manly firmness his invasions on the rights of the people.

He has refused for a long time, after such dissolutions, to 8
cause others to be elected; whereby the Legislative Powers, in-
capable of Annihilation, have returned to the People at large for
their exercise; the State remaining in the mean time exposed to all
the dangers of invasion from without, and convulsions within.

He has endeavoured to prevent the population of these States; 9
for that purpose obstructing the Laws of Naturalization of Foreigners; refusing to pass others to encourage their migration hither, and
raising the conditions of new Appropriations of Lands.

He has obstructed the Administration of Justice, by refusing 10
his Assent to Laws for establishing Judiciary Powers.

He has made Judges dependent on his Will alone, for the 11
tenure of their offices, and the amount and payment of their
salaries.

He has erected a multitude of New Offices, and sent hither 12
swarms of Officers to harass our People, and eat out their substance.

He has kept among us, in time of peace, Standing Armies with- 13
out the Consent of our Legislature.

He has affected to render the Military independent of and su- 14
perior to the Civil Power.

He has combined with others to subject us to jurisdiction for- 15
eign to our constitution, and unacknowledged by our laws; giving
us Assent to their acts of pretended Legislation:

For quartering large bodies of armed troops among us: 16

For protecting them, by a mock Trial, from Punishment for 17
any Murders which they should commit on the Inhabitants of these
States:

For cutting off our Trade with all parts of the world: 18

For imposing Taxes on us without our Consent: 19

For depriving us in many cases, of the benefits of Trial by 20
Jury:

For transporting us beyond Seas to be tried for pretended 21
offences:

For abolishing the free System of English Laws in a Neigh- 22
bouring Province, establishing therein an Arbitrary government,
and enlarging its boundaries so as to render it at once an example
and fit instrument for introducing the same absolute rule into these
Colonies:

For taking away our Charters, abolishing our most valuable 23
Laws, and altering fundamentally the Forms of our Governments:

For suspending our own Legislatures, and declaring themselves 24 invested with Power to legislate for us in all cases whatsoever.

He has abdicated Government here, by declaring us out of his 25 Protection and waging War against us.

He has plundered our seas, ravaged our Coasts, burnt our 26 towns, and destroyed the Lives of our people.

He is at this time transporting large Armies of foreign Mer- 27 cenaries to compleat the works of death, desolation and tyranny, already begun with circumstances of Cruelty & perfidy scarcely paralleled in the most barbarous ages, and totally unworthy the Head of a civilized nation.

He has constrained our fellow Citizens taken Captive on the 28 high Seas to bear Arms against their Country, to become the executioners of their friends and Brethren, or to fall themselves by their Hands.

He has excited domestic insurrections amongst us, and has en- 29 deavoured to bring on the inhabitants of our frontiers, the merciless Indian Savages, whose known rule of warfare, is an undistinguished destruction of all ages, sexes and conditions.

In every stage of these Oppressions We have Petitioned for Re- 30 dress in the most humble terms: Our repeated petitions have been answered only by repeated injury. A Prince, whose character is thus marked by every act which may define a Tyrant, is unfit to be the ruler of a free People.

Nor have We been wanting in attention to our British brethren. 31 We have warned them from time to time of attempts by their legislature to extend an unwarrantable jurisdiction over us. We have reminded them of the circumstances of our emigration and settlement here. We have appealed to their native justice and magnanimity and we have conjured them by the ties of our common kindred to disavow these usurpations, which would inevitably interrupt our connections and correspondence. They too have been deaf to the voice of justice and of consanguinity. We must, therefore acquiesce in the necessity, which denounces our Separation, and hold them, as we hold the rest of mankind, Enemies in War, in Peace Friends.

We, therefore, the Representatives of the United States of 32 America, in General Congress, Assembled, appealing to the Supreme Judge of the world for the rectitude of our intentions, do, in the Name, and by Authority of the good People of these Colonies, solemnly publish and declare, (That these United Colonies are, and of Right ought to be Free and Independent States; that they are Absolved from all Allegiance to the British Crown, and that all political connection between them and the State of Great Britain, is and ought to be totally dissolved;) and that as Free and Independent States, they have full power to levy War, conclude Peace, contract Alliances, establish Commerce, and to do all other Acts and Things which Independent States may of right do. And for the support of this Declaration, with a firm reliance on the protection of Divine Providence, we mutually pledge to each other our lives, our Fortunes and our sacred Honor.

Meanings and Values

1. For what practical reasons (other than the "decent respect to the opinions of mankind") did the Founding Fathers need to explain so carefully their reasons for declaring independence?

2. Many American colonials opposed the break with England and remained loyal to the Crown throughout the struggle for independence. What do you suppose could inspire such loyalty to a king whom most of them had never seen and who had shown little concern for their welfare?

Expository Techniques

1. The basis of the Declaration of Independence is deduction and can therefore be stated as a logical syllogism. The major premise, stated twice in the second paragraph, may be paraphrased as follows: When a government proves to be despotic, it is the people's right and duty to get rid of it.
   a. What, then, is the minor premise of the syllogism?
   b. Where is the syllogism's conclusion set forth? Restate it concisely in your own words.
   c. Write this resulting syllogism in standard form.

2. Twenty-eight pieces of inductive evidence are offered as support for one of the deductive premises.
   a. Which premise is thus supported?
   b. Demonstrate the meaning of "inductive leap" by use of materials from this selection. (Remember that the order of presentation in inductive or deductive writing is merely an arrangement for *telling*, not necessarily that of the original reasoning.)

3a. Why, according to the document itself, is the other premise not supported by any inductive reasoning?

b. Would everyone agree with this premise? If not, why do you suppose the Founding Fathers did not present inductive evidence to support it?

4. What benefits are gained in the Declaration by the extensive use of parallel structures? (See Guide to Terms: *Parallel Structure.*)

5. Show as specifically as possible the effects that a "decent respect for the opinions of mankind" apparently had on the selection and use of materials in the Declaration of Independence.

Diction and Vocabulary

1. Select five words or phrases from the Declaration of Independence to demonstrate the value of an awareness of connotation. (Guide: *Connotation/Denotation.*)

2. If not already familiar with the following words as they are used in this selection, consult your dictionary for their meanings: impel (par. 1); transient, usurpations, evinces, sufferance, constrains (2); inestimable (5); depository (6); dissolutions (8); mercenaries, perfidy (27); redress (30); magnanimity, conjured, consanguinity, acquiesce (31); rectitude, absolved (32).

Suggestions for Writing and Discussion

1. George Santayana, an American writer and expatriate, called the Declaration of Independence "a salad of illusion." Develop this metaphor into a full-scale analogy to explain his meaning. Without arguing the matter, attempt to assess the truth of his allegation.

2. Select one important similarity or difference between the rebellion of the American colonials and that of some other country in recent history. Use comparison or contrast to develop a theme on this subject.

3. Compare or contrast any one of the Declaration signers with one of the leaders of some other country's more recent severance of ties with a colonial power.

4. Give evidence from your knowledge of history to support, or to negate, the following statement by Patrick Henry, one of the signers of the Declaration: "It is impossible that a nation of infidels or idolators should be a nation of freemen. It is when a people forget God, that tyrants forge their chains. A vitiated state of morals, a corrupted public conscience, is incompatible with freedom."

(NOTE: Suggestions for topics requiring development by INDUCTION and DEDUCTION are on page 252, at the end of this section.)

PETER F. DRUCKER

PETER F. DRUCKER was born in Vienna and received most of his early education in Austria and Germany. He came to the United States in 1937, and he became an American citizen in 1943. For many years he served in positions as economist and consultant for banks and major business corporations in a variety of countries. Drucker has been awarded honorary degrees by several universities in this country and abroad, and is now Clarke Professor of Social Sciences at Claremont Graduate School and is a Professor of Management at New York University. Among the most recent of his many successful books are *The Age of Discontinuity* (1969), *Technology, Management and Society* (1970), and *Men, Ideas and Politics* (1971). Drucker has also produced two film series: *The Effective Executive* (1969), and *Managing Discontinuity* (1971).

How Best to Protect the Environment

"How Best to Protect the Environment," a more moderate approach than most to the ecological problem, was published first in *Harper's Magazine* and condensed for *Reader's Digest*, as reprinted here. The ease with which the average reader can understand Drucker's ideas is no indication of the careful planning that must go into their organization and presentation. The intertwining patterns of induction in this essay, for example, are quite complex — perhaps more so than your instructor will consider worth your time just now to analyze fully. But it is because of such advance work on the part of a serious author that his ideas can be presented clearly.

Everybody today is "for the environment." Yet the crusade to restore a balance between man and nature is in real danger of running off the tracks, much like its immediate predecessor, the so-called war on poverty. And, paradoxically, the most fervent environmentalists may be among the chief wreckers. For many are [1] confused about the causes of our crisis and the ways in which we might resolve it. They ignore the difficult decisions that must be made; they splinter the resources available for attacking environmental problems. Indeed, some of our leading crusaders seem almost perversely determined to sabotage their cause — and our future.

Consider, for example, the widespread notion that a clean environment can be obtained by reducing or even abolishing our dependence on "technology." This is a delusion. The truth is that most environmental problems require technological solutions — and dozens of them. To control just one major water pollutant, human wastes, we shall have to draw on all sciences and technologies from biochemistry to thermodynamics. Similarly, we need the most advanced technology for adequate treatment of the effluents that mining and manufacturing spew into the world's waters. It will take even more new technology to repair the damage caused by a third major source of water pollution in this country — the activities of farmers. Environmental control, in other words, requires technology at a level at least as high as the technology whose misuse it is designed to correct.

A second and equally dangerous delusion is the common belief that the cost of cleaning the environment can be paid for out of "business profits." After taxes, the profits of all American businesses in a good year come to $60 or $70 billion. And mining and manufacturing — the most polluting industries — account for less than half of this. But, at the lowest estimate, the cleanup bill, even for just the most urgent jobs, will be three or four times as large as all business profits.

We face an environmental crisis because for too long we have disregarded genuine costs. Now we must raise the costs, in a hurry, to where they should have been all along. The expense must be borne, eventually, by the great mass of the people as consumers and producers. The only choice we have is which of the costs will be borne by the consumer in the form of higher prices, and which by the taxpayer in the form of higher taxes.

THE IMPERATIVE OF INDUSTRIAL GROWTH

Closely related to the fallacy that "profit" can pay the environmental bill is the belief that we can solve the environmental crisis by reducing industrial output. In the highly developed affluent countries, it is true that we may be about to de-emphasize the "production orientation" of the past few hundred years. Indeed, the "growth sectors" of the developed economies are increasingly education, leisure activities or health care rather than goods. But, paradoxical as it may sound, the environmental crisis will force us to return to an emphasis on both growth and industrial output — at least for the next decade.

There are three reasons for this, each adequate in itself.   6

1. A great many environmental tasks demand huge amounts of   7
electrical energy, way beyond anything now available. Sewage treatment is just one example; the difference between the traditional and wholly inadequate methods and a modern treatment plant that gets rid of human and industrial wastes and produces reasonably clear water is primarily electric power, and large supplies of it. This poses a difficult dilemma. Power plants are themselves polluters. And one of their adverse side effects, thermal pollution, is something we do not yet know how to handle on the scale involved. I am a member of the Sierra Club, and I share its concern for the environment. But the Sierra Club, among other groups, is opposing many new power plants. If the building of new plants continues to be restricted, it will not be possible to perform other ecological tasks in years to come.

2. No matter how desirable a de-emphasis on production   8
might be, the next decade is the wrong time for it in all the developed countries and especially in the United States. The next decade will bring a surge in employment-seekers and the formation of young families — both the inevitable result of the baby boom of the late '40s and early '50s. Young adults need jobs; and unless there is a rapid expansion of jobs, there will be massive unemployment, especially among low-skilled blacks and other minority-group members. In addition to jobs, young families need goods — from housing and furniture to shoes for the baby. If this is resisted in the name of ecology, environment will become a dirty word in the political vocabulary.

3. If there is no expansion of output equal to the additional   9
cost of cleaning up the environment, the cost burden must be met by cutting the funds available for education, health care or the inner city, thus depriving the poor. It would be nice if the resources we

need could come out of defense spending. But of the six or seven percent of our national income that now goes for defense, a large part is the cost of past wars, that is, veterans' pensions and disability benefits (which, incidentally, most other countries do not include in their defense budgets — a fact that critics of "American militarism" often ignore). Even if we could — or should — cut defense spending, the "peace dividend" would be only one or two percent of national income.

But the total national outlay for education, health care and the inner city and other poverty areas comes to one fifth of total national income today. And, indeed, in their rejection of school budgets across the nation and in their desperate attempts to cut welfare costs, voters have already begun to look to these sectors for money. That the shift of resources is likely to be accomplished in large part through inflation — essentially at the expense of the lower-income groups — will hardly make the environmental cause more popular with the poor.

The only way to avoid these evils is to expand the economy, probably at a growth rate of four percent a year for the next decade, a higher rate than we have been able to sustain in this country in the postwar years. This undoubtedly entails great environmental risks. But the alternative is likely to mean no environmental action at all.

CARROTS YES, STICKS NO

The final delusion is that the proper way to bring about a clean environment is through punitive legislation. We do need prohibitions and laws forbidding actions that endanger and degrade the environment. But, more than that, we need incentives to preserve and improve it.

Punitive laws succeed only if the malefactors are few and the unlawful act is comparatively rare. Today every one of us is a polluter. Punitive laws and regulations can force automobile manufacturers to put emission controls into new cars, but they will never be able to force 100 million motorists to maintain this equipment.

What we should do is make it to everyone's advantage to reach environmental goals. Automobile owners who voluntarily maintain in working order the emission controls of their cars might, for instance, pay a much lower automobile registration fee. And if they were offered a sizable tax incentive, the automobile companies would put all their best energies to work to produce safer and emission-free cars, rather than fight delaying actions against punitive legislation.

Despite all the rhetoric on the campuses, we know by now   15 that "capitalism" has nothing to do with the ecological crisis. Pollution is fully as severe in the communist countries. Nor is the United States the world's *foremost* polluter; Japan holds this dubious honor by a good margin. No great American river is as much an open sewer as the lower Rhine, or the lower Dnieper and the Volga in the industrial Ukraine.

THE FRUITS OF SUCCESS

We should also know that "greed" has little to do with the en-   16 vironmental crisis. The two main causes are population pressures, especially the pressures of large metropolitan populations, and the desire — a highly commendable one — to bring a decent living at the lowest possible cost to the largest possible number of people.

The environmental crisis is the result of success — success in   17 cutting down the mortality of infants (which has given us the population explosion), success in raising farm output sufficiently to prevent mass famine (which has given us contamination by pesticides and chemical fertilizers), success in getting people out of the noisome tenements of the 19th-century city and into the greenery and privacy of the single-family home in the suburbs (which has given us urban sprawl and traffic jams). The environmental crisis, in other words, is largely the result of doing too much of the right sort of thing.

To overcome the problems that success always creates, one   18 must build on it. But where to start? Cleaning up the environment requires determined, sustained effort with clear targets and deadlines. It requires, above all, concentration of effort. Up to now we have tried to do a little bit of everything — and tried to do it in the headlines — when what we ought to do first is draw up a list of priorities.

Clean air should probably head the list. It's a worldwide prob-   19 lem, and getting worse. We don't know all the answers, but we do have the technological competence to handle most of the problems of foul air today. Within ten years we should have results to show for our efforts. Within ten years, too, we should get major results in cleaning up the water around big industrial cities, and we should have slowed (if not stopped) the massive pollution of the oceans, especially in the waters near our coastal cities.

AN END TO MANIFESTOS

As for research priorities, I suggest that the first is to develop birth-control methods that are cheaper, more effective, and more accept- 20 able to people of all cultures than anything we now have. Second, we need to learn how to produce electric energy with a minimum of pollution. A third priority is to devise ways of raising crops for a rapidly growing world population without at the same time doing irreversible ecological damage through pesticides and chemical fertilizers.

Until we get the answers, I think we had better keep on build- 21 ing power plants and growing food with the help of fertilizers and such insect-controlling chemicals as we now have. The risks are well known, thanks to the environmentalists. If they had not created a widespread public awareness of the ecological crisis, we wouldn't stand a chance. But such awareness by itself is not enough. Flaming manifestos and prophecies of doom are no longer much help, and a search for scapegoats can only make matters worse. The time for sensations and manifestos is about over. Now we need rigorous analysis, united effort and very hard work.

Meanings and Values

1a. What seems to be the author's attitude toward his subject matter?
  b. How does the essay's tone help in answering question 1a? (See Guide to Terms: *Style/Tone.*)
2. Sentimentality has been commonplace on both sides of the en-vironmental question. To what extent, if at all, does Drucker yield to this weakness? (Guide: *Sentimentality.*)
3a. Why does the assertion that environmentalists may endanger the program amount to a paradox? (Guide: *Paradox.*)
  b. You may find another paradox in paragraph 17. What is it?
4. Do you suppose that literally "every one of us" is a polluter (par. 13)? Cite any possible exceptions.

5. Supply other examples of "successes" that have caused environmental deterioration (par. 17).

6a. If you have read the Carson selection in Section 5, what characteristics do you find in common between the approach of the two authors?

 b. If any noticeable differences, what are they?

Expository Techniques

1. This whole essay is based on implied deduction:
    Major Premise: Any solution based on delusions could be disastrous.
    Minor Premise: The proposed solutions of many environmentalists are based on delusions.
    Conclusion: The proposed solutions of many environmentalists could be disastrous.
    The bulk of the essay's development, however, is devoted to inductive *support* for this implied syllogism.
    a. Which of the two premises seems to need such support?
    b. How many primary pieces of inductive evidence do you find used as this support?
    c. Briefly list, or mark, these and cite the paragraph in which each is to be found.

2. These primary pieces of inductive evidence are themselves in turn supported by further induction (although much less clear-cut).
    a. Briefly summarize that offered in paragraph 2, and show what it supports.
    b. A good small-scale induction complete in itself comprises paragraph 17. Briefly outline, or mark, the points of this induction, showing the conclusion drawn from them.

3a. What is gained, if anything, by the author's including the fact that he is a member of the Sierra Club (par. 7)?

 b. What is gained other than mere recording of fact, by the acknowledgment of valuable service by the environmentalists (par. 21)?

Diction and Vocabulary

1. Why does the author use quotation marks around several words in paragraphs 2, 3, 5, 9, 16?

2. Use the dictionary as necessary to acquaint yourself with the following words and their meanings: perversely (par. 1); biochemistry, thermodynamics, effluents (2); fallacy, affluent (5); dilemma, thermal (7); entails (11); punitive, incentives (12, 14); malefactors (13); manifestos (20).

Suggestions for Writing and Discussion

1. If you are familiar with the situation, explain how the "war on poverty" ran off the tracks (par. 1).

2. To what extent has the "liberation" of women contributed to the need for more and more jobs (not mentioned in par. 8), and hence to the need for more production, rather than less?

3. Our free enterprise system is often criticized for a so-called lack of concern for the underprivileged. How, if at all, can this criticism be justified in view of the statistics given in paragraph 10?

4. What precedents do we have that lend credence to Drucker's assertion that punitive laws can succeed only if the unlawful act is comparatively rare (par. 13)? Can you think of any examples that would tend to disprove this theory? Explain.

5. Do you agree that "greed has little to do with the environmental crisis" (par. 16)? Defend your answer.

(NOTE: Suggestions for topics reqiuring development by INDUCTION and DEDUCTION are on page 252, at the end of this section.)

ARTHUR C. CLARKE

Arthur C. Clarke (born 1917) was born and educated in England and served in the Royal Air Force during World War II. His varied early career included underwater photography in Ceylon and Australia, editing Physics Abstracts, and auditing. He has served as chairman of the Royal Astronomical Society and is recipient of many awards and honors including the Stuart Ballantine Medal of the Franklin Institute (1963) "for his soundly based and prophetic early concept of the application of satellites in the primary human endeavor of communication." Clarke is perhaps best known for his novel and screenplay 2001: A Space Odyssey. A prolific science-fiction writer, he has also published numerous non-fiction and juvenile books. Some of the latest are The Nine Billion Names of God (1967), The Lost Worlds of Zool (1971), and The Wind from the Sun (1972).

The Star of the Magi

"The Star of the Magi" first appeared in Holiday in 1954 and was republished in Clarke's Report on Planet Three in 1972. There he noted that he had not changed the opening paragraph, "because almost every Christmas Venus is a brilliant object either in the morning or the evening sky." In his considerations of the various explanations for the Bethlehem star, Clarke uses not only the inductive/deductive process but also several others of our patterns of exposition.

Go out of doors any morning this December and look up at the 1 eastern sky an hour or so before dawn. You will see there one of the most beautiful sights in all the heavens — a blazing, blue-white beacon, many times brighter than Sirius, the most brilliant of the

Reprinted by permission of the author and his agents, Scott Meredith Literary Agency, Inc., 580 Fifth Avenue, New York, N.Y. 10036, from Report on Planet Three, by Arthur C. Clarke (New York: Harper & Row). Copyright © 1972 by Arthur C. Clarke.

stars. Apart from the Moon itself, it will be the brightest object you will ever see in the night sky. It will still be visible even when the Sun rises; you will even be able to find it at midday if you know exactly where to look.

It is the planet Venus, our sister world, reflecting across the gulfs of space the sunlight glancing from her unbroken cloud shield. Every nineteen months she appears in the morning sky, rising shortly before the Sun, and all who see this brilliant herald of the Christmas dawn will inevitably be reminded of the star that led the Magi to Bethlehem.

What was that star, assuming that it had some natural explanation? Could it, in fact, have been Venus? At least one book has been written to prove this theory, but it will not stand up to serious examination. To all the people of the Eastern world, Venus was one of the most familiar objects in the sky. Even today, she serves as a kind of alarm clock to the Arab nomads. When she rises, it is time to start moving, to make as much progress as possible before the Sun begins to blast the desert with its heat. For thousands of years, shining more brilliantly than we ever see her in our cloudy northern skies, she has watched the camps struck and the caravans begin to move.

Even to the ordinary, uneducated Jews of Herod's kingdom, there could have been nothing in the least remarkable about Venus. And the Magi were no ordinary men; they were certainly experts on astronomy, and must have known the movements of the planets better than do ninety-nine people out of a hundred today. To explain the Star of Bethlehem we must look elsewhere.

The Bible gives us very few clues; all that we can do is to consider some possibilities which at this distance in time can be neither proved nor disproved. One of these possibilities — the most spectacular and awe-inspiring of all — has been discovered only in the last few years, but let us first look at some of the earlier theories.

In addition to Venus, there are four other planets visible to the naked eye — Mercury, Mars, Jupiter, and Saturn. During their movements across the sky, two planets may sometimes appear to pass very close to one another — though in reality, of course, they are actually millions of miles apart.

Such occurrences are called "conjunctions"; on occasion they may be so close that the planets cannot be separated by the naked eye. This happened for Mars and Venus on October 4, 1953, when for a short while the two planets appeared to be fused together to give a single star. Such a spectacle is rare enough to be very striking, and the great astronomer Johannes Kepler devoted much time to proving that the Star of Bethlehem was a special conjunction of Jupiter and Saturn. The planets passed very close together (once again, remember, this was purely from the Earth's point of view — in reality they were half a billion miles apart!) in May, 7 B.C. This is quite near the date of Christ's birth, which probably took place in the spring of 7 or 6 B.C. (This still surprises most people, but as Herod is known to have died early in 4 B.C., Christ must have been born before 5 B.C. We should add six years to the calendar for A.D. to mean what it says.)

Kepler's proposal, however, is as unconvincing as the Venus theory. Better calculations than those he was able to make in the seventeenth century have shown that this particular conjunction was not a very close one, and the planets were always far enough apart to be easily separated by the eye. Moreover, there was a closer conjunction in 66 B.C., which on Kepler's theory should have brought a delegation of wise men to Bethlehem sixty years too soon!

In any case, the Magi could be expected to be as familiar with such events as with all other planetary movements, and the Biblical account also indicates that the Star of Bethlehem was visible over a period of weeks (it must have taken the Magi a considerable time to reach Judea, have their interview with Herod, and then go on to Bethlehem). The conjunction of two planets lasts only a very few days, since they soon separate in the sky and go once more upon their individual ways.

We can get over the difficulty if we assume that the Magi were astrologers ("Magi" and "magician" have a common root) and had somehow deduced the birth of the Messiah from a particular configuration of the planets, which to them, if to no one else, had a unique significance. It is an interesting fact that the Jupiter-Saturn conjunction of 7 B.C. occurred in the constellation Pisces, the Fish. Now though the ancient Jews were too sensible to believe in astrology, the constellation Pisces was supposed to be connected with them. Anything peculiar happening in Pisces would, naturally, direct the attention of Oriental astrologers toward Jerusalem.

This theory is simple and plausible, but a little disappointing. One would like to think that the Star of Bethlehem was something

8

9

10

11

more dramatic and not anything to do with the familiar planets whose behavior had been perfectly well known for thousands of years before the birth of Christ. Of course, if one accepts as *literally* true the statement that "the star, which they saw in the east, *went before them, till it came and stood over where the young Child was,*" no natural explanation is possible. Any heavenly body — star, planet, comet, or whatever — must share in the normal movement of the sky, rising in the east and setting some hours later in the west. Only the Pole Star, because it lies on the invisible axis of the turning Earth, appears unmoving in the sky and can act as a fixed and constant guide.

But the phrase, "went before them," like so much else in the Bible, can be interpreted in many ways. It may be that the star — whatever it might have been — was so close to the Sun that it could be seen only for a short period near dawn, and so would never have been visible except in the eastern sky. Like Venus when she is a morning star, it might have risen shortly before the Sun, then been lost in the glare of the new day before it could climb very far up the sky. The wise men would thus have seen it ahead of them at the beginning of each day, and then lost it in the dawn before it had veered around to the south. Many other readings are also possible.   12

Very well, then, can we discover some astronomical phenomenon sufficiently startling to surprise men completely familiar with the movements of the stars and planets and which fits the Biblical text?   13

Let's see if a comet would answer the specification. There have been no really spectacular comets in this century — though there were several in the 1800s — and most people do not know what they look like or how they behave. They even confuse them with meteors, which any observer is bound to see if he goes out on a clear night and watches the sky for half an hour.   14

No two classes of object could be more different. A meteor is a speck of matter, usually smaller than a grain of sand, which burns itself up by friction as it tears through the outer layers of Earth's atmosphere. But a comet may be millions of times larger than the entire Earth, and may dominate the night sky for weeks on end. A really great comet may look like a searchlight shining across the stars, and it is not surprising that such a portentous object always   15 caused alarm when it appeared in the heavens. As Calpurnia said to Caesar:

> When beggars die, there are no comets seen;
> The heavens themselves blaze forth the death of princes.

Most comets have a bright, starlike core, or nucleus, which is   16
completely dwarfed by their enormous tail — a luminous appendage which may be in the shape of a narrow beam or a broad, diffuse
fan. At first sight it would seem very unlikely that anyone would
call such an object a star, but as a matter of fact in old records
comets are sometimes referred to, not inaptly, as "hairy stars."

Comets are unpredictable: the great ones appear without warn-   17
ing, come racing in through the planets, bank sharply around the
Sun, and then head out toward the stars, not to be seen again for
hundreds or even millions of years. Only a few large comets —
such as Halley's — have relatively short periods and have been
observed on many occasions. Halley's comet, which takes seventy-
five years to go around its orbit, has managed to put in an appearance at several historic events. It was visible just before the sack of
Jerusalem in A.D. 66, and before the Norman invasion of England
in A.D. 1066. Of course, in ancient times (or modern ones, for that
matter) it was never very difficult to find a suitable disaster to attribute to any given comet. It is not surprising, therefore, that their
reputation as portents of evil lasted for so long.

It is perfectly possible that a comet appeared just before the   18
birth of Christ. Attempts have been made, without success, to see
if any of the known comets were visible around that date. (Halley's, as will be seen from the figures above, was just a few years
too early on its last appearance before the fall of Jerusalem.) But
the number of comets whose paths and periods we do know is very
small compared with the colossal number that undoubtedly exists.
If a comet did shine over Bethlehem, it may not be seen again from
Earth for a hundred thousand years.

We can picture it in that Oriental dawn — a band of light   19
streaming up from the eastern horizon, perhaps stretching ver-
tically toward the zenith. The tail of a comet always points away
from the Sun; the comet would appear, therefore, like a great ar-
row, aimed at the east. As the Sun rose, it would fade into invisibility; but the next morning, it would be in almost the same
place, still directing the travelers to their goal. It might be visible

for weeks before it disappeared once more into the depths of space.

The picture is a dramatic and attractive one. It may even be the correct explanation; one day, perhaps, we shall know.

20

But there is yet another theory, and this is the one which most astronomers would probably accept today. It makes the other explanations look very trivial and commonplace indeed, for it leads us to contemplate one of the most astonishing — and terrifying — events yet discovered in the whole realm of nature.

21

We will forget now about planets and comets and the other denizens of our own tight little Solar System. Let us go out across *real* space, right out to the stars — those other suns, many far greater than our own, which sheer distance has dwarfed to dimensionless points of light.

22

Most of the stars shine with unwavering brilliance, century after century. Sirius appears now exactly as it did to Moses, as it did to Neanderthal man, as it did to the dinosaurs — if they ever bothered to look at the night sky. Its brilliance has changed little during the entire history of our Earth and will be the same a billion years from now.

23

But there are some stars — the so-called "novae," or new stars — which through internal causes suddenly become celestial atomic bombs. Such a star may explode so violently that it leaps a hundred-thousand-fold in brilliance within a few hours. One night it may be invisible to the naked eye; on the next, it may dominate the sky. If our Sun became such a nova, Earth would melt to slag and puff into vapor in a matter of minutes, and only the outermost of the planets would survive.

24

Novae are not uncommon; many are observed every year, though few are near enough to be visible except through telescopes. They are the routine, everyday disasters of the Universe.

25

Two or three times in every thousand years, however, there occurs something which makes a mere nova about as inconspicuous as a firefly at noon. When a star becomes a *super*nova, its brilliance may increase not by a hundred thousand but by a *billion* in the course of a few hours. The last time such an event was witnessed by human eyes was in A.D. 1604; there was another supernova in A.D. 1572 (so brilliant that it was visible in broad daylight); and the Chinese astronomers recorded one in A.D. 1054. It is quite possible that the Bethlehem star was such a supernova, and if so one can draw some very surprising conclusions.

26

We'll assume that Supernova Bethlehem was about as bright as 27 the supernova of A.D. 1572 — often called "Tycho's star," after the great astronomer who observed it at the time. Since this star could be seen by day, it must have been as brilliant as Venus. As we also know that a supernova is, in reality, at least a hundred million times more brillant than our own Sun, a very simple calculation tells us how far away it must have been for its *apparent* brightness to equal that of Venus.

It turns out that Supernova Bethlehem was more than three 28 thousand light years — or, if you prefer, 18 quadrillion miles — away. That means that its light had been traveling for at least three thousand years before it reached Earth and Bethlehem, so that the awesome catastrophe of which it was the symbol took place five thousand years ago, when the Great Pyramid was still fresh from the builders.

Let us, in imagination, cross the gulfs of space and time and go 29 back to the moment of the catastrophe. We might find ourselves watching an ordinary star — a sun, perhaps, no different from our own. There may have been planets circling it; we do not know how common planets are in the scheme of the Universe, and how many suns have these small companions. But there is no reason to think that they are rare, and many novae must be the funeral pyres of worlds, and perhaps races, greater than ours.

There is no warning at all — only a steadily rising intensity of 30 the sun's light. Within minutes the change is noticeable; within an hour, the nearer worlds are burning. The star is expanding like a balloon, blasting off shells of gas at a million miles an hour as it blows its outer layers into space. Within a day, it is shining with such supernal brilliance that it gives off more light than *all the other suns in the Universe combined*. If it had planets, they are now no more than flecks of flame in the still-expanding shells of fire. The conflagration will burn for weeks before the dying star collapses back into quiescence.

But let us consider what happens to the light of the nova, 31 which moves a thousand times more swiftly than the blast wave of the explosion. It will spread out into space, and after four or five years it will reach the next star. If there are planets circling that star, they will suddenly be illuminated by a second sun. It will give them no appreciable heat, but will be bright enough to banish night completely, for it will be more than a thousand times more luminous than our full Moon. All that light will come from a single blazing point, since even from its nearest neighbor Supernova Bethlehem would appear too small to show a disk.

Century after century, the shell of light will continue to expand 32 around its source. It will flash past countless suns and flare briefly in the skies of their planets. Indeed, on the most conservative estimate, this great new star must have shone over thousands of worlds before its light reached Earth — and to all those worlds it appeared far, far brighter than it did to the men it led to Judea.

For as the shell of light expanded, it faded also. Remember, by 33 the time it reached Bethlehem it was spread over the surface of a sphere six thousand light-years across. A thousand years earlier, when Homer was singing the song of Troy, the nova would have appeared twice as brilliant to any watchers further upstream, as it were, to the time and place of the explosion.

That is a strange thought; there is a stranger one to come. For 34 the light of Supernova Bethlehem is still flooding out through space; it has left Earth far behind in the twenty centuries that have elapsed since men saw it for the first and last time. Now that light is spread over a sphere ten thousand light-years across and must be correspondingly fainter. It is simple to calculate how bright the supernova must be to any beings who may be seeing it now as a new star in *their* skies. To them, it will still be far more brilliant than any other star in the entire heavens, for its brightness will have fallen only by 50 per cent on its extra two thousand years of travel.

At this very moment, therefore, the Star of Bethlehem may 35 still be shining in the skies of countless worlds, circling far suns. Any watchers on those worlds will see its sudden appearance and its slow fading, just as the Magi did two thousand years ago when the expanding shell of light swept past the Earth. And for thousands of years to come, as its radiance ebbs out toward the frontiers of the Universe, Supernova Bethlehem will still have power to startle all who see it, wherever — and whatever — they may be.

Astronomy, as nothing else can do, teaches men humility. We 36 know now that our Sun is merely one undistinguished member of a vast family of stars, and no longer think of ourselves as being at the center of creation. Yet it is strange to think that before its light fades away below the limits of vision, we may have shared the Star

of Bethlehem with the beings of perhaps a million worlds — and
that to many of them, nearer to the source of the explosion, it must
have been a far more wonderful sight than ever it was to any eyes
on earth.

What did they make of it — and did it bring them good tid-   37
ings, or ill?

Meanings and Values

1a. Illustrate the difference between objective and subjective writing by
     use of carefully selected sentences from this essay. (See Guide to
     Terms: *Objective/Subjective.*)
  b. Which, if either, predominates?
2.   What personal benefits, if any other than mere receipt of informa-
     tion, did you gain from reading this essay?
3.   Use the three-point system of evaluation to measure the success of
     "The Star of the Magi." (Guide: *Evaluation.*)

Expository Techniques

1a. As Clarke considers each possibility and disposes of it as un-
     worthy, what basic form of reasoning is he using? (It is not im-
     portant to this question that the evidence is often negative.)
  b. What seems to determine the order of presentation?
  c. How, if at all, is this a matter of emphasis? (Guide: *Emphasis.*)
2.   The author never moves directly from discussion of one possibility
     to that of the next.
  a. What seems to be the organic function of paragraph 5?
  b. Of paragraphs 12–13?
  c. Of paragraphs 20–21?
  d. Why would this not be an effective technique in certain other types
     of writing?
3.   This author employs several other patterns of exposition already
     studied. List these and cite at least one paragraph where each is to
     be found.
4.   How effective do you consider Clarke's two-paragraph closing?
     (Guide: *Closings.*) Why?
5.   If you have read the Drucker selection preceding this one, com-
     pare and/or contrast the styles of the two authors, as evinced by
     one or two representative paragraphs of each — e.g., the last two
     of each selection. (Guide: *Style/Tone.*)

Diction and Vocabulary

1. What steps does the author take to prevent astronomical terms from creating a communication block for his readers? Cite examples wherever possible.

2. Review your answer to question 5 of "Expository Techniques" to determine which stylistic differences, if any, are matters of diction. Provide specific examples to illustrate.

3. Use the dictionary as needed to understand the meanings of the following words: configuration (par. 10); portentous (15, 17); appendage (16); sack (17); denizens (22); quiescence (30).

Suggestions for Writing and Discussion

1. If you believe in astrology, you may wish to prepare a brief case refuting Clarke's implication that such a belief is not "sensible" (par. 10).

2. If your religious or private belief is in the literal interpretation of the Biblical account of the Bethlehem star, explain how you account for the presumable setting aside of the "normal movement of the sky" (par. 11).

3. Clarke says there are many other interpretations possible (par. 12). What are some of these? Discuss any which seem somewhat plausible.

4. Perhaps you would prefer to select some other passage from the Bible, or from the sacred book of another religion, and consider its various possible interpretations.

Writing Suggestions for Section 8
Induction and Deduction

Choose one of the following unformed topics and then form your central theme concerning it. This could express whatever view you prefer or allow for opposing views. Develop your composition primarily by use of induction, alone or in combination with deduction. But unless otherwise directed by your instructor, be completely objective and limit yourself to exposition, rather than engaging in argumentation.

1. Little League Baseball (or the activities of 4-H clubs, Boy Scouts, Girl Scouts, etc.) as a molder of character.
2. Conformity as an expression of insecurity.
3. The display of nonconformity as an expression of insecurity.
4. The status symbol as a motivator to success.
5. The hippie way of life as an effective "solution."
6. The liberal arts curriculum and its "relevance."
7. Student opinion as the guide to better educational institutions.
8. College education as a prerequisite for worldly success.
9. The values of education, beyond dollars and cents.
10. Knowledge and its relation to wisdom.
11. The right of the individual to select the laws he obeys.
12. Television commercials as a molder of morals.
13. The unpronounced death of ———— Church.
14. The important new role of ———— Church.
15. The "other" side of one ecological problem.
16. Complete freedom from worry as a desirable goal.
17. Decreased effectiveness of the home as an influence in adolescent development.

Explaining with the Help of *Description*

Although usually classed as one of the four basic forms of prose, description is used nearly always as a supporting device of one of the other three. Exposition, as well as argument and narration, can be made more vivid, and hence more understandable, with this support. Most exposition does contain some elements of description, and at times description carries almost the entire burden of the explanation, becoming a basic pattern for the expository purpose.

Description is most useful in painting a word-picture of something concrete, such as a scene or a person. Its use is not restricted, however, to what we can perceive with our senses; we can also describe (or attempt to describe) an abstract concept, such as an emotion or quality or mood. But most attempts to describe fear, for instance, still resort to the physical — a "coldness around the heart," perhaps — and in such concrete ways communicate the abstract to the reader.

In its extreme forms, description is either *objective* or *impressionistic* (subjective), but most of its uses are somewhere between these extremes. Objective description is purely factual, uncolored by any feelings of the author; it is the type used for scientific papers and most business reports. But impressionistic description, as the term implies, at least tinges the purely factual with the author's personal impressions; instead of describing how something *is,* objectively, he describes how it *seems,* subjectively. Such a description might refer to the "blazing heat" of an August day. Somewhat less impressionistic would be "extreme heat." But the scientist would describe it precisely as "115 degrees Fahrenheit," and this would be purely objective reporting, unaffected by the impressions of the author. (No examples of the latter are included in this section, but many textbooks for other courses utilize the technique of pure objective description, as do encyclopedias. The Petrunkevitch essay in Section 5 provides some good examples of objective description, although not entirely unmixed with colorful impressionistic details.)

The first and most important job in any descriptive endeavor is the selection of details to be included. There are usually many from which to choose, and the writer must constantly keep in mind the kind of picture he wants to paint with words — for *his* purpose and *his* audience. Such a word-picture need not be entirely visual; in this respect the writer has more freedom than the artist, for he can use strokes that will add the dimension of sound, smell, and even touch. Such "strokes," if made to seem natural enough, can help create a vivid and effective image in the reader's mind.

Most successful impressionistic description focuses on a single *dominant impression*. Of the many descriptive details ordinarily available for use, the author selects those which will help create a mood or atmosphere or emphasize a feature or quality. But more than the materials themselves are involved, for even diction can often assist in creating the desired dominant impression. Sometimes syntax is also an important factor, as in the use of short, hurried sentences to help convey a sense of urgency or excitement.

Actual structuring of passages is perhaps less troublesome in description than that in most of the other patterns. But some kind of orderliness is needed for the sake of both readability and a realistic effect. (Neither objective nor impressionistic description can afford not to be realistic, in one manner or another.) In visual description, orderliness is usually achieved by presenting details as the eye would find them — that is as arranged in space. We could describe a person from head to toe, or vice versa, or begin with his most noticeable feature and work from there. A scenic description might move from near to far or from far to near, from left to right or from right to left. It might also start with a broad, overall view, gradually narrowing to a focal point, probably the most significant feature of the scene. These are fairly standard kinds of description; but as the types and occasions for using description vary widely, so do the possibilities for interesting treatment. In many cases, the writer is limited only by his own ingenuity.

But ingenuity should not be allowed to produce *excessive*

description, an amazingly certain path to reader boredom. A few well-chosen details are better than profusion. Economy of words is desirable in any writing, and description is no exception. Appropriate use of figurative language and careful choices of strong nouns and verbs will help prevent the need for strings of modifiers, which are wasteful and can seem amateurish.

To even the experienced writer, however, achieving good description remains a constant challenge; the beginner should not expect to attain this goal without working at it.

SHARON CURTIN

SHARON CURTIN, a native of Douglas, Wyoming, was raised in a family of ranchers and craftsmen. She was trained as a nurse and has had varied experience in that field in Viet Nam, New York, and California. Ms. Curtin, a women's liberationist and political leftist, is a friend of such activists as Abbie Hoffman and Kate Millet. She now devotes much of her time to writing and to operating a small farm in Virginia.

Aging in the Land of the Young

"Aging in the Land of the Young" is the first part of Curtin's article by that title, as it appeared in *Atlantic* in July 1972. It is largely a carefully restructured composite of portions of her book *Nobody Ever Died of Old Age*, also published in 1972. It illustrates the subjective form of description, generally known as impressionistic.

Old men, old women, almost 20 million of them. They constitute 1 10 percent of the total population, and the percentage is steadily growing. Some of them, like conspirators, walk all bent over, as if hiding some precious secret, filled with self-protection. The body seems to gather itself around those vital parts, folding shoulders, arms, pelvis like a fading rose. Watch and you see how fragile old people come to think they are.

Aging paints every action gray, lies heavy on every movement, 2 imprisons every thought. It governs each decision with a ruthless and single-minded perversity. To age is to learn the feeling of no longer growing, of struggling to do old tasks, to remember familiar actions. The cells of the brain are destroyed with thousands of unfelt tiny strokes, little pockets of clotted blood wiping out memories and abilities without warning. The body seems slowly to give up, randomly stopping, sometimes starting again as if to torture and tease with the memory of lost strength. Hands become clumsy, frail transparencies, held together with knotted blue veins.

Sometimes it seems as if the distance between your feet and the floor were constantly changing, as if you were walking on shifting and not quite solid ground. One foot down, slowly, carefully force the other foot forward. Sometimes you are a shuffler, not daring to lift your feet from the uncertain earth but forced to slide hesitantly forward in little whispering movements. Sometimes you are able to "step out," but this effort — in fact the pure exhilaration of easy movement — soon exhausts you. 3

The world becomes narrower as friends and family die or move away. To climb stairs, to ride in a car, to walk to the corner, to talk on the telephone; each action seems to take away from the energy needed to stay alive. Everything is limited by the strength you hoard greedily. Your needs decrease, you require less food, less sleep, and finally less human contact; yet this little bit becomes more and more difficult. You fear that one day you will be reduced to the simple acts of breathing and taking nourishment. This is the ultimate stage you dread, the period of helplessness and hopelessness, when independence will be over. 4

There is nothing to prepare you for the experience of growing old. Living is a process, an irreversible progression toward old age and eventual death. You see men of eighty still vital and straight as oaks; you see men of fifty reduced to gray shadows in the human landscape. The cellular clock differs for each one of us, and is profoundly affected by our own life experiences, our heredity, and perhaps most important, by the concepts of aging encountered in society and in oneself. 5

The aged live with enforced leisure, on fixed incomes, subject to many chronic illnesses, and most of their money goes to keep a roof over their heads. They also live in a culture that worships youth. 6

A kind of cultural attitude makes me bigoted against old people; it makes me think young is best; it makes me treat old people like outcasts. 7

Hate that gray? Wash it away! 8
Wrinkle cream. 9
Monkey glands. 10

Face-lifting.   11
Look like a bride again.   12
Don't trust anyone over thirty.   13
I fear growing old.   14
Feel Young Again!   15
I am afraid to grow old — we're all afraid. In fact, the fear of   16
growing old is so great that every aged person is an insult and a
threat to the society. They remind us of our own death, that our
body won't always remain smooth and responsive, but will some-
day betray us by aging, wrinkling, faltering, failing. The ideal way
to age would be to grow slowly invisible, gradually disappearing,
without causing worry or discomfort to the young. In some ways
that does happen. Sitting in a small park across from a nursing
home one day, I noticed that the young mothers and their children
gathered on one side, and the old people from the home on the
other. Whenever a youngster would run over to the "wrong" side,
chasing a ball or just trying to cover all the available space, the
old people would lean forward and smile. But before any communication could be established, the mother would come over,
murmuring embarrassed apologies, and take her child back to the
"young" side.

Now, it seemed to me that the children didn't feel any par-   17
ticular fear and the old people didn't seem to be threatened by the
children. The division of space was drawn by the mothers. And the
mothers never looked at the old people who lined the other side of
the park like so many pigeons perched on the benches. These well-
dressed young matrons had a way of sliding their eyes over, around,
through the old people; they never looked at them directly. The
old people may as well have been invisible; they had no reality for
the youngsters, who were not permitted to speak to them, and they
offended the aesthetic eye of the mothers.

My early experiences were somewhat different; since I grew   18
up in a small town, my childhood had more of a nineteenth-century
flavor. I knew a lot of old people, and considered some of them
friends. There was no culturally defined way for me to "relate" to
old people, except the rules of courtesy which applied to all adults.
My grandparents were an integral and important part of the family
and of the community. I sometimes have a dreadful fear that mine
will be the last generation to know old people as friends, to have a
sense of what growing old means, to respect and understand man's

mortality and his courage in the face of death. Mine may be the last generation to have a sense of living history, of stories passed from generation to generation, of identity established by family history.

Meanings and Values

1. What is the general tone of this writing? (See Guide to Terms: *Style/Tone.*)

2. If you find it depressing to read about aging, try to analyze why (especially in view of the fact that you are very likely many years from the stage of "a fading rose").

3. Why do you suppose it is more likely to be the mothers than the children who shun old people (pars. 16–17)?

4a. Has this author avoided the excesses of sentimentality? (Guide: *Sentimentality.*)

 b. If not, where does she fail? If she does avoid them, try to discover how.

Expository Techniques

1a. Why should this writing be classed as primarily impressionistic, rather than objective?

 b. What is the dominant impression?

2a. Analyze the role which selection of details plays in creating the dominant impression.

 b. Provide examples of the type of details that could have been included but were not.

 c. Are such omissions justifiable?

3a. Paragraph 5 ends the almost pure description to begin another phase of the writing. What is it?

 b. How has the author provided for a smooth transition between the two? (Guide: *Transition.*)

4a. What particular method of gaining emphasis has been used effectively in one portion of the selection? (Guide: *Emphasis.*)

 b. How might the material have been presented if emphasis were not desired?

5. Which previously studied patterns of exposition are also used in this writing? Cite paragraphs where each may be found.

Diction and Vocabulary

1a. The author sometimes changes person — e.g., "they" to "you" after paragraph 2. Analyze where the changes occur.
 b. What justification, if any, can you find for each change?
2a. Which two kinds of figure of speech do you find used liberally to achieve this description? (Guide: *Figures of Speech*.)
 b. Cite three or more examples of each.
 c. As nearly as you can tell, are any of them clichés? (Guide: *Clichés*.)

Suggestions for Writing and Discussion

1. If Curtin is correct in her fears expressed in the last two sentences, what could be the consequences for society in general?

2. Discuss the pro's and con's of placing senile old people in rest homes, rather than letting them live alone or taking them to live with "the family." What other alternatives, if any, does the family have?

3. If you know some very old person who (apparently) is not affected by aging as the ones the author describes, what seems to be his, or her, formula for success?

4. If you are familiar with the Gray Power movement, or others like it, what exactly is it that they hope to accomplish?

5. If many people at age 60–65 are still efficient at their jobs, as is often argued, what practical reasons are there for forcing retirement at that age?

(NOTE: Suggestions for topics requiring development by use of DESCRIPTION are on page 281, at the end of this section.)

BARBARA W. TUCHMAN

BARBARA W. TUCHMAN, a widely respected author and journalist, was born in New York City. A graduate of Radcliffe
College, she has since been awarded honorary degrees from
numerous universities. For many years she was a foreign
correspondent both in Europe and in the Orient, where she
started the writing career which has been her abiding interest
for forty years. She has won two Pulitzer Prizes: one for *The
Guns of August* (1962) and the other for *Stilwell and the
American Experience in China, 1911–45* (1971). She is also
the author of *The Proud Tower* (1966) and *The Zimmerman
Telegram* (1958).

The Changed and Unchanging

"The Changed and Unchanging" was written for Associated
Press and later included in the author's book *Notes from
China* (1972). As did the rest of the book, this selection resulted from Tuchman's six-week visit to China in the summer
of 1972, and is typical of her quietly realistic style of reporting. You will find that her methods of description differ
greatly from those of the preceding author.

The two most striking physical features of China today are the new   1
tree-planting and the old transportation by animal- and man-
drawn cart.

Willows, sycamores, and countless varieties of poplars and   2
cypress in multiple and flourishing rows, often under-planted with
shrubs and hedges, supply shade and greenness in the city streets
and extend for miles along the roads outside. Trees have been
richly planted in parks, on campuses, factory grounds, new housing
lots, airports, military barracks, dam sites, river banks. In the new

part of Chengchow the avenues lined with double rows of sycamores already thirty feet high are spectacular. Nanking and
Suchow have no street without shade. Nurseries of thin saplings
can be seen everywhere. The "greening" campaign, as it is called,
is said to have lowered the implacable summer heat in the baked
cities of the north and the muggy cities of the Yangtse Valley by
two degrees. In the hills it has begun to get a grip on the soil that
had been allowed to erode and slide away in the rivers unchecked
for centuries.

Afforestation is one of those civic works that was simply not   3
undertaken in China before what is officially called "Liberation,"
that is, the Communist take-over in 1949. In Manchu times, local
officials lived by the cut they could take out of tax-collecting and
were disinclined to spend any of it on projects for the public welfare. After the Revolution of 1911, the "People's Welfare" was one
of the Three Principles of the Kuomintang Party founded by Sun
Yat-sen and inherited by Chiang Kai-shek, but it got lost in the
difficulties of consolidating political power and of invasion by the
Japanese. Until now the Yangtse was never bridged — not at
Nanking although it was the national capital during 1929–49; nor
upstream at the triple city of Wuhan where railroad cars on the
main north-south line had to be carried over by ferry; nor farther
up at Chungking, Chiang Kai-shek's war-time capital for eight
years. Now bridges carry traffic across the river at all three places.

In Honan, province of the ghastly famine of 1942–43, a canal   4
that took ten years to build has been cut through rock and mountain to carry water and electric power to stony Linhsien County
whose people used to walk six miles to fetch water by bucket. Less
spectacular but in the same spirit, a 400-man factory in Loyang has
developed from twelve original workers and one sewing machine
to make rubber-soled shoes for soldiers and peasants who once
walked on straw.

How far China remains from its goal of modernization, how-   5
ever, lies under one's eyes every day in the endless procession of
two-wheeled carts moving in and out of the provincial cities. This,
not the trucks that serve Canton, Shanghai, and Peking, is the
wider reality of China. Drawn by mixed teams or tandems of
donkey, mule, and horse or by the straining muscles of a man between the shafts, with added pulling rope around a shoulder pad,
the carts carry gravel, manure, bricks, building stone, sand, iron

pipes, bottled drinks, earthenware jars, mountainous piles of scallions, red onions, melons, and other produce, roped loads of tires, boxes, chairs, waste paper and rags, bags of grain, bags of fertilizer, blocks of ice, baskets of coal, heavy tree trunks twenty feet long, and everything else the country sends to the city and vice versa.

Some, pulled by children, carry grandma sitting under an umbrella; some, pulled by grandma, carry children. Every animal-drawn cart carries, in addition to the driver, a second figure sprawled asleep on top of the load. Whole lives must be thus spent plodding along the roads, at such creeping pace when the load is heavy that once we drove past two haulers of scrap iron in the morning and on returning three hours later saw the same men only a few blocks farther on. Though some of the plodders are brawny young men, most are thin, muscular, workworn, soiled, and sweating toilers who may no longer have a landlord to oppress them but whose labor has not been much alleviated since the old days. A scrawny old woman bent against the weight of a load of wire rods bears little relation to the sturdy rosy ever-smiling maiden idyllically picking grapes who represents ideal proletarian womanhood on China's magazine covers. Often the heaviest loads are pulled by the oldest men as if (whisper it not in Mao's land of "struggle") the Marxist young, like any other, may have little inclination for the hardest work.

In the canal area, transportation is by barge, much of this too propelled by manpower. While some barges in long trains are pulled by tug on the Grand Canal, others are dragged by rope by plodders along the bank. On the smaller canals, single scows are moved by a man poling at snail's pace or bending his back to an oar pushed back and forth on a fulcrum at the stern.

How will all this human labor be used when and if China's transportation gradually becomes mechanized? The goal is so far from realization that it is hardly a worry, yet there are already signs that urban labor is underemployed. China's boasted record of full employment, which they like to tell you is the result of a planned economy as against the evils of our competitive private enterprise, is only achieved by assigning large numbers to more or less nominal jobs with no real function. Retinues of junior assistants follow every "leading cadre" like a claque, and a superabundance of personnel stands around in hotel corridors vaguely waiting for something to do. No fewer than six staff members of a "Friendship" store for foreigners clustered around the foreign exchange desk to supervise the cashing of one American Express check. At the Nanking Observatory nine staff members at one time were engaged in moving a bag of sand — which one could have handled — to mend a terrace. The cost of keeping people employed must be as great if not greater than our system of supporting the unemployed on welfare. The burden looms heavily over the future.

Meanings and Values

1a. Does either the author's tone or her content indicate any bias in her reporting of conditions in China? If so, is it for or against the so-called Liberation?
 b. Justify your answer, citing specific references.
2. What irony, if any, do you see in the last sentence of paragraph 6? (See Guide to Terms: *Irony.*)
3a. Compose a brief sentence which clearly states the author's central theme. (Guide: *Unity.*)
 b. Does any part of the selection seem irrelevant to this theme?
 c. If so, does it indicate poor unity — or your poor statement of theme? Explain.

Expository Techniques

1a. If possible, illustrate the meaning of both objective and impressionistic description by citing specific sentences.
 b. Which kind predominates in this selection?
 c. If you have read the Curtin piece preceding this one, explain how the two authors' points of view helped dictate any differences in the predominant kind of description. (Guide: *Point of View.*)
2. What other patterns of exposition are also employed in this selection? Cite paragraphs wherein each may be found.
3a. Is the long, stringy sentence in paragraph 5 a bad sentence, as it is used? Explain.
 b. Comment on the effectiveness of the sentence in paragraph 1 and the first sentence of paragraph 6. What characteristics do the two have in common?
 c. Explain how both questions 3a and 3b above are related to syntax. (Guide: *Syntax.*)

Diction and Vocabulary

1a. If you have read the Curtin selection preceding this one, contrast its style of diction to that of Tuchman's. (Guide: *Diction; Style/Tone.*)
   b. How do these differences affect the impressionistic qualities of the respective writings?

2. Consult your dictionary as needed to determine meanings of the following words: implacable (par. 2); alleviated, idyllically, proletarian (6); nominal, retinues, cadre, claque (8).

Suggestions for Writing and Discussion

1. What do you think is the psychological reasoning behind the theory that the way to enlist and retain people's support is to advertise your cause as one of "struggle" (par. 6)? Why, at least to Americans, is this theory apt to seem paradoxical? (Guide: *Paradox.*)

2. If you had to choose between oppression by landlords (par. 6) and oppression by the government, which would be less objectionable? Why?

3. By cause/effect analysis (limited as it may be, of course, by your limited knowledge) try to determine potential consequences, to you personally, of increasingly friendly relations between China and the United States.

(NOTE: Suggestions for topics requiring development by use of DESCRIPTION are on page 281, at the end of this section.)

MICHAEL J. ARLEN

MICHAEL J. ARLEN, born in London in 1930, is a Harvard graduate and is the son of Michael Arlen, a well-known novelist of the twenties. He has been a television critic for *The New Yorker* and is a contributing editor to *Harper's*. Arlen has traveled to Vietnam and produced a disturbing critique of the war coverage by the American press. His books are *Exiles* (1970), a memoir of his famous parents; and *An American Verdict* (1973), on the Chicago Black Panther raid.

Griefspeak

"Griefspeak" is from Arlen's book *Living-Room War* (1969). It provides a unique illustration of highly impressionistic description. All elements of style, tone, and organization seem intended, at least, to contribute to the dominant impression, to the subtle central theme itself. Although not the type of writing most people have occasion to emulate, it does offer clear evidence of how the careful writer can use the means at his disposal to create exactly the effect he desires.

When Robert Kennedy was shot, the reporters were already there — the cameras, the lights, the heralds of the people standing upon chairs and tabletops, trailing wire and tape recorders, the black tube-like microphones stretched out arclike into the room (that kitchen). He was shot, and it was real — a life, a death, the *event*, confusion, motion, people running, the man on the floor, young girls in straw hats crying, policemen, people pushing, yelling, the man on the floor, dying, dead, dying. It was all there for a moment, for a short while (it is perhaps this moment, stretching out forward and backward in our imaginations, that now remains), this event, this God knows what it was, and then the hands of people began to touch it.

Inevitably, one will say. Inevitably. *Je suis touriste ici moimême.*[1]
Soft hands, tired hands, sincere hands, oh those sincere hands
touching it (and him), poking it, rubbing it, plumping it, patting it.
The men in rumpled shirts, hastily buttoned coats, were on the
tabletops (our witness-technicians), on sidewalks, in corridors,
holding aloft their microphones and cameras. The other men, in
better-fitting suits and serious expressions, were inside some room
— it all seemed like the same room (some underground chamber),
but it could not have been. They talked — to each other, out to us.
"I suppose," said Charles Kuralt, "we ought to be giving some comfort to the country in times like this. . . ." Griefspeak. "I don't know
about the rest of you," John Chancellor said, "but in the last few
hours I seem to have lost part of my self-respect." Somebody
handed a piece of paper to Edwin Newman. "I have some new information here," said Edwin Newman. "Sirhan has ordered two
books." He looked at the piece of paper. "One is by Madame
Blavatsky. The other is by C. W. Ledbetter. We don't know the
meaning of this as yet. Or whether it has anything to do with the
alleged, the — we want to remind you that all this is tentative, because in this country no man is guilty until judged by a court of
law." They talked of irony awhile. It was a time for discovering
ironies. It was ironic about "the family." It was ironic that he was
shot at the time of his "greatest triumph." It was ironic that "he
had spoken out so often against violence." It was ironic that only
yesterday he had rescued one of his children from the surf at
Malibu. "Excuse me, John," said Edwin Newman. "We just got this
on Madame Blavatsky. She lived from 1830 to 1891 and was a
Theosophist — although I want to say that we're not yet sure what
relationship, if any, this has to the . . ." "I just thought of another
irony," said Sander Vanocur. "In a speech just a few days ago
Senator Kennedy said, 'We were killed in Oregon. I hope to be
resurrected in Los Angeles.' " A psychiatrist appeared at some point
to say he thought the violence in our country derived from showing
films like *Bonnie and Clyde*. There were discussions across the
nation about brain surgery. "I think each one of us is guilty," Mike
Wallace said. Telephone calls from prominent people to the family
were duly logged and reported. CBS announced telephone calls
from President Johnson, Vice-President Humphrey, Governor Rea-

[1] French, meaning "I am a tourist (or visitor) here myself." [Ed.]

gan, and Senator Mansfield. NBC announced telephone calls from
President Johnson, Governor Reagan, Robert McNamara, and
Mayor Daley. The police chief of Los Angeles appeared before the
press and spoke calmly and effectively. "I'll give you boys a moment to get your machines adjusted," he said before beginning.
Prime Minister Harold Wilson was interviewed via satellite. The
BBC announced "prayers for America." There were scenes of the
coffin being placed into the plane in Los Angeles and being taken
out of the plane in New York. There was an interview with Card-
inal Cushing. Lord Harlech said that violence in America had become "an international scandal." There were interviews by satellite
with former Prime Minister Macmillan and Romain Gary. There
was an interview with an old gentleman seated in a chair upon a
lawn, who had once been Robert Kennedy's grade-school principal.
"I remember him very well," he said. "One day he brought one of
these animals to school with him. A little pig, I think it was." They
showed us the inside of the cathedral. Norman Mailer was standing
at vigil around the coffin. "I think Nick Katzenbach is there," said
an announcer. "There is George Plimpton. Ed, is that George
Plimpton?" "No," said Edwin Newman. "But I think Mayor Lind-
say is now coming down the aisle." They showed us Ethel Kennedy.
Mrs. Robert Kennedy was seated in church beside a child, her head
bent low over the child. The camera zoomed in. "How does one
comfort a child at a time like that?" asked Edwin Newman. There
was a Chevrolet ad. A man and a girl were seated on top of a con-
vertible singing about "the big new savings on all regular Chevro-
lets." The song ended. "And on Chevelles too," the girl with a
wink. CBS was running off a Western. A man and a very blond girl
with frizzy hair were hiding behind some curtains. There were advance shots of the route to be taken by the funeral procession.
There were shots of tree-lined streets in Washington. "He often enjoyed a brisk walk down streets such as these," a voice informed
us. There were pictures of the White House. Leonard Bernstein, it
was announced, would handle the musical arrangements. There
were more scenes of Ethel Kennedy in church. There were scenes
at Union Station. There were distant views of Hickory Hill. "He
liked fresh air," said another voice. Jerome Wilson of WCBS had a
number of people seated around him. "I realize it is hard for you
to talk at a time like this," he said to a young man who had been
a Citizen for Kennedy, "but what did you young people *especially*

like about him?" The young man thought for a moment. "We especially liked him because he had leverage," he said. "I think I can say that business would have been happy with Robert Kennedy," said Roswell Gilpatric. They showed us the crowds lined up outside Saint Patrick's. "Young and old alike are joined in grief," an announcer said. They showed us the flags flying on the office buildings on Park Avenue. Some were flying at half-mast, some were not. "The flags fly at half-mast all across this mourning city," an announcer said. They showed us people filing by the coffin. They showed us the train on the way to Washington. They showed us the railroad stations. They showed us the train tracks. "What was it . . . what was the *mystique* that the Kennedy family had?" asked Johnny Carson. "Ethel Kennedy must now begin to build anew," Gabe Pressman said. The Red Cross, one learned, had already distributed four thousand cups of cold drink. They showed us the Lincoln Memorial. They showed us the Joint Chiefs of Staff. "As time goes on," said Louis Nizer, "the pain from his passing will diminish." They showed us John Kennedy's widow in church. I watched the television on and off those days, and the strangely disconnected people on the streets, in crowds, in the lines that rolled around Saint Patrick's down to Forty-fourth Street. "The people have come by to pay their last respects," the voices said. "The people file by . . . the people wait . . . the people touch . . . the people grieve. . . ." They showed us that throng of men and women waiting outside the station at Trenton — kids with American flags, parents in their shirtsleeves, the long train tracks, the crowded platform. "The question," the announcer said, "is how much the train has been slowed down en route from Newark." No. The question all along (we had known three days ago who had been killed) was who was dead.

Meanings and Values

1. Briefly describe the dominant impression of this essay.
2a. What was the "it" that sincere hands began touching and patting?
 b. What symbolic function is served by the sincere hands? (See Guide to Terms: *Symbolism*.)
3. When Mike Wallace said that "each one of us is guilty," he was

merely echoing a rather common lament during those days. Why would people believe that?

4. Consider the "ironies" discovered by the announcers. Explain briefly why each was ironic. (Guide: *Irony*.)

5a. What did the young Citizen for Kennedy mean when he said Robert Kennedy had "leverage"?

   b. How was this comment also ironic, given at that time and in reply to that question?

6. Explain more fully the author's meaning in his last sentence.

7a. To what extent, if at all, does this essay disparage the real horror and grief at the tragedy itself?

   b. Do you suppose that the author intended any such disparagement?

   c. On what do you base your answer?

8a. If you watched television during those days, were your reactions in any way similar to those expressed by Arlen?

   b. Are they similar now, in retrospect?

   c. If your answers to 8a and 8b are different, what do you think accounts for the difference?

Expository Techniques

1. In highly impressionistic description such as this, the selection and placement of details (from the thousands available) are perhaps even more important than in most other types of writing. Comment briefly on each of the following details — i.e., the probable reason for its use and its effectiveness in helping to create the dominant impression.
   a. John Chancellor's self-respect.
   b. The various "ironies."
   c. The logging of telephone calls.
   d. The police chief's press appearance.
   e. The overseas comments.
   f. The Chevrolet commercial
   g. The various scenes "they" showed us.
   h. The cold drinks dispensed by the Red Cross.

2a. Clichés need not always be mere phrases nor do they require years to form by overuse. Show, using examples, how Arlen has made use of these facts. (Guide: *Clichés*.)

   b. How has he *used* sentimentality to serve his own purposes? (Guide: *Sentimentality*.)

3a. Besides a rather loose chronological system, what other principle apparently helped determine the arrangement of details?

   b. Can you think of another kind of arrangement that would have been more beneficial to the dominant impression? If so, explain it.

4a. Coherence is ordinarily a highly desirable quality in any kind of composition. (Guide: *Coherence*.) Does this essay have it? Justify your answer.

b. Does your answer indicate a weakness, or a virtue, in this writing? Justify your answer.

5a. Undoubtedly the author decided not to paragraph. (It would not be likely to "just happen," would it?) Was this a sound decision? Why, or why not?

b. Would it have been a good decision in any college writing you have done? Why, or why not?

6. Summarize the means, subtle or otherwise, by which the author achieved emphasis. (Guide: *Emphasis*.)

7a. How successful do you consider the terse and rather abrupt ending? Explain your reasons.

b. Which of the standard methods of signaling the end has the author adapted to his use? (Guide: *Closings*.)

c. Do you see the last sentence as sarcasm? Why, or why not? (Guide: *Irony*.)

Diction and Vocabulary

1a. Have you been able to determine the source of the coined word "Griefspeak"? If so, what is it?

b. Would we be correct to call it an allusion? (Guide: *Allusions*.)

c. What is its significance in this writing?

2. Explain why you think the author uses, or permits, so much repetition of sentence beginnings — e.g., "There were . . ." (Ten times); "They showed us . . ." (twelve times).

3a. What is the significance, here, of the French sentence "*Je suis . . .*"?

b. Was the author unwise to jeopardize rapport with his readers, many of whom do not read French? Why, or why not?

4a. What is a Theosophist?

b. What is meant by "mystique"? Why is it italicized?

5. There are few difficult words in this selection. Is that fact surprising? Why, or why not?

Suggestions for Writing and Discussion

1. What effect does the showing of films such as *Bonnie and Clyde* have on violence, or on public attitudes toward violence?

2. Develop the theme that we are all to blame for crimes such as the assassinations of the two Kennedys and of Martin Luther King, Jr.

(At the times these were popular self-accusations.) Or, if you prefer, show that it is a meaningless or purely emotional reaction.

3. Should photographers be permitted to film and to broadcast scenes
such as those of grieving relatives in church? Show the significance
of the problem, and, if you like, present both sides.

4. If you share Arlen's impressions of this sort of mass reaction, you
may be able to find one or more examples of similar social phenomena (not necessarily pertaining to death). Explain — without
trying to copy the author's style — the circumstances and the way
they impress you.

5. Why do people willingly stand for long, hot hours for such purposes
as watching a train go by?

(NOTE: Suggestions for topics requiring development by use of DESCRIP-
TION are on page 281, at the end of this section.)

MARTIN HOFFMAN

MARTIN HOFFMAN, born in 1935, is a staff psychiatrist at the Center for Special Problems at the San Francisco Health Department. He received a grant from the National Institute of Mental Health for the study of male homosexuals in the San Francisco Bay area and has taught a course on sexual deviance at both the undergraduate and graduate levels at the University of California, Berkeley. He is also experienced in psychoanalytic theory.

The Gay Bar

"The Gay Bar" is a portion of Hoffman's book *The Gay World* (1968), the controversial report on his three-year study of the homosexual scene in the San Francisco Bay area. In it, according to *Publisher's Weekly*, Hoffman "does for the homosexual subculture, its causes and patterns, what Vance Packard has done in more conventional areas" (see "New Directions of Marriage," Section 2). This selection provides us with a far different type of description than have the preceding two.

The gay bar has almost become a social institution in America. It is 1 the central public place around which gay life revolves and is to be found in all large and medium-sized cities across the country. We would like to describe here the "typical gay bar," although, of course, there is no such thing, any more than there is a "typical straight bar." Perhaps, narrowing our focus a bit, what we want to describe is what I call the "middle-class" gay bar, by which I mean not that all its members are necessarily middle-class socioeconomically, but rather that middle-class proprieties are observed and that there is nothing unique or specialized about the bar. We will not, for example, be concerned with the leather-jacket motorcycle bars,

Reprinted by permission of the publisher from Chapter 3 of *The Gay World*, by Martin Hoffman. © 1968 by Basic Books, Inc., Publishers, New York.

nor with the hustler bars so beautifully described by Rechy,[1] nor with those bars which provide entertainment such as drag shows and male go-go dancers.

Perhaps the most important fact about a gay bar is that it is a   2
sexual marketplace. That is, men go there for the purpose of seeking sexual partners, and if this function were not served by the bar there would be no gay bars, for, although homosexuals also go there to drink and socialize, the search for sexual experience is in some sense the core of the interaction in the bar. It should, however, be obvious that there must be more going on in the bar than simply people meeting and leaving; otherwise the bar could not exist as a commercial enterprise. People have to come there for a time long enough to drink, in order to make it profitable to the management to run these bars. And gay bars are very profitable and have sprung up in large numbers. It is estimated that there are about 60 gay bars in Los Angeles and about 40 in San Francisco. A number of heterosexuals have converted their own taverns into gay bars simply because they have found it more profitable to run a gay bar, even though they are sometimes not particularly delighted with the clientele. The gay bar plays a central role in the life of very many homosexuals — one which is much more important than the role played by straight bars in the life of all but a few heterosexuals. This is connected intimately with the use of the gay bar as a sexual marketplace and, of course, with the fact that homosexuals, as homosexuals, have really no place else where they can congregate without disclosing to the straight world that they are homosexual.

What does a gay bar look like? In the first place, unlike most   3
middle-class straight bars, it is almost exclusively populated by males. Sometimes non-homosexuals accidentally walk into a gay bar and it is usually this lack of women that makes them aware that they may have inadvertently walked into a homosexual setting. There are a few bars in which lesbians congregate along with male homosexuals, especially in cities which are not large enough to support a lesbian bar. But even in the larger cities, lesbian bars are not very common. They are never as large as the large metropolitan male gay bars. This is because female homosexuals are much less promiscuous than male homosexuals and really not able to support a sexual marketplace on the scale that males do.

---

[1] John Rechy, *City of Night* (1963).

Occasionally, "fruit flies," i.e., women who like to associate   4
with male homosexuals, are found in gay bars, although they are
not a very prominent part of any gay bar scene. Why a woman who
is not a lesbian would like to associate with male homosexuals is a
question which cannot be altogether answered in general, except to
say that some of these women obviously find homosexual men a
lot less threatening than heterosexual men, since the former are not
interested in them sexually. Since these women are not potential
sexual partners for the males, they are not potential sources of rejection for them either, and thereby they find themselves the subject of much attention by the male clientele. Consequently, they
are the beneficiaries of a great deal of sociability without being objects of seduction. Some women find this a very appealing position.

In the gay world there is a tremendous accent on youth and   5
this is reflected in the composition of the bar clientele. Youth is very
much at a premium and young men will go to the bars as soon as
they have passed the legal age limit. This varies from state to
state; it is 18 in New York and 21 in California. Along with the
younger men, there are somewhat older men who are trying to look
young. They attempt to accomplish this primarily by dress. The
typical bar costume is the same style of dress that an average college undergraduate might wear. It would consist of a sport shirt,
Levis, and loafers or sneakers. In this "typical" middle-class gay bar
which I am attempting to describe, extremely effeminate dress and
mannerisms are not well tolerated. Nevertheless, it would not be
correct to say that the scene in a gay bar looks like a fraternity stag
party. There is a tendency toward effeminacy in the overall impression one gets from observing the bar, although this may not necessarily be anything striking or flagrant. There is a certain softness
or absence of stereotypical masculine aggression present in the conversations and behavior of the bar patrons. Also, in spite of the
fact that the model bar costume is very much like that one would
see on a college campus, there is a good deal of special attention
paid by the bar patrons to their dress, so that they seem almost
extraordinarily well groomed. There is thus a feeling of fastidiousness about the appearance of the young men in the bar which, along
with their muted demeanor, rather clearly differentiates the overall
Gestalt of the gay bar from that which would be experienced upon
entering a gathering of young male heterosexuals. There are usually
a few clearly identifiable homosexuals, although the majority of

individuals in the bar are not identifiable and would not be thought homosexual in another setting. It seems to be the general consensus of gay bar observers that fights are less likely to break out in a gay than in a straight bar. This is, I think, probably attributable to the psychological characteristics of the clientele rather than to anything about the structure of the bar itself. Male homosexuals would certainly rather make love than war.

One of the clearest differences between the gay and the straight   6
bar is that in the gay bar the attention of the patrons is focused directly on each other. In a gay bar, for example, the patrons who are sitting at the bar itself usually face away from the bar and look toward the other people in the room and toward the door. When a new patron walks in, he receives a good deal of scrutiny, and people engaged in conversation with each other just naturally assume that their interlocutors will turn away from them to watch each new entering patron. All this is, of course, part of the pervasive looking and cruising which goes on in the bar.

There is a great deal of milling about in the bar and individuals   7
tend to engage in short, superficial conversations with each other. They try to make the circuit around the bar to see everyone in it, perhaps stopping to chat with their friends but usually not for very long. In a way, the shortness and superficiality of the conversations in the bar mirror that same brevity and shallowness of interpersonal relations which characterize gay life as a whole.

Heterosexual observers and even homosexuals who are not ha-   8
bitués of the bar scene often express great perplexity about the bars — they cannot quite understand what's going on there. They seem to be bewildered by the sight of all these young men standing around and communicating so little with one another. The patrons stand along the walls, it seems, for hours, without speaking. They move around the room and talk at length with almost no one. One heterosexual observer said that he felt as if everyone in the room were standing around waiting for some important figure to come in, but of course he never comes. He likened the scene to a reception for a foreign ambassador, where everyone stands around simply marking time until the dignitary arrives. In a sense, this observer was correct, for the young men *are* waiting for some important person to arrive, one who will never arrive — but it is not a foreign ambassador. Each is waiting for a handsome young prince to come and carry him off in his arms. They're waiting for the ideal sexual object, and if they don't find him they may very well go home

alone, in spite of the fact that there are sometimes hundreds of other attractive young men right there in the bar.

The gay bar, then, in a sense may be thought of as a stage on 9 which is played out a fantasy in which the hero never arrives. The reason why heterosexuals and even some homosexuals cannot understand what is going on is because they are not a party to this fantasy. They imagine that if you are going to a place to seek a sexual partner, you go in, look around a little bit, walk up to somebody that you like, engage in a conversation, and then go out together. And sometimes this is precisely what does occur in the gay bar. Very often, in fact, but the bewildering problem which confronts the uninitiated observer is why this does not happen more often: why, in fact, all these good-looking and well-dressed young men are standing around uncommunicative.

Sherri Cavan [2] has made the suggestion that in the homosexual 10 pickup bar it may happen that encounters are never begun because each party is waiting for the other to offer the first words of greeting. This is presumably due to the fact that when the situation involves two males, it is not clear who is expected to make the initial overture. One cannot deny the saliency of this observation. Nevertheless, I do not think it alone accounts fully for the strange situation in the gay bar, since one would expect the reverse to occur just as well, i.e., since both parties can make the initial overture, one would think that at least one of the members of the hypothetical pair could overcome his shyness. I think the sociological explanation fails to take into account the psychological factors involved. As many observers have noted, homosexuals are very much afraid of rejection, and hence, have an inordinate hesitancy about making an approach. I think this is due to the following reason: the only aspect of their self which male homosexuals are able to adequately present in a bar situation is their physical appearance. If they are rejected in making a conversational opening, this is interpreted (probably correctly) to mean a rejection of that crucial part of themselves, namely, their desirability as a sexual partner. Hence, their self-esteem is very much at stake and they have a great deal to lose by being rejected.

It must be remembered that in the gay world the only real 11 criterion of value is physical attractiveness; consequently, a rejec-

---

[2] Sherri Cavan, *Liquor License: An Ethnography of Bar Behavior* (1966), p. 192.

tion by a desired partner is a rejection of the only valued part of one's identity in that world. When we understand this, I think we understand why the fear of rejection is so prevalent among homosexual men.

The gay bar, is, then, a lot less licentious than people who are   12
not aware of what is going on there might be inclined to think. When heterosexual men enter a gay bar for the first time for the purpose of simply visiting it, they often seem afraid that somehow they will be rapidly approached, or perhaps even attacked, by the sexual deviants present inside the bar. This, of course, is about as far from reality as it is possible to imagine. It would not be unusual if none of the patrons would engage them in conversation during the entire course of the evening. If they are not young and handsome, they may well have great difficulty in communicating with anyone after even a great deal of effort on their part.

A word should be said, I suppose, about the function of the   13
gay bar as a source of group solidarity and as a place where one can meet one's friends and exchange gossip. I think, however, that this function is obvious and that it need not be elaborated upon. Many homosexuals frequent gay bars for reasons other than seeking sexual partners. If sex eventuates from the bar interaction, this is fine, but it is not the reason they went there in the first place. They went there for sociability. And yet this too must be qualified, for in the back of their minds is usually the thought that perhaps that special person will walk through the door tonight and they will meet him and go home with him.

The "cosmetic" quality of the gay bar is a result, in large part,   14
of the need for anonymity which pervades all the public places of the gay world. If one can only present the visible and non-identifying aspect of one's identity, one's physical appearance will be the central aspect that can be displayed to others. If homosexuals could meet *as homosexuals* in the kinds of social settings in which heterosexuals can (e.g., at school, at work) where the emphasis on finding sexual partners is not the controlling force behind all the social interaction which transpires, a great deal of the anonymous promiscuity which now characterizes homosexual encounters would be replaced by a more "normal" kind of meeting between two persons. Perhaps, then, the sexual relationships which develop would become more stable. Maybe the gay bar itself would not change — this can only be a matter for conjecture — but, at any rate, it would not be so central to gay life.

Meanings and Values

1a. Where would you place this writing on an objective-subjective continuum? (See Guide to Terms: *Objective/Subjective.*)

b. Is there a dominant impression? If so, what is it?

c. If there is a dominant impression, is it sufficient to give the description desirable unity?

2a. Explain more fully the meaning of "stereotypical masculine aggression" (par. 5).

b. If you have had some experience in a "typical straight bar," or in a similar setting, do you think one necessarily finds such "aggression" there? Explain.

3a. Clarify the author's meaning of the sentence beginning, "If homosexuals could meet . . ." (par. 14).

b. Do you think that this is a valid observation? (Consider, for instance, whether even heterosexuals ordinarily meet *as* heterosexuals in "social settings" such as school and work.)

4. At the outset the author states that his purpose is to "describe" the gay bar (par. 1), but description was obviously not his only purpose, perhaps not even his primary one.

a. What other do you think he had?

b. How well did he succeed?

c. Was it a worthwhile endeavor? Why, or why not? (Guide: *Evaluation.*)

Expository Techniques

1. What useful functions are served by the introductory paragraph, other than simply providing a way to start the essay?

2a. A rhetorical question begins the actual physical description. What is it? (Guide: *Rhetorical Question.*)

b. Why is it a rhetorical question?

3a. How effective do you think the author's choice of details is for his purposes?

b. If you think other details would have improved his descriptive analysis, what are they? Why are they needed?

c. Give several examples of details that might be desirable if the purpose had been to create a highly impressionistic description.

4a. What other patterns of exposition are used in this essay?

b. Cite two examples of each.

5a. Some of the paragraphs here are somewhat longer than those in most modern writing. Are they too long? If so, what is the disadvantage?

b. Select one of the longest, locate its topic sentence, and consider whether or not all parts of the paragraph are related to it. What, if anything, does this tell you about its unity? (Guide: *Unity*.)

c. If unity is lacking, how might this weakness be overcome? Be specific.

Diction and Vocabulary

1a. In the first paragraph Hoffman uses the editorial "we." Is this advantageous, or not? Why? (Guide: *Editorial "We."*)

b. Why do you think he did not continue its use throughout the essay?

2a. The seemingly excess wordiness of numerous passages in this essay might be criticized. Do any seem too wordy to you? (Guide: *Diction; Syntax*.)

b. If so, cite as many specific examples as you can.

c. Select one of these and rewrite it with the same exact meaning but with greater economy of language and therefore, perhaps, with greater clarity and more effective syntax.

3a. Hoffman uses several colloquial expressions, some so new that they cannot be found in some dictionaries. Cite five that you would classify as colloquial. (Guide: *Colloquial*.)

b. Why do they not alter the generally serious tone of the essay?

c. Would the writing be better, however, without them? Why, or why not?

4a. Why is "*Gestalt*" printed in italics (par. 5)?

b. What does it mean, as used here?

c. Is it really needed here, or would a more common word have done as well? If the latter, suggest one.

5. Study the author's uses of the following words, consulting the dictionary as needed: proprieties (par. 1); heterosexuals (2, and others); inadvertently, promiscuous (3); flagrant, fastidiousness, demeanor, consensus (5); interlocutors, pervasive (6); habitués (8); saliency, hypothetical, inordinate, crucial (10); criterion (11); licentious (12); eventuates (13); transpires, conjecture (14).

Suggestions for Writing and Discussion

1. If, through observation or serious reading, you have noticed any changes of public attitude toward homosexuality, describe such changes and what you believe to be the reasons for them. If you like, project these trends into the future.

2. What do you think should be the function of law in attempting to regulate private morality — e.g., between "consenting adults"?

3. What possible cause/effect relationship, if any, do you see between "hard-core" pornography and sexual deviation?

4. If you have read or heard authoritative and recent discussions on the causes of homosexuality, explain one or more of these theories. If you like, compare two of them.

5. Some religions have traditionally taught that homosexuality is a "sin against nature." How would you interpret the meaning of this dictum?

Writing Suggestions for Section 9
Description

1. Primarily by way of impressionistic description that focuses on a single dominant impression, show and explain the mood, or atmosphere, of one of the following:

   a. A county fair.
   b. A ball game.
   c. A rodeo.
   d. A wedding.
   e. A funeral.
   f. A riot.
   g. A ghost town.
   h. A cave.
   i. A mine.
   j. An antique shop.
   k. A party.
   l. A family dinner.
   m. A traffic jam.
   n. Reveille.
   o. An airport (or bus depot).
   p. A drag race (or horse race).
   q. A home during one of its rush hours.
   r. The last night of Christmas shopping.
   s. A natural scene at a certain time of day.
   t. The campus at examination time.
   u. A certain person at a time of great emotion — e.g., joy, anger, grief.

2. Using objective description as your basic pattern, explain the functional qualities or the significance of one of the following:

   a. A passenger train.
   b. A freeway system.
   c. A state park.
   d. A house for sale.
   e. A public building.
   f. A dairy barn.
   g. An ideal workshop (or hobby room).
   h. An ideal garage.
   i. A hippie-type commune.
   j. The layout of a town (or airport).
   k. The layout of a farm.
   l. A certain type of boat.

10

Using *Narration* as an Expository Technique

Attempts to classify the functions of narration seem certain to develop difficulties and end in arbitrary and sometimes fuzzy distinctions. These need not distress us, however, if we remember that narration remains narration — a factual or fictional report of a sequence of events — and that our only reason for trying to divide it into categories is to find some means of studying its uses.

In a sense, as we have already seen in Section 5, exposition by process analysis makes one important, if rather narrow, use of narration, since it explains in sequence how specific steps lead to completion of some process. But at the other extreme is narration that has very little to do with exposition: the story itself is the important thing, and instead of a series of steps leading obviously to a completed act, events *develop* out of each other and build suspense, however mild, through some kind of conflict. Here narration assumes importance in its own right as one of the four basic forms of prose, and it includes the novel and short story, as well as some news and sports reporting. Because we are studying exposition, however, we must avoid getting too involved with these uses of narration; they require special techniques, the study of which would require a whole course or, in fact, several courses.

Between the extremes of a very usable analysis of process and a very intriguing narration for the story's sake — and often seeming to blur into one or the other — is narration for *explanation's* sake, to explain a concept that is more than process and that might have been explained by one of the other patterns of exposition. Here only the form is narrative; the function is expository.

Fortunately, the average student seldom needs to use narration for major explanatory purposes, as it has been used in each of the following selections. But to learn the handling of even minor or localized narration, the best procedure (short of taking several college courses, or at least one that concentrates on the narrative form) is simply to observe how successful writers use it to perform various functions. Localized narration can sometimes be helpful as an aid in developing any of the other major patterns of exposition.

The most common problems can be summarized as follows:

1. *Selection of details.* As in writing description, the user of narration always has far more details available than he can or should use. Good unity demands that he select only those which are most relevant to his purpose and the effect he wants to create.

2. *Time order.* The writer can use straight chronology, relating events as they happen (the usual method in minor uses of narration); or he can use the flashback method, leaving the sequence temporarily in order to go back and relate some now-significant happening of a time prior to the main action. If flashback is used, it should be deliberate and for a valid reason — not merely because the episode was neglected at the beginning.

3. *Transitions.* The lazy writer of narration is apt to resort to the transitional style of a three-year-old: ". . . and then we . . . and then she . . . and then we. . . ." Avoiding this style may tax his ingenuity, but invariably the result is worth the extra investment of time and thought.

4. *Point of view.* This is a large and complex subject if dealt with fully, as a course in narration would do. Briefly, however, the writer should decide at the beginning whether the reader is to experience the action through a character's eyes (and ears and brain), or from an overall, objective view. This decision makes a difference in how much can be told, whose thoughts or secret actions can be included. The writer must be consistent throughout the narrative and include only information that could logically be known through the adopted point of view.

5. *Dialogue.* Presumably the writer already knows the mechanics of using quotations. Beyond these, his problems are to make conversation as natural-sounding as possible and yet to keep it from rambling through many useless details — to keep the narrative moving forward by *means* of dialogue.

As in most patterns of writing, the use of expository narration is most likely to be successful if the writer constantly keeps his purpose and his audience in mind, remembering that the only reason for using the method in the first place — for doing *any* writing — is to communicate ideas. Soundness, clarity, and interest are the best means of attaining this goal.

MARTIN GANSBERG

MARTIN GANSBERG, born in Brooklyn, N.Y., in 1920, received a
Bachelor of Social Sciences degree from St. John's University.
He has been an editor and reporter on the *New York Times*
since 1942, including a three-year period as editor of its international edition in Paris. He also served on the faculty of
Fairleigh Dickinson University for fifteen years. Gansberg has
written for many magazines, including *Diplomat*, *Catholic Digest*, *Facts*, and *U.S. Lady*.

38 Who Saw Murder Didn't Call the Police

"38 Who Saw Murder..." was written for the *New York
Times* in 1964, and for obvious reasons it has been anthologized frequently since then. Cast in a deceptively simple
news style, it still provides material for serious thought, as
well as a means of studying another use and technique of
narration.

For more than half an hour 38 respectable, law-abiding citizens in   1
Queens watched a killer stalk and stab a woman in three separate
attacks in Kew Gardens.

Twice their chatter and the sudden glow of their bedroom   2
lights interrupted him and frightened him off. Each time he returned, sought her out, and stabbed her again. Not one person
telephoned the police during the assault; one witness called after
the woman was dead.

That was two weeks ago today.   3

Still shocked is Assistant Chief Inspector Frederick M. Lussen,   4
in charge of the borough's detectives and a veteran of 25 years of
homicide investigations. He can give a matter-of-fact recitation on
many murders. But the Kew Gardens slaying baffles him — not be-

cause it is a murder, but because the "good per
the police.

"As we have reconstructed the crime," he
had three chances to kill this woman during a 35-n...
He returned twice to complete the job. If we had been called ...
he first attacked, the woman might not be dead now."

This is what the police say happened beginning at 3:20 A.M. in   6
the staid, middle-class, tree-lined Austin Street area:

Twenty-eight-year-old Catherine Genovese, who was called   7
Kitty by almost everyone in the neighborhood, was returning home
from her job as manager of a bar in Hollis. She parked her red
Fiat in a lot adjacent to the Kew Gardens Long Island Rail Road
Station, facing Mowbray Place. Like many residents of the neigh-
borhood, she had parked there day after day since her arrival from
Connecticut a year ago, although the railroad frowns on the prac-
tice.

She turned off the lights of her car, locked the door, and started   8
to walk the 100 feet to the entrance of her apartment at 82–70
Austin Street, which is in a Tudor building, with stores in the first
floor and apartments on the second.

The entrance to the apartment is in the rear of the building   9
because the front is rented to retail stores. At night the quiet neighborhood is shrouded in the slumbering darkness that marks most
residential areas.

Miss Genovese noticed a man at the far end of the lot, near a   10
seven-story apartment house at 82–40 Austin Street. She halted.
Then, nervously, she headed up Austin Street toward Lefferts
Boulevard, where there is a call box to the 102nd Police Precinct in
nearby Richmond Hill.

She got as far as a street light in front of a bookstore before   11
the man grabbed her. She screamed. Lights went on in the 10-story
apartment house at 82–67 Austin Street, which faces the bookstore.
Windows slid open and voices punctuated the early-morning stillness.

Miss Genovese screamed: "Oh, my God, he stabbed me! Please   12
help me! Please help me!"

From one of the upper windows in the apartment house, a man   13
called down: "Let that girl alone!"

The assailant looked up at him, shrugged, and walked down   14 tin Street toward a white sedan parked a short distance away. .iss Genovese struggled to her feet.

Lights went out. The killer returned to Miss Genovese, now 15 trying to make her way around the side of the building by the parking lot to get to her apartment. The assailant stabbed her again.

"I'm dying!" she shrieked. "I'm dying!" 16

Windows were opened again, and lights went on in many 17 apartments. The assailant got into his car and drove away. Miss Genovese staggered to her feet. A city bus, O–10, the Lefferts Boulevard line to Kennedy International Airport, passed. It was 3:35 A.M.

The assailant returned. By then, Miss Genovese had crawled 18 to the back of the building, where the freshly painted brown doors to the apartment house held out hope for safety. The killer tried the first door; she wasn't there. At the second door, 82–62 Austin Street, he saw her slumped on the floor at the foot of the stairs. He stabbed her a third time — fatally.

It was 3:50 by the time the police received their first call, from 19 a man who was a neighbor of Miss Genovese. In two minutes they were at the scene. The neighbor, a 70-year-old woman, and another woman were the only persons on the street. Nobody else came forward.

The man explained that he had called the police after much 20 deliberation. He had phoned a friend in Nassau County for advice and then he had crossed the roof of the building to the apartment of the elderly woman to get her to make the call.

"I didn't want to get involved," he sheepishly told the police. 21

Six days later, the police arrested Winston Moseley, a 29-year- 22 old business-machine operator, and charged him with homicide. Moseley had no previous record. He is married, has two children and owns a home at 133–19 Sutter Avenue, South Ozone Park, Queens. On Wednesday, a court committed him to Kings County Hospital for psychiatric observation.

When questioned by the police, Moseley also said that he had 23 slain Mrs. Annie May Johnson, 24, of 146–12 133d Avenue, Jamaica, on Feb. 29 and Barbara Kralik, 15, of 174–17 140th Avenue, Springfield Gardens, last July. In the Kralik case, the police are holding Alvin L. Mitchell, who is said to have confessed that slaying.

The police stressed how simple it would have been to have 24 gotten in touch with them. "A phone call," said one of the detectives, "would have done it." The police may be reached by dialing "O" for operator or SPring 7–3100.

Today witnesses from the neighborhood, which is made up of one-family homes in the $35,000 to $60,000 range with the exception of the two apartment houses near the railroad station, find it difficult to explain why they didn't call the police. 25

A housewife, knowingly if quite casually, said, "We thought it was a lover's quarrel." A husband and wife both said, "Frankly, we were afraid." They seemed aware of the fact that events might have been different. A distraught woman, wiping her hands in her apron, said, "I didn't want my husband to get involved." 26

One couple, now willing to talk about that night, said they heard the first screams. The husband looked thoughtfully at the bookstore where the killer first grabbed Miss Genovese. 27

"We went to the window to see what was happening," he said, "but the light from our bedroom made it difficult to see the street." The wife, still apprehensive, added: "I put out the light and we were able to see better." 28

Asked why they hadn't called the police, she shrugged and replied: "I don't know." 29

A man peeked out from a slight opening in the doorway to his apartment and rattled off an account of the killer's second attack. Why hadn't he called the police at the time? "I was tired," he said without emotion. "I went back to bed." 30

It was 4:25 A.M. when the ambulance arrived to take the body of Miss Genovese. It drove off. "Then," a solemn police detective said, "the people came out." 31

Meanings and Values

1. Why has this narrative account of old news (the murder provided its only headlines in 1964) retained its significance to this day?

2. Are you able to see in this event a sort of microcosm of any larger condition or situation? If so, explain, using examples as needed to illustrate your ideas.

3a. If one of the author's chief purposes was to propound such a central theme (as indicated in your answers to questions 1 and 2), how might he have done so without using narration at all? Specify what patterns of exposition he could have used instead.

b. Would any of them have been as effective as narration *for the purpose?* Why, or why not?

4. Show how this selection could be used as an illustration in an explanatory discussion of abstract and concrete writing. (See Guide to Terms: *Concrete/Abstract.*)

Expository Techniques

1a. What standard introductory technique is exemplified in paragraph 1? (Guide: *Introductions.*)
 b. How effective do you consider it?
 c. If you see anything ironic in the fact stated there, explain what the irony is. (Guide: *Irony.*)

2a. Where does the main narration begin?
 b. What, then, is the function of the preceding paragraphs?

3a. Study several of the paragraph transitions within the narration itself to determine Gansberg's method of advancing the time sequence (to avoid overuse of "and then"). What is the technique?
 b. Is another needed? Why, or why not?

4a. What possible reasons do you see for the predominant use of short paragraphs in this piece?
 b. Does this selection lose any effectiveness because of the short paragraphs?

5. Undoubtedly, the author carefully selected the few quotations from witnesses that he uses. What principle, or principles, do you think applied to his selection?

6. Explain why you think the quotation from the "solemn police detective" was, or was not, deliberately and carefully chosen to concude the piece. (Guide: *Closings.*)

7a. Briefly identify the point of view of the writing. (Guide: *Point of View.*)
 b. Is it consistent throughout?
 c. Show the relation, as you see it, between this point of view and the author's apparent attitude toward his subject matter.

8a. Does he permit himself any sentimentality? If so, where? (Guide: *Sentimentality.*)
 b. If not, specifically what could he have permitted that would have slipped into melodrama or sentimentality?

Diction and Vocabulary

1a. Why do you think the author used no difficult words in this narration?

b. Do you find the writing at all belittling to college people because of this fact? Why, or why not?

Suggestions for Writing and Discussion

1. Use both developed and undeveloped examples to show the prevalence, among individuals, of an anti-involvement attitude today. Or, if you prefer, show that this accusation is unjustified.

2. If this narration can be regarded as a sort of microcosm (see question 2 of "Meanings and Values"), select one example from the larger subject and develop it on whatever theme you choose. Your example could be from the international level, if you like (and if you don't mind becoming the center of a controversy) — e.g., the recent cries of "murder!" from numerous small countries. If you prefer, go into more distant (and therefore less controversial) history for your example.

3. If such a crime as the Genovese murder were happening in an area or a situation where police were not so instantly available, what do you think an observer should do about it? What would *you* do? Justify your stand on all possible grounds.

(NOTE: Suggestions for topics requiring development by NARRATION are on page 318, at the end of this section.)

DENNIS SMITH

DENNIS SMITH, born in New York City and raised in a slum tenement, knows well the area about which he writes. He quit school at 15 and for several years worked as delivery boy, cab driver, billing manager, and as a cowboy in Nevada. While serving four years in the Air Force as a radar operator, Smith passed his high school equivalency examination. He returned to New York City, where he joined the fire department and began attending New York University, from which he received a B.S. in English in 1970 and where he is now studying for a master's degree in communications. Smith and his family live in Washingtonville, N.Y.

Malicious False Alarms

"Malicious False Alarms" (editor's title) is an excerpt from Smith's book *Report from Engine Co. 82.* The use of narration differs here from the single-line reporting of the Genovese murder (in the preceding selection); its use is localized, confined to two separate events, both of which are closely related to the overall exposition. Smith's style is simple and, therefore, although entirely appropriate to the subject matter, can be deceptive to the student who still believes writing is ready to send right off to the printer (or the instructor) just as it comes from his head.

An average of eight firemen die each year while doing their duty in New York City. Only six died last year, and I don't want to think about how many will die this year, or next. Almost five thousand firemen were injured in the line of duty last year. The injuries cost the city 65,000 days in medical leaves. 1

There is a sign in the kitchen of my firehouse. It is inconspicuously hung, and it reads with a proper amount of ambiguity: THIS COULD BE THE NIGHT! We don't talk about the hazards of the 2 trade in the firehouse. There is no sense in talking about what we hope never becomes a reality for us, and for our families. It's all part of the job, and like committed Calvinists we accept what's written in the cards for us.

Just yesterday a man was killed. He was assigned to Rescue Company 1, and he was working on the roof of a burning warehouse. The roof had been weakened by the fire, and it gave in. The man fell through the roof and into an air shaft. He passed eight floors before he hit the bottom.

I was sitting in the kitchen of the firehouse when the bells came in. First five short rings, a pause, five more, a pause, another five, another pause, and the final five. Signal 5–5–5–5 has a special meaning to us. Put the flag at half mast, and listen to the department radio for the message.

There is a five-by-five cubicle at the front of the firehouse. Inside the small partition there is a man writing the signal in the department company journal. He turns the volume of the department radio up as we gather around it. This is the man assigned housewatch duty, and he knows what he has to do. After recording the signal, he moves to the outside of the firehouse and brings the colors to half-mast. He returns to the watch-desk and prepares to write the message in the company journal. His face is pensive, and he is asking himself the same question we all ask ourselves: I wonder if I know the guy?

The radio begins to squawk the message, and the housewatchman begins to write. *"The signal 5–5–5–5 has been transmitted, and the message is as follows: It is with deep regret that the department announces the death of Fireman 1st Grade Edward Tuite which occurred while operating at Box 583, at 1125 hours this date."*

None of us there knew the man personally, but we all felt the loss. We went about our work for the rest of the day without talking about it.

I had a friend we don't talk about either. His name was Mike Carr, and he was an upstanding kind of a guy. He was the union delegate of Engine 85. Only a few days before his death I had mentioned to him that we should clean out an old locker and use it for our union business. It was a shabby old locker, but it could be used to store medical forms, work contracts, information bulletins, and other union material. Mike thought it was a good idea,

and within the hour he had the locker cleared and had begun painting it. Anything that had the smallest benefit for firemen would
interest Mike, and he worked untiringly for the men in the firehouse.

    Then a nine-year-old boy reached up and pulled the alarm-   9
box handle. Kids do this a lot in the South Bronx. His friends gig-
gled, and they all ran up the street to watch the fire engines come.
The box came in on the bells — 2787 — Southern Boulevard and
172nd Street. Mike pulled himself up on the side step of the apparatus. The heavy wheels turned up Intervale Avenue, the officer's
foot pressing hard on the siren. At Freeman Street the apparatus
turned right, and Mike lost grip. He spun from the side like a top.
Marty Hannon and Juan Moran jumped off the apparatus even
before it came to a screeching stop. There was blood all over. They
could see that Mike had stopped breathing. Marty cleared some of
the blood away with a handkerchief, and began mouth-to-mouth
resuscitation. He told me all he remembers of those agonizing
minutes was the Battalion Chief's voice blaring over the Department radio: *"Transmit signal ten ninety-two for Box 2787. Malicious false alarm."*

    The following day the city's newspapers ran the story stating   10
that the Uniformed Firefighters Association was offering a thousand dollars reward for information leading to the arrest of the
person who pulled the box. That afternoon a nine-year-old boy
was led through the heavy iron doors of the Forty-first Precinct
House. News spreads quickly in the South Bronx, and the boy's
friends told their parents, who called the cops.

    While the boy was being questioned at the police station,   11
people from the Hoe Avenue Association, a neighborhood action
group, painted alarm box number 2787 black, and hung a sign
around it. The sign was in two parts, the top half in Spanish, and
the bottom in English. It read: A FIREMAN WAS KILLED WHILE COMING
HERE TO A FALSE ALARM. Before the paint was dry another false
alarm was pulled at the same box, and the men of Engine 85 took
the sign down.

    Mike had two sons, one seven, the other nine — two brave   12
and frightened boys now walking on either side of their mother,
walking slowly behind a shining red fire engine that moves between endless rows of their school chums, and hundreds of firemen. They look up at the flag-draped casket on top of the fire en-

gine and feel proud that their daddy is the cause of all this ceremony, but they are also frightened because they are old enough to realize that there is a tomorrow, and it is going to be different without him.

The young boy in the police station is frightened too, but in a 13 different way. He is confused, and wonders why everyone is so upset. All the kids pull false alarms. At least the kids he pals around with do. He came to this country from Puerto Rico five years ago, and the kids on the block taught him that you have to make your own fun in the South Bronx. You can play in the abandoned buildings, they told him, or in the towering trash heaps in the backyards, or in musty, rat-infested cellars. There used to be a boys' club in the neighborhood, but it burned down and never reopened. He learned, too, that pulling the handle of a fire-alarm box causes excitement, and a certain pleasure that comes with being responsible for all the noise, the sirens, the air horns. Why is everybody so upset?

I know why I am upset. My company alone, Engine 82, re- 14 sponded to over two thousand false alarms last year. Many of them were caused by kids like this. Kids with no place to go, nothing to do. Kids whose parents never talk to them, never have a surprise gift for them, or a warm squeeze. Kids whose real meaning in the family is that they symbolize a few extra dollars in the welfare check each month. Kids whose parents did not know anything about contraception to begin with, and never learned to love what they did not ask for. Kids born of poverty and ignorance into a system of deprivation.

What do you do with a nine-year-old boy who has pulled a 15 false alarm that has resulted in a death? It is easy to say that the death was unfortunate, but peripheral to the crime of pulling a false alarm. It is even easier to say that the perpetrator is only nine years old, and so should be made aware of the severity of his actions merely by being given over to the social services for guidance care. This, in fact, is what happened to the child.

I do not advocate cutting off the child's hand, but I do think 16 he should have been institutionalized for a year. I understand the sad social conditions in which this child has been forced to live, but I have lost sympathy for the cry that poverty founded the crime, not the boy. Anyone found guilty of pulling a malicious false alarm should be sent to jail for a year, or, if under sixteen, to a reform school. But, in the eight years I have been a fireman, I have seen only one man jailed, and I have responded to thousands of alarms that proved to be maliciously false.

In the city of New York last year, firemen responded to 72,060   17
false alarms — an average of 197 daily. Yet, the courts and the Police Department do not look on the pulling of a false alarm as a serious offense. Few are arrested, fewer are found guilty, and fewer still are punished.

Besides Mike Carr, I know of two other firemen who were   18
killed en route to false alarms in New York City in the past eight years. But, it is not just firemen who are victimized by false alarms. Often while firemen are answering a false alarm at one end of their district, a serious fire breaks out at the other end. Time is the most important factor in fighting fires. I can remember many fires where, had we been there a minute or two sooner, we probably would have saved someone's life. Three hundred and seven people died in New York City fires last year. Statistics are not available, but you can be sure that some of those deaths could have been avoided if firemen had not been answering a false alarm minutes before.

Mike Carr is dead, and his widow will have to make it on   19
just half the salary she was used to. It's strange, but had Mike come through the accident with a disabling injury, he would have been pensioned off with three-fourths of his salary. His wife would have been happy to have him alive. But he died, and she gets half his salary to support his family. The same will go to the widow of the man who fell through the roof yesterday.

We don't talk about Mike Carr in the firehouse. We think   20
about him often, but we don't talk about him. Words of sentiment and emotion do not come easily.

Meanings and Values

1. Why does the author consider the sign in the firehouse "ambig-uous," even properly so (par. 2)?

2. It seems to be normal to "talk about" tragedy, even the death of a relative or close friend. Why do you suppose firemen are different, at least in the situations narrated by Smith?

3a. There is a degree of irony, subtle perhaps, in the last sentence of paragraph 9. Why? (See Guide to Terms: *Irony.*)

   b. What kind is it?

4a. Show the importance of point of view in the overall effect of a writing, by demonstrating how "Malicious False Alarms" would have been a different piece altogether, even if comprising most of the same materials, if written by someone not a fireman himself. Use specific examples — e.g., the city treasurer, a sociologist, a fireman's wife. (Guide: *Point of View*.)

b. How, if at all, is emphasis involved? (Guide: *Emphasis*.)

Expository Techniques

1. Sometimes good coherence does come naturally, especially if the writer keeps always in mind the ease of his reader. But frequently some extra transitional device is needed, or some rearrangement of parts so that new developments can seem better linked to the old. (Guide: *Coherence, Transitions*.)

a. How is smooth transition provided — deliberately or not — for entry into the first narrative account (pars. 3–7)?

b. How is smooth transition accomplished into the second narrative (pars. 8–12)?

c. When this one ends, how has the author already provided for smooth transition to the scene at the police station?

2a. Comment on the choice of details — from the hundreds that must have been available — for paragraph 14 alone.

b. Could the author have found more effective details for his purpose? If so, provide examples.

3a. Paragraph 14 also contains several roughly parallel constructions. (Guide: *Parallel Structure*.) What is gained, or lost, by this treatment?

b. How is it a matter of syntax? (Guide: *Syntax*.)

4. Syntax can be made to create many special effects — although it should be noted that casual readers are seldom conscious of these at the time and certainly remain unaware of any manipulation to achieve them. (But readers will know whether, for them, the writing was successful — and that must depend greatly on the author's willingness to do his "homework.")

a. Study paragraph 3 and the middle portion of paragraph 9 to determine anything distinctive in the style of the sentences. What is unusual about them?

b. What effect is thereby created?

c. What other syntactic benefits, if any, are also achieved?

5a. Much of this selection, in the hands of a less competent writer, could easily have become slushy with sentimentality. Use the last part of paragraph 9 and all of paragraph 12, to analyze how Smith achieves strong emphasis in the process of *avoiding* sentimentality. (Guide: *Sentimentality/Emphasis*.)

b. Are the resulting style and tone consistent with the overall content and the author's particular point of view? (Guide: *Style/Tone.*) Why, or why not?

Diction and Vocabulary

1a. Cite examples of the numerous colloquial expressions in this writing. (Guide: *Colloquial.*)
 b. Why is their use appropriate, or not appropriate?
2. What justification can you find in the switching to present tense in certain portions of "Malicious False Alarms"?
3. Why is it not surprising that we find few, if any, "dictionary-type" words?

Suggestions for Writing and Discussion

1. What *should* be done with a nine-year-old who turns in a false alarm and thereby causes a death?
2. Do you think Smith is justified in losing sympathy for "the cry that poverty founded the crime, not the boy"?
3. Earlier in the book the author writes, "We are different from the rest of the people who work in this town: bankers, ad-men, truck drivers, secretaries, sellers and buyers, all have a high degree of assurance that they will return home from work in the evening the same way they left in the morning — on their feet. . . . Firemen are never sure." Then why do men choose to become firemen — or to continue as such after they learn what it is like?
4. Several other occupations, however — including some of those "in this town" — are as hazardous as being a fireman. What are some of them? Why do people still enter those occupations?
5. A reviewer in the Philadelphia *Bulletin* wrote: "Smith shows that the glue that holds firemen together is a combination of brotherhood and love — the sharing of common danger, and punishment, and dependence one upon the other that creates a bond that those outside the fire service cannot truly comprehend." What other human endeavors can create this kind of bond? Explain fully.

(NOTE: Suggestions for topics requiring development by NARRATION are on page 318, at the end of this section.)

GEORGE ORWELL

GEORGE ORWELL (1903–1950), whose real name was Eric Blair, was a British novelist and essayist, one of the best-known satirists of the twentieth century. He was born in India, educated at Eton in England, and then served for five years with the Imperial Police in Burma. During the 1930's, Orwell spent several years writing in Paris and one year fighting in the Spanish Civil War, during which he was wounded. He finally settled in England, where he wrote his best-known books, *Animal Farm* (1945), a satire on Soviet history, and *1984* (1949), a vivid picture of life in a projected totalitarian society. He was sharply aware of injustices in democratic societies and was consistently socialistic in his views. Many of Orwell's best essays are collected in *Critical Essays* (1946), *Shooting an Elephant* (1950), and *Such, Such Were the Joys* (1953).

A Hanging

"A Hanging" is typical of Orwell's essays in its setting — Burma — and in its subtle but biting commentary on colonialism, on capital punishment, even on one aspect of human nature itself. Although he is ostensibly giving a straightforward account of an execution, the author masterfully uses descriptive details and dialogue to create atmosphere and sharply drawn characterizations. The essay gives concrete form to a social message that is often delivered much less effectively in abstract generalities.

It was in Burma, a sodden morning of the rains. A sickly light, like yellow tinfoil, was slanting over the high walls into the jail yard. We were waiting outside the condemned cells, a row of sheds fronted with double bars, like small animal cages. Each cell mea-

1

sured about ten feet by ten and was quite bare within except for a plank bed and a pot for drinking water. In some of them brown, silent men were squatting at the inner bars, with their blankets draped round them. These were the condemned men, due to be hanged within the next week or two.

One prisoner had been brought out of his cell. He was a Hindu,   2
a puny wisp of a man, with a shaven head and vague liquid eyes. He had a thick, sprouting moustache, absurdly too big for his body, rather like the moustache of a comic man on the films. Six tall Indian warders were guarding him and getting him ready for the gallows. Two of them stood by with rifles and fixed bayonets, while the others handcuffed him, passed a chain through his handcuffs and fixed it to their belts, and lashed his arms tight to his sides. They crowded very close about him, with their hands always on him in a careful, caressing grip, as though all the while feeling him to make sure he was there. It was like men handling a fish which is still alive and may jump back into the water. But he stood quite unresisting, yielding his arms limply to the ropes, as though he hardly noticed what was happening.

Eight o'clock struck and a bugle call, desolately thin in the wet   3
air, floated from the distant barracks. The superintendent of the jail, who was standing apart from the rest of us, moodily prodding the gravel with his stick, raised his head at the sound. He was an army doctor, with a grey toothbrush moustache and a gruff voice. "For God's sake hurry up, Francis," he said irritably. "The man ought to have been dead by this time. Aren't you ready yet?"

Francis, the head jailer, a fat Dravidian in a white drill suit   4
and gold spectacles, waved his black hand. "Yes sir, yes sir," he bubbled. "All iss satisfactorily prepared. The hangman iss waiting. We shall proceed."

"Well, quick march, then. The prisoners can't get their break-   5
fast till this job's over."

We set out for the gallows. Two warders marched on either   6
side of the prisoner, with their rifles at the slope; two others marched close against him, gripping him by arm and shoulder, as though at once pushing and supporting him. The rest of us, mag-istrates and the like, followed behind. Suddenly, when we had gone ten yards, the procession stopped short without any order or warn-ing. A dreadful thing had happened — a dog, come goodness

knows whence, had appeared in the yard. It came bounding among us with a loud volley of barks and leapt round us wagging its whole body, wild with glee at finding so many human beings together. It was a large woolly dog, half Airedale, half pariah. For a moment it pranced round us, and then, before anyone could stop it, it had made a dash for the prisoner, and jumping up tried to lick his face. Everybody stood aghast, too taken aback even to grab the dog.

"Who let that bloody brute in here?" said the superintendent   7
angrily. "Catch it, someone!"

A warder detached from the escort, charged clumsily after the   8
dog, but it danced and gambolled just out of his reach, taking everything as part of the game. A young Eurasian jailer picked up a handful of gravel and tried to stone the dog away, but it dodged the stones and came after us again. Its yaps echoed from the jail walls. The prisoner, in the grasp of the two warders, looked on incuriously, as though this was another formality of the hanging. It was several minutes before someone managed to catch the dog. Then we put my handkerchief through its collar and moved off once more, with the dog still straining and whimpering.

It was about forty yards to the gallows. I watched the bare   9
brown back of the prisoner marching in front of me. He walked clumsily with his bound arms, but quite steadily, with that bobbing gait of the Indian who never straightens his knees. At each step his muscles slid neatly into place, the lock of hair on his scalp danced up and down, his feet printed themselves on the wet gravel. And once, in spite of the men who gripped him by each shoulder, he stepped lightly aside to avoid a puddle on the path.

It is curious; but till that moment I had never realized what it   10
means to destroy a healthy, conscious man. When I saw the prisoner step aside to avoid the puddle I saw the mystery, the unspeakable wrongness, of cutting a life short when it is in full tide. This man was not dying, he was alive just as we are alive. All the organs of his body were working — bowels digesting food, skin renewing itself, nails growing, tissues forming — all toiling away in solemn foolery. His nails would still be growing when he stood on the drop, when he was falling through the air with a tenth-of-a-second to live. His eyes saw the yellow gravel and the grey walls, and his brain still remembered, foresaw, reasoned — even about puddles. He and we were a party of men walking together, seeing, hearing,

feeling, understanding the same world; and in two minutes, with a sudden snap, one of us would be gone — one mind less, one world less.

The gallows stood in a small yard, separate from the main 11 grounds of the prison, and overgrown with tall prickly weeds. It was a brick erection like three sides of a shed, with planking on top, and above that two beams and a crossbar with the rope dangling. The hangman, a greyhaired convict in the white uniform of the prison, was waiting beside his machine. He greeted us with a servile crouch as we entered. At a word from Francis the two warders, gripping the prisoner more closely than ever, half led, half pushed him to the gallows and helped him clumsily up the ladder. Then the hangman climbed up and fixed the rope round the prisoner's neck.

We stood waiting, five yards away. The warders had formed 12 in a rough circle round the gallows. And then, when the noose was fixed, the prisoner began crying out to his god. It was a high, reiterated cry of "Ram! Ram! Ram! Ram!" not urgent and fearful like a prayer or cry for help, but steady, rhythmical, almost like the tolling of a bell. The dog answered the sound with a whine. The hangman, still standing on the gallows, produced a small cotton bag like a flour bag and drew it down over the prisoner's face. But the sound, muffled by the cloth, still persisted, over and over again: "Ram! Ram! Ram! Ram! Ram!"

The hangman climbed down and stood ready, holding the 13 lever. Minutes seemed to pass. The steady, muffled crying from the prisoner went on and on, "Ram! Ram! Ram!" never faltering for an instant. The superintendent, his head on his chest, was slowly poking the ground with his stick; perhaps he was counting the cries, allowing the prisoner a fixed number — fifty, perhaps, or a hundred. Everyone had changed colour. The Indians had gone grey like bad coffee, and one or two of the bayonets were wavering. We looked at the lashed, hooded man on the drop, and listened to his cries — each cry another second of life; the same thought was in all our minds; oh, kill him quickly, get it over, stop that abominable noise!

Suddenly the superintendent made up his mind. Throwing up 14 his head he made a swift motion with his stick. "Chalo!" he shouted almost fiercely.

There was a clanking noise, and then dead silence. The prisoner 15 had vanished, and the rope was twisting on itself. I let go of the dog, and it galloped immediately to the back of the gallows; but when it got there it stoped short, barked, and then retreated into a corner of the yard, where it stood among the weeds, looking timorously out at us. We went round the gallows to inspect the prisoner's body. He was dangling with his toes pointed straight downwards, very slowly revolving, as dead as a stone.

The superintendent reached out with his stick and poked the 16 bare brown body; it oscillated slightly. "*He's* all right," said the superintendent. He backed out from under the gallows, and blew out a deep breath. The moody look had gone out of his face quite suddenly. He glanced at his wrist-watch. "Eight minutes past eight. Well, that's all for this morning, thank God."

The warders unfixed bayonets and marched away. The dog, 17 sobered and conscious of having misbehaved itself, slipped after them. We walked out of the gallows yard, past the condemned cells with their waiting prisoners, into the big central yard of the prison. The convicts, under the command of warders armed with lathis, were already receiving their breakfast. They squatted in long rows, each man holding a tin pannikin, while two warders with buckets marched round ladling out rice; it seemed quite a homely, jolly scene, after the hanging. An enormous relief had come upon us now that the job was done. One felt an impulse to sing, to break into a run, to snigger. All at once everyone began chattering gaily.

The Eurasian boy walking beside me nodded towards the way 18 we had come, with a knowing smile: "Do you know, sir, our friend (he meant the dead man) when he heard his appeal had been dismissed, he pissed on the floor of his cell. From fright. Kindly take one of my cigarettes, sir. Do you not admire my new silver case, sir? From the boxwallah, two rupees eight annas. Classy European style."

Several people laughed — at what, nobody seemed certain. 19

Francis was walking by the superintendent, talking garru- 20 lously: "Well, sir, all hass passed off with the utmost satisfactoriness. It was all finished — flick! Like that. It iss not always so — oah, no! I have known cases where the doctor wass obliged to go beneath the gallows and pull the prissoner's legs to ensure decease. Most disagreeable!"

"Wriggling about, eh? That's bad," said the superintendent. 21

"Arch, sir, it iss worse when they become refractory! One 22 man, I recall, clung to the bars of hiss cage when we went to take him out. You will scarcely credit, sir, that it took six warders to dislodge him, three pulling at each leg. We reasoned with him, 'My dear fellow,' we said, 'think of all the pain and trouble you are causing to us!' But no, he would not listen! Ach, he wass very troublesome!"

I found that I was laughing quite loudly. Everyone was laugh-   23
ing. Even the superintendent grinned in a tolerant way. "You'd better all come out and have a drink," he said quite genially. "I've got a bottle of whisky in the car. We could do with it."

We went through the big double gates of the prison into the   24
road. "Pulling at his legs!" exclaimed a Burmese magistrate suddenly, and burst into a loud chuckling. We all began laughing again. At that moment Francis' anecdote seemed extraordinarily funny. We all had a drink together, native and European alike, quite amicably. The dead man was a hundred yards away.

Meanings and Values

1. What was the real reason for the superintendent's impatience?
2. On first impression it may have seemed that the author gave undue attention to the dog's role in this narrative.
   a. Why was the episode such a "dreadful thing" (par. 6)?
   b. Why did the author think it worth noting that the dog was excited at "finding so many human beings together"?
   c. Of what significance was the dog's trying to lick the prisoner's face?
3. Explain how the prisoner's stepping around a puddle could have given the author a new insight into what was about to happen (par. 10)?
4. Why was there so much talking and laughing after the hanging was finished?
5. What is the broadest meaning of Orwell's last sentence?

Expository Techniques

1. Cite examples of both objective and impressionistic description in the first paragraph.
2a. What time order is used primarily in this narrative?
   b. If there are any exceptions, state where.

3. Considering the relatively few words devoted to them, several of the characterizations in this essay are remarkably vivid — a result, obviously, of highly discriminating selection of details from the multitude of those that must have been available to the author. For each of the following people, list the character traits that we can observe, and state whether these impressions come to us through details of description, action, and/or dialogue.
   a. The prisoner.
   b. The superintendent.
   c. Francis.
   d. The Eurasian boy

4a. Why do you think the author included so many details of the preparation of the prisoner (par. 2)?
   b. Why did he include so many details about the dog and his actions?
   c. What is gained by the assortment of details in paragraph 10?

5. The tone of a writing such as this can easily slip into sentimentality or even melodrama without the author's realizing what is happening. (See Guide to Terms: *Sentimentality*.) Select three places in this narrative where a less-skilled writer might have had such trouble, and note by what restraints Orwell prevented sentimentality.

Diction and Vocabulary

1. A noteworthy element of Orwell's style is his occasional use of figurative language. Cite six metaphors and similes, and comment on their choice and effectiveness.

2. Orwell was always concerned with the precise effects that words could give to meaning and style.
   a. Cite at least six nonfigurative words that seem to you particularly well chosen for their purpose.
   b. Show what their careful selection contributes to the description of atmosphere or to the subtle meanings of the author.
   c. How is this attention to diction a matter of style? (Guide: *Style/Tone*.)

Suggestions for Writing and Discussion

1. Select *one* of the points of controversy over capital punishment and present both sides with equal objectivity.

2. Consider the dilemma of a person whose "duty" seems to require one course of action and "conscience" just the opposite course. Use concrete illustrations to show how serious such dilemmas can be.

3. Examine the moral right, or lack of it, of the people of one country to impose their laws on the people of another country.

4. Discuss one benefit of colonialism to the people colonized. Use specific illustrations.

5. Explain how, in your own experience, a seemingly minor incident led to much deeper insight into a matter not fully understood before.

(NOTE: Suggestions for topics requiring development by NARRATION are on page 318, at the end of this section.)

JACK KEROUAC

Jack Kerouac (1922–1969) was the first and probably most important of the "beatnik" authors of the fifties. Born in Lowell, Massachusetts, he went to Columbia University on scholarship and then began his nomadic life. An autobiographical author, he wrote of rootless youth in search of identity, casual sex and marijuana when they were still forbidden fruits. His books include *On the Road* (1955), *The Dharma Bums* (1958), *The Subterraneans* (1968), and *Visions of Cody*, published posthumously in 1972. Kerouac, an alcoholic, died in St. Petersburg, Florida, where he lived his last years with his mother, defensive against both the Establishment and the new "hippie" generation.

Alone on a Mountaintop

Many critics have admired Kerouac, but not all. Eugene Burdick (*The Ugly American, The Ninth Wave*) once wrote that Kerouac "is a bad writer and often a silly one. . . . He is like a sensitive eyeball that sweeps and perceives but is not connected to a brain." "Alone on a Mountaintop" was written for *Holiday* in 1958, and, being intended for "slick magazine" readers, is somewhat more conventional in style and structure than many of his works, particularly of that period. But students may see some evidence to support Burdick's criticism even in this selection. In it, Kerouac, using narration as a basic framework, puts to good use his rather unique descriptive style.

The Seattle City Light and Power boat leaves on regular schedule   1
from a little pier near Diablo Dam and heads north between steep
timbered rocky cliffs toward Ross Dam, about half an hour's ride.
The passengers are power employees, hunters and fishermen and
forestry workers. Below Ross Dam the footwork begins; you must

Reprinted by permission of The Sterling Lord Agency, Inc., from *Holiday* Magazine (October 1958). Copyright © 1965 by Jack Kerouac.

climb a rocky trail one thousand feet to the level of the dam. Here
the vast lake opens out, disclosing small resort floats offering rooms
and boats for vacationists, and just beyond, the floats of the U.S.
Forestry Service. From this point on, if you're lucky enough to be a
rich man or a forest-fire lookout, you can get packed into the North
Cascade Primitive Area by horse and mule and spend a summer of
complete solitude.

I was a fire lookout and after two nights of trying to sleep in
the boom and slap of the Forest Service floats, they came for me
one rainy morning — a powerful tugboat lashed to a large corral
float bearing four mules and three horses, my own groceries, feed,
batteries and equipment. The muleskinner's name was Andy and he
wore the same old floppy cowboy hat he'd worn in Wyoming
twenty years ago. "Well, boy, now we're gonna put you away
where we can't reach ya; you better get ready."

"It's just what I want, Andy, be alone for three solid months,
nobody to bother me."

"It's what you're sayin' now, but you'll change your tune
after a week."

I didn't believe him. I was looking forward to an experience
men seldom earn in this modern world: complete and comfortable
solitude in the wilderness, day and night, sixty-three days and
nights to be exact. We had no idea how much snow had fallen on
my mountain during the winter, and Andy said: "If there's not
enough it means you gotta hike two miles down that hard trail
every day or every other day with two buckets, boy. I ain't envyin'
you. I been back there. And one day it's gonna be hot and you're
about ready to broil, and bugs you can't even count 'em; and next
day a li'l' ole summer blizzard come hit you around the corner of
Hozomeen — which sits right there near Canada in your back
yard — and you won't be able to stick logs fast enough in that
potbelly stove of yours." But I had a full rucksack loaded with
turtleneck sweaters and warm shirts and pants and long wool socks
bought on the Seattle water front, and gloves and an earmuff cap,
and lots of instant soup and coffee in my grub list.

"Shoulda brought yourself a quart of brandy, boy," said
Andy, shaking his head as the tug pushed our corral float up Ross
Lake, through the log gate and around to the left dead north,
underneath the immense rain shroud of Sourdough Mountain and
Ruby Mountain.

"Where's Desolation Peak?" I asked, meaning my own moun- 7
tain (*A mountain to be kept forever,* I'd dreamed all that spring).

"You ain't gonna see it today till we're practically on top of 8
it," said Andy, "and by that time you'll be so soakin' wet you
won't care."

Assistant Ranger Marty Gohlke of Marblemount Ranger Sta- 9
tion was with us, too, also giving me tips and instructions. Nobody
seemed to envy Desolation Peak except me. After two hours pushing through the storming waves of the long rainy lake with dreary
misty timber rising steeply on both sides and the mules and horses
chomping on their feedbags patient in the downpour, we arrived
at the foot of Desolation Trail and the tugman (who'd been providing us with good hot coffee in the pilot cabin) eased her over
and settled the float against a steep muddy slope full of bushes and
fallen trees. The muleskinner whacked the first mule and she
lurched ahead with her double-sided pack of batteries and canned
goods, hit the mud with forehoofs, scrambled, slipped, almost fell
back in the lake and finally gave one mighty heave and went skit-
tering out of sight in the fog to wait on the trail for the other
mules and her master. We all got off, cut the barge loose, waved to
the tug man, mounted our horses, and started up, sad and dripping,
in the heavy rain.

At first the trail, always steeply rising, was so dense with 10
shrubbery we kept getting shower after shower from overhead and
from branches hit by our out-jutting knees. The trail was deep
with round rocks that kept causing the animals to slip. At one
point a great fallen tree made it impossible to go on until Old
Andy and Marty went ahead with **axes** and cleared a short cut
around the tree, sweating and cursing and hacking, as I watched
the animals. By-and-by they were ready, but the mules were afraid
of the rough steepness of the short cut and had to be prodded
through with sticks. Soon the trail reached alpine meadows pow-
dered with blue lupine everywhere in the drenching mists, and with
little red poppies, tiny-budded flowers as delicate as designs on a
tiny Japanese teacup. Now the trail zigzagged widely back and
forth up the high meadow. Soon we saw the vast foggy heap of a
rock-cliff face above and Andy yelled, "Soon's we get up high as
that we're almost there but that's another two thousand feet,
though you'd think you could reach up and touch it!"

I unfolded my nylon poncho and draped it over my head, and, 11 drying a little, or, rather, ceasing to drip, I walked alongside the horse to warm my blood and began to feel better. But the other boys just rode along with their heads bowed in the rain. As for altitude all I could tell was from some occasional frightening spots on the trail where we could look down on distant treetops.

The alpine meadow reached to timber line, and suddenly a 12 great wind blew shafts of sleet on us. "Gettin' near the top now!" yelled Andy. And now there was snow on the trail, the horses were chumping through a foot of slush and mud, and to the left and right everything was blinding white in the gray fog. "About five and a half thousand feet right now," said Andy, rolling a cigarette as he rode in the rain.

We went down, then up another spell, down again, a slow 13 gradual climb, and then Andy yelled, "There she is!" and up ahead in the mountaintop gloom I saw a little shadowy peaked shack standing alone on the top of the world and I gulped with fear:

"This my home all summer? And *this* is summer?" 14

The inside of the shack was even more miserable, damp and 15 dirty, leftover groceries and magazines torn to shreds by rats and mice, the floor muddy, the windows impenetrable. But hardy Old Andy, who'd been through this kind of thing all his life, got a roaring fire crackling in the potbellied stove and had me lay out a pot of water with almost half a can of coffee in it, saying, "Coffee ain't no good 'less it's *strong!*" and pretty soon the coffee was boiling a nice brown aromatic foam and we got our cups out and drank deep.

Meanwhile I'd gone out on the roof with Marty and removed 16 the bucket from the chimney and put up the weather pole with the anemometer and done a few other chores; and when we came back in Andy was frying Spam and eggs in a huge pan and it was almost like a party. Outside, the patient animals chomped on their supper bags and were glad to rest by the old corral fence built of logs by some Desolation lookout of the Thirties.

Darkness came, incomprehensible. 17

In the gray morning after they'd slept in sleeping bags on the 18 floor and I on the only bunk in my mummy bag, Andy and Marty left, laughing and saying, "Well, what ayou think now, hey? We been here twelve hours already and you still haven't been able to see more than twelve feet!"

"By gosh that's right, what am I going to do for watching 19 fires?"

"Don't worry, boy, these clouds'll roll away and you'll be able   20
to see a hunnerd miles in every direction."

I didn't believe it and I felt miserable and spent the day trying   21
to clean up the shack or pacing twenty careful feet each way in
my "yard" (the ends of which appeared to be sheer drops into
silent gorges), and I went to bed early. About bedtime I saw my
first star, briefly, then giant phantom clouds billowed all around
me and the star was gone. But in that instant I thought I'd seen a
mile below me gray-black Ross Lake where Andy and Marty were
back in the Forest Service boat which had met them at noon.

In the middle of the night I woke up suddenly and my hair   22
was standing on end: I saw a huge black shadow in my window.
Then I saw that it had a star above it, and realized that this was
Mt. Hozomeen (8080 feet) looking in my window from miles away
near Canada. I got up from the forlorn bunk with the mice scat-
tering underneath and went outside and gasped to see black mountain shapes gianting all around; and not only that but the billowing
curtains of the northern lights shifting behind the clouds. It was
a little too much for a city boy. The fear that the Abominable
Snowman might be breathing behind me in the dark sent me back
to bed where I buried my head inside my sleeping bag.

But in the morning — Sunday, July sixth — I was amazed and   23
overjoyed to see a clear blue sunny sky, and down below, like a
radiant pure snow sea, the clouds made a marshmallow cover for
all the world and all the lake while I abided in warm sunshine
among hundreds of miles of snow-white peaks. I brewed coffee and
sang and drank a cup on my drowsy warm doorstep.

At noon the clouds vanished and the lake appeared below,   24
beautiful beyond belief, a perfect blue pool twenty-five miles long
and more, and the creeks like toy creeks and the timber green and
fresh everywhere below and even the fishing boats of vacationists
on the lake and in the lagoons. A perfect afternoon of sun, and
behind the shack I discovered a snowfield big enough to provide
me with buckets of cold water till late September.

I had taken this job so I could round up a little grubstake and   25
take off for Mexico for a year, but also I wanted to be alone on the
top of a mountain and see what it was like, and besides, all the
mountain climbers and loggers I'd known on the West Coast had
told me not to miss the High Cascades.

My job was to watch for fires. One night a terrific lightning   26
storm made a dry run across the Mt. Baker National Forest without

any rainfall. When I saw that ominous black cloud flashing wrath-
fully toward me I shut off the radio and laid the aerial on the
ground and waited for the worst. Hiss! hiss! said the wind, bringing dust and lightning nearer. Tick! said the lightning rod, receiving a strand of electricity from a strike on nearby Skagit Peak.
Hiss! Tick! and in my bed I felt the earth move. Fifteen miles to the
south, just east of Ruby Peak and somewhere near Panther Creek,
a large fire raged, a huge orange spot. At ten o'clock lightning hit
it again and it flared up dangerously.

I was supposed to note the general area of lightning strikes.   27
By midnight I'd been staring so intently out the dark window I
got hallucinations of fires everywhere, three of them right in Lightning Creek, phosphorescent orange verticals of ghost fire that
seemed to come and go.

In the morning, there at 177°16' where I'd seen the big fire,   28
was a strange brown patch in the snowy rock showing where the
fire had raged and sputtered out in the all-night rain that followed
the lightning. But the result of this storm was disastrous fifteen
miles away at McAllister Creek where a great blaze had outlasted
the rain and exploded the following afternoon in a cloud that could
be seen from Seattle. I felt sorry for the fellows who had to fight
these fires, the smoke-jumpers who parachuted down on them out
of planes and the trail crews who hiked to them, climbing and
scrambling over slippery rocks and scree slopes, arriving sweaty
and exhausted only to face the wall of heat when they got there.
As a lookout I had it pretty easy and only had to concentrate on
reporting the exact location (by instrument findings) of every blaze
I detected.

Most days, though, it was the routine that occupied me. Up at   29
seven or so every day, a pot of coffee brought to a boil over a
handful of burning twigs, I'd go out in the alpine yard with a cup
of coffee hooked in my thumb and leisurely make my wind speed
and wind direction and temperature and moisture readings. Then,
after chopping wood, I'd use the two-way radio and report to the
relay station on Sourdough. At 10 A.M I usually got hungry for
breakfast, and I'd make delicious pancakes, eating them at my little
table that was decorated with bouquets of mountain lupine and
sprigs of fir.

Early in the afternoon was the usual time for my kick of the   30
day, instant chocolate pudding with hot coffee. Around two or

three, I'd lie on my back on the meadowside and watch the clouds float by, or pick blueberries and eat them right there. I had turned the radio loud enough to hear any calls for Desolation.

Then at sunset I'd roust up my supper out of cans of yams and Spam and peas, or sometimes just pea soup with corn muffins baked on top of the wood stove in aluminum foil. Then I'd go out to that precipitous snow slope and shovel my two pails of snow for the water tub and gather an armful of fallen firewood from the hillside like the proverbial Old Woman of Japan. For the chipmunks and conies I put pans of leftovers under the shack; in the middle of the night I could hear them clanking around. The rat would scramble down from the attic and eat some too. 31

Sometimes I'd yell questions at the rocks and trees, and across gorges, or yodel "What is the meaning of the void?" The answer was perfect silence, so I knew. 32

Before bedtime I'd read by kerosene lamp whatever books were in the shack. It's amazing how people in solitary hunger after books. After poring over every word of a medical tome, and the synopsized versions of Shakespeare's plays by Charles and Mary Lamb, I climbed up in the little attic and put together torn cowboy pocket books and magazines the mice had ravaged. I also played stud poker with three imaginary players. 33

Around bedtime I'd bring a cup of milk almost to a boil with a tablespoon of honey in it, and drink that for my lamby nightcap; then I'd curl up in my sleeping bag. 34

No man should go through life without once experiencing healthy, even bored solitude in the wilderness, finding himself depending solely on himself and thereby learning his true and hidden strength. Learning for instance, to eat when he's hungry and sleep when he's sleepy. 35

Also around bedtime was my singing time. I'd pace up and down the well-worn path in the dust of my rock singing all the show tunes I could remember, at the top of my voice, too, with nobody to hear except the deer and the bear. 36

In the red dusk, the mountains were symphonies in pink snow . . . Jack Mountain, Three Fools Peak, Freezeout Peak, Golden Horn, Mt. Terror, Mt. Fury, Mt. Despair, Crooked Thumb Peak, Mt. Challenger and the incomparable Mt. Baker bigger than the world in the distance . . . and my own little Jackass Ridge that completed the Ridge of Desolation. Pink snow and the clouds all 37 distant and frilly like ancient remote cities of Buddhaland splendor, and the wind working incessantly — whish, whish — booming, at times rattling my shack.

For supper I made chop suey and baked some biscuits and put   38
the leftovers in a pan for deer that came in the moonlit night and nibbled like big strange cows of peace — long-antlered buck and does and babies too — as I meditated in the alpine grass facing the magic moon-laned lake. And I could see firs reflected in the moon-lit lake five thousand feet below, upside down, pointing to infinity.

And all the insects ceased in honor of the moon.   39

Sixty-three sunsets I saw revolve on that perpendicular hill . . . 40
mad raging sunsets pouring in sea foams of cloud through unim-aginable crags like the crags you grayly drew in pencil as a child, with every rose tint of hope beyond, making you feel just like them, brilliant and bleak beyond words.

Cold mornings with clouds billowing out of Lightning Gorge   41
like smoke from a giant fire but the lake cerulean as ever.

August comes in with a blast that shakes your house and   42
augurs little Augusticity . . . then that snowy-air and woodsmoke feeling . . . then the snow comes sweeping your way from Canada and the wind rises and dark low clouds rush up as out of a forge. Suddenly a green-rose rainbow appears right on your ridge with steamy clouds all around and an orange sun turmoiling . . .

> *What is a rainbow,*
> *Lord? — a hoop*
> *For the lowly*

. . . and you go out and suddenly your shadow is ringed by the rainbow as you walk on the hilltop, a lovely-haloed mystery mak-ing you want to pray.

A blade of grass jiggling in the winds of infinity, anchored to a 43
rock, and for your own poor gentle flesh no answer.

Your oil lamp burning in infinity.   44

One morning I found bear stool and signs of where the mon-   45
ster had taken a can of frozen milk and squeezed it in his paws and bit into it with one sharp tooth, trying to suck out the paste. In the foggy dawn I looked down the mysterious Ridge of Starvation with its fog-lost firs and its hills humping into invisibility, and the wind blowing the fog by like a faint blizzard, and I realized that somewhere in the fog stalked the bear.

And it seemed, as I sat there, that this was the Primordial 46
Bear, and that he owned all the Northwest and all the snow and
commanded all the mountains. He was King Bear, who could crush
my head in his paws and crack my spine like a stick, and this was
his house, his yard, his domain. Though I looked all day, he would
not show himself in the mystery of those silent foggy slopes. He
prowled at night among unknown lakes, and in the early morning
the pearl-pure light that shadowed mountainsides of fir made him
blink with respect. He had millenniums of prowling here behind
him. He had seen the Indians and Redcoats come and go, and
would see much more. He continuously heard the reassuring rap-
turous rush of silence, except when near creeks; he was aware of
the light material the world is made of, yet he never discoursed, nor
communicated by signs, nor wasted a breath complaining; he just
nibbled and pawed, and lumbered along snags paying no attention
to things inanimate or animate. His big mouth chew-chewed in the
night, I could hear it across the mountain in the starlight. Soon he
would come out of the fog, huge, and come and stare in my window with big burning eyes. He was Avalokitesvara the Bear, and
his sign was the gray wind of autumn.

I was waiting for him. He never came. 47

Finally the autumn rains, all-night gales of soaking rain as I lie 48
warm as toast in my sleeping bag and the mornings open cold wild
fall days with high wind, racing fogs, racing clouds, sudden bright
sun, pristine light on hill patches and my fire crackling as I exult
and sing at the top of my voice. Outside my window a wind-swept
chipmunk sits up straight on a rock, hands clasped as he nibbles an
oat between his paws — the little nutty lord of all he surveys.

Thinking of the stars night after night I begin to realize "The 49
stars are words" and all the innumerable worlds in the Milky Way
are words, and so is this world too. And I realize that no matter
where I am, whether in a little room full of thought, or in this endless universe of stars and mountains, it's all in my mind. There's
no need for solitude. So love life for what it is, and form no pre-
conceptions whatever in your mind.

When I came down in September a cool old golden look had 50
come into the forest, auguring cold snaps and frost and the eventual
howling blizzard that would cover my shack completely, unless
those winds at the top of the world would keep her bald. As I
reached the bend where the shack would disappear and I would

plunge down to the lake to meet the boat that would take me out and home, I turned and blessed Desolation Peak and the little pagoda on top and thanked them for the shelter and the lesson I'd been taught.

Meanings and Values

1a. The author seems to devote a relatively large portion of this essay to the bear. Why do you suppose he considered it that important?
  b. Do you agree?
  c. Could that bear be considered a symbol? (See Guide to Terms: *Symbol*.) Why, or why not?
  d. If a symbol, what kind is it?

2a. Just what "lesson" did the author learn?
  b. If you had trouble answering question 2a, to what do you attribute the lack of clarity — e.g., was the author simply trying to be "subtle," and if so, why?

3. Judging from this rather atypical selection, do you think Burdick may have been right (see introductory remarks) about Kerouac's writing? Use specific details to support your stand.

Expository Techniques

1a. What time order did Kerouac employ for his narrative?
  b. Demonstrate how he might have used another instead.
  c. What would have been the advantages and/or disadvantages?

2. What functions are served by the brief dialogues with Andy?

3a. Often the movement of the narrative is almost obscured by description. Primarily what kind of description is it?
  b. How effective do you consider the description — for this particular writing? Why?
  c. In what kinds of writing, if any, would it be totally inappropriate?

4. The author achieves emphasis by various techniques. (Guide: *Emphasis*.) List them and cite at least one example of each.

5a. Kerouac has developed a style that, whatever critics may say of it, is all his own. Analyze the style and list the various elements that, blended together, make it distinctive. (Guide: *Style/Tone*.)
  b. Be prepared to cite enough examples to show the significance of each element.

Diction and Vocabulary

1. Explain the reference to the Abominable Snowman (par. 22).

2a. List, or mark, the figurative allusions in this essay. (Guide: *Figures of Speech.*)

  b. Realizing, as Kerouac must have, that most *Holiday* readers would not be familiar with these allusions (probably could not even find them if they went looking), why do you suppose he used them anyway?

  c. For you, is the meaning obscured because of them? Explain, citing examples.

3. One distinctive feature of Kerouac's style, of course, is his more-than-liberal use of figurative language. List, or mark, several of his most spectacular figures of speech (other than allusions), and comment on their originality and effectiveness.

4. He also coins his own words, if the dictionary offers none that suits his purpose — e.g., "gianting all around" (par. 22). Cite other examples of these and try to determine whether the writing is helped, or hindered, by them.

5. If you are unfamiliar with any of the following words, use your dictionary as necessary: alpine (par. 10); anemometer (16); scree (28); precipitous, conies (31); cerulean (41); augurs (42).

Suggestions for Writing and Discussion

1. In your own opinion, what *is* the "meaning of the void"?

2. If you too have experienced complete solitude, what were the short- and/or long-term effects on you?

3. Many ills of modern society are sometimes traced to this: millions of people grow up, live, and die with virtually no opportunity ever to be really alone, even for brief intervals. And undoubtedly it was different in the days of larger homes and smaller shops, of wood-sheds and barns and nearby fields. Discuss what seem to you the possible effects of this change — i.e., is it really necessary to be completely alone sometimes to "know" ourselves? (You may wish to show the opposite extreme by reference to the Wolfe essay in Section 4.)

Writing Suggestions for Section 10
Narration

Use narration as at least a partial pattern (e.g., in developed examples or in comparison) for one of the following expository themes or another suggested by them. You should avoid the isolated personal account that has little broader significance. Remember, too, that the essay's development itself should make your point, without excessive moralizing.

1. People can still succeed without a college education.
2. The frontiers are not all gone.
3. When people succeed in communicating, they can learn to get along with each other.
4. Innocent people can be executed by even "careful" use of capital punishment.
5. Judging by appearance and mannerisms is a poor way to recognize a homosexual as such.
6. True courage is different from boldness in time of sudden danger.
7. Prior conditioning to the realities of his job is as important to the policeman as training in the techniques of his profession.
8. It is possible for the employee himself to determine when he has reached his highest level of competence.
9. Wartime massacres are not a new development.
10. The issue of hair length still is not dead.
11. Worn-out land can be restored, without chemicals, to its original productivity.
12. Back-to-the-earth, "family" style communes can be made to work.
13. Such communes (as in 12 above) are a good (or poor) place to raise children.
14. Both heredity and environment shape the personality.

Essays for Further Reading and Analysis

ALEKSANDER I. SOLZHENITSYN

ALEKSANDER I. SOLZHENITSYN is a Soviet author and Nobel Prize winner. Although regarded by many people throughout the world as the greatest living Russian author, he is virtually an outcast in his own country, where none of his writing has been published in recent years. Solzhenitsyn was a political prisoner under Stalin, and one of his best-known books is an account of Soviet prison life: *One Day in the Life of Ivan Denisovich* (1962). Other books for which he is well known in the West are *Cancer Ward* and *The First Circle* (first published in the West in 1968, still unpublished in Russia); *We Never Make Mistakes* (1963); *For the Good of the Cause* (1964); *August, 1914* (1972). Solzhenitsyn has long been outspoken against literary censorship in the U.S.S.R; the following excerpt from his 1970 Nobel Prize address (1972) is partially a rationale for opposition to the repression of art in general and literature in particular.

The Heart of a Nation*

From time immemorial man has been made in such a way that his   1
vision of the world, so long as it has not been instilled under hypnosis, his motivations and scale of values, his actions and intentions are determined by his personal and group experience of life. As the Russian saying goes, "Do not believe your brother, believe your own crooked eye." And that is the most sound basis for an understanding of the world around us and of human conduct in it. And during the long epochs when our world lay spread out in mystery and wilderness, before it became encroached by common lines of communication, before it was transformed into a single, convulsively pulsating lump — men, relying on experience, ruled without mishap within their limited areas, within their communities,

Reprinted by permission of the Nobel Foundation from parts 4 and 5 of the Nobel Lecture by Aleksander Solzhenitsyn. © The Nobel Foundation 1972.
    * Editor's title.

within their societies, and finally on their national territories. At that time it was possible for individual human beings to perceive and accept a general scale of values, to distinguish between what is considered normal, what incredible; what is cruel and what lies beyond the boundaries of wickedness; what is honesty, what deceit. And although the scattered peoples led extremely different lives and their social values were often strikingly at odds, just as their systems of weights and measures did not agree, still these discrepancies surprised only occasional travellers, were reported in journals under the name of wonders, and bore no danger to mankind which was not yet one.

But now during the past few decades, imperceptibly, suddenly, mankind has become one — hopefully one and dangerously one — so that the concussions and inflammations of one of its parts are almost instantaneously passed on to others, sometimes lacking in any kind of necessary immunity. Mankind has become one, but not steadfastly one as communities or even nations used to be; not united through years of mutual experience, neither through possession of a single eye, affectionately called crooked, nor yet through a common native language, but, surpassing all barriers, through international broadcasting and print. An avalanche of events descends upon us — in one minute half the world hears of their splash. But the yardstick by which to measure those events and to evaluate them in accordance with the laws of unfamiliar parts of the world — this is not and cannot be conveyed via soundwaves and in newspaper columns. For these yardsticks were matured and assimilated over too many years of too specific conditions in individual countries and societies; they cannot be exchanged in mid-air. In the various parts of the world men apply their own hard-earned values to events, and they judge stubbornly, confidently, only according to their own scales of values and never according to any others.

And if there are not many such different scales of values in the world, there are at least several; one for evaluating events near at hand, another for events far away; aging societies possess one, young societies another; unsuccessful people one, successful people another. The divergent scales of values scream in discordance, they dazzle and daze us, and so that it might not be painful we steer clear of all other values, as though from insanity, as though from illusion, and we confidently judge the whole world according to our own home values. Which is why we take for the greater, more painful and less bearable disaster not that which is in fact greater, more painful and less bearable, but that which lies closest to us. Everything which is further away, which does not threaten this very day to invade our threshold — with all its groans, its stifled cries, its destroyed lives, even if it involves millions of victims — this we consider on the whole to be perfectly bearable and of tolerable proportions.

In one part of the world, not so long ago, under persecutions   4
not inferior to those of the ancient Romans', hundreds of thousands of silent Christians gave up their lives for their belief in God. In the other hemisphere a certain madman, (and no doubt he is not alone), speeds across the ocean to DELIVER us from religion — with a thrust of steel into the high priest! He has calculated for each and every one of us according to his personal scale of values!

That which from a distance, according to one scale of values,   5
appears as enviable and flourishing freedom, at close quarters, and according to other values, is felt to be infuriating constraint calling for abuses to be overthrown. That which is one part of the world might represent a dream of incredible prosperity, in another has the exasperating effect of wild exploitation demanding immediate strike. There are different scales of values for natural catastrophes: a flood craving two hundred thousand lives seems less significant than our local accident. There are different scales of values for personal insults: sometimes even an ironic smile or a dismissive gesture is humiliating, while at others cruel beatings are forgiven as an unfortunate joke. There are different scales of values for punishment and wickedness: according to one, a month's arrest, banishment to the country, or an isolation-cell where one is fed on white rolls and milk, shatters the imagination and fills the newspaper columns with rage. While according to another, prison sentences of twenty-five years, isolation-cells where the walls are covered with ice and the prisoners stripped to their underclothes, lunatic asylums for the sane, and countless unreasonable people who for some reason will keep running away, shot on the frontiers — all this is common and accepted. While the mind is especially at peace concerning that exotic part of the world about which we know virtually nothing, from which we do not even receive news of events, but only the trivial, out-of-date guesses of a few correspondents.

Yet we cannot reproach human vision for this duality, for this   6
dumfounded incomprehension of another man's distant grief, man
is just made that way. But for the whole of mankind, compressed
into a single lump, such mutual incomprehension presents the
threat of imminent and violent destruction. One world, one mankind cannot exist in the face of six, four or even two scales of
values: we shall be torn apart by this disparity of rhythm, this
disparity of vibrations.

A man with two hearts is not for this world, neither shall we   7
be able to live side by side on one Earth.

But who will co-ordinate these value scales, and how? Who will   8
create for mankind one system of interpretation, valid for good and
evil deeds, for the unbearable and the bearable, as they are differentiated today? Who will make clear to mankind what is really
heavy and intolerable and what only grazes the skin locally? Who
will direct the anger to that which is most terrible and not to that
which is nearer? Who might succeed in transferring such an understanding beyond the limits of his own human experience? Who
might succeed in impressing upon a bigoted, stubborn human creature the distant joy and grief of others, an understanding of dimensions and deceptions which he himself has never experienced?
Propaganda, constraint, scientific proof — all are useless. But fortunately there does exist such a means in our world! That means
is art. That means is literature.

They can perform a miracle: they can overcome man's detri-   9
mental peculiarity of learning only from personal experience so
that the experience of other people passes him by in vain. From
man to man, as he completes his brief spell on earth, art transfers
the whole weight of an unfamiliar, life-long experience with all its
burdens, its colours, its sap of life; it recreates in the flesh an
unknown experience and allows us to possess it as our own.

And even more, much more than that; both countries and whole   10
continents repeat each other's mistakes with time lapses which can
amount to centuries. Then, one would think, it would all be so obvious! But no; that which some nations have already experienced,
considered and rejected, is suddenly discovered by others to be the
latest word. And here again, the only substitute for an experience
we ourselves have never lived through is art, literature. They possess
a wonderful ability: beyond distinctions of language, custom, social

structure they can convey the life experience of one whole nation to another. To an inexperienced nation they can convey a harsh national trial lasting many decades, at best sparing an entire nation from a superfluous, or mistaken, or even disastrous course, thereby curtailing the meanderings of human history.

It is this great and noble property of art that I urgently recall   11
to you today from the Nobel tribune.

And literature conveys irrefutable condensed experience in yet   12
another invaluable direction; namely, from generation to generation. Thus it becomes the living memory of the nation. Thus it preserves and kindles within itself the flame of her spent history, in a form which is safe from deformation and slander. In this way literature, together with language, protects the soul of the nation.

(In recent times it has been fashionable to talk of the levelling   13
out of nations, of the disappearance of different races in the melting-pot of contemporary civilization. I do not agree with this opinion, but its discussion remains another question. Here it is merely fitting to say that the disappearance of nations would have impoverished us no less than if all men had become alike, with one personality and one face. Nations are the wealth of mankind, its collective personalities; the very least of them wears its own special colours and bears within itself a special facet of divine intention.)

But woe to that nation whose literature is disturbed by the   14
intervention of power. Because that is not just a violation against "freedom of print", it is the closing down of the heart of the nation, a slashing to pieces of its memory. The nation ceases to be mindful of itself, it is deprived of its spiritual unity, and despite a supposedly common language, compatriots suddenly cease to understand one another. Silent generations grow old and die without ever having talked about themselves, either to each other or to their descendants. When such as Achmatova and Zamjatin — interred alive throughout their lives — are condemned to create in silence until they die, never hearing the echo of their written words, then that is not only their personal tragedy, but a sorrow to the whole nation, a danger to the whole nation.

In some cases moreover — when as a result of such a silence   15
the whole of history ceases to be understood in its entirety — it is a danger to the whole of mankind.

ALEX HALEY

ALEX HALEY was born in Henning, Tennessee. He is the co-author of the critically acclaimed *Autobiography of Malcolm X*. His next book, *Roots*, will be a book-length treatment of the experiences recounted in the article below. It will also be made into a major motion picture. Haley is founder of the Kinte Foundation, a library of black genealogy, which is due to open in 1976 in Washington, D.C.

My Furthest-Back Person—"The African"

My Grandma Cynthia Murray Palmer lived in Henning, Tenn. (pop. 500), about 50 miles north of Memphis. Each summer as I grew up there, we would be visited by several women relatives who were mostly around Grandma's age, such as my Great Aunt Liz Murray who taught in Oklahoma, and Great Aunt Till Merriwether from Jackson, Tenn., or their considerably younger niece, Cousin Georgia Anderson from Kansas City, Kan., and some others. Always after the supper dishes had been washed, they would go out to take seats and talk in the rocking chairs on the front porch, and I would scrunch down, listening, behind Grandma's squeaky chair, with the dusk deepening into night and the lightning bugs flickering on and off above the now shadowy honeysuckles. Most often they talked about our family — the story had been passed down for generations — until the whistling blur of lights of the southbound Panama Limited train *whooshing* through Henning at 9:05 P.M. signaled our bedtime.

So much of their talking of people, places and events I didn't understand: For instance, what was an "Ol' Massa," an "Ol' Missus" or a "plantation"? But early I gathered that white folks had done lots of bad things to our folks, though I couldn't figure

out why. I guessed that all that they talked about had happened a
long time ago, as now or then Grandma or another, speaking of
someone in the past, would excitedly thrust a finger toward me,
exclaiming, "Wasn't big as *this* young 'un!" And it would astound
me that anyone as old and grey-haired as they could relate to my
age. But in time my head began both a recording and picturing of
the more graphic scenes they would describe, just as I also visualized David killing Goliath with his slingshot, Old Pharaoh's
army drowning, Noah and his ark, Jesus feeding that big multitude
with nothing but five loaves and two fishes, and other wonders that
I heard in my Sunday school lessons at our New Hope Methodist
Church.

The furthest-back person Grandma and the others talked of —   3
always in tones of awe, I noticed — they would call "The African."
They said that some ship brought him to a place that they pronounced " 'Naplis." They said that then some "Mas' John Waller"
bought him for his plantation in "Spotsylvania County, Va." This
African kept on escaping, the fourth time trying to kill the "hate-
ful po' cracker" slave-catcher, who gave him the punishment choice
of castration or of losing one foot. This African took a foot being
chopped off with an ax against a tree stump, they said, and he was
about to die. But his life was saved by "Mas' John's" brother —
"Mas' William Waller," a doctor, who was so furious about what
had happened that he bought the African for himself and gave him
the name "Toby."

Crippling about, working in "Mas' William's" house and yard,   4
the African in time met and mated with "the big house cook named
Bell," and there was born a girl named Kizzy. As she grew up her
African daddy often showed her different kinds of things, telling
her what they were in his native tongue. Pointing at a banjo, for
example, the African uttered, *"ko"*; or pointing at a river near the
plantation, he would say, *"Kamby Bolong."* Many of his strange
words started with a *"k"* sound, and the little, growing Kizzy
learned gradually that they identified different things.

When addressed by other slaves as "Toby," the master's name   5
for him, the African said angrily that his name was *"Kin-tay."*
And as he gradually learned English, he told young Kizzy some
things about himself — for instance, that he was not far from his
village, chopping wood to make himself a drum, when four men
had surprised, overwhelmed, and kidnaped him.

So Kizzy's head held much about her African daddy when at   6
age 16 she was sold away onto a much smaller plantation in North
Carolina. Her new "Mas' Tom Lea" fathered her first child, a boy
she named George. And Kizzy told her boy all about his African
grandfather. George grew up to be such a gamecock fighter that
he was called "Chicken George," and people would come from all
over and "bet big money" on his cockfights. He mated with Matilda,
another of Lea's slaves; they had seven children, and he told them
the stories and strange sounds of their African great-grandfather.
And one of those children, Tom, became a blacksmith who was
bought away by a "Mas' Murray" for his tobacco plantation in
Alamance County, N.C.

Tom mated there with Irene, a weaver on the plantation. She   7
also bore seven children, and Tom now told them all about their
African great-great-grandfather, the faithfully passed-down knowledge of his sounds and stories having become by now the family's
prideful treasure.

The youngest of that second set of seven children was a girl,   8
Cynthia, who became my maternal Grandma (which today I can
only see as fated). Anyway, all of this is how I was growing up in
Henning at Grandma's, listening from behind her rocking chair as
she and the other visiting old women talked of that African (never
then comprehended as *my* great-great-great-great-grandfather)
who said his name was *"Kin-tay,"* and said *"ko"* for banjo, *"Kamby
Bolong"* for river, and a jumble of other *"k"*-beginning sounds that
Grandma privately muttered, most often while making beds or
cooking, and who also said that near his village he was kidnaped
while chopping wood to make himself a drum.

The story had become nearly as fixed in my head as in Grand-   9
ma's by the time Dad and Mama moved me and my two younger
brothers, George and Julius, away from Henning to be with them
at the small black agricultural and mechanical college in Normal,
Ala., where Dad taught.

To compress my next 25 years: When I was 17 Dad let me   10
enlist as a mess boy in the U.S. Coast Guard. I became a ship's
cook out in the South Pacific during World War II, and at night
down by my bunk I began trying to write sea adventure stories,
mailing them off to magazines and collecting rejection slips for
eight years before some editors began purchasing and publishing
occasional stories. By 1949 the Coast Guard had made me its first

"journalist"; finally with 20 years' service, I retired at the age of 37, determined to make a full time career of writing. I wrote mostly magazine articles; my first book was "The Autobiography of Malcolm X."

Then one Saturday in 1965 I happened to be walking past the   11
National Archives building in Washington. Across the interim years I had thought of Grandma's old stories — otherwise I can't think what diverted me up the Archives' steps. And when a main reading room desk attendant asked if he could help me, I wouldn't have dreamed of admitting to him some curiosity hanging on from boyhood about my slave forebears. I kind of bumbled that I was interested in census records of Alamance County, North Carolina, just after the Civil War.

The microfilm rolls were delivered, and I turned them through   12
the machine with a building sense of intrigue, viewing in different census takers' penmanship an endless parade of names. After about a dozen microfilmed rolls, I was beginning to tire, when in utter astonishment I looked upon the names of Grandma's parents: Tom Murray, Irene Murray . . . older sisters of Grandma's as well — every one of them a name that I'd heard countless times on her front porch.

It wasn't that I hadn't believed Grandma. You just *didn't* not   13
believe my Grandma. It was simply so uncanny actually seeing those names in print and in official U.S. Government records.

During the next several months I was back in Washington   14
whenever possible, in the Archives, the Library of Congress, the Daughters of the American Revolution Library. (Whenever black attendants understood the idea of my search, documents I requested reached me with miraculous speed.) In one source or another during 1966 I was able to document at least the highlights of the cherished family story. I would have given anything to have told Grandma, but, sadly, in 1949 she had gone. So I went and told the only survivor of those Henning front-porch storytellers: Cousin Georgia Anderson, now in her 80's in Kansas City, Kan. Wrinkled, bent, not well herself, she was so overjoyed, repeating to me the old stories and sounds; they were like Henning echoes: "Yeah, boy, that African say his name was 'Kin-tay'; he say the banjo was 'ko,' and river 'Kamby-Bolong,' an' he was off choppin some wood to make his drum when they grabbed 'im!" Cousin Georgia grew

so excited we had to stop her, calm her down, 'You go' head, boy! Your grandma an' all of 'em — they up there watching what you do!'"

That week I flew to London on a magazine assignment. Since by now I was steeped in the old, in the past, scarcely a tour guide missed me — I was awed at so many historical places and treasures I'd heard of and read of. I came upon the Rosetta stone in the British Museum, marveling anew at how Jean Champollion, the French archeologist, had miraculously deciphered its ancient demotic and hieroglyphic texts . . .

The thrill of that just kept hanging around in my head. I was on a jet returning to New York when a thought hit me. Those strange, unknown-tongue sounds, always part of our family's old story . . . they were obviously bits of our original African "*Kintay's*" native tongue. What specific tongue? Could I somehow find out?

Back in New York, I began making visits to the United Nations Headquarters lobby; it wasn't hard to spot Africans. I'd stop any I could, asking if my bits of phonetic sounds held any meaning for them. A couple of dozen Africans quickly looked at me, listened, and took off — understandably dubious about some Tennesseean's accent alleging "African" sounds.

My research assistant, George Sims (we grew up together in Henning), brought me some names of ranking scholars of African linguistics. One was particularly intriguing: a Belgian- and English-educated Dr. Jan Vansina; he had spent his early career living in West African villages, studying and tape-recording countless oral histories that were narrated by certain very old African men; he had written a standard textbook, "The Oral Tradition."

So I flew to the University of Wisconsin to see Dr. Vansina. In his living room I told him every bit of the family story in the fullest detail that I could remember it. Then, intensely, he queried me about the story's relay across the generations, about the gibberish of "*k*" sounds Grandma had fiercely muttered to herself while doing her housework, with my brothers and me giggling beyond her hearing at what we had dubbed "Grandma's noises."

Dr. Vansina, his manner very serious, finally said, "These sounds your family has kept sound very probably of the tongue called 'Mandinka.'"

I'd never heard of any "Mandinka." Grandma just told of the   21
African saying *"ko"* for banjo, or *"Kamby Bolong"* for a Virginia
river.

Among Mandinka stringed instruments, Dr. Vansina said, one   22
of the oldest was the *"kora."*

"Bolong," he said, was clearly Mandinka for "river." Preceded   23
by *"Kamby,"* it very likely meant "Gambia River."

Dr. Vansina telephoned an eminent Africanist colleague, Dr.   24
Philip Curtin. He said that the phonetic *"Kin-tay"* was correctly
spelled *"Kinte,"* a very old clan that had originated in Old Mali.
The Kinte men traditionally were blacksmiths, and the women were
potters and weavers.

I knew I must get to the Gambia River.   25

The first native Gambian I could locate in the U.S. was named   26
Ebou Manga, then a junior attending Hamilton College in upstate
Clinton, N.Y. He and I flew to Dakar, Senegal, then took a smaller
plane to Yundum Airport, and rode in a van to Gambia's capital,
Bathurst. Ebou and his father assembled eight Gambia government
officials. I told them Grandma's stories, every detail I could remember, as they listened intently, then reacted. " *'Kamby Bolong'* of
course is Gambia River!" I heard. "But more clue is your fore-
father's saying his name was *'Kinte.'* " Then they told me something I would never even have fantasized — that in places in the
back country lived very old men, commonly called *griots*, who
could tell centuries of the histories of certain very old family clans.
As for *Kintes*, they pointed out to me on a map some family villages, Kinte-Kundah, and Kinte-Kundah Janneh-Ya, for instance.

The Gambian officials said they would try to help me. I re-   27
turned to New York dazed. It is embarrassing to me now, but
despite Grandma's stories, I'd never been concerned much with
Africa, and I had the routine images of African people living mostly
in exotic jungles. But a compulsion now laid hold of me to learn
all I could, and I began devouring books about Africa, especially
about the slave trade. Then one Thursday's mail contained a letter
from one of the Gambian officials, inviting me to return there.

Monday I was back in Bathurst. It galvanized me when the   28
officials said that a *griot* had been located who told the *Kinte* clan
history — his name was Kebba Kanga Fofana. To reach him, I discovered, required a modified safari: renting a launch to get upriver,
two land vehicles to carry supplies by a roundabout land route, and

employing finally 14 people, including three interpreters and four musicians, since a *griot* would not speak the revered clan histories without background music.

The boat Baddibu vibrated upriver, with me acutely tense: 29 Were these Africans maybe viewing me as but another of the pith-helmets? After about two hours, we put in at James Island, for me to see the ruins of the once British-operated James Fort. Here two centuries of slave ships had loaded thousands of cargoes of Gambian tribespeople. The crumbling stones, the deeply oxidized swivel cannon, even some remnant links of chain seemed all but impossible to believe. Then we continued upriver to the left-bank village of Albreda, and there put ashore to continue on foot to Juffure, village of the *griot*. Once more we stopped, for me to see *toubob kolong*, "the white man's well," now almost filled in, in a swampy area with abundant, tall, saw-toothed grass. It was dug two centuries ago to "17 men's height deep" to insure survival drinking water for long-driven, famishing coffles of slaves.

Walking on, I kept wishing that Grandma could hear how her 30 stories had led me to the *"Kamby Bolong."* (Our surviving storyteller Cousin Georgia died in a Kansas City hospital during this same morning, I would learn later.) Finally, Juffure village's playing children, sighting us, flashed an alert. The 70-odd people came rushing from their circular, thatch-roofed, mud-walked huts, with goats bounding up and about, and parrots squawking from up in the palms. I sensed him in advance somehow, the small man amid them, wearing a pillbox cap and an off-white robe — the *griot*. Then the interpreters went to him, as the villagers thronged around me.

And it hit me like a gale wind: every one of them, the whole 31 crowd, was *jet black*. An enormous sense of guilt swept me — a sense of being some kind of hybrid . . . a sense of being impure among the pure. It was an awful sensation.

The old *griot* stepped away from my interpreters and the 32 crowd quickly swarmed around him — all of them buzzing. An interpreter named A. B. C. Salla came to me; he whispered: "Why they stare at you so, they have never seen here a black American." And that hit me: I was symbolizing for them twenty-five millions of us they had never seen. What did they think of me — of us?

Then abruptly the old *griot* was briskly walking toward me. 33 His eyes boring into mine, he spoke in Mandinka, as if instinctively I should understand — and A. B. C. Salla translated:

"Yes . . . we have been told by the forefathers . . . that many 34
of us from this place are in exile . . . in that place called America
. . . and in other places."

I suppose I physically wavered, and they thought it was the 35
heat; rustling whispers went through the crowd, and a man brought
me a low stool. Now the whispering hushed — the musicians had
softly begun playing *kora* and *balafon*, and a canvas sling lawn seat
was taken by the *griot*, Kebba Kanga Fofane, aged 75 "rains" (one
rainy season each year). He seemed to gather himself into a physical
rigidity, and he began speaking the *Kinte* clan's ancestral oral
history; it came rolling from his mouth across the next hours . . .
17th- and 18th-century *Kinte* lineage details, predominantly what
men took wives; the children they "begot," in the order of their
births; those children's mates and children.

Events frequently were dated by some proximate singular 36
physical occurrence. It was as if some ancient scroll were printed
indelibly within the *griot's* brain. Each few sentences or so, he
would pause for an interpreter's translation to me. I distill here the
essence:

The *Kinte* clan began in Old Mali, the men generally black- 37
smiths ". . . who conquered fire," and the women potters and weavers. One large branch of the clan moved to Mauretania from where
one son of the clan, Kairaba Kunta Kinte, a Moslem Marabout holy
man, entered Gambia. He lived first in the village of Pakali N'Ding;
he moved next to Jiffarong village; ". . . and then he came here, into
our own village of Juffure."

In Juffure, Kairaba Kunta Kinte took his first wife, ". . . a 38
Mandinka maiden, whose name was Sireng. By her, he begot two
sons, whose names were Janneh and Saloum. Then he got a second
wife, Yaisa. By her, he begot a son, Omoro."

The three sons became men in Juffure. Janneh and Saloum 39
went off and found a new village, Kinte-Kundah Janneh-Ya. "And
then Omoro, the youngest son, when he had 30 rains, took as a
wife a maiden, Binta Kebba.

"And by her, he begot four sons — Kunta, Lamin, Suwadu, 40
and Madi . . ."

Sometimes, a "begotten," after his naming, would be accom- 41
panied by some later-occurring detail, perhaps as ". . . in time of
big water (flood), he slew a water buffalo." Having named those
four sons, now the *griot* stated such a detail.

"About the time the king's soldiers came, the eldest of these 42 four sons, Kunta, when he had about 16 rains, went away from this village, to chop wood to make a drum . . . and he was never seen again . . ."

Goose-pimples the size of lemons seemed to pop all over me. 43 In my knapsack were my cumulative notebooks, the first of them including how in my boyhood, my Grandma, Cousin Georgia and the others told of the African *"Kin-tay"* who always said he was kidnapped near his village — while chopping wood to make a drum . . .

I showed the interpreter, he showed and told the *griot*, who 44 excitedly told the people; they grew very agitated. Abruptly then they formed a human ring, encircling me, dancing and chanting. Perhaps a dozen of the women carrying their infant babies rushed in toward me, thrusting the infants into my arms — conveying, I would later learn, "the laying on of hands . . . through this flesh which is us, we are you, and you are us." The men hurried me into their mosque, their Arabic praying later being translated outside: "Thanks be to Allah for returning the long lost from among us." Direct descendants of Kunta Kinte's blood brothers were hastened, some of them from nearby villages, for a family portrait to be taken with me, surrounded by actual ancestral sixth cousins. More symbolic acts filled the remaining day.

When they would let me leave, for some reason I wanted to 45 go away over the African land. Dazed, silent in the bumping Land Rover, I heard the cutting staccato of talking drums. Then when we sighted the next village, its people came thronging to meet us. They were all — little naked ones to wizened elders — waving, beaming, amid a cacophony of crying out; and then my ears identified their words: *"Meester Kinte! Meester Kinte!"*

Let me tell you something: I am a man. But I remember the 46 sob surging up from my feet, flinging up my hands before my face and bawling as I had not done since I was a baby . . . the jet-black Africans were jostling, staring . . . I didn't care, with the feelings surging. If you really knew the odyssey of us millions of black Americans, if you really knew how we came in the seeds of our forefathers, captured, driven, beaten, inspected, bought, branded, chained in foul ships, if you really knew, you needed weeping . . .

Back home, I knew that what I must write, really, was our 47 black saga, where any individual's past is the essence of the millions'. Now flat broke, I went to some editors I knew, describing the Gambian miracle, and my desire to pursue the research; Doubleday contracted to publish, and Reader's Digest to condense the projected book; then I had advances to travel further.

What ship brought Kinte to Grandma's " 'Naplis" (Annapolis,   48 Md., obviously)? The old *griot's* time reference to "king's soldiers" sent me flying to London. Feverish searching at last identified, in British Parliament records, "Colonel O'Hare's Forces," dispatched in mid-1767 to protect the then British-held James Fort whose ruins I'd visited. So Kunta Kinte was down in some ship probably sailing later that summer from the Gambia River to Annapolis.

Now I feel it was fated that I had taught myself to write in the   49 U.S. Coast Guard. For the sea dramas I had concentrated on had given me years of experience searching among yellowing old U.S. maritime records. So now in English 18th Century marine records I finally tracked ships reporting themselves in and out to the Commandant of the Gambia River's James Fort. And then early one afternoon I found that a Lord Ligonier under a Captain Thomas Davies had sailed on the Sabbath of July 5, 1767. Her cargo: 3,265 elephants' teeth, 3,700 pounds of beeswax, 800 pounds of cotton, 32 ounces of Gambian gold, and 140 slaves; her destination: "Annapolis."

That night I recrossed the Atlantic. In the Library of Congress   50 the Lord Ligonier's arrival was one brief line in "Shipping In The Port Of Annapolis — 1748–1775." I located the author, Vaughan W. Brown, in his Baltimore brokerage office. He drove to Historic Annapolis, the city's historical society, and found me further documentation of her arrival on Sept. 29, 1767. (Exactly two centuries later, Sept. 29, 1967, standing, staring seaward from an Annapolis pier, again I knew tears). More help came in the Maryland Hall of Records. Archivist Phebe Jacobsen found the Lord Ligonier's arriving customs declaration listing, "98 Negroes" — so in her 86-day crossing, 42 Gambians had died, one among the survivors being 16-year-old Kunta Kinte. Then the microfilmed Oct. 1, 1767, Maryland Gazette contained, on page two, an announcement to prospective buyers from the ship's agents, Daniel of St. Thos. Jenifer and John Ridout (the Governor's secretary): "from the River GAMBIA, in AFRICA . . . a cargo of choice, healthy SLAVES . . ."

HENRY DAVID THOREAU

HENRY DAVID THOREAU (1817–1862) lived all but one year of his life in Concord, Massachusetts, where he was known as a nonconformist, an eccentric. He did some teaching and lecturing, gained a sound reputation as a naturalist, and, of course, as an author, contributing both verse and prose to magazines and newspapers of the day. His essay "Civil Disobedience" has long been read, pondered, acted upon in various parts of the world (e.g., by Mahatma Ghandi). However, *Walden*, his book of essays, is usually considered his masterpiece. Although it is partially an account of his "experiment in living" (alone in the woods at Walden Pond), it is also a careful study of nature, a critical view of then-modern society, and a work of much artistic merit.

From Where I Lived, and What I Lived For

I went to the woods because I wished to live deliberately, to front only the essential facts of life, and see if I could not learn what it had to teach, and not, when I came to die, discover that I had not lived. I did not wish to live what was not life, living is so dear; nor did I wish to practise resignation, unless it was quite necessary. I wanted to live deep and suck out all the marrow of life, to live so sturdily and Spartan-like as to put to rout all that was not life, to cut a broad swath and shave close, to drive life into a corner, and reduce it to its lowest terms, and, if it proved to be mean, why then to get the whole and genuine meanness of it, and publish its meanness to the world; or if it were sublime, to know it by experience, and be able to give a true account of it in my next excursion. For most men, it appears to me, are in a strange uncertainty about it, whether it is of the devil or of God, and have *somewhat hastily* concluded that it is the chief end of man here to "glorify God and enjoy him forever."

Still we live meanly, like ants; though the fable tells us that we were long ago changed into men; like pygmies we fight with

1

2

cranes; it is error upon error, and clout upon clout, and our best virtue has for its occasion a superfluous and evitable wretchedness. Our life is frittered away by detail. An honest man has hardly need to count more than his ten fingers, or in extreme cases he may add his ten toes, and lump the rest. Simplicity, simplicity, simplicity! I say, let your affairs be as two or three, and not a hundred or a thousand; instead of a million count half a dozen, and keep your accounts on your thumb-nail. In the midst of this chopping sea of civilized life, such are the clouds and storms and quicksands and thousand-and-one items to be allowed for, that a man has to live, if he would not founder and go to the bottom and not make his port at all, by dead reckoning, and he must be a great calculator indeed who succeeds. Simplify, simplify. Instead of three meals a day, if it be necessary eat but one; instead of a hundred dishes, five; and reduce other things in proportion. Our life is like a German Confederacy, made up of petty states, with its boundary forever fluctuating, so that even a German cannot tell you how it is bounded at any moment. The nation itself, with all its so-called internal improvements, which, by the way are all external and superficial, is just such an unwieldy and overgrown establishment, cluttered with furniture and tripped up by its own traps, ruined by luxury and heedless expense, by want of calculation and a worthy aim, as the million households in the lands; and the only cure for it, as for them, is in a rigid economy, a stern and more than Spartan simplicity of life and elevation of purpose. It lives too fast. Men think that it is essential that the *Nation* have commerce, and export ice, and talk through a telegraph, and ride thirty miles an hour, without a doubt, whether *they* do or not; but whether we should live like baboons or like men, is a little uncertain. If we do not get out sleepers, and forge rails, and devote days and nights to the work, but go to tinkering upon our *lives* to improve *them*, who will build railroads? And if railroads are not built, how shall we get to heaven in season? But if we stay at home and mind our business, who will want railroads? We do not ride on the railroad; it rides upon us. Did you ever think what those sleepers are that underlie the railroad? Each one is a man, an Irishman, or a Yankee man. The rails are laid on them, and they are covered with sand, and the cars run smoothly over them. They are sound sleepers, I assure you. And every few years a new lot is laid down and run over; so that, if some have the pleasure of riding on a rail, others have the misfortune to be ridden upon. And when they run over a man that is walking in his sleep, a supernumerary sleeper in the wrong position, and wake him up, they suddenly stop the cars, and make a hue and cry about it, as if this were an exception. I am glad to know that it takes a gang of men for every five miles to keep the sleepers down and level in their beds as it is, for this is a sign that they may sometimes get up again.

Why should we live with such hurry and waste of life? We are determined to be starved before we are hungry. Men say that a stitch in time saves nine, and so they take a thousand stitches to-day to save nine to-morrow. As for *work*, we haven't any of any consequence. We have the Saint Vitus' dance, and cannot possibly keep our heads still. If I should only give a few pulls at the parish bell-rope, as for a fire, that is, without setting the bell, there is hardly a man on his farm in the outskirts of Concord, notwithstanding that press of engagements which was his excuse so many times this morning, nor a boy, nor a woman, I might almost say, but would foresake all and follow that sound, not mainly to save property from the flames, but, if we will confess the truth, much more to see it burn, since burn it must, and we, be it known, did not set it on fire, — or to see it put out, and have a hand in it, if that is done as handsomely; yes, even if it were the parish church itself. Hardly a man takes a half-hour's nap after dinner, but when he wakes he holds up his head and asks, "What's the news?" as if the rest of mankind had stood his sentinels. Some give directions to be waked every half-hour, doubtless for no other purpose; and then, to pay for it, they tell what they have dreamed. After a night's sleep the news is as indispensable as the breakfast. "Pray tell me anything new that has happened to a man anywhere on this globe," — and he reads it over his coffee and rolls, that a man has had his eyes gouged out this morning on the Wachito River; never dreaming the while that he lives in the dark unfathomed mammoth cave of this world, and has but the rudiment of an eye himself.

For my part, I could easily do without the post-office. I think that there are very few important communications made through it. To speak critically, I never received more than one or two letters in my life — I wrote this some years ago — that were worth the postage. The penny-post is, commonly, an institution through which you seriously offer a man that penny for his thoughts which is so often safely offered in jest. And I am sure that I never read any memorable news in a newspaper. If we read of one man robbed, or murdered, or killed by accident, or one house burned, or one vessel wrecked, or one steamboat blown up, or one cow run over on the Western Railroad, or one mad dog killed, or one lot of grass-hoppers in the winter, — we never need read of another. One is enough. If you are acquainted with the principle, what do you care for a myriad instances and applications? To a philosopher all *news*, as it is called, is gossip, and they who edit and read it are old women over their tea. Yet not a few are greedy after this gossip. There was such a rush, as I hear, the other day at one of the offices to learn the foreign news by the last arrival, that several large squares of plate glass belonging to the establishment were broken by the pressure, — news which I seriously think a ready wit might write a twelvemonth, or twelve years, beforehand with sufficient accuracy. As for Spain, for instance, if you know how to throw in Don Carlos and the Infanta, and Don Pedro and Seville and Gra-nada, from time to time in the right proportions, — they may have changed the names a little since I saw the papers, — and serve up a bull-fight when other entertainments fail, it will be true to the letter, and give us as good an idea of the exact state or ruin of things in Spain as the most succinct and lucid reports under this head in the newspapers: and as for England, almost the last sig-nificant scrap of news from that quarter was the revolution of 1649; and if you have learned the history of her crops for an aver-age year, you never need attend to that thing again, unless your speculations are of a merely pecuniary character. If one may judge who rarely looks into the newspapers, nothing new does ever hap-pen in foreign parts, a French revolution not excepted.

What news! how much more important to know what that is   5
which was never old! "Kieou-he-yu (great dignitary of the state of Wei) sent a man to Khoung-tseu to know his news. Khoung-tseu caused the messenger to be seated near him, and questioned him in these terms: What is your master doing? The messenger answered with respect: My master desires to diminish the number of his faults, but he cannot come to the end of them. The messenger being gone, the philosopher remarked: What a worthy messenger! What a worthy messenger!" The preacher, instead of vexing the ears of drowsy farmers on their day of rest at the end of the week, — for Sunday is the fit conclusion of an ill-spent week, and not the fresh and brave beginning of a new one, — with this one other draggle-

tail of a sermon, should shout with thundering voice, "Pause! Avast! Why so seeming fast, but deadly slow?"

Shams and delusions are esteemed for soundless truths, while reality is fabulous. If men would steadily observe realities only, and not allow themselves to be deluded, life, to compare it with such things as we know, would be like a fairy tale and the Arabian Nights Entertainments. If we respected only what is inevitable and has a right to be, music and poetry would resound along the streets. When we are unhurried and wise, we perceive that only great and worthy things have any permanent and absolute existence, that petty fears and petty pleasures are but the shadow of the reality. This is always exhilarating and sublime. By closing the eyes and slumbering, and consenting to be deceived by shows, men establish and confirm their daily life of routine and habit everywhere, which still is built on purely illusory foundations. Children, who play life, discern its true law and relations more clearly than men, who fail to live it worthily, but who think that they are wiser by experience, that is, by failure. I have read in a Hindoo book, that "there was a king's son, who, being expelled in infancy from his native city, was brought up by a forester, and, growing up to maturity in that state, imagined himself to belong to the barbarous race with which he lived. One of his father's ministers having discovered him, revealed to him what he was, and the misconception of his character was removed, and he knew himself to be a prince. So soul," continues the Hindoo philosopher, "from the circumstances in which it is placed, mistakes its own character, until the truth is revealed to it by some holy teacher, and then it knows itself to be *Brahme*." I perceive that we inhabitants of New England live this mean life that we do because our vision does not penetrate the surface of things. We think that that *is* which *appears* to be. If a man should walk through this town and see only the reality, where, think you, would the "Mill-dam" go to? If he should give us an account of the realities he beheld there, we should not recognize the place in his description. Look at the meeting-house, or a court-house, or a jail, or a shop, or a dwelling-house, and say what that thing really is before a true gaze, and they would all go to pieces in your account of them. Men esteem truth remote, in the outskirts of the system, behind the farthest star, before Adam and after the last man. In eternity there is indeed something true and sublime. But all these times and places and occasions are now and here. God himself

culminates in the present moment, and will never be more divine in
the lapse of all the ages. And we are enabled to apprehend at all
what is sublime and noble only by the perpetual instilling and
drenching of the reality that surrounds us. The universe constantly
and obediently answers to our conceptions; whether we travel fast
or slow, the track is laid for us. Let us spend our lives in conceiving
then. The poet or the artist never yet had so fair and noble a design
but some of his posterity at least could accomplish it.

    Let us spend one day as deliberately as Nature, and not be   7
thrown off the track by every nutshell and mosquito's wing that
falls on the rails. Let us rise early and fast, or breakfast, gently and
without perturbation; let company come and let company go, let
the bells ring and the children cry, — determined to make a day of
it. Why should we knock under and go with the stream? Let us not
be upset and overwhelmed in that terrible rapid and whirlpool
called a dinner, situated in the meridian shallows. Weather this
danger and you are safe, for the rest of the way is down hill. With
unrelaxed nerves, with morning vigor, sail by it, looking another
way, tied to the mast like Ulysses. If the engine whistles, let it
whistle till it is hoarse for its pains. If the bell rings, why should we
run? We will consider what kind of music they are like. Let us
settle ourselves, and work and wedge our feet downward through
the mud and slush of opinion, and prejudice, and tradition, and
delusion, and appearance, that alluvion which covers the globe,
through Paris and London, through New York and Boston and
Concord, through Church and State, through poetry and philosophy
and religion, till we come to a hard bottom and rocks in place, which
we can call *reality*, and say, This is, and no mistake; and then begin,
having a *point d'appui*, below freshet and frost and fire, a place
where you might found a wall or a state, or set a lamp-post safely,
or perhaps a gauge, not a Nilometer, but a Realometer, that future
ages might know how deep a feshet of shams and appearances had
gathered from time to time. If you stand right fronting and face to
face to a fact, you will see the sun glimmer on both its surfaces, as
if it were a cimeter, and feel its sweet edge dividing you through
the heart and marrow, and so you will happily conclude your mortal
career. Be it life or death, we crave only reality. If we are really
dying, let us hear the rattle in our throats and feel cold in the extremities; if we are alive, let us go about our business.

    Time is but the stream I go a-fishing in. I drink at it; but while   8

I drink I see the sandy bottom and detect how shallow it is. Its thin current slides away, but eternity remains. I would drink deeper; fish in the sky, whose bottom is pebbly with stars. I cannot count one. I know not the first letter of the alphabet. I have always been regretting that I was not as wise as the day I was born. The intellect is a cleaver; it discerns and rifts its way into the secret of things. I do not wish to be any more busy with my hands than is necessary. My head is hands and feet. I feel all my best faculties concentrated in it. My instinct tells me that my head is an organ for burrowing, as some creatures use their snout and fore paws, and with it I would mine and burrow my way through these hills. I think that the richest vein is somewhere hereabouts; so by the divining-rod and thin rising vapors I judge; and here I will begin to mine.

A Guide to Terms

Abstract   (See *Concrete/Abstract.*)
Allusion   (See *Figures of Speech.*)
Analogy   (See *Section 4.*)
Argument is one of the four basic forms of prose. It usually employs one or all of the other forms — exposition, narration, description — sometimes becoming difficult to distinguish from them. The difference is in its basic motivation: argument assumes that there are two sides to the matter under discussion, but it aims to resolve the conflict by influencing the reader to favor one side.

A distinction is ordinarily made between *logical argument* (usually called simply "argument") and *persuasive argument* (usually termed "persuasion"). Whereas logical argument appeals to reason, persuasion appeals to the emotions. The aim of both is to convince, however, and they are nearly always blended into whatever mixture seems most likely to do the convincing. After all, reason and emotion are both important human elements — and we may have to persuade someone even to listen to our logic. The emphasis on one or the other, of course, should depend on the subject and the audience.

Some authorities make a somewhat different distinction: we argue merely to get someone to change his mind; we use persuasion to get him to *do* something about it — e.g., to vote a Republican ticket, not just agree with the party platform. But this view is not entirely inconsistent with the other. We can hardly expect to change a *mind* by emotional appeal, but we can hope to get someone to *act* because of it, whether or not his mind has been changed.

Cause   (See *Section 6.*)

Central Theme   (See *Unity.*)

Classification   (See *Section 2.*)

Clichés are tired expressions, perhaps once fresh and colorful, that have been overused until they have lost most of their effectiveness and become trite or hackneyed. (The term is also applied, less often, to trite ideas or attitudes.)

We may need to use clichés in conversation, of course, where the quick and economical phrase is an important and useful tool of expression — and where no one expects us to be constantly original. We are fortunate, in a way, to have a large accumulation of clichés from which to draw. To describe someone, without straining our originality very much, we can always declare that he is *as innocent as a lamb, as thin as a rail,* or *as fat as a pig;* that he is *as dumb as an ox, as sly as a fox,* or *as wise as an owl;* that he is *financially embarrassed* or *has a fly in the ointment* or *his ship has come in;* or that, *last but not least, in this day and age,* the *Grim Reaper* has taken him to *his eternal reward.* There is indeed *a large stockpile* from which we can draw for ordinary conversation.

But the trite expression, written down on paper, is a permanent reminder that the writer is either lazy or not aware of the dullness of stereotypes — or, even more damaging, it is a clue that his ideas themselves may be threadbare, therefore requiring threadbare language to express them.

Occasionally, of course, a writer can use obvious clichés deliberately, for his own purposes. (See Roiphe, par. 4; Sheehy, 12; Casler, 4; Allen, 14; Arlen.) But usually to be fully effective, writing must be fresh and should seem to have been written specifically for the occasion. Clichés, however fresh and appropriate at one time, have lost these qualities.

Closings are almost as much of a problem as introductions, and they are fully as important. The function of a closing is simply "to close," of course; but this implies somehow tying the entire writing into a neat package, giving the final sense of unity to the whole endeavor, and thus leaving the reader with a sense of satisfaction instead of an uneasy feeling that he ought to be looking around for another page.

There is no standard length for closings. A short composition may be effectively ended with one sentence — or even without any real closing at all, if the last point discussed is a strong or climactic one. A longer piece of writing, however, may be more slowly finished, perhaps through several paragraphs.

A few types of weak endings are so common that warnings are in order here. The careful writer will avoid these faults: (1) giving the effect of having suddenly become tired and quit; (2) ending on a minor detail or an apparent afterthought; (3) bringing up a new point in the closing; (4) using any new qualifying remark in the closing (if he wants his opinions to seem less dogmatic or generalized, he should go back to do his qualifying where the damage was done); (5) ending with an apology of any kind (if the author is not interested enough to become at least a minor expert in his subject, he should not be wasting the reader's time).

Of the several acceptable ways of giving the sense of finality to a paper, the easiest is the *summary*, but it is also the least desirable for most short papers. If the reader has read and understood something only a page or two before, he probably does not need to have it reviewed for him now. It is apt to seem merely repetitious. Longer writings, of course, such as research or term papers, may require thorough summaries.

Several other closing techniques are available to the writer. The following, which do not represent all the possibilities, may be usable at one time or another, and they are frequently employed in combinations with each other:

1. *Using word signals* — e.g., *finally, at last, thus, and so, in conclusion,* as well as more original devices suggested by the subject itself. (See Thurber, Casler.)

2. *Changing the tempo* — usually a matter of sentence length or pace. This is a very subtle indication of finality, and it is difficult to achieve. (For examples of modified use, see Clarke, Tuchman, Arlen.)

3. *Restating the central idea* of the writing — sometimes a "statement" so fully developed that it practically becomes a summary itself. (See Catton.)

4. *Using climax to end the writing* — a natural culmination of preceding points or, in some cases, the last major point

itself. This is suitable, however, only if the materials have been so arranged that the last point is noticeably outstanding. (See Catton, Kosinski, Kerouac, Haley.)

5. *Making suggestions*, perhaps mentioning a possible solution to the problem being discussed — a useful technique for exposition as well as for argument, and a natural signal of the end. (See Peter/Hull, Gregory, Casler, Allen.)

6. *Showing the topic's significance*, its effects, or the universality of its meaning — a commonly used technique that if carefully handled, is an excellent indication of closing. (Several selections are closed by this method; see, e.g., Gregory, Osgood, Hoffman.)

7. *Echoing the introduction* — a technique that has the decided virtue of improving the effect of unity since it brings the development around full circle, so to speak. The echo may be a reference to a problem posed or a significant expression, quotation, analogy, or symbol used in the introduction. (See Thurber, Sheehy, Franklin.)

8. *Using some rhetorical device* — a sort of catchall category, but a good supply source because it includes several very effective techniques: pertinent quotations, anecdotes and brief dialogues, metaphors, allusions, ironic comments, and various kinds of witty or memorable remarks. All run the risk of seeming forced, and hence amateurish; but properly handled they can do an effective job of closing. (See Gregory, Sheehy.)

Coherence is the quality of good writing that results from the presentation of all parts in logical and clear relations.

Coherence and unity are usually studied together and, indeed, are almost inseparable. But whereas unity refers to the relation of parts to the central theme (see *Unity*), coherence refers to their relations with each other. In a coherent writing, each sentence, each paragraph, each major division seems to grow out of those preceding it.

Several transitional devices (see *Transition*) help to make these relations clear, but far more fundamental to coherence is the sound organization of materials. From the moment he first begins to visualize his subject materials in patterns, the writer's goal must be clear and logical development. If it is, coherence is almost assured.

Colloquial expressions are characteristic of conversation and informal writing, and they are normally perfectly appropriate for those media. However, most writing done for college, business, or professional purposes is considered "formal" writing; and for such usage colloquialisms are too informal, too *folksy* (a word itself which most dictionaries label "colloq.").

Some of the expressions appropriate only for informal usage are *kid* (for child), *boss* (for employer), *flunk*, *buddy*, *snooze*, *gym*, *a lot of*, *phone*, *skin flicks*, *porno*. In addition, contractions such as *can't* and *I'd* are usually regarded as colloquialisms and are never permissible in, for instance, a research or term paper.

Slang is defined as a low level of colloquialism, but it is sometimes placed "below" colloquialism in respectability; even standard dictionaries differ as to just what the distinction is. (Some of the examples in the preceding paragraph, if included in dictionaries at all, are identified both ways.) At any rate, slang generally comprises words either coined or given novel meanings in an attempt at colorful or humorous expression. Slang soon becomes limp with overuse, however, losing whatever vigor it had to start with. In widely varying lengths of time, slang expressions either disappear completely or graduate to more acceptable colloquial status and thence, possibly, into standard usage. (That is one way in which our language is constantly changing.) But until their "graduations," all forms of slang and colloquialism have an appropriate function in formal writing only if used sparingly and for special effect. Because dictionaries frequently differ in matters of usage, the student should be sure he is using a standard edition approved by his instructor. (For further examples, see Gregory, Roiphe, Wolfe, Kosinski, Sheehy, Steinem, Allen, Brown, Smith.)

Comparison   (See *Section 3*.)

Conclusions   (See *Closings*.)

Concrete and **Abstract** words are both indispensable to the language, but a good rule in most writing is to use the concrete whenever possible. This policy also applies, of course, to sentences that express only abstract ideas, which can often be made clearer, more effective, by use of concrete examples. Many expository paragraphs are constructed with an abstract topic sentence and its concrete support. (See *Unity*.)

A concrete word names something that exists as an entity in itself, something that can be perceived by the human senses. We can see, touch, hear, and smell a horse — hence *horse* is a concrete word. But a horse's *strength* is not. We have no reason to doubt that strength exists, but it does not have an independent existence: something else must *be* strong or there is no strength. Hence, *strength* is an abstract word.

Purely abstract reading is difficult for the average reader; with no concrete images provided for him, he is constantly forced to make his own. Concrete writing helps the reader to visualize and is therefore easier and faster to read.

(See *Specific/General* for further discussion.)

Connotation and **Denotation** both refer to the meanings of words. Denotation is the direct, literal meaning as it would be found in a dictionary, whereas connotation refers to the response a word *really* arouses in the reader or listener. (See Wolfe, 14; or Osgood's concluding words.)

There are two types of connotation: personal and general. Personal connotations vary widely, depending on the experiences and moods that an individual associates with the word. (This corresponds with personal symbolism; see *Symbolism.*) *Waterfall* is not apt to have the same meaning for the happy young honeymooners at Yosemite as it has for the grieving mother whose child has just drowned in a waterfall. But general connotations are those shared by many people. *Fireside,* far beyond its obvious dictionary definition, generally connotes warmth and security and good companionship. *Mother,* which denotatively means simply "female parent," means much more connotatively.

A word or phrase considered less distasteful or offensive than a more direct expression is called a *euphemism,* and this is also a matter of connotation. (See Mitford.) The various expressions used instead of the more direct "four-letter words" are examples of euphemisms. (See Wolfe's "mounting" or Lawrence's "dirt.") *Remains* is often used instead of *corpse,* and a few newspapers still have people *passing away* and being *laid to rest,* rather than *dying* and being *buried.*

But a serious respect for the importance of connotations goes far beyond euphemistic practices. The young writer can hardly expect to know all the different meanings of words for all his potential readers, but he can at least be aware that they do *have* different meanings. Of course, this is most important in persuasive writing — in political speeches, in advertising copywriting, and in any endeavor where some sort of public image is being created. When President Franklin Roosevelt began his series of informal radio talks, he called them "fireside chats," thus putting connotation to work. An advertising copywriter trying to evoke the feeling of love and tenderness associated with motherhood is not seriously tempted to use *female parent* instead of *mother.*

In exposition, however, where the primary purpose is to explain, the writer ordinarily tries to avoid words that may have emotional overtones, unless these can somehow be used to increase understanding.

(For further connotative examples, see Gregory, Mitford, Brown.)

Contrast (See *Section 3.*)

Denotation (See *Connotation/Denotation.*)

Description (See *Section 9.*)

Diction refers simply to "choice of words," but, not so simply, it involves many problems of usage, some of which are explained under several other headings in this guide, e.g., *Clichés, Colloquial, Connotation/Denotation, Concrete/Abstract* — anything, in fact, which pertains primarily to word choices. But the characteristics of good diction may be more generally classified as follows:

1. *Accuracy* — the choice of words that mean exactly what the author intends.

2. *Economy* — the choice of the simplest and fewest words that will convey the exact shade of meaning intended.

3. *Emphasis* — the choice of fresh, strong words, avoiding clichés and unnecessarily vague or general terms.

4. *Appropriateness* — the choice of words that are appropriate to the subject matter, to the prospective reader-audience, and to the purpose of the writing.

(For contrasts of diction, see Thurber, Gregory, Wolfe, Allen, Carson, Brown.)

Deduction (See *Section 8.*)

Division (See *Section 2.*)

Editorial "We" is still used, although not as much as it used to be, by some editorial and column writers of newspapers and by the authors of some magazine departments, such as "The Talk of the Town" in *The New Yorker*. It has the advantage of avoiding the narrow, one-man implications of *I* or *me*, but it sometimes leads to the strange form *ourself* in avoiding the actual plural effect that *ourselves* would give.

(For examples of a somewhat modified usage, see Packard, Hoffman, and Casler.)

Effect   (See *Section 6*.)

Emphasis is almost certain to fall *somewhere*, and the author should be the one to decide where. He should make certain that a major point, not some minor detail, is emphasized.

Following are the most common ways of achieving emphasis. Most of them apply to the sentence, the paragraph, or the overall writing — all of which can be seriously weakened by emphasis in the wrong places.

1. By *position*. The most emphatic position is usually at the end, the second most emphatic at the beginning. (There are a few exceptions, including news stories and certain kinds of scientific reports.) The middle, therefore, should be used for materials that do not deserve special emphasis. (See Peter/ Hull, for the order of examples; Johnson; Catton, par. 16; Franklin; Clarke.)

A sentence in which the main point is held until the last is called a *periodic sentence;* in a *loose sentence*, the main point is disposed of earlier and followed by dependencies, e.g., "The house burned in the middle of the night."

2. By *proportion*. Ordinarily, but not necessarily, important elements are given the most attention and automatically achieve a certain emphasis because of this. (See Clarke's hypotheses, and Smith's proportionate attention to the second of his narrated examples.)

3. By *repetition*. Words and ideas may sometimes be given emphasis by reuse, usually in a different manner. If not cautiously handled, however, this method can seem merely repetitious, not emphatic. (See Thurber, Peter/Hull, Gregory, Lawrence, Arlen.)

4. By *flat statement*. Although an obvious way to achieve emphasis is simply to *tell* the reader what is most important, it is often least effective, at least when used as the

only method. Readers have a way of ignoring such pointers as "most important of all" and "especially true." (See Gregory; Catton, par. 16; Schweitzer; Drucker.)

5. By *mechanical devices*. Emphasis can be achieved by using italics (underlining), capital letters, or exclamation points. But too often these devices are used, however unintentionally, to cover deficiencies of content or style. Their employment can quickly be overdone and their impact lost. (See Lawrence, Franklin. Notice that Mitford, with more emphatic style than most, uses none of these devices.)

6. By *distinctiveness of style*. The author can emphasize subtly with fresh and concrete words or figures of speech, crisp or unusual structures, and careful control of paragraphs or sentence lengths. (These methods are used in many essays in this book; e.g., see Catton; Wolfe; Allen; Curtin, pars. 7–15; Arlen; Smith, 3, 9; Kerouac.) *Verbal irony* (See *Irony*), including *sarcasm* and the rather specialized form known as *understatement*, if handled judiciously, is another valuable means of achieving distinctiveness of style and increasing emphasis. (See Wolfe; Mitford; Lawrence; Smith, 12.)

Essay refers to a brief prose composition on a single topic, usually, but not always, communicating the author's personal ideas and impressions. Beyond this, because of the wide and loose application of the term, no really satisfactory definition has been arrived at.

Classifications of essay types have also been widely varied and sometimes not very meaningful. One basic and useful distinction, however, is between *formal* and *informal* essays, although many defy classification even in such broad categories as these. It is best to regard the two types as opposite ends of a continuum, along which most essays may be placed.

The formal essay usually develops an important theme through a logical progression of ideas, with full attention to unity and coherence, and in a serious tone. Although the style is seldom completely impersonal, it is literary rather than colloquial. (For examples of essays that are somewhere near the "formal" end of the continuum, see Johnson, Packard, Catton, Campa, Carson, Casler, Drucker. The Declaration of Independence, a completely formal document, is not classifiable as an "essay" at all.)

The informal, or personal, essay is less elaborately or-ganized and more chatty in style. First-person pronouns, con-tractions, and other colloquial or even slang expressions are usually freely used. Informal essays are less serious in ap-parent purpose than formal essays. Although most do contain a worthwhile message or observation of some kind, an im-portant purpose of many is to entertain. (See Baker, Thurber, Wolfe, Allen, Brown.)

The more personal and intimate informal essays may be classifiable as *familiar* essays, although, again, there is no well-established boundary. Familiar essays pertain to the author's own experiences, ideas, or prejudices, frequently in a light and humorous style. (See Roiphe, Curtin, Kerouac.)

Evaluation of a literary piece, like that of any other creative en-deavor, is meaningful only when based somehow on the answers to three questions: (1) What was the author's pur-pose? (2) How successfully does he fulfill it? (3) How worth-while was it?

An architect could hardly be blamed for designing a poor gymnasium if his commission had been to design a library. Similarly, if any author is trying to explain the need for in-creased technology in improving enivornment (as is Drucker), he cannot be faulted for failing to make the reader laugh. However, if his purpose is simply to amuse (a worthy enough goal, by the way), he should not be condemned for teaching little about disposal of wastes. (Nothing prevents his trying to explain an ecological problem through the use of humor, or trying to amuse by telling about the need for more electricity; but in these situations his purpose has changed — and grown almost unbearably harder to achieve.)

If the architect was commissioned to design a gymnasium, however, he could be justifiably criticized on whether the building is successful and attractive *as a gymnasium*. If an author is trying to explain the need for caution in "saving the environment" (as in Drucker) the reader has a right to expect sound reasoning and clear expository prose.

Many things are written and published that succeed very well in carrying out the author's intent — but simply are not worthwhile. Although this is certainly justifiable ground for unfavorable criticism, the reader should first make full allowance for his own limitations and perhaps his narrow range of interests, evaluating the work as nearly as possible from the standpoint of the average reader for whom the writing was intended.

Figures of Speech are short, vivid comparisons, either stated or implied; but they are not literal comparisons (e.g., "Your car is like my car," which is presumably a plain statement of fact). Figures of speech are more imaginative. They imply analogy but, unlike analogy, are used less to inform than to make quick and forceful impressions. All figurative language is a comparison of unlikes, but the unlikes do have some interesting point of likeness, perhaps one never noticed before.

A *metaphor* merely suggests the comparison and is worded as if the two unlikes were the same thing — e.g., the "strangling rope of Puritanism" (Michener, par. 6) and "a great chapter in American life" (Catton, 1). (For some of the many other examples in this book, see Roiphe; Mitford; Lawrence; Schweitzer; Drucker, 1, 16, 21; Clarke; Kerouac.)

A *simile* (which is sometimes classified as a special kind of metaphor) expresses a similarity directly, usually with the word *like* or *as* — e.g., "feeling dangerously like a broken-field runner on an asphalt gridiron" (Baker, par. 2). (For further illustrations, see Roiphe, 2; Sheehy, 10; Allen, 14; Franklin, 1; Curtin, 1; Orwell, 1, 2; Kerouac.)

A *personification*, which is actually a special type of either metaphor or simile, is usually classified as a "figure" in its own right. In personification, inanimate things are given the qualities or powers of a person to describe their function or appearance — e.g., "that big, beautiful, bountiful black bitch," with which the Brown essay is finished. (Also see Baker, par. 6.) Some people would also label as personification any characterization of inanimate objects as animals, or of animals as humans — e.g., the many descriptions and "love displays" of the Thurber piece.

An *allusion* is literally any casual reference, any alluding, to something; but rhetorically it is limited to a figurative reference to a famous or literary person or event, and it should be distinguished from the casual reference that has a literal function in the subject matter. Hence, casual mention of Judas Iscariot's betrayal of Jesus is merely a reference, but calling a modern traitor a "Judas" is an allusion. A rooster might be referred to as "the Hitler of the barnyard," or a lover as a "Romeo." Many allusions refer to mythological or biblical persons or places. (See Wolfe, title and par. 1; Petrunkevitch, 9; Kerouac, 31, 46.)

Irony and paradox (both discussed under their own headings) and analogy (see *Section 4*) are also frequently classed as figures of speech, and there are several other, less common types that are really subclassifications of those already discussed.

General   (See *Specific/General*.)

Illustration   (See *Section 1*.)

Impressionistic Description   (See *Section 9*.)

Induction   (See *Section 8*.)

Introductions give readers their first impressions, and these often turn out to be lasting ones. In fact, unless an introduction succeeds in somehow attracting a reader's interest, he probably will go no further. Its importance is one reason that its writing is nearly always difficult.

Sometimes, when the writer remains at a loss to know how to begin, he should forget about the introduction for a while and go ahead with the main body of his writing. Later he may find that a suitable introduction has suggested itself or even that the way he did start is actually introduction enough.

Introduction may vary in length from one sentence in a short composition to several paragraphs or even several pages in longer and more complex expositions, such as research papers and reports of various kinds.

Good introductions to expository writings have at least three and sometimes four functions:

1. *To identify the subject and sets its limitations,* thus building a solid foundation for unity. This function usually includes some indication of the central theme, letting the reader know what point is to be made about the subject. Unlike the other forms of prose, which can often benefit by some degree of mystery, exposition has the primary purpose of explaining, so the reader has a right to know from the beginning just *what* is being explained.

2. *To interest the reader,* and thus ensure his attention. To be sure of doing this, the writer must analyze his prospec-

tive readers and their interest in his subject. The account of a new X-ray technique would need an entirely different kind of introduction if written for doctors than if written for the campus newspaper.

3. *To set the tone* of the rest of the writing. (See *Style/ Tone.*) Tones vary greatly in writing, just as the tones of a person's voice vary with his attitudes. One function of the introduction is to let the reader know the author's attitude since it may have a subtle but important bearing on the communication he is about to receive.

4. *Frequently*, but not always, *to indicate the plan of organization.* Although seldom important in short, relatively simple compositions and essay examinations, this function of introductions can be especially valuable in more complex papers.

Besides failure to perform these necessary functions, introductions are subject to several common weaknesses that can be easily overcome: (1) Avoid referring to the title, or even assuming that the reader has seen it. Make the introduction do all the introducing. (2) Avoid crude and uninteresting beginnings, such as "This paper is about. . . ." (3) Avoid going too abruptly into the main body — smooth transition is at least as important here as anywhere else. (4) Avoid overdoing the introduction, either in length or in extremes of style.

Fortunately, however, there are many good ways to introduce expository writing, and several of the most useful may be illustrated by the selections in this book. Many writings, of course, combine two or more of the techniques into interesting introductions.

1. *Stating the central theme,* which is sometimes fully enough explained in the introduction to become almost a preview-summary of the exposition to come. (See Baker, Thurber, Petrunkevitch, Tuchman.)

2. *Showing the significance of the subject,* or stressing its importance. (See Packard, Catton, Wolfe, Carson, Casler, Hoffman.)

3. *Giving the background of the subject,* usually in brief form, in order to bring the reader up to date as early as possible for a better understanding of the current matter. (See Peter/Hull, Packard, Campa, Casler, Arlen.)

4. *"Focusing down"* to one aspect of the subject, a tech-

nique similar to that used in some movies, showing first a broad scope (of subject area, as of landscape) and then progressively narrowing views until the focus is on one specific thing (perhaps the name "O'Flinnigan Jones" on a mailbox by a gate — or the specific "choice" that has to be made, as in the selection by Carson. (See also Toffler, Arlen.)

5. *Using a pertinent rhetorical device* that will attract interest as it leads into the main exposition — e.g., an anecdote, analogy, allusion, quotation, or paradox. (See *Time*, Carson, Sheehy, Casler.)

6. *Using a short but vivid comparison or contrast* to emphasize the central idea. (See Thurber, *Time*, Petrunkevitch.)

7. *Posing a challenging question,* the answering of which the reader will assume to be the purpose of the writing. (See Kosinski.)

8. *Referring to the writer's experience with the subject,* perhaps even giving a detailed account of that experience. Some writings, of course, especially descriptive or narrative essays, are simply continuations of experience so introduced, perhaps with the expository purpose of the telling made entirely evident only at the end or slowly unfolding as the account progresses. (See Peter/Hull, Roiphe, Orwell.)

9. *Presenting a startling statistic or other fact* that will indicate the nature of the subject to be discussed. (See Thurber, Gregory, Smith.)

10. *Making an unusual statement* that can intrigue as well as introduce. (See Baker, Thurber, Berne, Roiphe, *Time*, Wolfe, Hemingway, Kosinski, Sheehy, Brown, Gansberg.)

11. *Making a commonplace remark* that can draw interest because of its very commonness in sound or meaning. (See Peter/Hull, Berne.)

Irony, in its verbal form sometimes classed as a figure of speech, is saying one thing on the surface but meaning exactly (or nearly) the opposite — e.g., "this beautiful neighborhood of ours" may mean that it is a dump. (For other illustrations, see Thurber, Wolfe, Mitford.)

Verbal irony has a wide range of tones, from the gentle, gay, or affectionate to the sharpness of outright *sarcasm,* which is always intended to cut. It may consist of only a word or phrase, it may be a simple *understatement* (see Mitford), or it may be sustained as one of the major components of satire.

Irony can be an effective tool of exposition if its tone is consistent with the overall tone and if the writer is sure that his audience is bright enough to recognize it as irony. In speech, a person usually indicates by voice or eye-expression that he is not to be taken literally; in writing, the words on the page have to speak for themselves.

In addition to verbal irony, there is also an *irony of situation*, in which there is a sharp contradiction between what is logically expected to happen and what does happen — e.g., a man sets a trap for an obnoxious neighbor and then gets caught in it himself. Or the ironic situation may simply be some discrepancy that the observer can see that those involved can not. (Much of the Arlen essay has this kind of irony, as does the principle itself in "The Peter Principle." For other examples of irony of situation, see Thurber; Gregory, par. 12; Roiphe, 2; Toffler, 7; Carson, 5; Kosinski, 7; Sheehy, 9; Tuchman, 6; Smith, 9.)

Logical Argument   (See *Argument*.)
Loose Sentences   (See *Emphasis*.)
Metaphor   (See *Figures of Speech*.)
Narration   (See *Section 10*.)
Objective writing and **Subjective** writing are distinguishable from each other by the extent to which the author's personal attitudes or emotions enter into them. The difference is usually one of degree, as few writing endeavors can be completely objective or subjective.

Objective writing, seldom used in its purest form except in business or scientific reports, is impersonal and concerned almost entirely with straight narration, with logical analysis, or with the description of external appearances. (For somewhat objective writing, see Berne, Packard, *Time*, Toffler.)

Subjective writing (in description usually called "impressionistic" — see *Section 9*) is more personalized, more expressive of the beliefs, ideals, or impressions of the author. Whereas in objective writing the emphasis is on the object being written about, in subjective writing the emphasis is on how the object is seen and interpreted by the author. (For some of the many examples in this book, see Gregory, Michener, Roiphe, Ashton-Warner, Mitford, Wolfe, Schweitzer, Lawrence, Brown, Arlen, Hoffman, Smith, Kerouac.)

Paradox is a statement or remark that, although seeming to be contradictory or absurd, may actually contain some truth. Michener's assertion that Mickey Mouse was "one of the most disastrous cultural influences ever to hit America" undoubtedly seems paradoxical to many people. (See also Carson, par. 6; Drucker, 1, 17.)

Paragraph Unity   (See *Unity.*)

Parallel Structure refers in principle to the same kind of "parallelism" that is studied in grammar: the principle that coordinate elements should have coordinate presentation, as in a pair or a series of verbs, prepositional phrases, gerunds. It is often as much a matter of "balance" as it is of parallelism.

But the principle of parallel structure, far from being just a negative "don't mix" set of rules, is also a positive rhetorical device. Many writers use it as an effective means of stressing variety or profusion in a group of nouns or modifiers, or of emphasizing parallel ideas in sentence parts, in two or more sentences, or even in two or more paragraphs. At times it can also be useful stylistically, to give a subtle poetic quality to the prose.

(For illustrations of parallel parts within a sentence: see Berne, par. 5; Roiphe, 2, 14; Osgood, 3; Toffler, 8; Wolfe, 1, 4; Kosinski, 2, 4; Schweitzer, 6, 8; Allen; Tuchman, 1, 6; Smith, 17; Kerouac. Of sentences themselves: Peter/Hull; Berne, 4; Catton, 14; Allen, 15, 18–22; Franklin; Jefferson; Arlen. Of both parts and sentences: Smith, 14; Arlen. Of paragraphs: Jefferson; Allen, 18–22.)

Periodic Sentence   (See *Emphasis.*)

Personification   (See *Figures of Speech.*)

Point of View is simply the position of the author in relation to his subject matter. Rhetorical point of view, our only concern here, has little in common with the grammatical sort and differs somewhat from that important to fiction.

A ranch in a mountain valley is seen differently by the practical stockman working at the corral, by his wife deciding where to plant her petunias, by the artist or poet viewing the ranch from the mountainside, and by the careful geographer in a plane above, map-sketching the valley in relation to the entire range. It is the same ranch, but the positions and attitudes of the viewers are varied.

So it is with expository prose. The position and attitude of the author are the important lens through which the reader also sees the subject. Consistency is important, because if the lens is changed without sufficient cause and explanation, the reader will become disconcerted, if not annoyed.

Obviously, since the point of view is partially a matter of attitude, the tone and often the style of writing are closely linked to it. (See *Style/Tone.*)

The selections in this book provide examples of numerous points of view. Ashton-Warner is the lover of children and creativity; Mitford is the debunking prober; Smith is the fireman in action. In each of these (and the list could be extended to include all the selections in the book), the subject would seem vastly different if seen from some other point of view.

Process Analysis (See *Section 5.*)

Purpose that is clearly understood by the author before he starts to write is essential to both unity and coherence. A worthwhile practice, certainly in the training stages, is to write down the controlling purpose before even beginning the outline. Some instructors require both a statement of purpose and a statement of central theme. (See *Unity.*)

The most basic element of a statement of purpose is the commitment to "explain," or perhaps for some assignments to "convince" (argument), to "relate" (narration), or to "describe." But the statement of purpose, whether written or only decided upon, goes further — e.g., "to explain that most employees are promoted until they are on their level of incompetence, where they remain" (Peter/Hull) or "to explain that love is a learned emotion" (Casler).

Qualification is the tempering of broad statements to make them more valid and acceptable, the author himself admitting the probability of exceptions. This qualifying can be done inconspicuously, to whatever degree needed, by the use of *possibly, nearly always* or *most often, usually* or *frequently, sometimes* or *occasionally.* Instead of saying that "freshman composition is the most valuable course in college," it may be more accurate and defensible to say that it is for *some people* or that *it can be* the most valuable.

Time uses such qualifiers. Peter and Hull's "principle" states that "every employee *tends* to rise to his level of incompetence." (You may decide that some authors should have made greater use of qualification than they did.)

Rhetorical Question is one posed with no expectation of receiving an answer; it is used solely as a structural device to launch or to further a discussion. Questions that are formulated as an integral part of the subject itself (such as those in the Kerouac essay) would *not* be considered rhetorical questions. (See Baker, par. 8; Berne, title; Roiphe, 4, 6; Ashton-Warner, 2; Kosinski, 2, 5; Sheehy; Lawrence; Tuchman, 8; Smith, 15.)

Sarcasm   (See *Irony.*)

Sentimentality, also called *sentimentalism,* is an exaggerated show of emotion, whether intentional or caused by lack of restraint. An author can oversentimentalize almost any situation, but the trap is most dangerous when he writes of time-worn emotional symbols or scenes — e.g., a broken heart, mother love, a lonely death, the conversion of a sinner. However sincere the author may be, if his reader is not fully oriented to the worth and uniqueness of the situation described, he may be either resentful or amused at any attempt to play on his emotions. Sentimentality is, of course, one of the chief characteristics of melodrama. (For example of writing that, less adeptly handled, could easily have slipped into sentimentality, see Catton, Campa, Brown, Curtin, Gansberg, Smith. Gregory comes dangerously close at times, as does Kerouac in his last sentence. Arlen, on the other hand, *uses* sentimentality to accomplish his own purposes.)

Simile   (See *Figures of Speech.*)

Slang   (See *Colloquial.*)

Specific and **General** terms, and the distinctions between the two, are similar to concrete and abstract terms (as discussed under their own heading), and for our purpose there is no real need to keep the two sets of categories separated. Whether *corporation* is thought of as "abstract" and *Ajax Motor Company* as "concrete," or whether they are assigned to "general" and "specific" categories, the principle is the same: in most writing, *Ajax Motor Company* is better.

But "specific" and "general" are relative terms. For instance, the word *apple* is more specific than *fruit* but less so than *Winesap*. And *fruit*, as general as it certainly is in one respect, is still more specific than *food*. Such relationships are shown more clearly in a series, progressing from general to specific: *food, fruit, apple, Winesap;* or *vehicle, automobile, Ford, Mustang*. Modifiers and verbs can also have degrees of specificity: *bright, red, scarlet;* or *moved, sped, careened*. It is not difficult to see the advantages to the reader — and, of course, to the writer who needs to communicate an idea clearly — in "the scarlet Mustang careened through the pass," instead of "the bright-colored vehicle moved through the pass."

Obviously, however, there are times when the general or the abstract term or statement is essential — e.g., "a balanced diet includes some fruit," or "there was no vehicle in sight." But the use of specific language whenever possible is one of the best ways to improve diction and thus clarity and force-fulness in writing.

(Another important way of strengthening general, abstract writing is, of course, to use examples or other illustrations. See *Section 1*.)

Style and **Tone** are so closely linked to each other, so often even elements of each other, that it is best to consider them together.

But there is a difference between them. Think of two young men, each with his girl friend on separate moonlight dates, whispering in nearly identical, tender and loving tones of voice. One young man says, "Your eyes, dearest, reflect a thousand sparkling candles of heaven," and the other says, "Them eyes of yours — in this light — they really bug me." Their *tones* were the same; their *styles* considerably different.

The same distinction exists in writing. But naturally, with more complex subjects than the effect of moonlight on a maiden's eyes, there are more complications in separating the two qualities, even for the purpose of study.

The tone is determined by the *attitude* of the writer toward his subject and toward his audience. He, too, may be tender and loving, but he may be indignant, solemn, playful, enthusiastic, belligerent, contemptuous — the list could be as long as a list of the many "tones of voice." (In fact, wide ranges of tone may be illustrated by essays of this book. Compare, e.g., those of Ashton-Warner and Mitford or Gregory and Brown.)

Style, on the other hand, expresses the author's individuality through his choices of word (see *Diction*), his sentence patterns (see *Syntax*), and his selection and arrangement of his basic materials. (All these elements of style are illustrated in the contrasting statements of the moonstruck lads.) These matters of style are partially prescribed, of course, by the adopted tone, but they are still bound to reflect the writer's personality and mood, his education and general background.

(Some of the many widely varying styles — partially affected by and affecting the tones — represented by selections in this book are those of Thurber, Gregory, Ashton-Warner, Wolfe, Schweitzer, Allen, Lawrence, Brown, Arlen, Smith, Kerouac.)

Subjective Writing   (See *Objective/Subjective.*)

Symbol refers to anything that, although real itself, also suggests something broader or more significant — not just in greater numbers, however, as a man would not symbolize a group or even mankind itself, although he might be typical or representative in one or more abstract qualities. On the most elementary level, even words are symbols — e.g., *bear* brings to mind the furry beast itself. But more important is that things, persons, or even acts may also be symbolic, if they invoke abstract concepts, values, or qualities apart from themselves or their own kind. Such symbols, in everyday life as well as in literature and the other arts, are generally classifiable according to three types, which, although terminology differs, we may label *natural*, *personal*, and *conventional*.

In a natural symbol, the symbolic meaning is inherent in the thing itself. The sunrise naturally suggests new beginnings to most people, an island is almost synonymous with isolation, a cannon automatically suggests war; hence these are natural symbols. It does not matter that some things, by their nature, can suggest more than one concept: Although a valley may symbolize security to one person and captivity to another, both meanings, contradictory as they might seem, are inherent, and in both respects the valley is a natural symbol.

The personal symbol, depending as it does on private experience or perception, is meaningless to others unless they are told about it or allowed to see its significance in context as in literature. Although the color green may symbolize the outdoor life to the farm boy trapped in the gray city (in this respect perhaps a natural symbol), it can also symbolize romance to the girl proposed to while wearing her green blouse, or dismal poverty to the woman who grew up in a weathered green shanty; neither of these meanings is suggested by something *inherent* in the color green, so they are personal symbols. Anything at all could take on private symbolic meaning, even the odor of marigolds or the sound of a lawnmower. The sunrise itself could mean utter despair, instead of fresh opportunities, to the man who has long despised his daily job and cannot find another. (Even Kerouac's bear seems to have had some private symbolic meaning to him.)

Conventional symbols usually started as personal symbols, but continued usage in life or art permits them to be generally recognized for their broader meanings, which depend on custom rather than any inherent quality — e.g., the olive branch for peace, the flag for love of country, the cross for Christianity, the raised fist for black power.

Symbols are used less in expository writing than in fiction and poetry, but a few authors represented in this book have made effective use of symbolism to help convey their ideas, or at least to give them added significance. (See also Hemingway, Arlen.)

Syntax is a very broad term — too broad, perhaps, to be very useful — referring to the arrangement of words in a sentence. Good syntax implies the use not only of correct grammar but also of effective patterns. These patterns depend on sentences with good unity, coherence, and emphasis, on the use of subordination and parallel construction as appropriate, on economy, and on a consistent and interesting point of view. A pleasing variety of sentence patterns is also important in achieving effective syntax.

Theme (See *Unity*.)
Thesis (See *Unity*.)
Tone (See *Style/Tone*.)

Transition is the relating of one topic to the next, and smooth transition is an important aid to the coherence of a sentence, a paragraph, or an entire writing. (See *Coherence*.)

The most effective coherence, of course, comes about naturally with sound development of ideas, one growing logically into the next — and that virtue depends on sound organization. But sometimes beneficial even in this situation, particularly in going from one paragraph to the next, is the use of appropriate transitional devices.

Readers are apt to be sensitive creatures, easy to lose. (And, of course, the writer is literally the loser since he is the one who presumably has something to communicate.) If the reader gets into a new paragraph and the territory seems familiar, chances are that he will continue. But if there are no identifying landmarks, he will often begin to feel uneasy and will either start worrying about his slow comprehension or take a dislike to the author and subject matter. Either way, a communication block arises, and very likely the author will soon have one less reader.

A good policy, then, unless the progression of ideas is exceptionally smooth and obvious, is to provide some kind of familiar identification early in the new paragraph, to keep the reader feeling at ease with the different ideas. The effect is subtle but important. These familiar landmarks or transitional devices are sometimes applied deliberately but more often come naturally, especially when the prospective reader is kept constantly in mind at the time of writing.

An equally important reason for using some kinds of transitional devices, however, is a logical one: while functioning as bridges between ideas, they also assist the basic organization by pointing out the *relationship* of the ideas — and thus contributing still further to readability.

Transitional devices useful for bridging paragraph changes (and, some of them, to improve transitional flow within paragraphs) may be roughly classified as follows:

1. *Providing an "echo"* from the preceding paragraph. This may be the repetition of a key phrase or word, or a pronoun referring back to such a word, or a casual reference to an idea. (See Thurber; Mitford; Wolfe, especially from pars. 1 to 2, and 4 to 5). Such an echo cannot be superimposed on new

ideas, but, by careful planning, must be an organic part of them.

2. *Devising a whole sentence or paragraph* to bridge between other important paragraphs or major divisions. (See Peter/Hull, par. 30; Gregory, 4; Brown, 6; Clarke, 12–13, 20–21.)

3. *Using parallel structure* between an important sentence of one paragraph and the first sentence of the next. This is a subtle means of making the reader feel at ease in the new surroundings, but it is seldom used because it is much more limited in its potential than the other methods of transition.

4. *Using standard transitional expressions,* most of which have the additional advantage of indicating relationship of ideas. Only a few of those available are classified below, but nearly all the reading selections of this book can amply illustrate such transitional expressions:

Time — soon, immediately, afterward, later, meanwhile, after a while.

Place — nearby, here, beyond, opposite to.

Result — as a result, therefore, thus, consequently, hence.

Comparison — likewise, similarly, in such a manner.

Contrast — however, nevertheless, still, but, yet, on the other hand, after all, otherwise.

Addition — also, too, and, and then, furthermore, moreover, finally, first, third, etc.

Miscellaneous — for example, for instance, in fact, indeed, on the whole, in other words.

Trite (See *Clichés.*)

Unity in writing is the same as unity in anything else — in a picture, a musical arrangement, a campus organization — and that is a *oneness,* in which all parts contribute to an overall effect.

Many elements of good writing contribute in varying degrees to the effect of unity. Some of these are properly designed introduction and closing; consistency of point of view, tone, and style; sometimes the recurring use of an analogy or thread of symbolism; occasionally the natural time boundaries of an experience or event, as in the Mitford and Saint-Exupéry selections.

But in most expository writing the only dependable unifying force is the *central theme*, which every sentence, every word, must somehow help to support. (The central theme is also called the *central idea* or the *thesis* when pertaining to the entire writing. In an expository paragraph it is the same as the *topic sentence*, which may be implied or, if stated, may be located anywhere in the paragraph, but is usually placed first.) As soon as anything appears which is not related to the central idea, then there are *two* units instead of one. Hence, unity is basic to all other virtues of good writing, even to coherence and emphasis, the other two organic essentials. (See *Coherence; Emphasis*.)

An example of unity may be found in a single river system (for a practical use of analogy), with all its tributaries, big or little, meandering or straight, flowing into the main stream and making it bigger — or at least flowing into another tributary that finds its way to the main stream. This is *one* river system, an example of unity. But now also picture another, nearby stream that does not empty into the river but goes off in some other direction. There are now two systems, not one, and there is no longer unity.

It is the same way with writing. The central theme is the main river, flowing along from the first capital letter to the very last period. Every drop of information must find its way into this theme-river, or it is not a part of the system at all. It matters not even slightly if the water is good, the idea-stream perhaps deeper and finer than any of the others: if it is not a tributary, it has no business pretending to be relevant to *this* theme of writing.

And that is why most students are required to state their central idea, usually in solid sentence form, before even starting to organize their ideas. If the writer can use only tributaries, it is very important to know from the start just what the river is.

To the student:

As publishers, we realize that one way to improve education is to improve textbooks. We also realize that you, the student, largely determine the success or failure of textbooks. Although it is the instructor who assigns them, it is the student who buys and uses them. If enough of you don't like a particular book and make your feelings known, the chances are your instructor will not assign it again.

Usually only instructors are asked about the quality of a text; their opinion alone is considered as revisions are planned or as new books are developed. Now, Little, Brown would like to ask you about Randall Decker's *Patterns of Exposition 4:* how you liked or disliked it; why it was interesting or dull; if it taught you anything. Would you fill in this form and return it to us at: Little, Brown and Co., College Division, 34 Beacon Street, Boston, Mass. 02106. It is your chance to directly affect the publication of future textbooks.

School:_____

Course title:_____

Other texts required:_____

1. Did you like the book?_____

2. CONTENT: Was it too easy?_____

                   Too difficult?_____

Did you read it all?_____

Which selections did you like most?_____

_____

_____

Which selections did you like least?_____

_____

_____

)

3. Did you like the cover design?_____

4. Were the exercises useful?_____

   How might they be changed?_____

   _____

5. Did you find the headnotes to each selection helpful?_____

   How might they be improved?_____

   _____

6. Do you feel the instructor should continue to assign this book

   next year?_____

7. Will you keep this book for your library?_____

8. Please add any general comments or suggestions. _____

   _____

   _____

   _____

   _____

   _____

   _____

9. May we quote you in our promotion efforts for this book?

   _____yes   _____no

   _____   _____
   date   signature

   _____
   school

   _____
   address